Embracing Your Past

To

Empower Your Future

Four Families Descended from Slaves Reflect on Stories of Strength, Love, and Gratitude

By

Lori Ann LaRocco, Abby Wallace

This book is dedicated to

"Polleete", Pote, Pollee and Rose Allen

Egya Amkwandoh

Sukey Bay

Esau and Sylvia Brooks

Richard Henry B rooks

Coreen

Jim Madison

Mandy

Cecilia Quander

Charles Henry Quander

Nancy Carter Quander

May their stories bring a voice to the contributions of the tens of millions of enslaved men, women, and children who were silenced in bondage. May they be acknowledged, for without them, this nation would not have been built. And may the souls of those who perished traveling the Middle Passage be remembered and honored.

Table of Contents

Author Comments

"Embracing Your Past to Empower Your Future" was an idea born from a mother-daughter history trip. After touring the homes of U.S Presidents George Washington, Thomas Jefferson, and James Madison, we were left with more questions than answers on the enslaved men, women, and children who were viewed as property and worked in bondage. While yes, we learned about their working and living conditions, little was known about *who* they were.

Monticello and Montpelier tour guides showed us fingerprints intentionally placed in bricks made by the hands of enslaved women and children. Once you see these fingerprints, you cannot unsee them.

Enslaved Fingerprints in Bricks

President Thomas Jefferson's Monticello   President James Madison's Montpelier

We decided after our trip to embark on a journey to find descendants of the enslaved who would want to share and tell their family's history. After a couple of years, our dream of compiling some of these stories became a reality. This is a labor of love and a celebration of the human spirit. In the darkest shadows of our American history, there was light.

This light could be found in the enslaved's perseverance, love, and determination. The power of their determination and knowing their self-worth is engrained in the DNA of their descendants. This is not an embellished statement but a fact. Their contributions to society by these enslaved descendants are just some examples.

The stories you are about to read were lovingly told by the family historians of some enslaved men, women, and children who helped build America. There are *millions* of more stories that have yet to be told.

FOREWORD

There is an African Proverb called "Each One Teach One", which exemplifies the spirit and determination of the enslaved. This saying started during slavery when the enslaved were precluded from learning to read. If an enslaved person was taught, or learned how to read, it became their *duty* to teach someone else.

This proverb was more than an inspirational saying; it was a call to action. I can personally tell you this call to action is embedded in my family's DNA because, like many Black Americans, my loved ones were denied education. But this repudiation did not stop the drive of my family to rise above oppression and succeed.

My family roots in America were in the segregated South, and I have seen firsthand how life comes full circle. I am a real estate developer whose family worked the land as farmers in the 1800's and early 1900's. I am a hotel owner whose grandfather, Thomas Willoughby, worked 60 hours a week as a hotel doorman. My ancestors sacrifices and accomplishments have built the foundation of who I am today.

My family tree in the United States was first publicly recorded in the 1880 census North Carolina where my maternal great-great-great- grandparents, Andrew Holloman, (born in North Carolina in 1812), was documented as a farmer, and his wife, Tiena, (Tiny) Holloman (born in North Carolina in 1814), was listed as a homemaker. Neither could read or write. There was no question in the state's census if residents owned or rented land. Tiena's family tree unfortunately stops with her. This break in family history is not uncommon for Black Americans, whose families were robbed of their past because of slavery.

The African Proverb I mentioned earlier proved to be true for my family when my maternal great-great grandparents, Charles Trummel and Martha Ann Trummel (born Pierce), were listed in the 1900 North Carolina census as not attending school, but they could read and write, meaning someone had taught them. Charles was a farmer who owned his land and was paying a mortgage, and Martha stayed at home.

On my father's side, in the 1880 Virginia Census, my great-great-great-great-grandfather, Henry Peebles (born in 1820), was a farmer, and his wife, Onnie Williams (circa 1818), was a homemaker. They, too, were listed as not being able to read or write. Their oldest daughter, Evelena, who was 20, also could not read or write. Their son, William H (age 18), and Virginia A. (age 15), could read and write, and were laborers. Their youngest, Mary L. Peebles, was attending an all-Black school at the age of twelve.

The power of reading and writing is exponential. My ancestors knew reading and writing would help them as they navigated life. It would lead them to better paying jobs. Eventually, when my family members attended school, they combined their book knowledge with their inner self drive to overcome obstacles. Each generation that overcame oppression offered words of wisdom to the next generation. The values, beliefs, and motivational support I grew up with were a byproduct of what was said and taught to my parents when they were young.

We are all a product of our past. I know I am. My entrepreneurial spirit comes from my mother Ruth

Yvonne Willoughby. Her father, Thomas, was a doorman at The Wardman Park Hotel in Washington, D.C. Her mom, Mammie Doris Newsome, was a stay-at-home mother. Neither of her pa rents, nor my mother, attended college. My mom met my father, Roy Donahue Peebles when she was 16 and they wed that same year and had me when she was 19. I was five when my parents divorced, and I watched my mom, as head of the household, be a fearless provider in her middle twenties.

My mother started her career as a secretary, and her career in real estate began almost by accident. The spark of her entering an industry dominated by White men was when she was buying us a home in suburban Maryland. In the closing documents, she reviewed how much the real estate broker made. She then thought, why not me? My mom attended night school and passed the real estate test to obtain her sales license. She became an agent and within a couple of years, she had her own real estate brokerage. She also took college classes to advance in her career. I watched in awe at my mother's drive. She inspired me.

If my mom could wear multiple hats, so could I. My alarm would go off at 4:30am so I could get ready and catch the bus for my 6am classes at Capitol Page High School on the top floor of the Library of Congress. Classes would be over by 10:30, and then I would go to work at the U.S. Capitol. In my senior year, I was a staff aide for a powerful member of Congress. Those two years provided me with a unique exposure and inviable opportunity to build long term relationships with some of our nation's most influential leaders. The knowledge I gained and the relationships I built would be instrumental to me later in life as an entrepreneur.

I honed my teambuilding skills as a player on the school's basketball and chess teams. Coming home at 10pm was nothing unusual, and then I would sit down to do my homework and study, go to bed at midnight and wake up at 4:45 am to start the next day. At that time, I wanted to emulate my uncle and become a doctor. And I knew I had to have good grades to get into college and be well-rounded. I was brought up with the notion that nothing will ever be handed to you. You need to earn it. There are no handouts in life. If you are faced with a challenge, think of a solution, create your own opportunities, and rise above. I was taught that nothing was impossible.

My relenting drive was fueled by seeing the injustice my parents suffered because of racism. They never let obstruction and indignities stop them from obtaining their goals. I will never forget when my mom was hired over the phone for a job as a sales director for a real estate project. She was so excited for this new chapter in her career. But, when she showed up for work and they saw she was Black, they did not give her the job. She was told by the person who hired her the real estate market and sales staff were not ready for a Black women to be the director of sales. Disappointed, but not deterred, my mother looked for a new job, and was hired at Fannie Mae as a secretary; within twelve months she was promoted to a low-level executive. Two years later she would start her own consulting role. However, she was never the same after her loss of career opportunity because of racism.

My dad grew up in a rural town in segregated Virginia. Opportunities were not just denied to black people there, they were blatantly made to feel like third class citizens in every aspect of life. My grandfather was a part-time farmer and full-time janitor at a local school restricted to educating white students. Despite not having much in the way of formal education, my dad was an innately hard worker with significant raw intelligence. He was keenly aware of how few opportunities he had based upon the color of his skin. While his father did the best he could to provide a stable and loving environment, my father's self-esteem suffered tremendously in the discriminatory landscape of the south and the ambitions he did have as a child were slowly extinguished as he approached adulthood. Like many Black men his age, he enlisted in the military. After he was discharged, he relocated to Washington, DC where his mother had relocated after divorcing my grandfather. He secured a job as an auto mechanic. After marrying my mom and with the help of his father-in-law, Thomas Willoughby, he obtained a job as a file clerk for the federal government. During the week, he held his government post, and, on the weekends, he worked as an auto mechanic to provide an additional revenue stream.

While both my grandfathers were in the service industry, one worked in an environment where he was able to open doors, literally and figuratively, and cultivate relationships with elected officials and prominent Washingtonians. Relationships that would provide opportunities for his children and grandchildren to become politically engaged and tap into the economic empowerment of our nation's capital. While my paternal grandfather, persistently meant to feel inferior to those around him, was resigned to being good enough to clean an all-white educational institution, but not good enough to have his own child attend.

These experiences instilled in me a sense of awareness on how to not allow society to impose any limitations on me and my dreams. I was also determined to assist others. I originally thought being a doctor would be that answer. Instead, I realized after my first year at Rutgers University, I wanted to make a difference in society in an industry I grew up in- real estate. So, I went to back to Washington, D.C., attended college part time while I studied and passed the exam for my real estate salesperson's license and became a real estate appraiser. My upbringing enabled me to have that confidence and make that career pivot. My clients included the United States Department of Housing & Urban Development and major financial and banking institutions.

When I started my real estate development career in 1986, I looked for locations with untapped potential that were being overlooked. The one hundred -thousand square foot office building I chose to develop was in one of Washington, D.C.'s most economically depressed neighborhoods. This development would not only create jobs but spark much needed socio- economic change in an area that needed to be lifted up. *This* was one of my ways of creating positive change.

I have dedicated my life, not only to my family and career, but to challenge, and eliminate limitations in society. We need structural changes, or the wide divides we see economically, socially, and educationally will continue. This means real and equal access to capital for Black American entrepreneurs, families and businesses in both the public and private sector as well as access to quality education and internships. The history of the Black American workforce is filled with entrepreneurs. I am a firm believer in mentorships and exposure. It is imperative today's youth have the opportunity to have hands on experience so they can learn and know what opportunities are out there for them. There are so many Black entrepreneurs to inspire today's youth.

O. W. Gurley, a Mississippi principal and grocery store owner, decided to sell his successful business and purchase 40 acres of land in Tulsa Oklahoma designated for Black people. He developed that land and it would become known as "the Black Wall Street." Maggie Lena Walker was the first Black American woman to charter a bank in the United States. Madam C.J. Walker was one of the first Black American women to become a self-made millionaire. She made her fortune by developing a specialty beauty and hair product line for Black women which was developed by her own company, Madam C.J. Walker Manufacturing. Booker T. Washington was founder of the National Negro Business League. Arthur Gaston was a leading employer of Black Americans in the 1960's. He established the Citizens Savings and Loan Association, the A.G. Gaston Construction Co., and CF Bancshares.

These men and women broke barriers and positively impacted society. They were not afraid to fail. I was faced with pushback and backlash when I wanted to diversify the South Florida real estate market. It was all-white at the time. I was a disruptor and up for the challenge.

Building my real estate company in the 1990's was daunting. Even with the passage of The Fair Housing Act in 1968, both economic and social hurdles made it challenging not only for black homeownership but for developers as well. About thirty years after this legislation was passed, Black Americans had enough of being excluded from Miami's mainstream tourism and hospitality industries. These spirited Americans flexed their economic power with national tourism boycott in Miami that lasted 1,000 days where Black Americans demanded change and a seat at the table.

The campaign cost the county an estimated $20 million to $50 million in tourism revenue. This economic boycott created an opportunity I seized upon. The city commission was accepting bids for the development of a hotel by a Black developer.

Economic inclusion and social inclusion are a must for a productive society.

Five years after I won that bid, The Royal Palm Hotel, became Miami Beach's first Black-owned hotel. Thousands of scholarships in hotel management were also created for Black Miamians interested in going to college to learn the business. Simply put, economic inclusion and social inclusion are a must for a productive society.

I committed to providing job opportunities for Black Americans in the hotel industry and it's a passion that has only intensified through the years. I am lucky to have my son, Roy Donahue, III by my side to continue my legacy of paying it forward. My mother taught me it was my obligation as a successful Black man to lift up others in my journey of life. This is a lesson my wife, Katrina and I have engrained in our children. It is our responsibility to teach the lessons we have learned in life. Our loved ones who have passed, live on in our actions today. Paying it forward is the best way to honor them.

This is a time of transformation. Everyone needs to do their part to make the world more inclusive. I would encourage young people to get engaged and to help them change America for the better. Our ancestors wanted a better future for us. The future of tomorrow is now charged in the hands of today's youth. If history shows us, change does not happen overnight. It takes time and a population of people who want to evoke change by challenging the system. We *all* have the positive disruptive ability to make a better tomorrow.

Mr. Peebles engages in practices of Affirmative Development™ to provide transformative economic inclusion for minority and woman owned businesses within their multi-billion dollar portfolio of projects in New York, Boston, Washington D.C., Charlotte, Atlanta, Miami, and Los Angeles.

Mr. Peebles is a passionate proponent of mentoring programs that expose youth to the value of entrepreneurship, as well as an active political supporter and fundraiser for local, state, and federal campaigns of both major parties.

Previously, he has served on the National Finance Committees of Presidents Barack Obama and Bill Clinton, he is the former Chairman of the Congressional Black Caucus Foundation.

PART ONE

"Polleete", Pollee "Pote," and Rose Allen- Survivors of The Clotilda and Co-Founders of Africatown

The Clotilda was the last slave ship to bring African captives to America illegally in July 1860. The two-masted schooner was discovered by reporter Ben Raines in 2018, and in May 2019, the Alabama Historical Commission confirmed that this ship was indeed the Clotilda. The ship since then has been included on the National Register of Historic Places.[1] "Polleete" Pollee and Rose Allen were survivors of the Clotilda and were enslaved by their human trafficker, Captain Timothy Meaher. Once emancipated, "Polleete" Pollee and Rose Allen were cofounders of Africatown. This community is now on the National Register of Historic Places, where 32 Clotilda survivors created the municipality three miles north of downtown Mobile, Alabama.

Author's note: In a book interview published in 1914, Pollee requested to have him referred to by his African name, "Polleete," in hopes that if the book reached Africa, his loved ones would know he was alive and okay. Pollee was his adopted Americanized version of his name. His friends and neighbors called him by the nickname "Pote." Historical documents have variations in spelling for Pollee. The family says his name was spelled with 2 "L"'s, not one.

Vernetta Henson was interviewed for this story. Mrs. Henson is the family historian for her family line and is the great-great-granddaughter of "Polleete", Pollee, "Pote," and Rose Allen.

"We know not why these troubles came upon us, but we are all God's children- we not always see the way, but his hands guide us and shape our ends."- "Polleete", "Pote", Pollee Allen

---

[1] Verbatim from Alabama Historical Commission's Clotilda National Registry form: The substantially intact archaeological remains of the wooden-hulled, 120-ton, two-masted schooner Clotilda (1Ba704) rest in mud and shallow fresh water off the banks of the Mobile River. It is located in the exact spot where its voyage ended, in a landscape that has remained essentially unchanged from 1860, when the schooner was scuttled at the site following an illegal voyage to bring captive men, women and children from Africa for the purposes of enslavement. The intact lower hull, the interior of the hull, with intact bulkheads forming compartments, including that in which the captives were held and transported against their will in harsh, brutal conditions, survive. The wreck retains a high degree of structural and archaeological integrity, representing as much as two-thirds and perhaps more of its original structure. Archaeological remains including physical evidence, including DNA, likely survive in the sealed, anaerobic conditions inside the hull, which is filled with silt. It rests in its original setting and is the only known and identified American vessel engaged in the illegal slave trade of the 19th century. As of this time, it is the only archaeological example of an American slave trading vessel lost in the context of the transatlantic slave trade. The exact location of Clotilda is restricted in order to protect the resource from looting.

"Polleete", Pollee, "Pote" and Rose Allen Family Tree

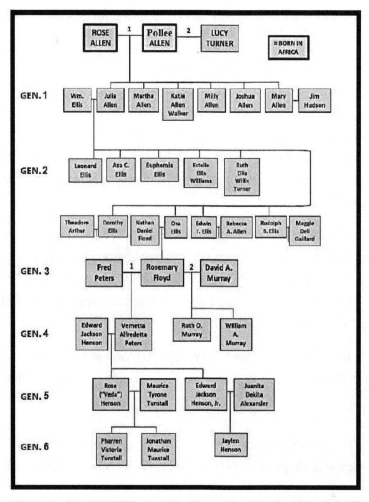

Source: Llewellyn (Lew) M. Toulmin, PhD, FRGS, FN '04 , The Pollee, Rose and Lucy Allen Lines: Genealogical Descents from Africa, the Slave Ship Clotilda, and Africatown, Alabama to the Present by Africatown, Alabama Silver Spring, Maryland August 2022; 2nd Edition

Chapter One
Surviving the Middle Passage and Enslavement

Because the men, women, and children on the Clotilda were illegally smuggled into Colonial America, there was an opportunity after emancipation to interview some of them. Firsthand accounts of life in Africa and the journey through the Middle Passage, the ocean route that carried slaves from West Africa to Colonial America, are very rare. Details surrounding Pollee and Rose's life are one of these accounts.

Pollee's story started in the inland village of Tarkar (or what is known today as Ghana). Pollee said his village was "many days from the water"[2] when he was interviewed for the 1914 book, "Historic Sketches of the South." He said the community was peace-loving and supported by agriculture. The author's accent was different from other former enslaved people with a southern accent. The Clotilda descendants' dialect was similar to an Italian-American dialect where a constant "a" sound was at the end of their words.[3] For example, "looka, worka, pulla". They described their sentences as well as "short and vivid."

Pollee explained their tribe raised cows, sheep, and hogs and planted vegetables like yams, beans, and corn. The forests were lush and fragrant with the scents of the bountiful fruit that grew unincumbered. Their big crop was palm oil.

Pollee came from the same town in Africa with at least two other Clotilda captives, Kazoola/Kossola (later known as Cudjo Lewis) and Abache (later known as Clara Turner). Pollee's future wife, Rose, was also on the Clotilda but came from another African town. Rose was born around 1841 in Africa, possibly near Lake Chad (what is considered northeast Nigeria or southwest Chad today).

Pollee and Kazoola/Kossola explained the construction of their African homes in great detail. They said the homes they built and lived in were "of superior quality and had the advantage of withstanding fire."[4] The foundation was a circular trench, and in that trench, the first of three wall sections built on top of each other were assembled. Each wall section was made of mud and was four feet in height and a foot and a half in width. The walls were made in three stages so that each section could dry. Once finished, these dwellings were twelve feet in height. Their rooves were thatched and were also covered with mud.

In that interview, Pollee and the survivors said honesty was a tribal characteristic.[5] Stealing was unheard of; all tribal members worked and had all the basic necessities of life to make them happy. Homes were never locked. If someone did commit theft, the King would say, "You are strong- you have two arms to work- you suffer for nothing- why have you stolen?" The offender would be imprisoned, and Pollee and the other Tarkars said that the culprit would no longer steal once they were released.

---

[2] Emma Langton Roche, "Historic Sketches of the South" page 75
[3] Emma Langton Roche, "Historic Sketches of the South" page 75
[4] Emma Langton Roche, "Historic Sketches of the South" page 76
[5] Emma Langton Roche, "Historic Sketches of the South" page 76

A person's social status had no influence in the eyes of the law, even with royalty. Everyone was equal under Tarkar law. Pollee stressed, "Money don't plea you there." [6]

The Tarkars were polygamists. Some had as many as three wives. The women in Tarkar owned the same amount of property as the men and did the same amount of work to keep the extra family members from being burdened. If they felt too tired or old, the wives could approach their husbands and offer them another wife[7]. Once a man was married, he only looked at his own wives and was considered their protector.

They believed in the Ahla-ahra, the Spirt of Good, and the Ahla-bady-oleelay, the Spirit of Evil. "Do right, and you will go to Ahla-ahra; do wrong, and you go Ala-bady-oleelay."[8] They followed the religions of Islam, Vodun, or the Orisa.

White men were not found in his area of Africa. White men were considered cannibals, and African parents would make sure their children would not go far from where they lived so they could not be kidnapped. The White men were called *yovo, anasarca, bature,* or *oyinbo.*[9]

African Culture

In African culture, the identities of the men and women were represented not only by their clothes but by their ornate hairstyles. It was a way of telling their ethnicity, family, social status, and profession. Hair was braided, woven, rolled, sculpted, or partly shaven. Feathers, precious metals like gold and silver, combs, pins, seeds, shells, fibers, and beads adorned their hair.

Teeth and earrings also had special meaning. Pollee's own smile was distinctive.[10] His two upper front teeth had been pecked off to form an inverted V. He had one small hoop in each ear, signifying to others that he completed his religious initiation of the *Orisa* religion.

Religious students like Pollee would have shaved entirely during the nine-month Orisa initiation. They would receive a new name, and it is said Kupollee was his initiation name, not his birth name. The "Ku" in Yoruba meant "death," and "Pollee" meant, "one born after the death of the chief of the house".[11] Pollee would also have tattoos of their respective *orisa* on their face, neck, and shoulders. These tattoos were considered ritual scarifications. Pollee and his fellow novices would have also learned a new language only known to the initiates. The group lived together away from their family during the initiation process. Food could be sent to them, but no direct contact was allowed.

---

[6] Emma Langton Roche, "Historic Sketches of the South" page 77
[7] Emma Langton Roche, "Historic Sketches of the South" page 78
[8] Emma Langton Roche, "Historic Sketches of the South" page 80
[9] "Dreams of Africa", page 54
[10] "Dreams of Africa", page 44
[11] Llewellyn (Lew) M. Toulmin, PhD, FRGS, FN '04, The Polee, Rose and Lucy Allen Lines: Genealogical Descents from Africa, the Slave Ship Clotilda, and Africatown, Alabama to the Present (Africatown, Alabama and Silver Spring, Maryland: August 2022, 2nd Edition

Once the religious initiation was completed, the devotees sang and danced for their family and friends in elaborate raffia costumes. In addition to the specific tattoos, a bracelet of cowry shells, sometimes accompanied by a double row of black beads or an earring, signified that the religious initiation had been completed. Once he accomplished his religious rite, Pollee was allowed to marry. Pollee proudly wore his gold hoop earrings, signifying his religious initiation in his adulthood. In fact, in the only drawing of Pollee the family has, he is wearing those earrings.

Drawing of "Polleete" Pollee Allen circa 1914
artist: Emma Roche, "Historic Sketches of
the South" (Knickerbocker Press, 1914)

Pollee was kidnapped in 1860 when he was approximately 18 years old.

Captive

The Tarkar tribe Pollee and Kazoola were members of were reportedly victims of a Dahomian Army dawn raid.[12]

---

[12] Narrative of events by Kazoola "Cudjo Lewis" in Emma Langton Roche, "Historic Sketches of the South", page 81

In the early morning hours, the female warriors of the Dahomeyans surrounded the sleeping village and attacked. Those who tried to flee were killed. The others were taken into captivity.[13] Infants were torn away from their mothers and held captive. The Elderly was taken as well.[14] Pollee, Kazoola, and the other captured Tarkars marched to the coast, where they saw their friends' heads dangling on poles. A map drawn by Kazoola detailed the horrific journey through the towns of Eko, Budigree, Adache, Whydah, and Grere.

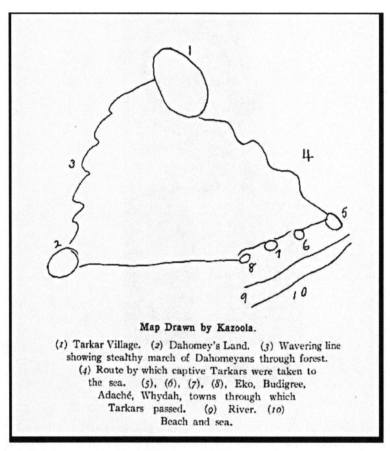

Map Drawn by Kazoola.

(*1*) Tarkar Village. (*2*) Dahomey's Land. (*3*) Wavering line showing stealthy march of Dahomeyans through forest. (*4*) Route by which captive Tarkars were taken to the sea. (*5*), (*6*), (*7*), (*8*), Eko, Budigree, Adaché, Whydah, towns through which Tarkars passed. (*9*) River. (*10*) Beach and sea.

Source: Historic Sketches of the South, by Emma Langdon Roche 1914.

Pollee and his fellow captives remembered seeing a white house at the end of the long march. They were now on the "Slave Coast" in West Africa: Ouidah. The slave trade thrived for 60 years in the late 17th century.[15] Once they arrived at that site, the Clotilda survivors said they were locked in the "barracoons", the African word for "slave cage", for about three weeks and were fed rice. The men and women held captive would shout to each other in the neighboring barracoons. They were in these cages for around three weeks until a white man named Captain Foster came to buy them.[16]

---

[13] Narrative of events by Kazoola "Cudjo Lewis" in Emma Langton Roche, "Historic Sketches of the South", page 81
[14] Narrative of events by Kazoola "Cudjo Lewis" in Emma Langton Roche, "Historic Sketches of the South", page 81
[15] "Ouidah slave Port" The Slave Kingdoms, PBS
https://www.pbs.org/wonders/Episodes/Epi3/ouidah.htm#:~:text=Ouidah%20was%20a%20densely%20populated,kingdom%20of%20Dahomey%20in%201727
[16] Emma Langton Roche, "Historic Sketches of the South", page 87

Middle Passage

Pollee and his fellow kidnapped Africans had no idea what was in store for them. The water that the slaves traveled on from Africa to colonial America was called the "Middle Passage." Little was known about the human trafficking voyage, as there were no firsthand accounts since many were brought to the United States a hundred years prior. It was not until the interviews with the survivors of the Clotilda that firsthand accounts could be recorded.

Oral history says in 1859, while gambling, Alabama steamship owner Captain Timothy Meaher made a bet of approximately $1,000 (the equivalent of $37,854.71 today) that he could smuggle Africans as slaves into the United States without being caught.

This would be illegal under the Act Prohibiting Importation of Slaves, which was enacted on March 2, 1807. The legislation was promoted by President Thomas Jefferson, who called for its enactment in 1806. The law took effect on January 1, 1808. If found guilty, the punishment was execution.

But Meaher was blinded by money and driven by ego. What enticed Meaher was a story he read on November 9th, 1858, of the *Mobile Press Register.* The article told of the quarreling of tribes on the Sierra Leone River and the King of Dahomey, who was "driving a brisk trade in slaves at from fifty to sixty dollars apiece at [the African town of] Whydah. Immense numbers of negroes were collected along the coast for export."[17]

There were several vessels Meaher owned, but he was most confident that his schooner, the Clotilda, was the fastest, and believed the vessel, which was equipped with extra sails, could outrun any of the several U.S. and British Naval squadrons that patrolled the waters in Africa to identify and stop any slave smugglers. He purchased that vessel for around $35,000 (the equivalent of $1,320,650.74 today) from shipbuilder Captain William Foster. He also recruited Foster to be the captain of the illegal voyage. Meaher also financed the trip.

The Clotilda was no ordinary schooner. The centerboard schooner had slightly larger dimensions than the average Gulf-built schooner, so it could not only carry more cargo, but also had the versatility of still accessing shallow water ports due to her hull shape and travel further in deep water to access more distant ports.[18] The vessel's copper sheathing on the outside of the vessel enabled this type of travel.[19]

Captain William Foster was the builder who co-owned the vessel with Meaher. The vessel that carried commodities such as lumbar and cotton would need to be retrofitted with a false deck to accommodate the human cargo. But that modification was not difficult to do. To give the appearance of a full vessel, the goods that would be used during the transatlantic voyage would be covered by lumber. This would not attract attention since lumber was a regularly transported item on the schooner.

---

[17] "Historic Sketches of the South", 1914
[18] SEARCH Inc., Final Report "Archeological Investigations of 1Ba704, A nineteenth-Century Shipwreck in the Mobile River
[19] SEARCH., Final Report "Archeological Investigations of 1Ba70r, A nineteenth-Century Shipwreck in the Mobile River

The self-assured Meaher told his brothers, James and Burns (also known as Byrnes), and his friends Thomas Buford and John M. Dabney about his illegal venture.

Meaher hired Captain William Foster for the trip, and Meaher himself financed it. Captain Foster obtained papers with the false claim he was delivering lumber.[20] During the time the Clotilda was on its trip to Africa, Captain Meaher made sure he had documented voyages of his own in the U.S. to maintain his innocence of any wrongdoing.

Captain Foster wrote down the voyage of the Clotilda in a letter to Mr. Donaldson.[21] It was under the cover of night in March of 1860 that Captain Foster set sail for Africa.

"Fitted out for the coast of Africa to purchase a cargo of Slaves; cleared and sailed from Mobile March 4th with the following cargo: 26 casks of Rice, 80 casks of augident Rum, 30 bbl. *[barrels]* Beef, 40 bbl. [barrels] Pork, 23 bbls [barrels] Sugar, 25 bbls [barrels] Flour, 4 bbl [barrels] Bread, 4 bbl [barrels] Molasses, 25 Boxes dry goods and sundries, 125 casks [barrels] water, and nine thousand ($9,000) dollars in gold; 9 men for the mast, first and second mates and myself made 12 in all on board."[22]

The only other modification needed for the transatlantic transportation of enslaved people would be in the main hold to confine people. In order to give the impression of a full hold, slaving goods were covered with lumber.

In Captain Foster's diary, there is an interesting entry he wrote the gold bars. Captain Foster remarked on the "magnetization" of the $9,000 in gold bars impacting the ship's compass. He wrote one night, early in the voyage, he looked at the stars and realized the vessel had gone off course. He blamed the bars and had them moved away from the compass so it would work properly. Captain Foster's account in his diary is incorrect.

Gold is not magnetic. If the bricks Meaher gave to Captain Foster to buy the enslaved were **pure gold**, the bricks could not impact a ship's compass. But, if the gold bars were **mixed** with alloyed metals such as zinc, copper, iron, cadmium aluminum, platinum-palladium, and/or aluminum, the bars might display magnetic properties. [23] If the bars did indeed impact the ship's compass, that would mean Timothy Meaher intentionally devalued the gold bars by mixing the gold with other metals, making them magnetic. The bars *looked* like $9,000 in gold, but in reality, they were not.

The trip to Africa almost didn't happen when Captain Foster was faced with mutiny. After a hurricane, the crew had to make repairs on the Clotilda and found the false deck. When this happened, the crew refused to work for ten days, but when Captain Foster offered to double their wages, they agreed to continue

---

[20] SEARCH., Final Report "Archeological Investigations of 1Ba704, A nineteenth-Century Shipwreck in the Mobile River
[21] Account of the Clotilda by Captain William Foster, "Last Slaver from U.S. To Africa. A.D. 1860" Mobile Public Library Digital Archives http://digital.mobilepubliclibrary.org/items/show/1802
[22] Account of the Clotilda by Captain William Foster, "Last Slaver from U.S. To Africa. A.D. 1860" Mobile Public Library Digital Archives http://digital.mobilepubliclibrary.org/items/show/1802
[23] "Does Gold Magnetize?" Stanford Magnets.com

working.[24] After the voyage, Captain Foster did not keep his promise of giving his crew more money. In his written account, he paid the crew the original amount first agreed upon in Mobile before the voyage: $8,000.[25] His wife once said the captain had a saying, "Promises were like pie crust- made to be broken."[26]

According to Captain Foster's written accounts, they arrived at Whydah, Africa, on May 15, 1860, at 4:00 pm. The sea was rough, yet Captain Foster said the native boats, approaching him so they could take him to shore, were easily cutting the water. Captain Foster wrote that the boats, which were about 60 feet long and manned by 20 men, "darted through the waves like fish." He boarded one of those boats to meet with the Prince and King to discuss exchanging commodities and trade for the slaves.

It was agreed between Captain Foster and the King for Captain Foster to pay one hundred dollars per head for one hundred and twenty-five men, women, and children. Captain Foster was there for eight days before they took him to a warehouse where four thousand captives were held. The captives were all in various states of nudity.[27] It was there Captain Foster selected the men, women, and children.[28]

Pollee, Rose, and the others held in the barracoons underwent invasive evaluations by human traffickers to determine their health. Survivors remembered in vivid detail the white men running their calloused hands over their arms and legs to assess their strength and virility and their fingers probing inside their mouths and intrusively examining their private parts to make sure the men and women did not have any venereal diseases.[29] The kidnapped men, women, and children were selected if they were deemed fit and healthy.

The Clotilda survivors were fed a big meal and were told they would be going on a long trip.[30] The chosen men and women would then have their hair shaved off for fear of lice. This was a serious violation in the Clotilda captives' eyes. Their hair was a major part of their identity. Survivors said they were outraged and demoralized. Their clothing was taken away, stripping away any remaining dignity.

The King offered to brand the slaves for him, but Captain Foster refused. Foster purchased gold and merchandise for 125 African men, women, and children for $9,000 (the equivalent of $341,856.90 today).

Captain Foster wrote in his account that he told his interpreter to have the enslaved men, women, and children leave the warehouse on the beach, be loaded on small boats, and delivered to the Clotilda by 10:00 am.

---

[24] Account of the Clotilda by Captain William Foster, "Last Slaver from U.S. To Africa. A.D. 1860" Mobile Public Library Digital Archives http://digital.mobilepubliclibrary.org/items/show/1802
[25] Account of the Clotilda by Captain William Foster, "Last Slaver from U.S. To Africa. A.D. 1860" Mobile Public Library Digital Archives http://digital.mobilepubliclibrary.org/items/show/1802
[26] Emma Langton Roche, "Historic Sketches of the South"
[27] Zora Neale Hurston, "Barracoon"
[28] Account of the Clotilda by Captain William Foster, "Last Slaver from U.S. To Africa. A.D. 1860" Mobile Public Library Digital Archives http://digital.mobilepubliclibrary.org/items/show/1802
[29] Zora Neale Hurston, "Barracoon"
[30] Zora Neale Hurston, "Barracoon"

Pollee, Rose, and the others were gathered between 5 and 6 am to prepare the group for this transfer.[31] Firsthand accounts said they were then separated by gender. The men were chained one behind the other. The women were in a separate line. They looked across the great green lawn of the property on which they were held captive to a scene that would forever be burned in their minds. Two long lines of captured men and women slowly waded through the river to reach a beach where crew boats were waiting, with white men pulling them onto the small boats to take them to the Clotilda, anchored in the ocean.

Slowly, the men and women waded in the river. The water quickly rose, and they fought the weight of the chains, pulling them down into the soft sand below. This weight got heavier with every step. At one point, one of Pollee's fellow captives, Cudjo, thought he would drown as the weight of the chains held his body down. He fought against the water, which was up to his neck.[32]

Once they were deep enough where the boats were staged, the human traffickers picked them up and took off their chains because the collective weight of all the chains could sink the boat. The Dahomeyans, who would row their small boats out to the Clotilda to unload the human cargo, aggressively and viciously tore off the clothes of the captives. They told them, "You go where you can get plenty of clothes."[33] Decades later, this memory still haunted the Clotilda survivors who told their story to the author.[34] They were very modest and proud people. To be stripped of their clothes was humiliating.[35] The small boats then rowed out in methodical procession to the Clotilda to unload the human cargo.

Once on the Clotilda, survivors said they were led down below deck. According to the survivors, the hull was hot and suffocating, and you could not stand up if you were tall.[36] If you were a man of smaller stature, you were able to stand erect.[37] Once the top of the hole of the hull was shut, the captives were enveloped in complete darkness.

The small boats moving the captives were constant. While two boats were in the process of moving thirty-five enslaved onto the Clotilda, Captain Foster saw vessels changing their course and heading toward them to intercept the vessel. Fearing capture, they stranded 15 kidnapped Africans, kept 110 on board, and set course for colonial America. Amongst those on the Clotilda were Pollee and Rose Allen.

Survivors said the rolling of the waves in the darkness and the boat's pitch made them feel that the vessel was airborne and the crest of the waves, only to come crashing down.[38]

---

[31] "Barracoon"
[32] "Barracoon"
[33] Roche, Emma Langton, "Historic Sketches of the South"
[34] Roche, Emma Langton, "Historic Sketches of the South"
[35] Roche, Emma Langton, "Historic Sketches of the South"
[36] "Barracoon"
[37] Roche, Emma Langton, "Historic Sketches of the South"
[38] "Barracoon"

The Clotilda survivors were given a gill of water (four ounces) a day.[39] In one particular interview, Pollee and the other Clotilda survivors described the water as tasting like vinegar.[40] They were also given some food.[41] The only company the survivors had were each other and the howling wind.

On the thirteenth day of their journey, survivors said the crew brought them out of the hull, where they could walk around the deck. This was no easy task. Their legs could not support them after sitting for so long, and they had grown so weak that they could not stand without assistance. The crew members had to help each captive individually and support them while they walked on their weak, unsteady legs. It took some time for the captives to be able to walk on their own. When they had a chance, the survivors looked around and saw nothing but the vast ocean. Africa, their beloved homeland, was gone.

The ship's journey back to Mobile was around 45 days. In Captain Foster's written account, he detailed how they were able to thwart being captured by numerous vessels, for news was about the Clotilda and the illegal mission.

"… disguised our vessel by taking down square sail yards, and fore topmast; appearing as a common coaster and sailed for Mobile, coming through Prilaboy channel into lake Pontchartrain, and anchored off "Point of Pines" Grand Bay, Miss."[42]

Captain Foster and the captives arrived in Alabama around July 8, 1860. He paid a local resident $25 for a horse and buggy ride to Mobile. [43] There, he hired a tug to push the Clotilda up the Spanish River into the Alabama River at "Twelve Mile Island."

The tug enabled Captain Foster to evade U.S. Customs by moving her upriver. This failure to report to evade U.S Customs was a federal crime.[44] This crime would be in addition to the illegal transportation of slaves.

Once at their desired river location, the enslaved Africans were transferred onto the Steamboat Czar[45], which was owned by Timothy Meaher's brother, Byrnes (aka Burns) Meaher. Pollee and the other Clotilda survivors watched Meaher and Burns set fire to the Clotilda.

"I transferred my Slaves to a river steamboat and sent them up into the canebrake to hide them until further disposal. I then burned my schr. (schooner) to the water's edge and sunk her."[46]

---

[39] Roche, Emma Langton "Historic Sketches of the South"
[40] Roche, Emma Langton "Historic Sketches of the South"
[41] Roche, Emma Langton "Historic Sketches of the South"
[42] Account of the Clotilda by Captain William Foster, "Last Slaver from U.S. To Africa. A.D. 1860" Mobile Public Library Digital Archives http://digital.mobilepubliclibrary.org/items/show/1802
[43] Account of the Clotilda by Captain William Foster, "Last Slaver from U.S. To Africa. A.D. 1860" Mobile Public Library Digital Archives http://digital.mobilepubliclibrary.org/items/show/1802
[44] SEARCH., Final Report "Archeological Investigations of 1Ba704, A nineteenth-Century Shipwreck in the Mobile River
[45] "Dreams of Africa in Alabama"
[46] Account of the Clotilda by Captain William Foster, "Last Slaver from U.S. To Africa. A.D. 1860" Mobile Public Library Digital Archives http://digital.mobilepubliclibrary.org/items/show/1802

Once in the canebrake, the naked Clotilda survivors were given clothes to wear. They were not the beautiful and customized garbs they wore at home. Instead, they were made of thick, coarse fabric, which hung loosely on their thin frames.

The enslaved Africans were then hidden in the swamp located on John Dabney's Mount Vernon plantation. They slept under a wagon shed at night and were brought to the swamp before daybreak, where they stayed until darkness fell.

Meaher secretly sent word to prospective buyers of the kidnapped men, women, and children. He lined them up, women on one side, men on the other. The potential white male buyers would run their rough hands over Clotilda's survivors' arms and legs to inspect their strength and health.[47] The White men would look at their teeth. The group of Clotilda survivors got smaller and smaller as they were sold off. The remaining survivors would grieve for their former life, speaking softly to each other at night.

Finally, Meaher decided to divide up the group because the hiding place in the swamp was too thick with mosquitos.[48] The group, which bonded strongly over the treacherous journey, sang a parting song with tears rolling down their faces as they were separated. Some of its words were *'lona se wu'* or 'no danger on the road.'[49]

Captain Tim Meaher took 32 captives (16 men and 16 women), and Byrnes Meaher, Tim's brother, took ten couples. James John Dabney and Foster were all given enslaved people from the Clotilda. Some were sold up the river in the town of de Bogue Chitto.[50]

Some stories said the Clotilda survivors were sold, but in an interview, Augustine Meaher, Jr., Captain Tim Meaher's grandson, said that the Clotilda men, women, and children were only rented, despite some stories they were sold.[51]

"Slave prices were too high," said Augustine Meaher, Jr. "It cost as much as $2,000 (approximately $73,283.61 today) for a field hand and $5,000 (approximately $183,209.04 today) for a butler. You could get a cow for $2 ($73.28) then."[52]

Meaher's enslaved people worked on his plantation and steamboats. Pollee and Rose were laborers on one of Meaher's Mobile area plantations.[53] The Magazine Point land was fertile, and they were "astonished" to see a mule behind a plow.[54] Pollee's ancestors say he was paired up with Rose and then married to her.

---

[47] Emma Langton Roche, "Historic Sketches of the South" page 100
[48] "Dreams of Africa in Alabama"
[49] "Dreams of Africa in Alabama"
[50] "Dreams of Africa in Alabama"
[51] Roger Rapoport, "African Descendants Still Live in Plateau", The Southern Courier, June 17-18, 1967
http://www.southerncourier.org/hi-res/Vol3_No25_1967_06_17.pdf
[52] Roger Rapoport, "African Descendants Still Live in Plateau", The Southern Courier, June 17-18, 1967
http://www.southerncourier.org/hi-res/Vol3_No25_1967_06_17.pdf
[53] Emma Langton Roche, "Historic Sketches of the South"
[54] Emma Langton Roche, "Historic Sketches of the South"

The captives were ½ female and ½ male, and all enslaved were married so that they could procreate more enslaved workers for their new masters.

The Clotilda survivors who were given to Byrnes Meaher told stories of great hardship. They were given one pair of shoes, sent to the field at daybreak, and worked until night when they returned to their homes by torchlight.[55]

Global Headlines

Stories about the illegal importation of slaves were reported both locally and in international news. The Nashville Tennessean reported on July 10, 1860, "New Orleans, June 9-The Schooner Clotilda with 103 Africans arrived in Mobile Bay and a steamboat took the Negroes up the river".[56]

The other newspaper articles appeared in The Baltimore Daily Exchange on July 11, 1860; The Wilmington Daily Herald on July 12, 1860; and the Montgomery Weekly Post on July 18, 1860. The Janesville Daily Gazette, July 14, 1860, also reported on the crime.[57] Human trafficking also became international news with an entry in The London Morning Post on October 5, 1860.[58]

The U.S. reports prompted a search for the Clotilda by the US Government.

Thaddeus Sanford, the US Collector in Mobile, wrote to Howell Cobb, the Secretary of the Treasury, on July 17, 1860, alerting, "the evidence that the schooner Clotilde [sic], Capt. Foster, from the coast of Africa…entered this bay with a cargo of slaves about a week ago, is pretty near conclusive".

Sanford reported the Clotilda was towed up the "Tensaw River," and the people on board were sold or distributed to local residents and "speculators:"[59]

"Under a very strong belief of the truth of this report, I felt it my duty to advise the charter of a small steamer to pursue this vessel and cooperate with the US Marshal in his endeavors to capture her. To this end, Mr. Godbold started in the steamer yesterday evening to explore the rivers, creeks, inlets, etc., with which the upper waters of our bay abound and with which M. Godbold the Marshal is well acquainted. It is believed that Clotilde [sic] is secreted in someone of these by-placed, and should this be true, M. Godbold will be certain to overtake her."[60]

But it was too late. The Clotilda was destroyed. There were no enslaved persons found, and the ship was never located. By then, the Clotilda captives were all working on various plantations and could not be

---

[55] Emma Langton Roche, "Historic Sketches of the South"
[56] SEARCH., Final Report "Archeological Investigations of 1Ba704, A nineteenth-Century Shipwreck in the Mobile River
[57] SEARCH., Final Report "Archeological Investigations of 1Ba704, A nineteenth-Century Shipwreck in the Mobile River
[58] SEARCH., Final Report "Archeological Investigations of 1Ba704, A nineteenth-Century Shipwreck in the Mobile River
[59] SEARCH., Final Report "Archeological Investigations of 1Ba704, A nineteenth-Century Shipwreck in the Mobile River
[60] SEARCH., Final Report "Archeological Investigations of 1Ba704, A nineteenth-Century Shipwreck in the Mobile River

tracked. Captain William Foster admitted to the burning of the Clotilda[61] to destroy any evidence of the ship or any traces of enslaved people on board (the layers of human feces in the hull of the ship).

Account of the *Clotilda* by Captain William Foster, "Last Slaver from U.S. To Africa. A.D. 1860" Mobile Public Library Digital Archives http://digital.mobilepubliclibrary.org/items/show/1802

In 1861, Meaher and his co-conspirators were eventually charged with illegally smuggling slaves into the country, but the charges were dismissed for a "lack of evidence." Captain Foster was punished with a $1,000 fine for evading customs and not filing his documentation from the voyage.[62]

---

[61] Account of the Clotilda by Captain William Foster, "Last Slaver from U.S. To Africa. A.D. 1860" Mobile Public Library Digital Archives http://digital.mobilepubliclibrary.org/items/show/1802
[62] SEARCH., Final Report "Archeological Investigations of 1Ba704, A nineteenth-Century Shipwreck in the Mobile River

After five years of enslavement, the Union Forces freed the slaves in the Mobile area in April of 1865. Pollee and Rose finally had the liberty to live their own lives. None of the Clotilda survivors adopted the last name of their enslaver, which was common for enslaved people after Emancipation. Pollee instead adopted an American version of his African name, Kupollee, and became Pollee Allen. The surname Allen was a common last name adopted by free Black men.[63]

In the Yorba tradition, a male's name would be in the following order: the first name was of their grandfather, then the first name of their father, and finally adding, their own first name.[64] The American tradition of a person's first name followed by a surname was a foreign concept to them.

It is said Pollee was proud of his African name and did not want to take an American name. He would be very patient and repeat his name several times to census takers and clerks to make sure his name was written down for posterity.[65] This is why, based on the different documents, you will see a variation in spelling: Polee, Pollee, Pollyon, Poe L. In the community, he was also referred to as "Pollee, the elder."[66] The community was very tight, and they highly respected one another. Cudjo and his wife Celia named their third child Pollee in honor of Pollee.[67] The Allen children called Cudjo "Uncle Cudjo".

Pollee and Rose did not want to continue to work on the land for Meaher, so they left his plantation. Pollee found work as a lumber stacker at one of Blackshear Mill, which Meaher owned.[68] According to one of Pollee's great-granddaughters, the Meahers demanded they work an extra hour daily for free. Pollee worked 10 hours a day for one dollar.[69]

According to historical and survivor accounts, when the Clotilda survivors who worked for Meaher asked for land, he refused. He told them they would have to pay for it.

Meaher was a wealthy man after the Civil War. In the 1870 Census, his assets included $20,000 in land and personal property.[70] His son, Augustine, was listed in a 1905 newspaper article as a "multi-millionaire".

At the beginning of Emancipation, Pollee, Rose, and the other Clotilda survivors wanted to return to Africa and attempted to file an application to be accepted into a return program organized by the American

---

[63] Sylviane A. Diouf, "Dreams of Africa" page 134
[64] "Dreams of Africa" page 133
[65] "Dreams of Africa", page 132
[66] "Dreams of Africa", page 136
[67] "Dreams of Africa", page 137
[68] Addie Pettaway, "Africatown, U.S.A. Some Aspects of Folklife and Material Culture of an Historic Landscape", Wisconsin Department of Public Instruction, Bureau for Equal Educational Opportunity, 1985
[69] "Dreams of Africa, page 131
[70] Toulmin, op cit.

Colonization Society (ACS[71]). They were denied. Unable to relocate, Pollee and the other Clotilda male survivors formally announced their intention to become naturalized US citizens in 1868. The women would gain their U.S. citizenship through their husbands.

Since the Clotilda survivors were not born in the United States, they had to become naturalized citizens because the 14th amendment was only for men born in the U.S. or naturalized citizens who could own land. Pollee became a naturalized citizen in 1868.

Name	Polee Allen	
Birth	Circa 1847	
Arrival	1868	
	📍 Mobile Co., Alabama	
Age	21	
Document type	Immigrant Record	
Accession #	9999965143	
Gale Id	578795	
Source publication code	6009.2	
Source	Passenger and Immigration Lists Index	

Source: Passenger and Immigrant Lists Index, MyHeritage

The Clotilda survivors decided they would create their own town and that they would work hard to buy the land they were leasing from Meaher.[72] The land they wanted was perfect. It was near the river that they traveled on when they were purchased and held captive in the Clotilda's hull. The land was located in the already existing town of Plateau.

---

[71] ACS was the idea of Reverend Robert Finley, a Presbyterian minister from New Jersey. Early supporters included Henry Clay, Daniel Webster, and Francis Scott Key, President Thomas Jefferson, James Monroe, and James Madison.
[72] Alabama Baldwin County Clotilda Historical Registry form

Some of the Africatown Founders

Source: Historic Sketches of the South, by Emma Langdon Roche 1914, drawings by Author

The families were frugal and ate molasses on bread to save their money[73]. They also ate cornbread or mush (which was boiled cornmeal).[74] They worked hard in the shipyards and mills. Pollee worked at the sawmill owned by Meaher, his former enslaver. One of Pollee's daughters, Eva Allen Jones, recounted in a 1983 newspaper article that Pollee earned 50 cents a day at that sawmill.[75] Their pay was far less than their sawmill counterparts.

The wage for a sawmill worker in Alabama at that time ranged between $1 to $3 a day.[76] Young boys made less than 10 cents an hour in the planning mill.[77] General laborers earned approximately 14 cents an hour in the mill, planing mill, and the railyard.[78] Pollee and Rose saved their money. On October 21, 1872, Pollee purchased two acres of land for $200 from James M. and Sarah E. Mear and Timothy and Mary C. Meaher.[79] [80]

---

[73] Barracoon

[74] "Historic Sketches of the South"

[75] Jeff Hardy, "Mobile's Africatown Experiencing Renewal," Birmingham Post-Herald, 14 February 1983, https://www.newspapers.com/image/794849356/?terms=africatown&match=1

[76] Matt Parbs, "Museum Works to Profile Sawmill Workers" Clinton Herald, April 14, 2018

[77] Matt Parbs, "Museum Works to Profile Sawmill Workers" Clinton Herald, April 14, 2018

[78] Matt Parbs, "Museum Works to Profile Sawmill Workers" Clinton Herald, April 14, 2018

[79] "Dreams of Africa", page 189

[80] Toulmin, op cit.

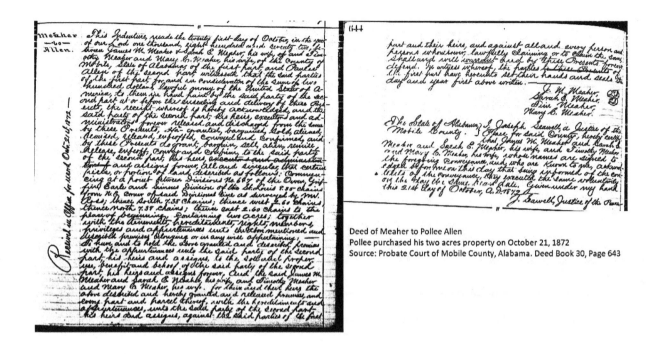

Deed of Meaher to Pollee Allen
Pollee purchased his two acres property on October 21, 1872
Source: Probate Court of Mobile County, Alabama. Deed Book 30, Page 643

According to Pollee's granddaughter, Ivory Hill, Pollee "carried the wood on his back" from the sawmill to the site where he was going to build the home.[81]

Based on historical documents, Pollee likely built his house and paid off his loan in a short period of time. By 1910, records show Pollee owned his house with no mortgage attached.[82]

On September 30, 1872, Africatown, Alabama, was founded by 32 survivors of The Clotilda. They believed they would bring Africa to the United States if they could no longer go back to Africa. Africatown, also known as Plateau, was originally 50 acres two miles north of Mobile, Alabama. Founders said in interviews that they were considerate of one another, and the town's foundation was built on the bricks of "kindness, charity, and harmony."[83]

The women of Africatown elected not to work in white households. Instead, they would stay home with their children, grow fruit and vegetables, and sell their crops in open markets in the county. Eventually, the 32 cofounders of Africatown had enough money to buy their land.

The Africatown founders were very proud of their cleanliness and appearance.[84] Their homes were always clean inside, and their attire and hair were also kept clean and tidy.[85] One of their strongest objections

---

81 Toulmin, op cit.
82 Toulmin, op cit.
83 "Historic Sketches of the South"
84 "Historic Sketches of the South"
85 "Historic Sketches of the South"

at that time was about the look of the former Black enslaved persons born in America. They considered them unclean based on their appearance.[86]

Africatown was developed in two stages.[87] The first stage (1866-1900) was in the southern portion of the district. The five-mile square community constructed homes that were close together so they could form a sharing community like the one they had back in Africa.

According to the United States Department of the Interior National Park Service National Register of Historic Places, these homes were erected in "unplanned" city building standards.[88] The streets were considered "irregularly shaped" and followed the curve of the land versus the traditional grid pattern. The streets were also not in proportion to what was considered as custom.

"A few streets in the oldest portion of the district are only 15 feet wide. The streets are lined with rectangular lots averaging a frontage of 50 feet by 150 feet deep. Occasionally, lots have been doubled or subdivided. Houses in the district are set back 15 to 20 feet, with a few set back 30 feet and with informally landscaped yards, although a few are more heavily planted and well-shaded. In a few instances, houses are situated so that their entrances are at right angles to the street."[89]

The Africatown founders made sure their children would also prosper, and they knew one way to help them on this path of prosperity was land. The founders would purchase land and divide it amongst their children.

The Pollee Allen land, where he and Rose lived, was located south of Bay Bridge Road and across from the south end of Peter Lee Street. The Allen land ran over to the east, as far as the east side of South Magazine Road. With the annexation of land, the exact location of the Pollee and Rose Allen house was what is known today as South Magazine Road, on the east side of that street.

"When Pollee started to buy property, he would get a property for his children," explained Vernetta. "You would find whole families living together on the same street or around the corner. The family was all together."

Vernetta said one of the reasons why the founders created Africatown was its close proximity to the water.

"They felt like they could use the river to board a vessel and go back home."

---

[86] "Historic Sketches of the South"

[87] United States Department of the Interior National Park Service National Register of Historic Places Continuation Sheet Africatown Historic District Name of Property Mobile County, AL, NPS Form 10-900-a OMB No. 1024-0018

[88] United States Department of the Interior National Park Service National Register of Historic Places Continuation Sheet Africatown Historic District Name of Property Mobile County, AL, NPS Form 10-900-a OMB No. 1024-0018

[89] United States Department of the Interior National Park Service National Register of Historic Places Continuation Sheet Africatown Historic District Name of Property Mobile County, AL, NPS Form 10-900-a OMB No. 1024-0018

Africatown was a tight-knit community that kept to themselves. The 30 homes that made up Africatown ranged from log cabins to shotgun-style homes[90]. They were built close together in a five-mile radius. The closeness resembled the sharing community they grew up in when they lived in Africa. Resources and food were easily shared among the Africatown residents. Pollee had a modest shotgun-style home that was 12 feet wide and 16 feet long.[91]

In the 1880 Census, Pollee was listed as working at the sawmill and was recorded as not being able to read. Rose could not read or write, according to the Census. Other Africatown residents, who were Clotilda survivors, were also listed as illiterate.

On March 15, 1880, Pollee and Rose were officially married in the eyes of the state of Alabama. Cudjo Lewis was present for their marriage. According to additional marriage documents, Pollee was also listed on Cudjo Lewis' license.

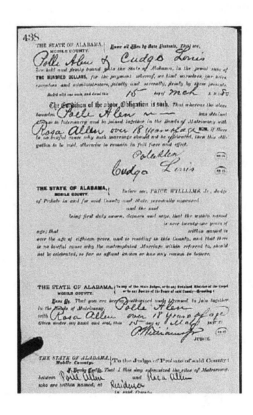

By the time the government recognized their union, Pollee and Rose already had four of their six children. In the 1880 census, their oldest child, Julia (recorded as "Eulia" in the census), was 14 years old.

---

90 A house where all of the rooms are directly behind one another, named this way because if someone were to shoot a gun through the house, the bullet would go through every room.
91 Toulmin, op cit.

Mary, age 7, Milly, age 5, and Joshua, age 2, were also listed. Julia is Vernetta's great-grandmother. Rose was known as "Maum," and Pollee was affectionately called "Poppa" by his children.[92]

Pollee and Rose's children were hard workers. They either worked at the lumber mill or on the land. Mary Allen, one of Pollee's daughters, was a baker. Her son Clarence would sell her pies and cakes at the R.H. Benner Mill, where he worked and sold them.[93] Pollee's children taught their children to be proud of their heritage and to be self-sufficient. Mary's two daughters, Rosina Celestine and Viola Elizabeth, both worked. Rosina was a waitress, and Viola worked at the lumber mill.[94]

Pollee had a thriving garden and was an expert beekeeper. Rows of onions, garlic, scuppernong grapes, peanuts, watermelons, cantaloupes, bananas, pears, plums, apples, figs, and okra were grown. He also tended to his bees and used the honey for medicine and nutrition. Pollee also raised livestock. Chickens, cows, hogs, and horses were on his property. He also did carpentry work if hired. Africatown founders were known to have a "high reputation for honesty and industry."[95] Their lessons of hard work and reputation were examples for their children.

In an interview, daughter Eva Allen Jones fondly remembered her father, Pollee, saying her father grew watermelons and corn. She said Pollee grew the corn because, out of all his children, she loved popcorn the most. One of her greatest joys as a kid and adult was hearing the kernels bang against the pot.[96]

The second phase in Africatown's expansion was a second seven-acre plot just a mile west of the settlement. It was called "Lewis Quarters" in honor of one of its founders, Charlie Lewis.

Africatown Governance and Equity

The founders of Africatown established a system of government based on the African law they all grew up with in Africa and was based on three judges.

Gumpa (also known as African Peter or Peter Lee), Charlee (or "Orsey" in Tarkar), and Jaybee were the judges who presided over Africatown.[97] If a disagreement came up, the judges would be notified, and a meeting would happen at night at one of the judge's homes. They were not considered to be above reproach.

If there was a disagreement and there was no resolution, both sides would have a hearing before the whole town. Each side would then be reprimanded and warned to keep the peace. If they didn't, they would be punished. Jaybee, Gumpa, or Charlee would then whip the offender.[98]

---

[92] Toulmin, op cit.
[93] Addie Pettaway, "Africatown, U.S.A. Some Aspects of Folklife and Material Culture of an Historic Landscape", Wisconsin Department of Public Instruction, Bureau for Equal Educational Opportunity, 1985
[94] Toulmin, op cit.
[95] Toulmin, op cit.
[96] Jeff Hardy, "Mobile's Africatown Experiencing Renewal," Birmingham Post-Herald, 14 February 1983, https://www.newspapers.com/image/794849356/?terms=africatown&match=1
[97] "Historic Sketches of the South"
[98] "Historic Sketches of the South"

United Front for Diversity

Emancipation may have freed the survivors of the Clotilda from their human traffickers and enslavers, but that did not mean the racial tensions between the communities or their being targets of hate would stop. In 1874, Pollee, Cudjo Lewis, and Charlie Lewis said they attempted to vote for the first time at several local polling locations, only to have Timothy Meaher, who followed them on horseback, intimidate them.

Firsthand accounts detailed how Timothy Meaher got election workers to turn the three men away, saying the three men were not eligible to vote. Pollee, Cudjo, and Charlie walked to a second location, but Meaher again prevented them from voting, saying to the poll workers, "See those Africans? Don't let them vote. They are not of this country."[99]

Meaher followed the men on a horse to another polling place and said, "Don't let those Africans vote- they have no right- they are not of this country."[100]

Pollee, Cudjo Lewis, and Charlie Lewis were strong-willed men and had a devoted faith in God. The three men put their hands together and raised them to the sky.[101] They then prayed to God that he would permit them to vote. They believed that the power of God would help them achieve what they were legally allowed to do- vote. The next polling place they decided to walk to was in Mobile. They walked one behind the other (which was a Tarkar custom), and they headed to the St. Francis Street polling place. The men explained to the poll workers their situation, and they were told if they paid one dollar, they could vote.[102]

The poll tax was the equivalent of one day's wage, but they did not care. They paid the poll tax and voted. The three men cast their ballot for Lincoln, who supported the full rights for blacks – the Republican Party. They were proud of their accomplishment, and the paper they received in exchange for their vote became one of their greatest treasures.

The unity and cohesiveness of Africatown helped the community thrive and prosper despite the racial tensions and challenges.

---

[99] "Historic Sketches of the South"
[100] "Historic Sketches of the South"
[101] "Historic Sketches of the South"
[102] "Historic Sketches of the South"

Combining African Culture with Colonial America

Pollee Allen, who completed the religious rites of Orisa, and Cudjo Lewis, who was raised in a different African faith, gradually accepted Christianity. But they merged their Christian beliefs with their African principles.

Once emancipated, some of the survivors of the Clotilda, including Pollee and Rose, wanted to feed their spirit with religion. Pollee, Rose, and other Africatown residents first attended what they called "a little white Methodist Church in Toulminville."[103]

Years later, Pollee, Rose, and other Africatown residents turned to the Baptist Faith.[104]

The Baptist faith was popular amongst former enslaved persons as it was introduced to them either during their time in enslavement or by the Baptist missionaries and pastors who traveled from Virginia, South Carolina, and Tennessee.[105]

Pollee, Rose, and other Africatown residents would walk around four miles[106] to attend Stone Street Baptist Church, the first Black Baptist Church in the state.[107] This church was a semi-independent church of the Stone Street Baptist Church for Whites. The initial Stone Street Baptist church for Black worshippers was constructed of bush tops and straw, which was held up by connecting poles. The church was also referred to as "The African Church."[108] Pollee, Rose, and the other Africatown residents who attended Stone Street were baptized and united in faith under Reverend Benjamin Burke, who was the pastor at that time.[109] Their love of God extended beyond Sundays, where they held prayer meetings in different homes.[110]

Pollee, Rose, and other Africatown cofounders desired to create their own local church. The trustees of Stone Street Baptist Church--James Henderson, George Byrd, and Fred Jones--had 2.5 acres of land in their location, and they told Pollee and Cudjo they would allow them to use the land and sell it to them so they could build their own church. The price would be $10 (the equivalent of $347.38 today).

The church was officially named the "Old Baptist Church" in 1872, and the congregation chose Reverend Henry McGray as their pastor to lead the church.[111] They called the location *the Praying Ground,*

---

[103] Addie Pettaway, "Africatown, U.S.A. Some Aspects of Folklife and Material Culture of an Historic Landscape", Wisconsin Department of Public Instruction, Bureau for Equal Educational Opportunity, 1985

[104] Addie Pettaway, op cit.

[105] "Black Baptists in Alabama", Encyclopedia of Alabama

[106] Calculation based on Google Maps

[107] Stone Street Baptist Church was organized in 1806, thirteen years before Alabama became a state.

[108] Stone Street Baptist Church plaque, The African American Heritage Trail of Mobile

[109] Addie Pettaway, op cit.

[110] Addie Pettaway, op cit.

[111] Addie Pettaway, op cit.

and Stone Street Church owned it until the congregation of Africatown could purchase it[112]. The co-founders of Africatown set off to save their money. In 1903, the name of the church was changed to Union Baptist Church, and Reverend Watson became their first pastor.[113]

Pollee, Rose, and other Africatown residents finally saved enough money collectively to purchase the land. On November 28, 1904, Pollee Allen, Nick Caffey, and Cudjo Lewis became Union Baptist Church's official trustees.[114] Also stipulated in the deed, "and their successors forever."[115] Allen, Caffey, and Lewis did not sign the document. Their dream of having their own church became a reality.

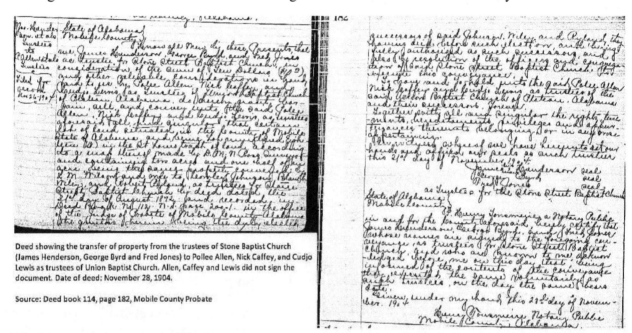

Deed showing the transfer of property from the trustees of Stone Baptist Church (James Henderson, George Byrd and Fred Jones) to Pollee Allen, Nick Caffey, and Cudjo Lewis as trustees of Union Baptist Church. Allen, Caffey and Lewis did not sign the document. Date of deed: November 28, 1904.

Source: Deed book 114, page 182, Mobile County Probate

Before there were church facilities, Baptisms were done in Three Mile Creek near the Cochrane Bridge and in a creek near the hardwood yard facing East.[116] This was a big occasion, and many residents would come out to watch and celebrate.

The original Union Baptist church was a white wooden structure and was rebuilt twice to accommodate the growing congregation.[117] Both of those structures were built by the residents of Africatown. The first

---

[112] Deed book 114, page 181, Mobile County Probate- in this portion of the bill of sale, the land is referred to as a parcel owned by the Church and the deed was dated August 31, 1872.

[113] Addie Pettaway, "Africatown, U.S.A. Some Aspects of Folklife and Material Culture of an Historic Landscape", Wisconsin Department of Public Instruction, Bureau for Equal Educational Opportunity, 1985

[114] Deed book 114, page 181, Mobile County Probate- in this portion of the bill of sale, the land is referred to as a parcel owned by the Church and the deed was dated August 31, 1872.

[115] Deed book 114, page 181, Mobile County Probate- in this portion of the bill of sale, the land is referred to as a parcel owned by the Church and the deed was dated August 31, 1872.

[116] Addie Pettaway, op cit.

[117] Addie Pettaway, op cit.

church faced the East.[118] [119] The second church was the same style as the first and faced Green Avenue.[120] The shade of trees flanked the church.

Cudjo, who lived next to the church, had a fence with eight gates, symbolizing the eight gates surrounding their Tarkar village. Cudjo was the Sexton of the church and was responsible for ringing the church bell as well as opening the building for meetings. Cudjo taught the younger children how to ring the bell as he got older.[121]

The Africatown congregation was very proud of their church and kept the church very clean. The church was swept before every service on Wednesday, Friday, and Sunday night.[122] The first white church did not have electricity, so they used oil lamps. Every week, the lamps were cleaned outside until they sparkled.[123] The children of the congregation would come in with scrub buckets and clean the church. The congregation received Communion once a month. Church business during that time was still conducted at Stone Street Baptist Church.[124]

There is an undated photo of one of the white churches, which includes the congregation. The photo depicts a celebration of Baptism. The children were wearing white, which is the signature color of Baptism.

In the photo, Pollee can be distinctly seen under the archway of the door of the church, wearing his thin tie and jacket. It is similar to the one seen in the sketch. The facial features were exact. The authors can confirm the existence of this photo because it was shown to one of them by Union Baptist Pastor Derek Tucker[125]. Vernetta and Veda were not aware of the photo. Pastor Derek Tucker is in possession of the photo.

The church was also a site of communal gatherings. Picnics on the church grounds would be a time when families could get together. When they built the first church, a long shed was also created. In this shed they stored a long table that was used for the picnics.[126] For $1.20 (approximately $36.39 today), a family could eat no matter what size. The night before a picnic, the men would dig a pit where they would barbeque hogs, goats, and cows. There was a house built behind the church where things would be stored and

---

[118] Addie Pettaway, op cit.
[119] Early Christian churches constructed churches facing East based on historical documents that one should turn to the East to pray.
[120] Addie Pettaway, op cit.
[121] Addie Pettaway, op cit.
[122] Addie Pettaway, op cit.
[123] Addie Pettaway, op cit.
[124] Addie Pettaway, op cit.
[125] In person conversation with Union Baptist Church Pastor Derrick Tucker, August 14, 2023
[126] Addie Pettaway, op cit.

prepared.[127] On the day of the barbeque, the women of the congregation would serve plates of food on the long table.

The brick church, which currently stands and is in current use, was constructed from 1943 to 1955.

Practicing Faith Using the Foundation of African Principles

The Baptist parish founded by the Clotilda survivors was devout. Services were held every Sunday night and Friday night, with Sunday school on Sunday morning at the church. They would have one pastoral service a month. Attendance was important to the church elders.

The Africatown residents ran their church with the same communal involvement as they did when they lived in Africa. Based on half a dozen church ledger books spanning from the 1900s to the 1930s, the congregation kept copious notes providing keen insight into the church's happenings and its members' participation. Earlier ledgers dating to the late 1880s were not found. All of these ledgers are in possession of Pastor Tucker. Vernetta and her daughter Veda did not know these ledgers existed until Pastor Tucker showed the books to the author.

Every Sunday was annotated. Neatly and methodically written down in lists were the number of weekly dues individual members paid, an account of which members did not pay their dues, attendance, an itemized account of Church expenses such as utilities, as well as what hymns and scriptures were read. Donations to the poor were also included. Dues were collected and recorded by the Deacons or "Ward Leaders."

According to the documents, a meeting would be called to order before each church service. This meeting would follow the "Robert's Rules of Order."[128] In addition to hearing about the church's business affairs, the congregation would also evaluate and vote on much more serious issues.

Like their laws in Africa, where an offender would have to go before the entire community if a fellow parishioner violated the church's code of conduct, the congregation would hear the offense and vote on a punishment they deem appropriate.

Based on church ledger records, if a member was found in violation, they could pay a hefty fine, be expelled by the congregation for a length of time (one account had one member expelled for a month), or if the parishioner committed a serious offense or multiple offenses, they would be expelled permanently. The founding congregation of the church was also very strict on behavior and did not allow dancing or drinking. By the 1930s, however, there were wine purchases listed in the ledger under church expenses.

The ledgers also showed how the congregation would help one another if members were in need. A year before Cudjo passed away, the church gave him $27 (the equivalent of about $494.23 today). Other

---

[127] Addie Pettaway, op cit.
[128] Robert's Rules of Order was published in 1876 and named after Colonel Henry Martyn Robert who was a military engineer in the U.S. Army. The rules were designed to conduct a meeting effectively. The most important are main motions, which are brought before an organization, for a 2/3 vote. Once there is a vote, another member has to second that motion.

members were given smaller sums of assistance through the years. Loans were also made and repaid. Reports of sacrifice to help the congregation were also recorded. During the Spanish Flu and World War I, Pastor Joiffu (Reverend Joyful) Keeby, son of Africatown cofounders Ossa and Annie Keeby, did not take a salary for one year in order for the church to use the money elsewhere.[129] Vernetta said members of the Africatown church were also very charitable, bringing preachers peaches along with other fruits and vegetables.

Pollee's granddaughter Viola explained in an interview the word "Reverend" was not used at the beginning of the church.[130] If it was, Pollee would have been called a Reverend. Instead, he was referred to being a church Elder. As an elder, he would sometimes preach during mass. His sermons were not the fist-pounding "fire and brimstone." After church services, some members would go to the homes of Pollee, Cudjo, or Abache, where they would discuss the current matters of the day but would also end every conversation with a story about their beloved hometowns in Africa.

Pollee's religious faith was strong, and he always carried a small, worn copy of the New Testament with him. It was referred to as Pollee's "constant companion."[131] Researchers found a small New Testament Bible dating back to Pollee's time in the old white church before they tore it down, but it remains unknown if it belongs to Pollee. Pastor Tucker said the Bible is in his possession. Family Bibles were an important part of family record keeping where births, marriages, deaths, and important milestones were recorded.

Pollee was once asked to reflect on his personal journey of kidnapping, slavery, and emancipation. His response was steeped deep in faith. "We know not why these troubles came upon us, but we are all God's children- we not always see the way, but his hands guide us and shape our ends."[132]

This deep faith was passed down to future generations, including Vernetta's.

Like most churches in Black communities, Union Baptist Church served a dual purpose- nourishing the spirit and the mind. Black children were normally taught in churches, and in Africatown, this was no exception. The Africatown residents did not wait for "white people's assistance" in building a school.[133] They viewed themselves as independent and frowned upon how other "colored people" would wait for "white handouts."[134] Once they had a structure built, they asked the county for a Black female teacher.[135]

The first school, called The Plateau Normal and Industrial Institute for the Education of the Head, Heart, and Hands of the Colored Youth, was established at the Union Baptist Church. This education also helped Pollee, as oral history said he learned how to read and write from his children.

---

[129] Union Baptist Church ledger
[130] Addie Pettaway, op cit.
[131] Toulmin, op cit.
[132] "Historic Sketches of the South"
[133] "Dreams of Africa", page 177
[134] "Dreams of Africa", page 177
[135] "Dreams of Africa", page 178

The founders of Africatown built a schoolhouse in 1910, and the county designated a teacher for the school. The school was then renamed Mobile County Training School *(MCTS)*. Today, it is known as "the cradle or birthplace of Black public high schools"[136] because it was the first high school in Mobile for Blacks. Five of the six public high schools in Mobile have ties to MCTS. It is the oldest county training school in Alabama and is still in operation today.

Even though their children were taught and educated in English, Pollee and Rose spoke Yoruba, their native tongue in their home, as well as their six children. Their daughter, Julia, married William Ellis on March 18, 1886.

It was common in Africatown for the residents to generally speak in their native tongue. They did not learn to speak English fluently. It was part of their unique bond and promotion of African culture. Part of their culture was their walking gait. Just like it was custom to walk in single file, the Africatown men always walked with a very straight back, and their shoulders were squared with confidence. This distinct walking gait set them apart from other Black men and women. Pollee, himself, always walked at a quick pace.

In 1889 or 1890, Pollee lost his wife, Rose, at around the age of 48.[137] A family photo of Rose has her holding her grandson, Leonard, when he was a young child.

---

[136] Joe Womack, "Africatown's High School - The Cradle of Mobile's Black Education" June 11, 2017, Bridge the Gulf https://bridgethegulfproject.org/blog/2017/africatowns-high-school-cradle-mobiles-black-education
[137] Toulmin, op cit.

**Rose Allen & her
grandson Leonard Ellis**

Source: Llewellyn (Lew) M. Toulmin, PhD,
FRGS, FN '04, The Polee, Rose and Lucy Allen
Lines: Genealogical Descents from Africa, the
Slave Ship Clotilda, and Africatown, Alabama
to the Present

Rose and Pollee's daughter, Julia, was not listed with a job in the 1900 Census, but her husband, William, was registered as a carpenter. Their oldest of five children, Leonard, was documented as being in school. According to the census, both Julia and William could read and write.

William Ellis and Julia Allen Ellis

Source: Llewellyn (Lew) M.
Toulmin, PhD, FRGS, FN '04
"The Polee, Rose and Lucy
Allen Lines: Genealogical
Descents from Africa, the Slave
Ship Clotilda, and Africatown,
Alabama to the Present"
Africatown, Alabama and
Silver Spring, Maryland August
2022; 2nd Edition

On December 17, 1891, Pollee married 19-year-old Lucy Turner. She was the daughter of Clotilda survivor Abache, "Clara," Aunspaugh Turner. Lucy was born in Alabama on September 10, 1872, and was at least 30 years younger than Pollee.[138] Together, they had 13 children. Unlike Rose, whose native tongue was Yoruba, Lucy could not speak Yoruba fluently, so she and her children spoke English.

Pollee and Lucy had ten children, and he was a wonderful provider for his large family. Even though Lucy did not speak Yoruba, their children did have African names, and were used in the house. But that did not mean the children would use those names in public.

In 1894, their daughter, "Joko"[139] was born. "Joko" was an abbreviation of "Bamijoko." In Yoruba, it means "stay with me[140]" or "sit with me"[141]. Outside of the home, she went by Eva. In an interview, she recalled her father's devotion to providing for their family. When she would go tell her father it was time for dinner, he would tell her, "Go tell your mama I can eat by lamplight, but I can't do no planting by lamplight."[142] Pollee worked from six to six.[143] After work, he would either come home and tend to the fruits and vegetables in the garden, or he would be building things for his children. One of the things he made was a swing made out of wood and iron bars. The swing would have a floor in it, so babies could swing in it as well. In addition to his personal farm, he also worked at times as a carpenter.

All of Pollee's children learned about his life in Africa, which was described as a paradise with a bounty of fruits and vegetables.[144] The children would listen to stories by their father, who would have tears in his eyes. They would also see him, along with "Uncle Cudjo," crying about going home. They were told how bananas, coconuts, and oranges grew in abundance. Pollee refused to eat any of these fruits in Mobile. His daughter Eva believed if he ate the fruits, it would make him homesick.

Officially Making the Map

In 1889, Africatown was first identified on an official map of Mobile.[145] Paul Charles Boudousquie, who was an architect, map publisher, and civil engineer in the Mobile District from 1870 to 1900, added "African Colony" at Magazine Point in the 1889 revision of his map.

---

[138] Data from Familysearch.org

[139] Clara E. Jones Obituary, The Pittsburgh Press, Wednesday, February 12, 1992, page 20

[140] "Dreams of Africa", page 137

[141] Earnshaw Desmond Bamijoko Palmer, UK, comment section of "What's in an African Name?" BBC, December 15, 2003 http://news.bbc.co.uk/2/hi/africa/3314075.stm#:~:text=In%20Yoruba%2C%20Joko%20is%20to,have%20meaning%20which%20children%20are

[142] "Dreams of Africa", page 189

[143] Addie Pettaway, op cit.

[144] "Dreams of Africa", page189

[145] United States Department of the Interior National Park Service National Register of Historic Places Continuation Sheet Africatown Historic District Name of Property Mobile County, AL County and State NPS Form 10-900-a OMB No. 1024-0018

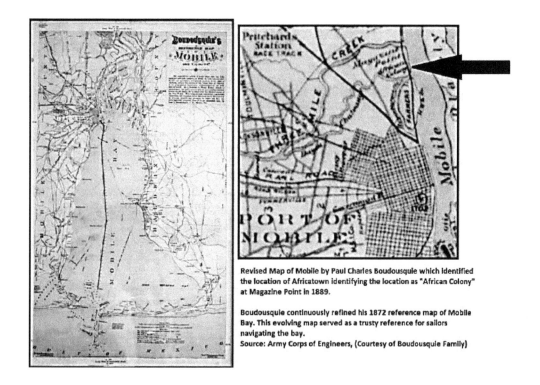

Revised Map of Mobile by Paul Charles Boudousquie which identified the location of Africatown identifying the location as "African Colony" at Magazine Point in 1889.

Boudousquie continuously refined his 1872 reference map of Mobile Bay. This evolving map served as a trusty reference for sailors navigating the bay.
Source: Army Corps of Engineers, (Courtesy of Boudousquie Family)

Those who met Pollee said his face never changed expression. It was his eyes that did. They were the window to his soul. His eyes were described as being small and deep-set, and he watched you thoughtfully.[146]

Pollee passed away on August 19, 1922, after battling pneumonia for 20 days. The death certificate listed the approximately 80-year-old Pollee's occupation as a sawmill laborer. The death certificate also inaccurately listed his age at the time of death as 58. This discrepancy would most likely be Lucy's age at the time of Pollee's passing.

---

[146] "Historic Sketches of the South"

CERTIFICATE OF DEATH

STATE OF ALABAMA—BUREAU OF VITAL STATISTICS
STATE BOARD OF HEALTH

File No. for State Register Only.

1 PLACE OF DEATH
County
Town or City of ____ No. ____ St. ____ Ward ____
Registration District No. ____ Registered No. ____

(If death occurred in a hospital or institution, give its NAME instead of street and number)

2 FULL NAME Palee Allen
(a) Residence, No. ____ St., ____ Ward ____
(Usual place of abode)
Length of residence in city or town where death occurred ____ yrs. ____ mos. ____ ds. How long in U. S., if of foreign birth? ____ yrs. ____ mos. ____ ds.
(If nonresident, give city or town and State)

PERSONAL AND STATISTICAL PARTICULARS

3 SEX Male
4 COLOR OR RACE Colored
5 SINGLE, MARRIED, WIDOWED, OR DIVORCED (Write the word) Married

5a If married, widowed, or divorced HUSBAND of (or) WIFE of Lucy Allen

6 DATE OF BIRTH (month, day, and year)

7 AGE Years 58 Months ____ Days ____ If LESS than 1 day ____ hrs. ____ or ____ min.

8 OCCUPATION OF DECEASED
(a) Trade, profession or particular kind of work Saw mill Laborer
(b) General nature of industry, business, or establishment in which employed (or employer)
(c) Name of employer

9 BIRTHPLACE (city or town) (State or country) Africa

10 NAME OF FATHER Don't Know
11 BIRTHPLACE OF FATHER (city or town) (State or country) Don't Know
12 MAIDEN NAME OF MOTHER Don't Know
13 BIRTHPLACE OF MOTHER (city or town) (State or country) Africa

14 Informant Lucy Allen (Address)

15 Filed Aug 21, 1922 Geo Bryars Registrar

MEDICAL CERTIFICATE OF DEATH

16 DATE OF DEATH (month, day, and year) Aug. 19, 1922

17 I HEREBY CERTIFY, That I attended deceased from Aug. 7, 1922 to Aug. 19, 1922
that I last saw h— alive on Aug. 19, 1922
and that death occurred, on the date stated above, at 10:30 a. m.
The CAUSE OF DEATH was as follows:

CONTRIBUTORY (Secondary)

18 Where was disease contracted if not at place of death?
Did an operation precede death? No Date of
Was there an autopsy?
What test confirmed diagnosis?
(Signed) ____ M. D.
(Address)

*State the DISEASE CAUSING DEATH, or in deaths from VIOLENT CAUSES, state (1) MEANS AND NATURE OF INJURY, and (2) whether ACCIDENTAL, SUICIDAL, or HOMICIDAL. (See reverse side for additional information.)

19 PLACE OF BURIAL, CREMATION, or REMOVAL Plateau, Ala.
DATE OF BURIAL Aug 21, 1922
20 UNDERTAKER Johnson — Alb.
ADDRESS Plateau, Ala.

Lucy lived in Africatown until she passed on November 19, 1952.

32

Vernetta was raised by her grandmother, Ora Anna Ellis Floyd, and grandfather, Nathan Daniel Floyd, after her parents, Rosemary Floyd Peters and Fred Peters, divorced. Rosemary was the oldest of Ora and Nathan's 11 children. She was baptized at Union Baptist Church in Plateau (Africatown), and she graduated from Tuskegee University with her degree in Nursing and her Master's Degree and Nurse Practitioner certificate from Georgetown University. Rosemary was also an Ordained Minister.

Peters Family Photo
(Left to Right) Fred Peters, Rosemary holding baby Vernetta
Source: Henson Family

Vernetta was born a preemie and arrived at her grandparent's home at around six months of age. She was considered one of their children. Her grandfather, Nathan, worked at the R.H. Bemmer Sawmill[147] as a young adult and then as a porter at Seamen's Club in Mobile. He later worked at Mobile General Hospital as a custodian. Grandmother Ora had her own small business in Africatown, where she sold her produce and dairy products.

"My grandmother had a book that logged what people purchased from her, but if they never paid, she understood," said Vernetta. "Many people in Africatown had small businesses but operated out of their homes. My grandmother had a storefront."

Ora closed her store once she moved into a new 15-room home her sons built for her in Toulminville. The town was three miles away from Africatown, where Vernetta grew up grew up three miles away from Africatown.

---

[147] World War I Selective Service System Draft Registration Cards, Draft Board: Mobile County; Eager, George-Sellers, J. M.

On weekends Vernetta would stay with her aunts, Estelle Wilson and Ruth Turner, in Africatown so she could attend church and spend time with her family. When either of her aunts entertained, she would stay at one of their houses to help them cook and serve meals.

Here, Aunt Estelle Wilson had a potbelly wood stove in her bedroom and a second one in her kitchen. Vernetta would spend the night in that bedroom, and in that stove, her aunt would cut up a chicken in a skillet, and when she woke up, the warm smell of chicken would fill her nostrils. The chickens she cooked were ones her aunt raised. The tender chicken, thick gravy, and biscuits would warm her young belly.

"You knew you were in for a good day when you smelled her biscuits waking up," laughed Vernetta.

Africatown was a vibrant area when Vernetta was growing up. There were a series of mom-and-pop stores. Additional Clotilda descendants also had stores.

Some of the businesses that flanked the business district of Africatown were Hubbard's grocery, a service station, and the Williams Motel. The residents would receive their mail by A.T. Days, who ran the one-man post office.

Williams Motel, August 14, 2023

"There is so much history out there you don't realize it until you start talking about it," said Vernetta. "We don't realize how rich our history is. It needs to be told."

Vernetta grew up listening to her grandmother speak of the lessons she learned as a child from her mother, Julia Allen, Pollee's daughter. Vernetta called this type of raising "Generational Training." Each generation was taught the same principles of living a good life, and they never strayed from those principles. This was how Vernetta taught her own children.

The lesson that was handed down from her great-great-grandfather Pollee was to live a life where you were always there for your neighbor. This way of life was learned by Julia, who watched her parents, Rose and Pollee, live by example and create a society that was built on this principle. This was the way of Africatown.

"I came up in a society where everybody on the street was your friend, your neighbor, your parents, so to speak," said Vernetta. "My grandmother was one of those people who believed that adults didn't need to lie to you. If they said you did something that wasn't approved, you did it and didn't have any backtalk. You didn't dispute what the elders said about you. Whatever the neighbors told you to do, you had to do that. The last thing my family said to me when I left the house was, 'Have a good day, and don't do anything to embarrass me.'"

Vernetta was taught her friends were a reflection of who she was. Her grandfather would speak with them, asking about who they were, where they came from, their parents, etc.

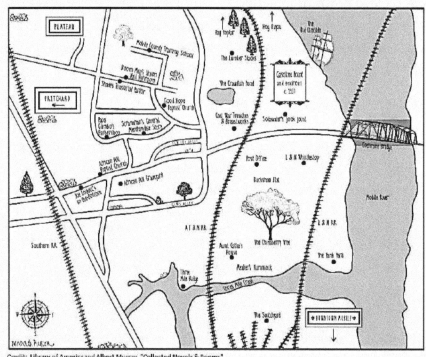

Credit: Library of America and Albert Murray, "Collected Novels & Poems"

One example of this respect for one another is one that deals with one of Vernetta's great cousins, Clara Eva Bell Allen Jones, one of Pollee's children with Lucy Turner. In her obituary, it said, "Mrs. Jones known as 'Momma Eva' because she frequently took care of the children of others…Anybody who was going anywhere or had to leave the area left their children with Momma Eva. She helped raise 63 other children."

Vernetta said this communal support was the cementing foundation of Africatown. The common ideology that everyone mattered **equally** was essential to the town's perseverance in both hard times and good times.

"Back then, everybody wanted the best for *everybody*," she stressed. "And we're in a situation now where we only want our own children to shine, and we don't worry about anybody else. We need that to change. We are stronger together."

Just like the gatherings at Pollee's home after Sunday church services, that type of community and familial bonding continued during Vernetta's rearing. "Big Momma" was the affectionate term for the matriarch of the family. "Big Momma" was Ora in her family.

Ora Anna Ellis Floyd, Pollee and Rose Allen's Granddaughter and Vernetta's Grandmother
Source: Henson Family

"On Sundays, there would probably be at least 20 people at Big Momma's house," said Vernetta. "She'd have homemade ice cream where she would make the custard on the stove and then make it into ice cream with the hand crank freezer. She would either do sweet potato pies or jelly cakes. Sometimes, Blackberry and dumplings. That's how the children stayed close."

Ora lived by the Allen mantra of always finding ways to help her neighbor. She passed this down to all of her children, including Vernetta. As a child, Vernetta would go to the grocery store to pick up bags of groceries for her neighbors. Under her grandmother's instruction, she was never to take a nickel from them. She was taught you are helping your neighbor out of the goodness of your heart. Vernetta said her grandmother always gave away her extra produce during harvest time. They also raised chickens, cows, pecan trees, and fruit trees.

"My grandmother would always pray to the Lord and ask who to send her bounty to," said Vernetta. "He would put somebody on her heart, and she would go and take a dozen eggs or flour and tell them, 'I brought you this bag of flour or brown eggs.' That family would be so happy because they didn't know where their next meal was coming from. Her example influenced me into who I am today."

Vernetta remembered Ora and other Africatown women always wearing a double-sided apron with a pocket on each side. Back in those days, the egg and vegetable man would stop by to sell and drop off their produce or dairy. Her grandmother would keep track of the money for each man in the respective pocket.

Ora's double-sided apron

Source: Vernetta Henson

Ora's highest level of education was the seventh grade.[148]

"They may not have had college degrees, but they were very learned in the organization," said Vernetta. "They always followed a plan and would have eggs, bacon, and grits every morning. Every Sunday, we knew we were going to eat fried chicken, macaroni and cheese, and the whole works. Sometimes, we had stew meat with rice with chicken giblet gravy. On wash day, they prepared a simple meal of boiled peas or beans with cornbread because they had to be outdoors to do their wash. The peas or beans would be slow-cooked with salt meat. For dessert, we would have Jell-O with a fruit cocktail in it. They were very organized and stuck to whatever they were brought up with."

They also planned morning meals. Ora would make preserves from the figs and pear trees, and Vernetta ate biscuits with jelly and sausage in the morning.

One of Vernetta's greatest treasures is one of her grandmother's last aprons. The other treasure is the family quilt. The fabric that makes up the various quilted squares came from her ancestor's military clothes, dresses, and worn clothing. The aprons were also made from various materials. No fabric was wasted.

Floyd family double-sided quilt

Source: Vernetta Henson

---

[148] 1940 Census

Thriftiness was a way of life. This was a skill passed down the Allen family. Just like Pollee and Rose, who saved up money all those years ago to buy their home, land for the church, and for the town's first school, Ora was very careful with her money.

"My grandmother kept what we called the mattress account," Vernetta said. "Whatever money she got, she would wrap it up in a handkerchief and put it in between the two mattresses at the end. Whenever she got ready to buy something, she would open her mattress account, go to the store, and pay cash for it. That's what a lot of people did back then because they didn't have credit or a bank account. African Americans had to save their money, and they called it a mattress account."

The various pieces of fabric that complete this tapestry tell of the Pollee and Rose Allen story and of the descendants who have contributed to society. Asa Ellis, one of the sons of Julia Allen, served as a private in the US Army in World War I. On rainy days, Vernetta said that the children would cut up the fabric so it could be used in the quilts and aprons. Flour sacks were cut and sewn into dresses, either with prints like flowers or even plain flower sacks. There was an intention in every piece of fabric.

"The squares on the quilt speak a language of love, sorrow, and triumph," she said. "I feel blessed because of her upbringing, and I'm trying to pass it on to my children, Edward and Veda."

When they did get "new" clothes, Vernetta said you had to take extra care of them, for they would eventually be passed down to someone else in the family. The baby dolls that Vernetta played with were homemade. A white rope would be affixed onto soda water bottles, and they would curl the rope to make hair. They could not draw faces on the dolls, but it didn't matter. She loved them. Other dolls were made out of clothes pins. They would draw faces on them, and, at nose level, they would place four leaf clovers and flowers, and that would be the doll's clothes. Jacks, marbles, jump rope, and hopscotch were other fun favorites that did not cost a lot of money.

"Black dolls were given to us young girls during Christmas," smiled Vernetta.

Faith

Vernetta said she was put on this earth to do God's will, and this strong sense of faith was passed down from Pollee.

"He (Pollee) was very strong on the spiritual aspects of life and following the Bible," said Vernetta. "Treat everybody with the same respect; reach out to people and don't always look for what you can get out of it. Look at the *good* that it does (your actions) to somebody."

Vernetta said Pollee was known to be helpful to everyone.

The lesson of the Allen family was simple, "whatever was good for you is good enough for me."

Vernetta said that, when she was growing up, Africatown residents did not compare themselves to their neighbors. There was no 'keeping up with the Joneses.' Instead, there was more reverence and admiration.

If neighbors were able to survive tough situations, certainly they too should be able to survive challenging situations as well.

Ora's faith was strong, and she followed the Bible, telling Vernetta to look at the good *you* can do for someone and *never* expect anything in return.

"This is training that I received from my grandmother, who was told by her mother, Julia, and her mother learned from her mother, Rose Allen. This training helped me get to where I am today," said Vernetta.

Choosing Love Instead of Hate

Growing up in Africatown had its challenges, both financially and socially. The animosity between Whites and Blacks was very high during the Jim Crow era when Vernetta was growing up. The enslavers' family still lived in the neighboring town. Violence against Blacks in her area was not uncommon.

"When I went out with my grandmother or when I went out with my friends or by myself, my grandmother always told me, 'Don't look at White people and always say yes, ma'am.' But she never raised me to have hate in my heart against White people. She was wise enough to not let that happen. So, I was fortunate in that respect because I have a lot of friends who developed a serious hatred for White people. Not having that hate gave me the freedom to move ahead. Hate can weigh you down and hold you back."

Growing up as a child, Vernetta said the "Colored" and "White" water fountains and bathrooms were just a part of her life. If she wanted to go to the lunch counter over at S.H. Kress, she had to go through the back door and sit at the designated lunch counter for Black patrons. Vernetta held no ill will in her heart. It was too full of love.

Ora was a civil rights activist in her own way, keeping up with the latest news to stay informed. As a family, they would listen to WMOZ, which was geared to the Black American audience. Her uncle, Vernon Clinton Floyd, was the first Black radio station engineer when it opened in 1956. Vernon was a Black American broadcast pioneer. He went on to found three black radio stations in Mississippi. One of them, WORV-AM, was a part of the company he founded, Circuit Broadcasting Company. WORV-AM was the state's first Black American-owned and operated radio station in 1969. The programming was geared towards the Black American listener. He later added the gospel station, WGDQ, in Sumrall, Mississippi, and WJMG in Hattiesburg, Mississippi.

Vernon was considered a civil rights champion, not only for giving a voice to the Black community but also for using his stations to encourage the Black community to vote. During voter registrations for various elections, the stations would encourage Black Americans to register to vote and to cast their ballots. That same fire his great-grandfather Pollee had to cast his vote in 1874 was burning inside Vernon. He wanted to make sure no Black man or woman would be denied the opportunity to vote. A U.S. Army veteran, Vernon served in World War I and graduated from Tuskegee Institute (now Tuskegee University).

Education and Knowing Family History

Vernetta was lucky to know her family history. Not all of her cousins knew growing up they were descendants of Clotilda survivors. She explained how the history of the Clotilda, Africatown, and slavery were not taught in her history class at school.

"We learned our history and slavery through family," said Vernetta. "Keeping us straight and keeping us at arm's length from White people. Slavery and our story of family was not a subject talked about every day. It was a dinner meal conversation."

Learning about her history and being raised with the values of Pollee and Rose have helped shape Vernetta, but she wished she knew more about what happened to them on that ship.

"I've heard the stories how they were shackled for so many hours on the Clotilda, and they had no clothes, and they were served food, but as far as treatment, I don't know anything," said Vernetta. "When they described the men having good strong backs, that bothered me when I first read it."

If Vernetta had extra time, her grandparents would tell her to "read a book." The family had a set of encyclopedias that she and her grandma read. Vernetta would read the morning paper to her grandmother and the evening paper to her grandfather. This would help her learn the proper pronunciation of words.

"Granddaddy would never tell me how to pronounce a word," said Vernetta. "Sometimes it would take three or four times till I got it right. That was their way of teaching me how to read."

Ora and Nathan made sure all of their children had access to college.

"They knew the power of higher education," said Vernetta. "My grandparents passed down the value of education to her kids, and their kids have also passed it down. Our family is blessed with teachers, electrical engineers, pharmacists, and even members who have obtained doctorates!"

Education was paramount in the household. While there was time for fun, there was one thing Ora was very strict about- dancing. No dancing was allowed in her home. This is a direct link to Pollee and Rose's strict religious beliefs that were passed down.

Ora's husband called her "Kid." Every time he would catch Vernetta doing the Twist or another popular dance, Vernetta would hear him shout, "Kid, she's dancing again! Get that girl and tell her to come in and read!"

Vernetta lived in Toulminville and attended Central High School. Each year, she would go to the back door of Anders bookstore, located on Government Street in Mobile at that time, to buy their used textbooks for school. She would pay three to five dollars for the books. They never stayed in her locker at school. They always came home with her so she could read them, regardless of homework.

"The government gave the new books to the White students," said Vernetta. "We had to purchase the used leftovers, so we didn't have any current history."

Vernetta knows of one person who learned about the Clotilda during school and wrote a book report.

"The only boats we learned about were the Mayflower," said Vernetta.

One of the reasons behind Vernetta's limited history education was the fact it was censored. History books in the South were "UDC-approved." The UDC is the United Daughters of the Confederacy, a powerful force that re-shaped the historical narrative of the Civil War and slavery in textbooks. The group was heavily involved in both writing and publishing textbooks for school-age children.[149] They also were active in banning books that they believed painted the South in the wrong light. This was part of the United Daughters of the Confederacy's pursuit of preserving the history of the Confederacy [150] , otherwise called the "Lost Cause"[151].

In 1919, at the United Confederate Veterans reunion, a committee was created to make sure pro-Confederate ideology was written in textbooks.[152] The United Confederate Veterans, the United Daughters of Confederates, and the Sons of Confederate Veterans (SCV) appointed five members to form the new committee.[153] Because of its most high-profile and vocal member, Mildred Lewis Rutherford, the committee unofficially became known as the "Rutherford Committee." Rutherford was the UDC's historian from 1911-1916. Her speeches made her well-known in the South.

In defending slavery, Rutherford said, "Slavery was no disgrace to the owner or the owned... In all the history of the world, no peasantry was ever better cared for, contented, or happier. These wrongs must be righted, and the Southern slaveholder defended as soon as possible."[154]

Rutherford also praised the Ku Klux Klan as defenders of the white woman.[155]

Popular history books for students attending Alabama schools during the 1950s and 1960s were called "Know Alabama" and "Alabama History for Schools."

In the fourth-grade history book, "Know Alabama," authors Frank L. Owlsey, John Craig Stewart, and Gordon T. Chappell wrote that slaves were "content in captivity," and the Ku Klux Klan as "loyal white

[149] Thurgood Marshall Institute, "Whose History? How Textbooks Can Erase the Truth and Legacy of Racism" https://tminstituteldf.org/books-censorship-black-history/
[150] Scott Morris, "Racist Textbooks Endured Presenting Alternative 'History' to Alabama Students for 70 Years" September 2, 2020. https://birminghamwatch.org/racist-textbooks-endured-presenting-alternate-history-alabama-students-70-years/
[151] Lost Cause: an interpretation of the American Civil War viewed by most historians as a myth that attempts to preserve the honor of the South by casting the Confederate defeat in the best possible light., Encylcopedia Britannica https://www.britannica.com/topic/Lost-Cause
[152] Greg Huffman, "Twisted Sources: How Confederate Propaganda Ended Up in the South's Schools" Facing South, April 10, 2019 https://www.facingsouth.org/2019/04/twisted-sources-how-confederate-propaganda-ended-souths-schoolbooks
[153] Greg Huffman, "Twisted Sources: How Confederate Propaganda Ended Up in the South's Schools" Facing South, April 10, 2019 https://www.facingsouth.org/2019/04/twisted-sources-how-confederate-propaganda-ended-souths-schoolbooks
[154] Rutherford, Mildred Lewis, "Historical Sins of Omission and Commission", United Daughters of the Confederacy, "Address", Friday, October 22, 1915, Civic Auditorium Hall, San Francisco, California https://archive.org/details/addressdelivered04ruth/page/n1/mode/2up
[155] Rutherford, Mildred Lewis, "Historical Sins of Omission and Commission", United Daughters of the Confederacy, "Address", Friday, October 22, 1915, Civic Auditorium Hall, San Francisco, California https://archive.org/details/addressdelivered04ruth/page/n1/mode/2up

men of Alabama" who "...knew they had to do something to bring back law and order, to get the government back in the hands of honest men who knew how to run it."

"The Civil War" was never referenced in the book. Instead, the term "War Between the States" was used. This was based on the influence of the United Daughters of the Confederacy (UDC). Even today, on its website, the UDC does not reference the "Civil War" and continues to have the "War Between the States." in its' place.[156] It wasn't until the 1970 version of the "Civil War" was adequately documented in the "Know Alabama" textbook.[157] It took a U.S. Senate Hearing and protests from Black families to have the real history printed in the book.[158]

In "Alabama History for Schools," it wrote about the "positives" of slavery.[159] "With all the drawbacks of slavery, it should be noted that slavery was the earliest form of social security of the United States." Lynching was not discussed in the book. Segregation was also reportedly not discussed, and the Black political leaders during the Reconstruction period were not included.

What was mentioned in the "Alabama History for Schools" was the story of the Clotilda (identified as the Clotilde"). In the few paragraphs it detailed, it said that there were slave traders who were "willing to take their chances with the law in order to make large profits." Also mentioned was how "Meaher found it impossible to sell most of the slaves he brought in his ship. The War Between the States finally overtook the arguments as to what do to with the slaves, and these Negroes were settled in Africky Town in Mobile County."[160]

---

[156] "Reaffirmation of the Objectives of the United Daughters of the Confederacy", United Daughters of the Confederacy" https://hqudc.org/
[157] Reich, Kenneth, "Some Still Unhappy with History Book", The Los Angeles "The Tuscaloosa News", February 23, 1971 https://news.google.com/newspapers?nid=1817&dat=19710223&id=8gwdAAAAIBAJ&sjid=FpwEAAAAIBAJ&pg=2768,41 62894&hl=en
[158] Kenneth Reich, op cit.
[159] Lyman, Brian, "When the textbooks lied, Black Alabamians turned to each other for history", December 3, 2020 https://www.montgomeryadvertiser.com/story/news/education/2020/12/03/blacks-alabama-turned-each-other-history-when-textbooks-lied/3729292001/
[160] Summersell, Charles Grayson, "Alabama History for Schools", 1961

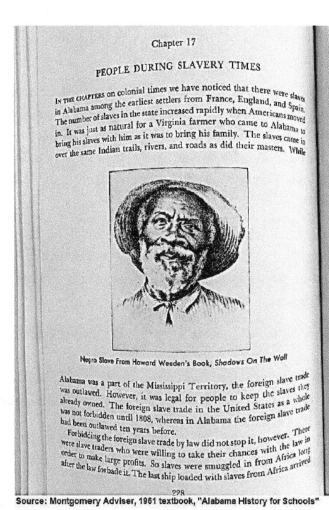

Chapter 17

PEOPLE DURING SLAVERY TIMES

IN THE CHAPTERS on colonial times we have noticed that there were slaves in Alabama among the earliest settlers from France, England, and Spain. The number of slaves in the state increased rapidly when Americans moved in. It was just as natural for a Virginia farmer who came to Alabama to bring his slaves with him as it was to bring his family. The slaves came in over the same Indian trails, rivers, and roads as did their masters. While

Negro Slave From Howard Weeden's Book, *Shadows On The Wall*

Alabama was a part of the Mississippi Territory, the foreign slave trade was outlawed. However, it was legal for people to keep the slaves they already owned. The foreign slave trade in the United States as a whole was not forbidden until 1808, whereas in Alabama the foreign slave trade had been outlawed ten years before.

Forbidding the foreign slave trade by law did not stop it, however. There were slave traders who were willing to take their chances with the law in order to make large profits. So slaves were smuggled in from Africa long after the law forbade it. The last ship loaded with slaves from Africa arrived

298

Timothy Meaher found it impossible to sell most of the slaves he had brought in his ship. The War Between the States finally overtook the arguments as to what to do with the slaves, and these Negroes were settled in Africky Town in Mobile County. This is now called Plateau, and descendants of these former slaves still live in Plateau. Captain Meaher was a native of Maine who was living in Alabama when he determined to bring in the *Clotilde* and her slave cargo. Most of the slave trading ships were owned and operated by Northerners. While the Negro was badly treated as a rule in the foreign slave trade, he was generally very well treated by Alabama farmers.

DRIVERS AND OVERSEERS

On large plantations the work of the slaves was supervised by a driver, or an overseer, or both. The driver was a Negro slave himself, selected to boss the others because of his intelligence, his ability as a leader, and also his ability to carry out orders of his master. The overseer of a plantation was a white man who managed the plantation affairs, including the workers. Most overseers were Southerners. Very rarely did a Northerner get a position as overseer. This was because the plantation owner wanted an overseer who had had years of experience in the problems of the plantation and its workers.

In age overseers ranged from 17 to 60, but most of them were young men between 20 and 25, according to the historian, James B. Sellers. Sometimes an overseer worked on a percentage of the crop. At other times he received a fixed salary (payable when the cotton was sold), such as $400 per year plus his room and board. The master supervised both the driver and the overseer. Occasionally a master had a pair of binoculars and watched distant workers from the upper story of his plantation house. Thus the stage was set for some lazy field hand who went to sleep beside his job to get the surprise of his life from the master who had been watching him with the field glasses!

FIELD HANDS AND DOMESTIC SERVANTS

The two principal divisions of Negro slaves were field hands and domestic servants. The work of the domestic servants depended, of course, upon the size of the plantation house and the wealth of the master. The servants recognized some of the jobs as carrying more prestige than others, such as that of butler, seamstress, nurse, coachman, or cook. However, most

229

Source: Montgomery Adviser, 1961 textbook, "Alabama History for Schools"

Developing Spiritual Knowledge

The principles of Africatown, according to Vernetta, were spiritual, and it was said they had visions and signs given to them by God.

"They were God-fearing people, and God would show them signs and wonders through their dreams," she said. "My grandmother strongly believed in her dreams. She felt if the Lord was showing her something, it would come through a dream. And she would say, I don't know what this means right now. But when it happens, I won't be thrown off guard."

Vernetta said looking at the signs embedded in the songs about freedom and the underground railroad and the singing in the fields of the plantation are just some examples of how enslaved African Americans communicated with their White enslavers, knowing they were communicating with one another.

Vernetta gave three examples of the power of dreams and acting on them. The first involved her grandmother. Ora told Vernetta when she was a little girl, she was in the house with her mom when a strong wind started to blow hard, and the single candle on the kitchen table started to flicker.

Her mother, Julia, yelled to Ora, 'Go get the baby! Go get the baby!', who was outside. Ora started to run to the locked front door.

"But when she (Ora, my grandmother) got to the door, the Lord just opened the door without her need to unlock it," said Vernetta. "My grandmother told me she told her mother that day she saw this imagery in a dream before but didn't know what it was about."

The second example was in 1977, and it involved Vernetta. Her children would go to her grandmother's home after school, and she would normally pick them up after she was done with her work as a secretary. One day, she decided to go home first and take a different route. It was then her grandfather, who passed away in 1975, appeared to her in the passenger seat and told her in a strong voice not to go home but to "Go get them children."

Without questioning him, Vernetta changed lanes to take her normal route back to her grandmothers. She looked in the review mirror, saw no one was coming, and changed into the right lane. As soon as she switched lanes, a car in the lane she was previously in ran the red light and crashed into a fence. If she did not move out of that lane, the car would have smashed into her.

"That was my God telling my granddad to tell me to get out of the way," she said.

Vernetta also recalled two dreams that were a premonition of things to come.

Vernetta and her grandmother were trying to find information on her mother's sister, Vernetta's Aunt Dorothy Ann, when she didn't arrive as expected. Vernetta had a dream that Aunt Dorothy Ann knocked on the door in the morning wearing a pink suit. The dream felt so real. Vernetta got out of bed and went to the door. She then called her Uncle Vernon in Mississippi and told him about her dream. He said he had not heard anything. The next day, there was a knock on the door, and it was her Aunt Dorothy Ann wearing that pink suit in Vernetta's dream. Both Vernetta and her grandmother started to cry.

"The Lord has shown me things in realistic ways," said Vernetta.

The other vision Vernetta recalled was the night of her grandfather passing away.

Vernetta was restless that night. She kept telling her grandmother she did not know why, but she was not able to sleep. It was two am.

"Something inside me was conflicted," she said. "We finally laid down to sleep, and less than an hour later, we got a call from the hospital that he passed at two am. This is how the Lord has worked through me."

Ora would lean on "spirit songs," now called the African American Spirituals, when presented with any conflict. Some of these songs have been around since the days of slavery. The song *"Free at Last,"* which you may have heard sung, is considered a Spiritual. They were folk music not written by any one or two people. The spiritual Vernetta heard her grandmother sing was written in the 1930s called "Peace in the Valley", and this spiritual was sung by Black songwriter Thomas A. Dorsey.

"PEACE IN THE VALLEY"

I am tired and weary, but I must toil on
Till the Lord come to call me away
Where the morning is bright and the Lamb is the light
And the night is fair as the day

There'll be peace in the valley for me someday
There'll be peace in the valley for me
I pray no more sorrow and sadness or trouble will be
There'll be peace in the valley for me

There the flow'rs will be blooming, the grass will be green
And the skies will be clear and serene
The sun ever shines, giving one endless beam
And the clouds there will ever be seen

There, the bear will be gentle, the wolf will be tame
And the lion will lay down by the lamb
The host from the wild will be led by a Child
I'll be changed from the creature I am

No headaches or heartaches or misunderstands
No confusion or trouble won't be
No frowns to defile, just a big, endless smile
There'll be peace and contentment for me

Ora's singing of this spiritual left Vernetta amazed. She would also see how her grandmother would start her day with a morning meditation while sitting alone in her garden.

Throughout the years, Vernetta has also learned to tap into that peace. Her sanctuary is her porch, where she sits in peace and watches the birds in thankfulness.

"I always have a red bird that comes whenever God and I are on the same page."

In 1983 her grandmother, Ora, had a disabling stroke. Vernetta moved in to take care of her. Vernetta's husband took care of their two children, who were then in high school and middle school. The teens would come over to help as well.

"I was able to employ a lot of that training she told me, which I passed on to my kids on compassion and suffrage. They showed their love and respect by helping and being there."

Chapter Four
Africatown Divided, Clotilda Found, Vernetta's Cry for Unity

Because Africatown was bordered by water on three sides, it became an attractive area for manufacturing and transportation. To the east is the Mobile River, to its north is the Chickasaw Creek and Hog Bayou, and to the South is the Three Mile Creek. Sawmills and shipbuilding businesses provided employment for some of the Africatown residents like Pollee. Eventually, additional industries came in. This included paper mills, a lumber yard, the Hog Bayou gas-fired plant, and an oil refinery. This industry was just the beginning of Africatown's industrial encroachment and environmental injustice.

For almost 100 years, the Meaher family rented approximately 500 shotgun houses in Plateau to the descendants of Africatown.[161] The homes had three rooms and a water pump. The tenants would receive electricity later. The homes at that time, according to Augustine Meaher Jr., grandson of Timothy Meaher, were cheap to make, costing approximately $300 to build. The roads were dirt; there were no sewers.[162] They charged $1 a week for rent.[163]

Beginning in the 1920s, the Meaher family still owned large swaths of property, and they started to sell off their land, once worked on by the enslaved, to heavy industry. This added to their wealth. Through the years, more than 500 homes, which they once rented out, were destroyed and replaced by industries. International Paper opened a plant in 1929 on land the Meaher family owned. The company built a second plant in the town a decade later. At that time, International Paper had built the largest paper mill in the world in Africatown. Scott Paper Company also set up shop in the mid-1940's, which displaced renters.

The town, once filled with dreams of Africa, unwillingly became a part of Alabama's "Chemical Corridor." 26 large chemical companies dotted the 50-mile stretch of land. The Mobile Chamber's "Amazing Alabama" marketing brochure to attract business boasts the area as the "Pipeline to Prosperity"[164]. But, this "prosperity" did not include the residents of Africatown.

The manufacturing led to the destruction of the once prosperous community both financially and environmentally. The paper mills, which flanked Africatown, generated a lot of revenue, and became an acquisition target for the city of Mobile.

"The city of Mobile started to take over parts of the town where the manufacturing was located to capture its tax revenue," said Vernetta. "We were defenseless."

---

[161] Roger Rappaport, "Grandson of Slave Ship's Captain Rents Houses to Negro Families", The Southern Courier, June 17-18, 1967 http://www.southerncourier.org/hi-res/Vol3_No25_1967_06_17.pdf

[162] Roger Rappaport, op cit.

[163] Roger Rappaport, op cit.

64 Mobile Chamber, "Pipeline to Prosperity" Alabama Gulf Coast Chemical Corridor https://mobilechamber.com/wp-content/uploads/2014/07/Alabama_Chemical_Corridor_Brochure.pdf

The community once built and founded to sustain life and prosperity through a culture of sharing and inclusion was reduced to poverty after a series of eminent domain land acquisitions from the city of Mobile. The land belonging to Pollee, Gumpa (Peter Lee), and Cudjo Lewis was purchased in the mid-1920's to build a two-lane Bay Bridge Road. That road was built through the center of the town and divided the once thriving community in two. The homes of Pollee, Gumpa, and Cudjo were destroyed. Businesses were gone. That road was created to shorten travel to the Eastern Shore. Cars and trucks could use the new vertical lift Cochrane Bridge, which opened in 1927. Ironically, the name of the bridge was in honor of the head of the Chamber of Commerce for Mobile at that time.

Africatown land was swallowed up by the city of Mobile in three different phases. With each phase, more of the city's identity was destroyed. According to city records, a section of Africatown was annexed in 1945, followed by 1956, and, finally, in 1960, the rest of it was folded into Mobile. A February 5, 1955 article in the Press Register reported with the boom in population and traffic, the city's leaders intended to remedy the lack of space by "Tripling the size of the City of Mobile was proposed Saturday by City Coms. Joseph N. Langan and Henry R. Luscher."

Residents of Africatown hoped that by being a part of Mobile, their quality of life would get better. They had no indoor plumbing or running water.

They voted for annexation in 1960 so they could be connected to the municipal water system, because their wells were contaminated by pollutants. [165] Even with annexation, city sewer, water, and garbage pick-up were denied in Africatown until the Mid-1960's.[166]

---

[165] Roger Rappaport, op cit.
[166] Roger Rappaport, op cit.

TWO PLATEAU HOUSES

Source: *The Southern Courier*, photo featured on page four,
"African Descendants Still Live in Plateau", June 17-18, 1967

When the Meahers were told by the city of Mobile they would need to update their shotgun shacks so they could provide running water and sewage for the Africatown residents who rented them, Meaher had the homes torn down. Augustine Meaher Jr. said that the updates would cost more than the homes themselves.[167] 80 of the 100 shacks were torn down. He spoke with the press in June of 1967 and March of 1968 on his decision, which made headlines.

The bigotry towards his tenants was just as palpable as his grandfather to his former enslaved workers.

"Of course, we'll probably leave a few three for the old darkies that worked for us," said Augustine Meaher, Jr., in an interview with the *Southern Courier*. He also said he didn't charge the elderly tenants rent but regretted that decision. "The government has softened them up in their old age these days. With those old-age pensions, you can't get them to work as hard anymore."[168]

Once the homes were not going to be renovated, the city of Mobile rezoned Meaher's residential property into industrial, and Augustine Meaher, Jr. leased that property to Scott Paper Company.[169] Displaced residents told *The Southern Courier* that they didn't know where they were going to go.

---

[167] Roger Rappaport, op cit.
[168] Roger Rappaport, op cit.
[169] Jonathan Gordon, "Hard Times for Poor Folks", The Southern Courier, March 16-17, 1968
http://www.southerncourier.org/low-res/Vol4_No11_1968_03_16.pdf

Augustine Meaher, Jr. told the reporter he moved the tenants to the Meaher owned community "Saraland".[170] According *The Southern Courier*, Meaher explained he persuaded the city of Mobile to annex Saraland, which at that time was unincorporated. Meaher, Jr. said it was done so the neighboring town of Satsuma would not tax the homes. Since the homes had no foundation or plumbing, they were picked up and moved by truck.[171]

"This annexation agreement gives us ten years to bring the houses up to the (minimal housing) code. Of course, we may sell the land to industry by then."[172]

When the reporter questioned Augustine Meaher, Jr. about the relocation of residents, he defended his decision. "These people don't mind. Saraland is like Magazine Point (another Black Community near Plateau)." He continued to say, "You know, that's the way with niggers. They'll be happy in a community—everybody together. They try and go back to the African tribal life. He don't need garbage service—a darkie will feed it to his pigs. He don't need a bathtub- he'd probably store food in it. Wouldn't know how to use it."[173]

In the 1970's, the city of Mobile started to expand its rezoning of residential land to business/industrial use. This created further financial inequity for the Africatown residents, and increased wealth for the Meaher family.

Vernetta left the area to move to New Jersey with her husband from 1969 to 1974. When they returned home, she was shocked to see what happened to her beloved Africatown.

"It was in complete disarray," said Vernetta. "People had stopped keeping up their yards. It looked like the dignity of the people had been diminished, and they just didn't care whether they kept it up or not. They forgot the land came the descendants who worked hard to save that money and pass on that land to them."

In 1978, Vernetta was driving her young children in Mobile when she saw Ku Klux Klan members wearing their white hoods in the middle of the street she was driving on. She told her children to lay down on the floor in the back of the car, because she was going to have to go through the red light where they were standing. Her heart was in her throat, and she slowly drove through the red light. It turned out the group of KKK members were collecting money in the middle of the day.

It was then that she told her children then, ages, 7 and 9, about segregation.

---

[170] Jonathan Gordon, op cit.
[171] Jonathan Gordon, op cit.
[172] Jonathan Gordon, op cit.
[173] Jonathan Gordon, op cit.

"I told them you don't ever want to stop for Ku Klux Klan. If you see them, you need to hold your head down and get out of the way."

Mobile Expansion, Africatown's Demise

The dismantling of Africatown continued with the expansion of Bay Bridge Road. The two-land road, which destroyed the homes of Pollee, further expanded into a four-lane major highway in the 1980's and was completed in 1992.[174] That expansion wiped out Africatown's central business district, and the city of Mobile used eminent domain to take that land. This permanently divided the main Africatown communities of Plateau and Magazine Point, and the retail businesses would never be re-established. The business district of Africatown no long exists.

Bay Bridge Road Built Through Africatown

The destruction of the town can be seen off the property of Clotilda survivor and Africatown cofounder, "Gumpa" or Peter Lee. According to family patriarch, James Lee, the property originally went up to the second lane of the four highway closest to the property.

---

[174] United States Department of the Interior National Park Service National Register of Historic Places Continuation Sheet Africatown Historic District Name of Property Mobile County, AL, NPS Form 10-900-a OMB No. 1024-0018

This chimney is the only original portion of Africatown left. "Gumpa," Peter Lee, was descended from Dahomean kings Gele and Benhazin. Today, great-great grandson James Lee meticulously maintains the family property where three homes formerly stood. He had a cement platform made and had the chimney lifted in hopes of preserving the structure. The home was torn down years ago by the family.

Source: Lewis Family

Environmental Racism

Through the years of land leases and sales by the Meaher-owned Chippewa Lakes LLC, Africatown became surrounded by asphalt and petrochemical plants, pipelines, paper plants, and coal terminals. There was no escape from the encroaching industrialization. For example, the land owned by the family of Clotilda survivor, Charlie Lewis, was surrounded by the Gulf Lumber Company.[175]

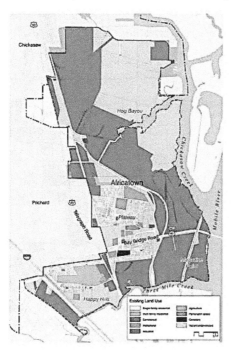

A map of current land use in Africatown. The historic core of Africatown is in the Plateau and Magazine Point neighborhoods, now surrounded by industry (purple) and hemmed in and bisected by highways and the Bay Bridge Road and Cochrane–Africatown USA Bridge. Further isolated and now separated by Interstate 165 is Lewis Quarters in the Happy Hills census tract (bottom left).

Credit: The City of Mobile's 2016 Community and Housing Development Department

One Africatown resident, Joe Womack, a prominent environmental justice activist and Sierra Club member, championed Africatown residents' rights for clean air and water. In an interview, he spoke of the pollutants generated by the International Paper mill falling from the sky coating surfaces with ash.[176]

In other interviews, additional residents described the ash emitted from the plant as so thick it you "couldn't see three feet in front of you." [177] Cars would rust out in out in a couple of years because of the pollution, the residents said. The residents' vegetable gardens were covered in ash. Finally, pollution

[175] Vickii Howell, "Efforts and Gaps | Neighborhood Development Plans" American Roundtable https://archleague.org/article/africatown-neighborhood-development-plans/
[176] "Alabama Power's Plan to Perpetuate Injustice" Sierra Club, Alabama Chapter, June 24, 2020 https://www.sierraclub.org/alabama/blog/2020/06/alabama-power-s-plan-perpetuate-injustice
[177] Lauren Zanolli, 'Still fighting': Africatown, site of last US slave shipment, sues over pollution, January 26, 2019, The Guardian https://www.theguardian.com/us-news/2018/jan/26/africatown-site-of-last-us-slave-ship-arrival-sues-over-factorys-pollution

controls were implemented in the 1980s and 1990's, but it was too late. The pollution had taken infected the town. Cancer became the disease that took many lives.

Ironically, in 1989, the Alabama Department of Conservation and Natural Resources opened Meaher State Park. The land was donated by Timothy Meaher's son, Augustine Meaher Sr., in 1952, instructing it to be used for public recreation. According to Encyclopedia of Alabama, the park was "Named after John Meaher, a noted Alabama steamboat operator during the nineteen century."[178] Research into the Meaher family tree[179] shows that John Cheverus Meaher, one of Timothy Meaher's brothers, was born on April 24, 1825 in Whitefield, Maine, and died unmarried on October 9, 1853. He fell ill in Mobile when he was going to work in the office of the Meaher family business.[180] John was 28 years old and was not a "noted Alabama steamboat operator." The only "noted Alabama steamboat operator" in the family during that time was Timothy Meaher.

In 1992, a report in the Birmingham News said 53,000 pounds of chloroform were released into the air.[181] International Paper closed its plant in 2000. Cancer cases started to increase in Africatown residents. In 2006, the Pastor of Africatown's Yorktown Missionary Baptist Church had services for at least 20 residents due to cancer. After a questionnaire went out to survey how many families knew of someone in their family with cancer, 100 out of 150 said yes.[182]

Today, the EPA has identified several environmentally contaminated sites in Africatown called "brownfields." These sites, according to EPA documents, "include a 40-acre former manufacturing plant and multi-family housing complex, a former paper manufacturer, and a historic sawmill."[183]

---

[178] "Meaher State Park", Encyclopedia of Alabama, https://encyclopediaofalabama.org/article/meaher-state-park/
[179] Timothy Meaher Family Tree, MyHeritage, https://www.myheritage.com/research/record-1-424015211-1-500146/timothy-meaher-in-myheritage-family-trees
[180] John C. Meaher, Memorial ID: 35291502, Find a Grave https://www.findagrave.com/memorial/35291502/john-cheverus-meaher
[181] Nick Tabor Africatown and the 21st-Century Stain of Slavery. The New Yorker. n.d.
[182] Lauren Zanolli, 'Still fighting': Africatown, site of last US slave shipment, sues over pollution, January 26, 2019, The Guardian https://www.theguardian.com/us-news/2018/jan/26/africatown-site-of-last-us-slave-ship-arrival-sues-over-factorys-pollution
[183] EPA Selects Three Alabama Entities to Receive Share of $897,000 for Brownfields Cleanup and Assessment, May 6, 2020, EPA https://www.epa.gov/newsreleases/epa-selects-three-alabama-entities-receive-share-897000-brownfields-cleanup-and

The Power of Unity

Residents have banded together to fight environmental injustice after seeing their friends and family die of various forms of cancer as a result of industrial pollution. Emissions data from the Environmental Protection Agency in the 1980's and 1990's ranked Mobile County, which Africatown is a part of, in the top five counties for air pollution in the nation.[184][185] Almost all the pollution recorded was in Africatown.

Stronger federal air quality regulations under President Clinton in the 1990's helped, but the Africatown residents wanted more to protect future environmental hazards.

Residents helped found the Mobile Environmental Justice Action Coalition in September 2013 to fight the building of an oil storage tank farm for Canadian tar sand oil in 2015. This paved the way for the launch of Africatown~CHESS (Clean Health Educated Safe and Sustainable Africatown). The environmental justice organization was created to partner with the HBCU Gulf Coast Equity Consortium. The partnership would study and address environmental issues through the lens of equity and racial justice.

CHESS would be tested when the Alabama Public Service Commission approved a 2.2-mile crude oil pipeline in Mobile County.[186] The $14.4 million dollar product was by Plains Mobile, a subsidiary of Plains All-American. It was to replace a 40-year-old existing pipeline.

Residents believed the town would be protected and spared of any additional industry because it was listed on the National Register of Historic Places in 2012. To their horror, they weren't.

Infrastructure Apartheid

In a blog written by Joe Womack, an Africatown resident and president and CEO of CHESS, residents found out after meeting with Public School Superintendent Martha Peek. It was in that meeting that the Africatown residents found out the school district was not surprised by the construction. In fact, they were aware of it.

The pipeline carved out trenches through the school yard and the historic baseball field where Cleon Jones, one of the 1968 "Amazing Mets," learned to play ball.

In an effort to bridge understanding and trust, Rick McMichael, director of operations for Plains All-American, donated approximately $75,000 to restore the school grounds, and monies to enhance student

---

[184] EPA Complaint Africatown May 8, 2023
https://www.epa.gov/system/files/documents/2023-05/08R-23-R4%20Complaint_Redacted.pdf
[185] Ben Raines, "Inside Africatown's Fight to Create a National Monument for the Enslaved "https://lithub.com/inside-africatowns-fight-to-create-a-national-monument-for-the-enslaved/
[186] Kim Chandler, Public Service Commission Approve Oil Pipeline in Mobile County, November 5, 2013 AL.com
https://www.al.com/wire/2013/11/public_service_commission_appr_1.html

academics.[187] He also purchased a new welcome center sign. Protests by the Mobile Bay Sierra Club and Tar Sands Mobile Coalition helped put on hold two additional projects that were slated to be located in Africatown--The Plains Southcap Pipeline, which would have passed through the Big Creek Lake watershed, and the American Tank & Vessel project to build tar sands storage tanks.

The group was successful in stopping a hazardous waste disposal facility that was proposed on a contaminated paper mill site.

In 2017, Africatown residents filed a suit against International Paper, alleging the plants produced hazardous chemicals, such as dioxins and furans, which ended up in the air, water, and ground.[188] 248 individuals who owned or occupied residential property in the community were a part of this case. Eventually, a total of 1,000 residents joined in the legal fight. In the suit, it is alleged the chemicals exceeded EPA limits and are causing cancer amongst the residents. The suit also alleged the company failed to properly clean up the site when it was closed 20 years prior. The company denied any wrongdoing.

Topographical samples in Africatown were collected by Mobile's Baheth Research and Development Laboratories. Additional historical studies for Polychlorinated biphenyls, (highly carcinogenic chemical compounds), and effects on water, soil, and wildlife were also taken.[189] A report was given to the Mobile Environmental Justice Action Coalition, and the law firm representing the plaintiffs, Stewart and Stewart.

In the early days of COVID, in a letter dated May 29, 2020, Stewart and Stewart urged the plaintiffs to settle, for the soil testing did not show significant levels of dioxin and furan pollution.[190] It was explained 95 percent of their clients needed to agree to the settlement by no later than August 21, 2020. If not, no one would receive settlement funds. The attorneys described the settlement as "satisfactory." Monies were considered confidential and not to be disclosed, but a report said the highest amount amongst those who received a settlement was $8,000. Others reportedly received $200. No information was given on attorney fees. 1,090 plaintiffs agreed to the settlement, and a joint dismissal of the complaint was filed Nov. 2, 2020. International Paper, in a statement, said itdenied the allegations, but in the best interest of the company, the claim would be settled.

---

[187] Sharp, John, "Plains All-American invests $75,000 for school work, Africatown welcoming center" February 13, 2014 AL.com https://www.al.com/live/2014/02/plains_all-american_invests_75.html
[188] Samuel Adams, et al., Plaintiffs, v International Paper Company, et al., Defendants, U.S. District Court for the Southern District of Alabama Southern Division, May 5, 2017, https://law.justia.com/cases/federal/district-courts/alabama/alsdce/1:2017cv00105/60740/26/
[189] Kevin Lee, "America's Cancerous Legacy for the Descendants of the Kidnapped Africans Who Arrived on the Last Slave Ship" January 31, 2021, The Daily Beast https://www.thedailybeast.com/americas-cancerous-legacy-for-the-descendants-of-the-kidnapped-africans-who-arrived-on-the-last-slave-ship
[190] Kevin Lee, "America's Cancerous Legacy for the Descendants of the Kidnapped Africans Who Arrived on the Last Slave Ship" January 31, 2021, The Daily Beast https://www.thedailybeast.com/americas-cancerous-legacy-for-the-descendants-of-the-kidnapped-africans-who-arrived-on-the-last-slave-ship

This was just one fight the residents of Africatown banded together to seek environmental justice. The EPA awarded Africatown, along with two other state entities, grants to clean up and redevelop the 40-acre former manufacturing plant and multi-family housing complex, a former paper manufacturer, and a historic sawmill.[191]

Africatown residents saw a small victory in 2022 when the U.S. Environmental Protection Agency struck down an air pollution permit for a chemical plant.[192] The EPA said the state of Alabama needed to do a better job responding to public questions about the permit since it was required to do by law. The EPA also formally objected to a permit by the Alabama Department of Environmental Management issued last year for the UOP LLC chemical manufacturing plant in Mobile County, which Honeywell International owns.[193]

Africatown Today

Vernetta said it was the power of togetherness and support that provided the foundation for the town's early success. In the early 1900's, Africatown was the fourth largest community in the country that Black Americans governed.

"Their unity is what gave them their strength," said Vernetta. "They built their own school for their children since the Whites did not want to give them one. They didn't back down from their right to vote, and they even built their own church. It was their togetherness that created their power."

When you walk through Africatown today, the barber shops, grocery stores, movie theatres, and restaurants are long gone. Baseball, which was a popular sport for some of the Africatown boys, produced two major league players.

They were a part of the 1969 "Miracle Mets." Cleon Jones and Tommie Agee won the World Series that year. They both grew up and were educated in Africatown. Jones was the outfielder who caught the last out in that series. Today, Jones' nonprofit Last Out Foundation is raising funds to create and provide youth programs for Africatown as well as combat blight, refurbish, and build affordable homes. After he retired from baseball, the legend moved back to his beloved hometown.

Jones and his fellow Africatown descendants welcomed the opening of the Africatown Heritage House in July of 2023 to tell the story of the Clotilda.

---

[191] EPA Selects Three Alabama Entities to Receive Share of $897,000 for Brownfields Cleanup and Assessment, May 6, 20202 https://www.epa.gov/newsreleases/epa-selects-three-alabama-entities-receive-share-897000-brownfields-cleanup-and
[192] Notice of intent to sue for EPA's failure to perform non-discretionary duty under the Clean Air Act to respond to petition requesting that the Administrator object to the Barry Plant Title V operating permit in Mobile County, Alabama https://www.epa.gov/system/files/documents/2022-04/plant-barry-noi-04082022.pdf
[193] PETITION NO. IV-2021-6 Before the Administrator United States Environmental Protection Agency, In the Matter of UOP LLC https://www.epa.gov/system/files/documents/2022-05/UOP%20Order_4-27-22.pdf

Africatown native Reverend Julius C. Hope was the first Director of Religion for the NAACP National Organization and former National Football League Defensive rookie of the year. Houston Oilers Hall of Famer Robert Brazell also called Africatown home[194].

Clotilda Found

Since the ship's sinking, there had been searches for the Clotilda. Finally, on March 5, 2019, Ben Raines, an environmental journalist, filmmaker, and charter captain, found her[195]. A blizzard in January of 2018 created low tides, which exposed part of the wreck alongside an island where Captain William Foster wrote in his correspondence he had burned and sank the Clotilda.

At first, the wreck found was so large, that researchers originally believed the vessel was "simply too big"[196] to be the Clotilda. But Florida archaeologists Greg Cook and John Bratten wanted to study the wreck more. They got the proper permits, and Raines went back to the site where he, along with Monty Graham, head of Marine Sciences at the University of Southern Mississippi, Joe Turner, and a team from Underwater Works Dive Shop explored that wreck.

On April 13, 2018, Raines pulled up the first piece of Clotilda to see the light of day in 160 years. Raines shared the coordinates of the wreck along with the survey data with the Alabama Historical Commission. The committed hired Search Inc., to verify the find. For a year, the discovery was under wraps.

---

[194] Joe Womack, "Africatown Notables" September 9, 2014 https://bridgethegulfproject.org/blog/2014/africatown-notables
[195] Vessels in maritime are referred to as a "she" not it.
[196] Raines, Ben, "Wreck found in Delta not the Clotilda, the last American slave ship" March 5, 2018

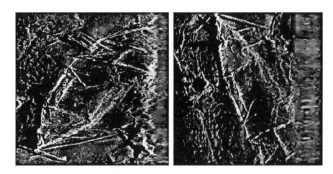

Sonar images of the underwater wreck of the *Clotilda* – now listed on the National Register of Historic Places in 2021. This vessel was conclusively identified as the *Clotilda* by a team led by James P. Delgado of SEARCH, Inc. and Fellow of The Explorers Club, and with the involvement and backing of the Alabama Historical Commission, National Geographic Society, Smithsonian's National Museum of African American History and Culture and its Slave Wrecks Program, Divers with a Purpose, the Black Scuba Divers Association, and the George Washington University Maritime Archaeology Department. The team's efforts led to the listing on the National Register.

Source: POLEE AND ROSE ALLEN OF THE SLAVE SHIP CLOTILDA AND AFRICATOWN, ALABAMA
by Llewellyn "Lew" Toulmin, PhD, FRGS, FN '04, April 4, 2022

They wanted to make sure the verification was complete. Finally, on May 22, 2019, it was announced by the Alabama Historical Commission the wreckage of the *Clotilda* was indeed found.

The size of the schooner hit the Africatown residents hard. Everyone thought the Clotilda would be smaller.

State studies show the Clotilda is largely intact, which has increased calls on the vessel being raised.[197] A 172-page report was released on the findings and analysis of the Clotilda conducted by SEARCH Inc. between December 12 and 15, 2018, and on January 28, 2019. The report concluded the vessel is likely the Clotilda.

The discovery and confirmation of the vessel are highly significant because out of the more 20,000 ships that were involved in the global slave trade, the Clotilda is only one of 13 ever located worldwide. She[198] is also the only slave ship ever found that was involved in the U.S. slave trade.

Raines chose not to fight for ownership of the vessel and deferred ownership of the Clotilda to the State of Alabama. Officials at that time promised in media interviews they would dig up the vessel and put her on display in Africatown.[199]

---

[197] Raines, Ben "History Demands We Preserve the Wreck of America's Last Slave Ship" Time Magazine February 18, 2022 https://time.com/6148417/clotilda-preserve-americas-last-slave-ship/
[198] A vessel is referred to as a "she" in maritime terms.
[199] Raines, Ben "History Demands We Preserve the Wreck of America's Last Slave Ship" Time Magazine February 18, 2022 https://time.com/6148417/clotilda-preserve-americas-last-slave-ship/

The Clotilda Alabama Historical Commission has not released its final study to see if the raising of the vessel is feasible, as well as the best ways to preserve the vessel. The report is long past due. The Alabama Historical Commission explained in an email for this book, "The ongoing scientific research will tell us if raising the wreck is even possible without destroying it and inform our path forward in preserving the site."[200]

The AHC said since they are still in the process of conducting research and consultation on queries if a water site would be built in the event the vessel is not raised.

"We are still trying to determine the best path forward."[201]

The discovery of the schooner has thrusted Africatown into the spotlight and with mixed feelings. While the story of their loved ones has been told in a Netflix documentary and in hundreds of stories around the world, the residents of Africatown are still faced with economic disparity.

The big corporations and authors who have been written about the town and its founders have made profits off the story. The companies and authors have not shared that wealth with the residents of Africatown.

The blight that has infected the community is a stark reminder of the generational financial disparity.

Boarded up homes in Africatown, August 14, 2023

The town's population is so small that the Department of Labor for the state of Alabama explained it does not meet the population standards for the state to track and calculate employment data.[202]

---

[200] AHC email correspondence with author on July 19, 2023
[201] AHC email correspondence with author on July 19, 2023
[202] Alabama Department of Labor, August 14, 2023 email to author

New Beginnings and Justice

The doors of the long awaited Africatown Heritage House and "*Clotilda*: The Exhibition" opened on July 8, 2023. This day holds deep in the hearts of descendants, for it's the day marking the arrival of their loved ones in 1860.

Vernetta is hopeful this energy will infuse a bond of solidarity the town needs so it can be strengthened to is former glory.

"We are stronger and better together," stressed Vernetta.

As a descendant, Vernetta explained the word justice is a hard word to define.

"What we call justice is equal footing, equality," said Vernetta, "We would like to be recognized for our contributions, be it small or large. We would like to be able to use our talents to enhance the population. In the end, we would like to be afforded the same opportunities as everybody else."

Vernetta says the residents of Africatown need to unite like their forefathers did.

"In the past, the (Clotilda) descendants were a very solidified group of people who stuck together," stressed Vernetta. "Their families are taken care of each other and employed one another. In our quest for freedom, we became greedy as African Americans. We'd love the slogan 'all for one', and it turned into 'we want to do this ourselves; we're the top of the line,' and it is not what our fore parents instilled in us."

Vernetta said with a heavy heart the values that made Africatown strong was unity. A city is about the people, not the buildings.

"There were two lines of thinking growing up in Africatown: knowing where you came from, Africans cherish the community and support each other, using their strength to lift everyone up. The other way of living was never looking back, denying your African heritage, and moving forward," she explained. "This has created division."

"This has been lost among some of the descendants," warned Vernetta. "Part of it is because people make their children superior to other people. I can say this because I came up in a society where everybody on the street was your friend. In Africatown, most of the families had larger families. My grandmother had nine children. She had a brother who had 12 children. Their parents had seven children. So, that's how the population of Africatown grew. But the respect for your neighbors was there. Your neighbors, and your parents, all raised their children with the same principles. I miss this today."

Vernetta says children learn what they live. "I told my children growing up, 'You don't have to do anything I tell you to do. But you do have to do what you *see* me do.' That will be my legend in life."

Looking back, she said she didn't know her family was not "rich" in social brackets, but they all had their basic needs met. This helped drive her and her children to strive for more and not be laid back, thinking things are owed to them.

"My grandparents taught me to be proud, and I taught my children to be proud as well," stressed Vernetta. "Nobody owes us anything but the opportunity to do good. I am not in favor of reparations because I don't think that's a part of the way we were brought up."

This echoes the days of the beginnings of Africatown, where the Clotilda survivors did not wait for "the Whites" to build a school.

Vernetta's opinions do differ from some of her Allen cousins, who are in favor of reparations. She asked a cousin who was in favor of reparations, how do they really quantify the value of their loved one's hard labor during slavery? She asked how you compound that figure with the interest rate over the years and how that number would really be fair and equitable? Vernetta said the response to her questions was laughter.

Vernetta says the key to Africatown's success is unification and honoring the accomplishments of its residents to encourage the community.

In a recent conversation with Pat, a former classmate, Vernetta told her friend what a positive influence she was on so many people and how she has taken everything in her life in stride.

"She then shared with me that she had been on a podium with Coretta Scott King back in the sixties. I said this is a story that needs to be brough out during Black History month because someone can hear that story and say, 'Well, if they can do that, I can do that.' That was my grandmother's philosophy, anybody can do it, you can do it."

Just Say Hello

Saying hello, Vernetta says, is the quickest way to form a community.

"I'm guilty of stopping people on the street to say hello, and I wouldn't change it," said Vernetta. "It's important for all of us to keep abreast of the people in your community. It's equally important to remember where you came from. *Who* are the people in your family? The generations before us helped guide us to *who* we are today. *Embrace* those values. This was the success of Africatown."

Going back to the teachings of Pollee and how he, along with the Africatown cofounders, built the town together so all could be successful, Vernetta was reminded of an African proverb whose origins date back to slavery when education was denied to them.

"The proverb is 'Each One, Teach One,'" said Vernetta. "When someone learned how to read or write back then, it became *their* responsibility to teach someone else and to spread that knowledge. By sharing your knowledge, it would strengthen your community. This should be the mindset for all generations, young and old, no matter where you are from. It's time to take back that responsibility and help others. For in the end, it will only create new opportunities for everyone.

PART TWO

Mandy, and Coreen

"Always remember—you're a Madison. You come from African slaves and a

president."

Bettye Kearse, MD, was interviewed for this story. Dr. Kearse is the eighth-generation *griotte* (oral historian), for her family.

"Our white ancestors laid the foundations for this country, but our dark-skinned ancestors built it. They worked the fields, nursed babies, preached sermons, and fought in wars. They played music, owned businesses, cured sickness, and worked on railroads. They taught their children everything important about life in this world. They taught their children about God." - John Chester

—

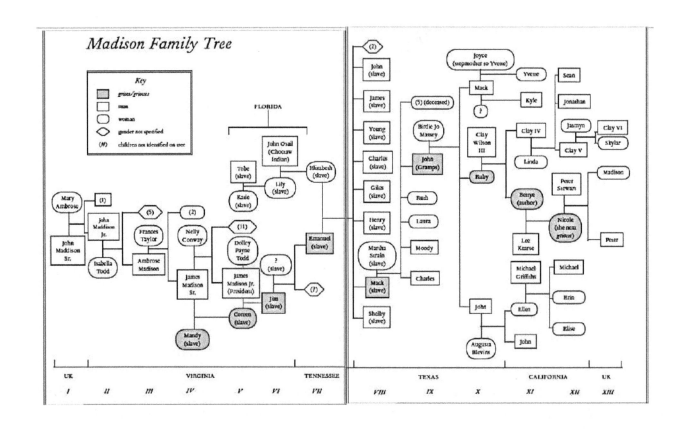

Madison Family Tree

Key
- grises/grieuses
- man
- woman
- gender not specified
- (#) children not identified on tree

FLORIDA

John Ouail (Choctaw Indian)

Tobe (slave)
Lily (slave)
Katie (slave)
Elizabeth (slave)

Mary Ambrose
(1)
John Maddison Jr.
(5)
Frances Taylor
(2)
Nelly Conway
(11)
Dolley Payne Todd
Emanuel (slave)

John Maddison Sr.
Isabella Todd
Ambrose Madison
James Madison Sr.
James Madison Jr. (President)
? (slave)
(?)

Corteen (slave)
Jim (slave)

Mandy (slave)

(2)
John (slave)
James (slave)
Young (slave)
Charles (slave)
Giles (slave)
Henry (slave)
Martha Strain (slave)
Mack (slave)
Shelby (slave)

(5) (deceased)
Birdie Jo Massey
John (Gramps)
Ruth
Laura
Moody
Charles
John

Ruby

Joyce (stepmother to Yvette)
Mack
?
Yvette
Kyle

Clay Wilson III

Bettye (author)

Augusta Blevins

Sean
Jonathan
Clay IV
Linda

Lee Kearse

Michael Griffiths
Ellen
John

Peter Stewart
Nicole (the next griotte)

Jasmyn
Clay V

Madison
Peter

Clay VI
Skylar

Michael
Erin
Elise

UK | VIRGINIA | TENNESSEE | TEXAS | CALIFORNIA | UK

I | II | III | IV | V | VI | VII | VIII | IX | X | XI | XII | XIII

Chapter One
Always Remember—You're a Madison

A *griot* is responsible for *accurately preserving* and passing along the family's history. This is an ancient West African tradition brought to America by the men and women who were kidnapped from Africa. While referred to as storytellers, these men and women are their families' historians. The stories they tell are not fables—they are real moments, told orally. Through the generations and with the help of modern technology, the *griottes* (women) *or griots* (men) build onto their family history and make it more tangible through documents and photos. Bettye's family stores these precious family treasures in a special box for safe keeping.

In this story, you will learn the family's story and how *griots* and *griottes* embrace their responsibilities and use their talents to make those stories more tangible through the new information they each discovered.

The story of Mandy, Dr. Bettye Kearse's great-great-great-great-great-grandmother, began in a small village in Ghana. Kidnapped as a teenager in the 1750s, Mandy was forced onto a slave ship.

According to the family's oral history, Mandy was not her real name.[203] The Madison family renamed her using an English name. Along with hundreds of African men, women, and children, Mandy traveled across the Atlantic Ocean to Colonial Virginia aboard a cramped slave ship on a route known as the *Middle Passage*[204]. Approximately 12.5 million Africans were transported along the Middle Passage (transatlantic trade) route between 1500 and 1866. Approximately 1.8 million of them perished during the journey.[205]

Mandy was confined to the lower deck of the slave ship. Historical reports say the men and women were separated from each other, with men sitting side by side, crowded together, and shackled at the ankle.[206] Women and children were not shackled, but they, too, were crammed against each other. The only daylight they saw was through air holes in the ship that provided fresh air and light. The holes were kept closed in bad weather, and the captives sat in the dark.[207] Because of the lack of food and crowded and unsanitary conditions, the mortality rate for this approximately 80-day journey was between 10 and 20 percent.[208] Other historians have estimated the rates at between 15 and 25 percent, accounting for those who perished on slave ships, their bodies thrown overboard.

---

[203] Bettye Kearse, The Other Madisons, March 24, 2020
[204] The Middle Passage is the Africa to Atlantic route of the slave trade where millions of Africans were kidnapped and transported on slave ships.
[205] Encyclopedia Virginia, slave ships
[206] Encyclopedia Virginia, slave ships
[207] U.S. History, b. Middle Passage.
https://www.ushistory.org/us/6b.asp#:~:text=Slaves%20were%20fed%20twice%20daily,dead%20were%20simply%20thrust%20overboard.
[208] Encyclopedia Virginia, slave ships

Mandy arrived in Colonial Virginia, the largest of the continental societies that used slave labor, where she was examined by a doctor to determine her worth. [209] She then stood on an auction block and was purchased by a slave trader who in turn, sold her to James Madison Sr., a prominent planter, enslaver, politician, and colonel in the militia during the American Revolutionary War. He was also the father of James Madison, Jr., the future president of the United States.

James Madison, Sr. was the son of Ambrose Madison and his wife, Frances. The couple also had two daughters, Elizabeth and Frances.[210] In 1732, when James, Sr. was nine, the family moved to a plantation Ambrose named Mount Pleasant, later renamed Montpelier. To clear and cultivate his land, Ambrose purchased additional slaves.

That summer, Ambrose fell ill. After a couple of months, he died of a lingering illness that the court determined to be the result of being poisoned.[211] Two of his wife's enslaved workers, a man named Turk, and a woman named Dido, along with a neighbor's slave, Pompey, were charged and convicted on September 6, 1732.

The day after their conviction, Pompey was hanged for murder. Because slaves were considered property, not persons, Pompey was appraised for £30 (approximately $8,150 in today's dollars) and the county government had to pay that appraisal price to Ambrose's wife Francis to compensate her for the loss of her property. Turk and Dido each received 29 lashes on their bare backs and were then sent back to work on the farm now run by Ambrose's widow, Frances.[212]

With Ambrose's passing, his widow became head of the household and never remarried. This was uncommon at the time, and once James Sr. turned 18 in 1741, he inherited the plantation and the enslaved workers. James Sr. purchased additional land, bringing the total to five-thousand additional acres, becoming the largest landowner in the county. More slaves, including Mandy, were acquired to clear and cultivate the property. James Sr. and his mother operated the plantation jointly until her death in 1761.

While tobacco was the cash crop in Virginia, the Madisons also produced a small amount of cotton, according to oral history. Family oral history says James Madison Sr. was attracted to Mandy because she was the fastest at picking cotton. She worked from sunrise to sunset in that remote cotton field.[213]

Sometime during 1760s and 1770s, James Madison Sr.'s attraction to Mandy resulted in the birth of a daughter, Coreen, Bettye's fourth-great-grandmother.[214] During this time, he was married to Eleanor Rose

---

[209] The Journal of Interdisciplinary History Vol. 5, No. 3 (Winter, 1975), pp. 383-412

[210] http://www.jamesmadisonfamily.com/docs/AmbroseMadison.pdf

[211] Douglas B., Chambers Murder at Montpelier: Igbo Africans in Virginia, Oxford, Mississippi: University Press of Mississippi, 2005, pp. 5-9

[212] Anne Miller, "The Short Life and Strange Death of Ambrose Madison", published by the Orange County (Va.) Historical Society,

[213] Bettye Kearse, The Other Madisons, March 24, 2020

[214] https://www.ancestry.com/genealogy/records/coreen-slave-24-525lcl

"Nelly" Conway, and together, they had twelve children, including their oldest, James Madison Jr., who would go on to become president of the United States in 1809.

Mandy raised Coreen while she continued to work in the fields. Oral history says Mandy taught Coreen that "no one can really own you—only you can own you."[215] Mandy, Coreen, and the following generation of family members, who were enslaved, all believed in this mantra. They never believed they were property. Instead, they saw themselves as people who wanted to make their mark on the world—they had dreams, strengths, hopes, and a fire burning in their souls. For eight generations, that message has been passed down.

The other lesson Mandy taught her daughter and successive generations was to be "fighting mad." When something went against your values, you needed to fight for what you believed in. These lessons all originated with knowing your worth as a human being.

Oral history says Coreen joined her mother, Mandy, in the fields to pick cotton when Coreen was eight years old.[216] Three years later, Coreen left those hot fields to work in the sweltering kitchen, chosen by the head cook to work in the cookhouse. At that time, kitchens were not attached to the main house because of the threat of fire. Colonial-era kitchens were open-hearth with two or three bake ovens and a large fireplace to roast meats and cook meals. All these fires would be burning simultaneously, requiring constant attention to keep temperatures consistent. While the large hearth kept the building comfortable during cooler months, the fires could burn at more than 1,000 degrees in the summer.[217] Cooking staff normally awoke at 4 a.m. to get the fire started and draw fresh water.

Coreen, known for her apple pies, would have to work the fire constantly to ensure her desserts would not be undercooked or burned. Leaving a fire unattended was not an option regardless of the temperature inside the kitchen.

When James Madison Jr. became an adult, he turned to politics and returned to Montpelier when breaks in his schedule allowed. During the Revolutionary War, he was a Virginia House of Delegates member and later a Virginia Representative in the Continental Congress.

In the late 1780s he lived in New York, where Congress was located. He followed when Congress was relocated to Philadelphia in the early 1790s. There are numerous stories in the family's oral history that James Madison Jr. favored apple pie. As mentioned above, Coreen was known for her apple pies and desserts, making it likely that the future president was enjoying one of Coreen's creations.

---

[215] Bettye Kearse, The Other Madisons, March 24, 2020
[216] Bettye Kearse, The Other Madisons, March 24, 2020
[217] Kelley Fanto Deetz, Bound to the Fire How Virginia's Enslaved Cooks Helped Invent American Cuisine, November 17, 2017)

Again, according to family oral history, James Madison Jr. became attracted to Coreen and her talent for making apple pies.[218] It is unknown if he was aware Coreen was his younger half-sister, but his attraction to her resulted in the birth of a son, Jim, around 1792.

Madison's correspondence and other documents confirm that James Madison Jr. returned to Montpelier on September 11, 1791, stayed until mid-October, then returned to Philadelphia.[219] Montpelier documents also show that James Madison Jr. arrived in Montpelier in May of 1792, after meeting President Washington at Mount Vernon. Madison Jr. stayed at Montpelier until October of 1792, when he again departed for Philadelphia. This travel pattern was common for Madison during the Continental Congress sessions.

In 1794, during a trip to Philadelphia, Madison Jr. asked Aaron Burr to introduce him to young widow Dolley Payne Todd. In less than a year, and despite their seventeen-year age difference and his Episcopalian religious background (Dolley was a Quaker), the couple married on September 15, 1794. "Our hearts understand each other," Dolley later wrote to her husband.[220]

While the pair never had children of their own, Madison Jr. would be a father figure to Dolley's son, Payne. They lived in a spacious three-story house in Philadelphia until 1796, when John Adams was elected president. After Adams' election, Madison Jr. announced his retirement, and moved his family back to Montpelier. In 1797, he added a thirty-foot extension and a Tuscan portico to build space and create privacy for his parents, who were still living at Montpelier, and his own family.

According to family oral history, during Jim's childhood, James Madison Jr. allowed his son with Coreen to listen in on the lessons of Dolley's nieces, Victoria and Susan.[221] Jim hid behind the door during their reading, writing, and arithmetic lessons. Ruby, the seventh family *griotte*, Bettye's mother, told her, "[this] was Madison's way of showing love for his son."

According to family oral history, when Victoria was twelve, she was told by Dolley she could no longer be around boys, especially those who were slaves. At the time, Jim worked in the Madison home.[222]

The Madisons loved to entertain, and the cooking staff and enslaved workers prepared meals for the Madisons and their many guests. Breakfast was not served at one sitting—guests and family members ate at different times based on their preferences. Coreen and her fellow enslaved workers would bake bread before dawn; the meats they served were likely left from the day before.[223]

Some guests recorded their culinary experiences at Montpelier and noted they were served hot bread at breakfast along with cold meats, pastry, tea, and coffee. This demonstrates how enslaved workers like Coreen had to wake up before first light to make sure hot, fresh bread was served. The cooking methods

---

[218] Bettye Kearse, The Other Madisons, March 24, 2020
[219] "Madison Chronology, 1723-2003," Montpelier Research Files, Montpelier Foundation, Orange, Virginia.
[220] Allida Blac, The First Ladies of the United States of America," Copyright 2009 by the White House Historical Association.
[221] Bettye Kearse, The Other Madisons, March 24, 2020
[222] Bettye Kearse, The Other Madisons, March 24, 2020
[223] Montpelier Research Department

they used were exhaustive. A single dinner could include roasting, boiling, baking, and frying. For example, one visitor wrote in 1835, "There was before us – soup, a roast turkey, boiled beef, chicken pie, potatoes fried with grease, turnips. Then cranberry pie, custards, preserves."[224] Another visitor in 1836 noted "good soups, flesh, fish, and vegetables, well cooked-dessert."[225] A visitor in 1825 wrote, "We had a good, neat little dinner at noon, with artichokes and other vegetables."[226] A visitor in 1816 wrote, "French cookery ... made a part of every day's fare!"[227]

When his father died in 1801, James Jr. inherited Montpelier. When James Madison Sr.'s library was inventoried, there were two cookbooks that most likely belonging to his wife, Nelly, *The Compleat Housewife* by E. Smith (Williamsburg, 1742) and *The Country Housewife and Lady's Director* by Richard Bradley (London, 1736). It is likely that some of the dishes Coreen prepared were featured in those books.

Two popular cookbooks published during Dolley's lifetime were *The Art of Cookery, Made Plain and Easy* by Hannah Glass, and *The Virginia House-wife* by Mary Randolph. Even though Coreen was not able to read, it was likely she prepared some of the recipes featured in these two volumes.

The Madisons always had an abundance of pies on their table: apple, cranberry, and even Périgord (pie stuffed with partridges and truffles). Unfortunately, there are very few historic records of specific recipes Coreen prepared because nineteenth century cooks did not rely on written recipes. In addition, cookbooks may have been destroyed when the Madisons' personal belongings were destroyed, the result of the White House being burned to the ground by British troops on August 24, 1814.

Madison Jr.'s retirement didn't last long. He was named Secretary of State for President Thomas Jefferson in 1801. and ran for president himself in 1808. Oral history says when Madison won the presidential election and moved to Washington, D.C. with Dolley, Victoria, and Susan in 1809, he brought Coreen and Jim with them.[228]

---

[224] George C. Shattuck, Diary, 1834-1842, Massachusetts Historical Society, Boston, Massachusetts.
[225] Charles Jared Ingersoll, "A Visit to Mr. Madison at Montpelier, May 2, 1836," The Globe (Washington, DC), August 12, 1836.
[226] Diary of Lukas Vischer (excerpts), June 11-12, 1825, Private Collection
[227] Richard Rush to Charles Jared Ingersoll, October 9, 1816, Historical Society of Pennsylvania, Philadelphia, Pennsylvania. The quotations in this paragraph were excerpted from Hilarie M. Hicks, "All the Delicacies That the Most Fastidious Gourmand Could Ever Sigh For:" Cooking and Cooks at Montpelier, unpublished research report, 2018, Montpelier Foundation, Orange, Virginia.
[228] Bettye Kearse, The Other Madisons, March 24, 2020

To accommodate the Madisons' summer visits and immense entertaining schedule, President Madison commissioned a renovation of his house at Montpelier from 1808 through 1812, adding two large one-story wings on the north and south sides of the mansion and cellar kitchens under each wing.

The south kitchen was the traditional kitchen for Madison Jr.'s mother, Nelly. Coreen was a cook in the south kitchen, but she could have worked in both kitchens to prepare the food for Dolley's lavish Montpelier social gatherings.[229]

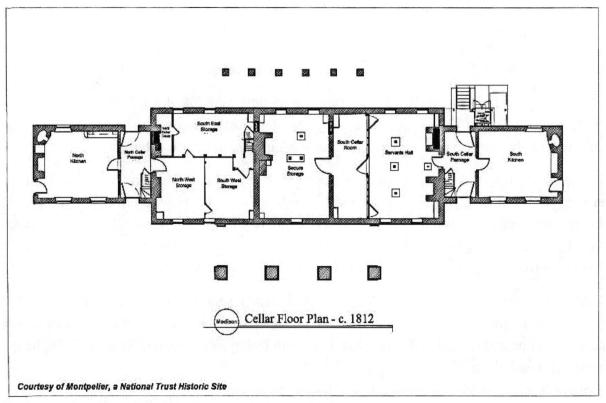

Cellar Floor Plan - c. 1812

Courtesy of Montpelier, a National Trust Historic Site

The north kitchen was the "modern" kitchen. Dolley's enslaved cooks also used an additional kitchen outbuilding north of the house. These kitchens contributed to creating large quantities of culinary dishes, which set the standard for the Madisons' well known southern hospitality.

The cellars of these kitchens housed additional facilities, including a workroom, called a "servants' hall," where cooks ate or performed tasks, like polishing silver, sewing, or spinning, while they awaited their next task from the Madisons. Most of the foods served were typically Virginian (such as ham and BBQ). French and other imported wines and liquors were also featured regularly since President Madison had an affinity for them.

Social gatherings expanded beyond the D.C. political gatherings Dolley hosted. During Madison's presidency, these gatherings in D.C. were known as "drawing rooms" Sometimes large, sometimes small, these weekly gatherings were essentially open houses where guests met the Madisons, had refreshments, and mingled. When the gathering was crowded, it was sometimes called a "squeeze." During the summer, President Madison and Dolley lived at Montpelier, where their dinners and large social events continued. Oral history states that Coreen was part of the staff that created the food served at these events.

In an 1816 letter to her sister, Anna Cutts, Dolley described an Independence Day party at Montpellier:

Yesterday we had ninety persons to dine with us at one table, fixed on the lawn, under a thick arbor. The dinner was profuse and handsome, and the company very orderly... half a dozen only staid all night, and are now about to depart... I am less worried here with a hundred visitors than with twenty five in Washington.[230]

   ***

Oral history recounts that Victoria did not listen to her aunt and her warnings to stay away from Jim. She continued to meet up with him in D.C, and the two would share their deepest thoughts and feelings while hiding in armoires in house's family bedrooms. The two ended up falling in love.

A maid found out about their relationship and told Victoria and Jim that they needed to stay away from each other. Because he was afraid the maid would report them to Dolley, Jim told his mother what was going on. Coreen cried when he poured his heart out to her. She knew her son would be sold or killed if Dolley found out.

Coreen came up with a plan to keep Jim and Victoria apart. She persuaded a steward to allow Jim to work in the kitchen so she could keep an eye on him. However, Victoria followed him. An enslaved chef warned her if she didn't stop sneaking into the kitchen, he would be forced to tell the mistress of the home.

During this time, on June 18, 1812, the U.S. declared war on Great Britain. On August 24, 1814, British soldiers and Black men who had been freed and recruited to fight alongside them advanced on Washington. Dolley instructed Jim to save the American flag that was flown at the White House. After Dolley handed him the flag, Jim folded it and hid it under his shirt. He then ran into the nearby woods and hid with the other slaves.

Years after the war, Ruby told Bettye, "Jim told his children how worried he was that lightning and flames from the burning city would reveal his hiding place."

Two months later, under the glitter of candlelight, Dolley threw a party to celebrate the signing of the peace treaty between Britain and the U.S. The glamourous ambiance was created by Jim and other male slaves Dolley had ordered to stand along the walls like statues, holding rushlights.

---

[230] Dolley Payne Todd Madison to Anna Payne Cutts, July 5, 1816, Cutts Family Collection of Papers of James and Dolley Madison, Library of Congress, Washington, D.C.

A decade later, when Jim was a father, he told his children that despite being forced to stand in place for hours on end, he would never forget the beauty of that evening, including the music and dancing, and the ambience he helped create

Shortly after that celebration, Victoria once again sneaked into the kitchen—this time, the enslaved chef followed through on his threat. Dolley was furious and arranged to sell Jim immediately. Family history, said President Madison objected, albeit meekly.

Before he stepped onto the wagon that would take him to his new enslaver, Coreen grabbed Jim and embraced him tightly. Her tears soaked his shirt. Through her weeping, she told him in her strongest voice: "Always remember — you're a Madison."

This was how the family credo originated—it was a tool they hoped could help find torn-away loved ones.

Victoria drove herself by wagon to see Jim at the new plantation. Dolley found out and pleaded with his enslaver to sell him, but this time further away to Gibson County, Tennessee.

Jim never saw his mother or Victoria again. But he never forgot the family credo and would make sure he would pass on his family history to the next generation as the third griot. He wanted to be sure they never forgot where they came from.

Chapter Two
Always remember—you're a Madison. You come from a president.

Tax records from the 1820s and 1830s showed Jim's son Emanuel lived in Tennessee and was the property of Jeptha Billingsley. He was identified as the only "black poll" (taxable slave). In 1834, a bill of sale showed Jeptha purchased a wife for him. Emanuel's name was listed on the bill of sale.

Elizabeth Quail, the enslaved worker purchased, was of French, African, and Native American lineage. "Ma Madison," as she is referred to, is a beloved member of the family.[231] The photo below is the first photo the family found of an ancestor. It is considered a treasured family heirloom and one Bettye always keeps with her.

Madison Family photo: *Elizabeth Madison (1815–1911)*

Elizabeth's grandmother, Katie, was from the French-speaking Senegambia region of Africa. Oral history says that on a trip back from Port Harcourt, Katie was on a footbridge, and two Black men grabbed her.[232] She was in her teens when she was put on a slave ship bound for the east coast of Florida. Katie was purchased by Edward Jackson, the owner of a plantation in Pensacola.

Katie was a personal servant to Mrs. Jackson. She taught Katie to sew and embroider, as well as to bake cookies and fancy cakes. The mistress enjoyed showing off her dainty, French-speaking slave. Katie pretended not to understand English.

---

[231] Bettye Kearse, The Other Madisons, March 24, 2020
[232] Bettye Kearse, The Other Madisons, March 24, 2020

Oral history says Katie did this to have an excuse for avoiding work she did not want to do, or in the event she made a mistake.[233] Mr. Jackson eventually caught her speaking English to another slave named Toby. Deciding to make an example of what would happen if he was ever deceived again, he beat her with a switch until she was bloody, on the house's veranda in front of the other slaves. Many months later, Toby asked Mr. Jackson if he could "jump the broom" with Katie and marry her. While Jackson agreed, he would not allow them to live together. Toby was a field slave on one of Jackson's plantations. Katie was a domestic slave and lived in the house. They saw each other on Sundays and whenever Toby was able to sneak away from his quarters. In 1817, less than a year after they were married, their daughter Lily was born. Lily was a shy domestic slave and worked in the house with her mother.

One day, while on her way back from town after summoning the doctor for Mr. Jackson, Lily met John Quail, a Choctaw Indian. The stranger tried to engage her in conversation, but Lily ignored him. Eventually she relented, and the two started a conversation. Oral history says it was love at first sight.

Lily and John were eventually allowed to jump the broom, but Mr. Jackson would not write up free papers for the bride. She continued to work as an enslaved domestic worker, even though her husband was a free man. The couple had a daughter, Elizabeth.

Three years later, Jackson died, the result of failing health. Faced with a number of outstanding debts, his widow was forced sell several slaves, including Lily and Elizabeth. John was not aware of the sale. His wife and daughter were taken away while he was delivering grain to a nearby plantation. For months, John searched for his family. He never saw them again.

Elizabeth was purchased by Augustus King, the owner of a plantation in Gibson County, Tennessee. It is unknown if he purchased Lily. A bill of sale from 1834 shows King sold Elizabeth to Jeptha Billingsley. Details of the paperwork revealed the two plantation owners agreeing to give their property, Emanuel and Elizabeth, the freedom to decide if they wanted to get married.

---

[233] Bettye Kearse, The Other Madisons, March 24, 2020

Elizabeth ("Betsey") Madison's bill of sale, 1834

The agreement stated Billingsley would keep "a certain Negro slave name, "Betsey" (Elizabeth) of a light mulatto complexion of seventeen years old" for one year specifically to become a mate for a "Negro boy named Manuel." Elizabeth answered "Betsey" from her enslaver. Still, amongst family and friends, King would be required to provide Elizabeth and any children she might have with "good clothing." After the year, if either Emanuel or Elizabeth did not want to stay together, Elizabeth would be returned to King. The couple decided to stay together. "Elizabeth, Ma Madison" taught her family the value of love, hard work, and honesty. A woman of strong Christian faith, she also lived by example, showing their children that actions in life must reflect your faith.

Elizabeth had between twelve and fourteen children, but only eight were listed in the 1860 census. The family did not know whether they had died or were sold.

***

Billingsley property data showed Elizabeth, Emanuel, and their surviving five children lived in Tennessee until 1848. The family was then relocated to Texas to work for Billingsley's son Jesse.

75

Jeptha's son Jesse was a Captain of the First Regiment Texas Volunteers at San Jacinto[234] and was a friend of David Crockett. Jesse received twenty-two hundred acres of land for his leadership in the military and allotted some of his land to his father. Emanuel and his oldest sons Shelby, Mack, Henry, and Giles were needed to work that land.

The trip was not easy for the family. Oral history says one day in the faint morning light, Emanuel, Elizabeth, and their four oldest sons were getting ready to go out to the cotton fields to work when a white man they did not recognize appeared in their cabin doorway. Four-year-old Charles was still sleeping on his pallet.[235]

The stranger told the family to wake the child and gather their things because they were going to Texas. Before they could do that, the man walked over to the sleeping child and carried him out to the wagon. Fear she would never see her baby boy again, Elizabeth ran out of the house to join her son Charles with Emanual, Shelby, Mack, Henry, and Giles behind her.

The family piled onto the wagon without being able to gather any food, clothing, or supplies. There were two men on that wagon. One held a shotgun. The other held ropes he tied around Emanuel's wrists. He then locked heavy iron chains around the ankles of all the family members except for young Charles.

The trip from Tennessee to Texas was made during the night to escape the intense summer heat. But traveling in the dark came with its own risks because it was a well-known fact that thieves hid on roads to kidnap slaves. Even though they were shackled, the family was held at gunpoint to ensure they would not escape.

The canopy of trees snuffed out any moonlight. In the darkness, Charles would cry from hunger. Concerned his cries would alert thieves, the guard holding the shotgun pointed his weapon at Elizabeth's chest and whispered, "If you want everybody to get to Texas, you better shut that boy up." Elizabeth taught her young son to cry silently.

Because the family left with no supplies, Elizabeth was unable to hide her menstrual flow. The guard and driver would laugh at her as the blood dripped down her legs into a pool on the wagon floor. Elizabeth fought through the degradation with grace. She would repeatedly tell herself she was blessed to have her whole family still together. "God is good. God is amazing," She would repeat to herself.

The trip took three weeks, and the lack of food and water took a toll on the once strong family. The tight ropes around Emanuel's wrist carved deep, bloody wounds into his skin. Sores developed under their iron shackles. When they arrived at their destination, Jeptha was horrified to see the family he was told was healthy was not much more than skeletons. In fact, they were so weak they could not stand, let alone walk, their clothes and skin caked in layers of dirt and mud, and bugs crawling in their hair. Jeptha was concerned his "investment" was in jeopardy.

---

[234] San Jacinto Museum of History
[235] Bettye Kearse, The Other Madisons, March 24, 2020

Nine years later, on January 13, 1857, the ownership of Emanuel, Elizabeth, and their now eight boys was transferred to Jesse. This deed, a piece of family history, is kept in the family's box of treasures. The document listed their approximate ages and description of skin color. Emanuel was 52, and Elizabeth was 37 at the time of the purchase. Their children aged from four to twenty-two were: Shelby (22), Mack (19), Henry (17), Giles (15), Young (13), Charles (11), James (9), and John (4). Jesse paid his father, Jeptha, nine-thousand dollars for the enslaved family ($306,492.41 in today's dollars).

Also in the box is a copy of the 1860 slave census. Bettye's mother, the seventh griotte, wrote their names in her copy of the document. This was the last slave census before the Emancipation Proclamation of 1863.

The ninth boy and baby girl listed either passed away or were sold. The family does not know what happened to them.

Emanuel received permission to teach his children how to read. Jesse Billingsley was an advocate for the literacy of the enslaved.[236] The Madisons read the Bible every day. Allowing Emanuel to teach his children how to read was unusual because, after the Nat Turner Rebellion, most southern states had passed laws making it illegal to promote literacy in slaves.[237]

As the fourth *griot*, one of the greatest life lessons Emanuel taught his children was that they needed to know their family history and be proud of their name because they had come from a president. It was at this time the credo was expanded to:

"Always remember—you're a Madison. You come from a president."

This was the first time the credo—originally used as a tool to find a torn-away loved one—was being used as a source of inspiration.

***

Freedom for the enslaved men and women in Texas did not happen with the preliminary Emancipation Proclamation Lincoln issued on September 22, 1862[238], or with the Emancipation Proclamation of 1863, that "slaves within any State, or designated part of a State…in rebellion…shall be then, thenceforward, and forever free."[239]

Even though telegraph messages shared the news of the Emancipation Proclamation when it was issued, and despite the Civil War ending in April of 1865, the freedom of the enslaved population would not have happened without enforcement by the Union Military.[240]

On June 19, 1865, the Union Army officially occupied Texas. Major General Gordon Granger of the Union Army read federal orders in the city of Galveston that declared the enslaved were free. Texas was the last state in the Confederacy where the enslaved population gained their freedom, a full 66 days after President Lincoln's assassination.

On June 25, 1865, Union troops raised the American flag in Austin[241], the state's capital. Austin is 25 miles from Cedar Creek, Bastrop County, home to Jesse Billingsley's plantation, where the Madisons were enslaved. It was around this time that the Madisons learned they were now free.

---

[236] Texas State Historical Association

[237] Nat Turner was an enslaved man who was a literate preacher and led a rebellion of enslaved people on August 21, 1831. Around 55 white men, women, and children were killed.

[238] The Library of Congress: "On September 22, 1862, partly in response to the heavy losses inflicted at the Battle of Antietam, President Abraham Lincoln issued a preliminary Emancipation Proclamation, threatening to free all the enslaved people in the states in rebellion if those states did not return to the Union by January 1, 1863. The extent of the Proclamation's practical effect has been debated, as it was legally binding only in territory not under Union control. In the short term, it amounted to no more than a statement of policy for the federal army as it moved into Southern territory."

[239] National Archives "The Emancipation Proclamation"

[240] Juneteenth History: Why Doesn't Everyone Know About Texas? June 8, 2021, CU Denver News

[241] The Breakup: The Collapse of the Confederate Trans-Mississippi Army in Texas, 1865. Southwest Historical Quarterly. Vol. CVIII

During that year, 51,000 Union troops were mobilized to regain control over the state. Within five years (March of 1870), that number had dropped to 3,000[242]. As a result, violence against Blacks was widespread, including 375 Blacks murdered between 1865 and 1868.

For the state of Texas to be readmitted to the Union, they had to follow a convention process in which provisional governors would oversee the state to create a new constitution, repeal secession ordinances, and repudiate their war debt. Voters would then have to approve the results and elect a new governor and legislators who would then ratify the 13th Amendment to the U.S. Constitution.

The 1866 Constitutional Convention resulted in the bare minimum needed to start the process of readmission into the Union. The Reconstruction Period was filled with hate, turbulence, and intimidation. Even though the 13th and 14th Amendments were passed, the Texas State Legislature did not support the laws. They wanted things to go back to the way they were before the Civil War.[243]

The newly elected 11th Texas Legislature refused to ratify the 13th and 14th amendments during the 1866 Constitutional Convention. There were no Black delegates representing the newly freed Black Americans. That Convention only gave Black men the right to be sued or to sue, acquire land or pass on property, obtain equal criminal prosecution under the law, and testify in any case involving another Black American.[244]

Freedom may have finally been a reality to the Madisons, but the ugly truth behind that freedom was fear and poverty. Freedom did not solve Madison's problems; it enhanced them. The Amendments were not enforceable.

The 11th Texas State Legislature also created the Black Codes in 1866. These codes prohibited Blacks from marrying whites, kept them segregated on railroads and in public facilities (bathrooms), and kept them from sharing public school funds and receiving distribution of public land.[245] Sharecropping was supposed to free the newly emancipated Black people from slavery-era gang labor. These contracts, however, were structured to favor the landowner, who usually was the former enslaver.

The Madisons heard the stories about the Ku Klux Klan and the oppression Black citizens faced, including paying exorbitant prices to rent land from their former enslavers. Yet Emanuel, the patriarch of the family, told his sons, "We've come far, but we've got far to go. Your great-grandfather was president of this country. You can do great things, too, so make something of yourselves now that you have that chance. Tell your children and tell them to tell *their* children: Always remember: you're a Madison. You come from a president."

Emanuel and his family instilled the premise that freedom was a responsibility, and it was up to them to make a future for themselves. Emanuel reminded his adult children about Mandy, Coreen, and Jim. He

---

[242] Reconstruction in Texas Digital History ID 3680 and Texas State Historical Association
[243] Texas State Library and Archives Commission, The 1860's: Reconstruction
[244] Texas State Library and Archives Commission, The 1860's Reconstruction
[245] Texas State Historical Association, Black Codes

told them that with hard work, those dreams could become a reality if you believe in yourself and your dreams. The freedom allowed the Madisons to pursue their dreams.

They now had free will, and it was their responsibility to seize upon it. They decided what jobs they wanted to pursue to care for and educate their families. Their futures were blank sheets of paper—writing their own stories was up to them. The stories of Emanuel and Elizabeth were many, but they all had a common theme: giving back to the community.

Some of the couple's sons became ministers who inspired and nourished the souls of their parishioners. Giles was a tenant farmer[246]', Mack became a large landowner, and Henry Green Madison broke social boundaries.

Henry was twenty-three when emancipation came. At that time, he was married to another enslaved worker, Louisa. Together they had a daughter, Elizabeth. He wanted a better life for his family, so he traveled twenty-five miles to Austin to learn the carpentry trade.

Louisa and Elizabeth stayed in Cedar Creek and lived with Henry's parents. Henry traveled back to chop down trees every weekend with his brothers Giles and Mack. They loaded the logs onto Henry's horse-drawn wagon and hauled them to Austin so he could build his family a log cabin. Once the twelve-by-twelve cabin was completed, between 1865 and 1866, he brought his family to their first home. Through the years, as Henry prospered, he built the log house.

More than a century later, the original cabin was discovered when an Austin demolition crew tore down the old frame home, revealing the log cabin. In 1968, the city moved the cabin to Rosewood Park, where it became a monument honoring the significant contributions slaves and ex-slaves made to American history. The home received a historical marker in 1974 from the National Trust for Historic Preservation.

---

[246] A tenant farmer is a famer who rented land.

Henry Green Madison's cabin in Rosewood Park, Austin, Texas

Henry inherited Mandy's fiery spirt and determination. He remembered Mandy's words passed down to him through his father: never back down from anything that you believe in. He was a passionate Unionist[247] , and during the Civil War in 1867, Henry was president of the Austin chapter of the Union League, a secret organization formed in 1863 in the North to support the policies of President Abraham Lincoln.[248]

***

The next Texas Constitutional Convention was in June of 1868. This time, ten Black men were elected to the ninety-delegate convention. Henry Green Madison was an assistant and aided the ten Black members.[249] This was the first time in Texas history Black people had a voice in state government.[250] This Constitution expanded the rights of Black men to not only vote, but to also serve in office, and participate

---

[247] Southerners living in the Confederate States of America opposed to secession
[248] Texas State Historical Association
[249] Texas State Library and Archives Commission- Madison, Henry Green (1843-1912)
[250] Texas State Library and Archives Commission

in the legal process as a member of a jury. In addition to these rights, Black citizens could now own land. According to the journals of the 1868 Convention, on August 29, 1868:

Be it ordained by the people of Texas in Convention assembled, that Africans, and descendants of Africans, now residing in Texas, shall receive land as follows: Every head of a family shall be entitled to one hundred and sixty acres, and every single man of the age of twenty-one years and upwards, shall be entitled to eighty acres; provided, however, that it shall be the duty of the Legislature to set apart and cause to be sectionized so much of the vacant public domain lying in the unsettled portion of this State, as in the judgment of that body shall be sufficient for the execution of this ordinance.

The Convention also added an article to allow Black households to be taxed so those monies could be used to create schools for Black children. This version of the state's constitution, in which Henry participated, was ratified in November of 1869. Despite the expansion of political freedoms being offered to Black men, the state did not formally ratify the 13th Amendment.

This state constitution swung the political pendulum further away from the bondage of slavery. It was just eighty years earlier when Henry's great-great-grandfather, James Madison Jr., introduced the twelve amendments he wrote to the first congress in 1789. Ten of those amendments would later become the Bill of Rights.

The 13th and 14th Amendments were not formally ratified by the State of Texas until February 18, 1870. Until then, the state's official position was that the 13th Amendment already had been implicitly adopted.[251] This finally satisfied the state's requirements to rejoin the Union.

Within months of Texas' readmission into the Union, Governor Edmund J. Davis and the 12th Legislature, in its first called session in 1870, created the Frontier Forces (June 13), the State Guard and Reserve Militia (June 24), and the State Police (July 1), all of which were commanded by a newly restored state Adjutant General. [252] Three state military rolls[253] showed that Henry served as Captain of the all-Black unit, Company B, in the sixth regiment of the Texas State Guard.[254]

---

[251] The Handbook of Texas explains, "[T]he members agreed that the Thirteenth Amendment, by then a part of the Constitution, had abolished slavery and that since they had taken the oath to support that Constitution, they had indirectly abolished slavery. They reasoned, therefore, that a direct and formal ratification of the amendment was not necessary and voted to allow the taking of the constitutional oath to suffice."- The Texas Politics Project U.S. Constitution Civil War amendments
[252] Texas Archives
[253] Texas Adjutant General's Department Reconstruction military rolls Company B (Austin, Travis County) (Capt. Henry G. Madison), undated [1870], Company B (Austin, Travis County) (Capt. Henry G. Madison), August 30, 1870, Company B (Austin, Travis County) (Capt. Henry G. Madison), September 30-October 31, 1870
[254] Adjutant General's Records, Texas State Library and Archives, Austin, Company b, 6th Regiment, Folder 10, Box 401-727; State Guard Military Rolls, Reconstruction Military Rolls; Austin city Council Meeting Archives

On February 1, 1871, the governor also appointed Henry as the first Black Alderman. At that time, Austin City records showed that Henry was a shoemaker in Austin's Ward 5.[255] He was reappointed in November of 1872.[256]

Henry Green Madison (1843-1912)
Source: Austin Public Library, Austin Beginnings An Exhibit of Memorable Austin Firsts

Henry's civic leadership extended to numerous other roles. He was one of twelve members of the temporary governing body, the Travis County Executive Committee. As a city councilman, he fought for infrastructure. He was on committees for streets and cemeteries and crafted legislation regarding the city's water supply. Henry was also a champion of the legal system. He voted to raise the salaries of law enforcement personnel as well as the city attorney and to ban lotteries within the city limits.

Henry was fearless. In 1871, during Reconstruction, he volunteered to serve as a registrar of voters in Travis County. This was considered especially dangerous for a Black man because of the opposition to Black civil rights.

The police department in Austin was not established until 1862 when an ordinance establishing it and the office of chief of police was created.[257] Henry became a police officer in the 1880s. With a growing population, the city experienced more crime. New ordinances were passed, giving more authority to the police to curb disorderly conduct. When Henry was serving in the police department, crime was particularly brutal. The city of Austin experienced a series of vicious, unsolved serial murders that lasted from 1883 until 1885. The serial killer was known as The Servant Girl Annihilator, *Austin* Axe Murderer, and the Midnight Assassin.[258]

---

[255] Austin Library, "Austin Beginnings" An Exhibit of Memorable Austin Firsts
[256] Austin City Council
[257] Austin Police Department Guide, Sources of Information Relating to the Austin Police Department, Austin History Center, Compiled by Bob Rescola and Rusty Heckaman, updated by Toni Cirilli, 2018
[258] Fort Worth Daily Gazette. September 29, 1885

***

Freedom provided Mack the opportunity as *griot* to offer future generations the chance to learn their family story through physical evidence. He brought his family's stories to life with letters, documents, and photographs. By reading their words, reviewing land deeds, and looking into the eyes of photographs of their loved ones, family members could now see how the family flourished, despite the odds.

Mack married Martha Murchison Strain in 1837. Her mother, Mahala, moved to Austin with the Murchison family as an enslaved child and is believed to be the first Black person in Austin.

Mahala Murchison (1824–1912)

Martha's brother, Frank Strain, made history as a free Black man. In December of 1871, he was the first Black porter on the first train to make a trip to Austin.[259] Despite breaking down barriers, Frank encountered racism on a daily basis. Because he had fair skin and wavy hair, his supervisor required Frank to remove his shirt while serving his patrons, to reveal to them that he was Black.

---

[259] Texas History Portal

During their union, Martha and Mack had ten children, five of whom survived to adulthood: Ruth, Laura, Moody, Charles, and John Chester. Charles was born enslaved and was emancipated at around three years of age, but his brothers and sisters were the first Madisons born free. This made Mack's responsibilities as a *griot* even more consequential: His children were the first generation of Madisons who would grow up as free citizens. He raised them to be productive and respected members of society and wanted them to know their ancestors and how their hard work and perseverance helped pave the road they were on and would continue to build for future generations.

Source: Madison Family Archives, composite photo. Right- studio portrait of Moody (standing Left) John Chester (standing right), Seated left t right: Laura and Ruth). On the Left standing alone is Charlie

Parenting in the post-enslavement era was a challenge. Mack lived by the words of Mandy to stand up for what you believed in. When the 14th Amendment granted citizenship to the previously enslaved, tensions between white and Black communities were high.

Mack was a proud member of the Negro Loyal League. The group was created by forty black men after Lincoln's proclamation was read in Texas. The purpose of the organization was to protect the status of the Black community.

Every Saturday night, Mack and his fellow Negro Loyal League members met at the Cedar Creek Street Store and performed drills up and down the road. They carried whatever they could get their hands on that could be considered weapons, including sticks and rocks. Some white men who watched these drills viewed them as acts of rebellion and a threat to their community.

One evening before a Negro Loyal League meeting, Mack was stopped by Peter Murchison, his white cousin, through his marriage to Martha. They had had a cordial relationship, but that night, Peter was transformed into an angry man Mack didn't recognize. Peter pointed a gun at Mack's chest and refused to let him pass to attend his meeting. Peter saw Mack as a threat to his white way of life. Mack missed that evening's meeting and promised himself he would never miss another one. He would not let "white hate" win. Eventually, Jesse Billingsley urged Governor Edmund Davis to break up the League. Unfortunately, that did not lessen tensions.

The resentment toward Blacks hit a high in 1888 after a historic election in which two Black men were voted into the offices of Justice of the Peace and Constable of Cedar Creek. Orange Wicks was elected Justice of the Peace for Bastrop County's Precinct 3, and in his role of judge, he was set to reside over the trial of Frank Litton, a white man, accused of assaulting a Black woman. [260] Litton refused to sit in the courtroom while the jury deliberated and sealed his fate. Outside of Wick's courtroom, a shoot-out started, resulting in the death of four men, two Black and two white.[261]

John Chester, Mack's youngest son, who was seven at the time, watched the scene with friends from the top of a smoke house. From their vantage point, the boys witnessed Mack scrambling and then firing a pistol. Once the gun fire stopped, John Chester and his friends climbed down from the rooftop and headed home. Their parents hugged them, relieved they were okay.

The shooting fueled additional anxiety amongst the white population and sparked riots—local white residents swore revenge on every Black person connected to the murder of the two white men. One by one, the Black men were murdered in acts of revenge—or they were forced to flee the area.[262]

Justice Wicks and several other men were charged with murder even though everyone who saw the shooting said Wicks was unarmed. He was convicted of murder twice, but eventually, the convictions were overturned.[263] After the court battles, Wicks returned to teaching in Bastrop County.

***

Mack's children knew how important education was. Mack told them he learned math, reading, and writing from his father, who was taught by their grandfather, Jim. Mack's acumen in math and his strong literacy skills made him an asset in the business world. Once freed, the education he received from his father, Emanuel enabled Mack to become Jesse Billingsley's business manager. As Jesse's right-hand man, Mack took the cotton crop to the cotton gin, where he negotiated deals and handled the proceeds.

Like his brother Giles, Mack was part of a group of tenant farmers known as "halvers[264]" because half of the income generated by the tenant farmer's crop production would be turned over to the landowner. Mack signed an agreement with Jesse Billingsley and saved his earnings for nine years. By 1874 he had $192 in gold (about $5,000 in today's dollars)—enough to buy a ninety-six-acre farm. Mack was a savvy

---

[260] Thompson, Cal, Texas State Historical Association
[261] "Bastrop Country's First Black Justice of the Peace Gets Tombstone", Nov. 11, 2017, Austin American Statesman
[262] Thompson, Cal, Texas State Historical Association
[263] "Bastrop Country's First Black Justice of the Peace Gets Tombstone", Nov. 11, 2017, Austin American Statesman
[264] Texas Beyond History, Osborn Farm, World of the Tenant Farmer"…after Emancipation and the abolishment of slavery in 1865, cotton growers turned to tenant farming as a means of securing the needed labor. The tenant system was popular throughout the latter part of the nineteenth century and into the first half of the twentieth century."

Businessman. He flipped that same farm for $394 the following year (more than $10,000 in today's present value) and purchased two hundred acres for $400. Those deeds are part of the family's box of heirlooms.

Mack wanted to make sure the documents were preserved so future generations would know that through determination and grit—traits instilled in the family beginning with Mandy, combined with a focus on education instilled in them by Jim—you could achieve anything.

Mack chose to live close to his parents in Cedar Creek, knowing and appreciating how lucky he was to be near his family members. He knew many former enslaved men and women were still looking for their loved ones after their families had been ripped apart.

MACK MADISON
(1837-1912)

Moody became a janitor at the State House in Austin. Mack Madison saved enough to be able to put his children through college. Laura, Ruth, and John Chester all attended and graduated from college, the first Madisons to do so. Because John Chester did not want to use his father's hard-earned money, he paid for college himself. College was not accessible for many Black men and women during that time because they either didn't qualify or didn't have the monetary resources. In Texas, there were four colleges created for Black Americans between 1872 and 1878, all of which were focused on trade work.

During the 1870s and 1880s, many white Texans opposed integrating public schools or even providing educational opportunities for Black children.[265] They believed an educated Black population would aspire to higher paying jobs and reduce the pool of cheap agricultural and industrial labor they relied on. They also felt that integrating schools could lead to interracial marriages.

---

[265] Texas State Historical Association: Black Colleges

At the beginning of Reconstruction, the Freedmen's Bureau[266] helped establish elementary and secondary schools for former slaves. General Oliver Otis Howard was the commissioner of the Freedmen's Bureau during the bureau's period of operation (September 1865 through July 1870). During that time, five men served as assistant commissioners. Howard regarded Texas as his biggest challenge in the country. In his autobiography[267], he recalled that when appointing the first assistant commissioner to the state, it was "to be the post of greatest peril."

Colleges in the South were created by Northern missionary and religious groups. About a dozen were established. The first Black private college in Texas, Paul Quinn College, was established in Austin on April 4, 1872.[268] The school was named after an African Methodist Episcopal (AME) Church Bishop who served a church on the western frontier. John Chester attended Paul Quinn College but commuted.

Wiley College was founded in 1873 by the Freedmen's Aid Society of the Methodist Episcopal Church. Tillotson College was established in 1877 in Austin and opened to students in January 1881. It was founded by the AMA, the American Missionary Association, and offered elementary, secondary, and college training. Ruby and her brothers lived on campus and attended Tillotson. Bettye's mother, Ruby, later transferred to Prairie View State Normal School (now called Prairie View A&M University), where she studied home economics so she could become a dietician. The college curriculum for Black students generally consisted of teacher training, as well as agricultural and vocational training. Many whites were opposed to more expansive educational offerings, so choices remained purposely limited.[269] Prairie View was a byproduct of the state Constitution of 1876 whereby the legislature was required to create an institution for higher education for Black youth. The expectation that Prairie View would expand its educational offerings as part of the University of Texas never materialized. Political pressure and litigation ensued.

The Black community and organizations, including the Colored Teachers State Association of Texas, pushed for a Black State University at Austin. In 1882, it was proposed and authorized by ballot, but the Texas legislature never took action to begin construction. In 1897, the Colored Teachers State Association of Texas pressured the legislature to pass a bill authorizing the use of 50,000 acres of public land to build a Black State University of Austin. The Texas Supreme Court invalidated that action in 1898 by prohibiting the land commissioner from using more land for education.[270] It became clear a separate Black university

---

[266] Freedmen's Bureau was a temporary agency established by congress in March 1865 as a branch of the U.S. Army. They were to supervise affairs related to newly freed slaves in the southern states; provide relief to thousands of Black and White refugees left homeless after the Civil War. The Bureau operated in Texas from late September 1865 until 1870.
[267] Autobiography of Oliver Otis Howard, Major-General, United States Army, Vol. 1, Vol. 2
[268] Paul Quinn College, "About Paul Quinn College"
[269] Texas State Historical Association, Black Colleges
[270] Texas General Land Office: In Hogue v. Baker (1898) the Texas Supreme Court declared that there was no more vacant and unappropriated land in Texas. In 1900 an act was passed "to define the permanent school fund of the State of Texas, to partition the public lands between said fund and the State, and to adjust the account between said fund and said state; to set apart and appropriate to said school fund, the residue of the public domain…" Thus all of the remaining unappropriated land was set aside by the legislature for the benefit of public schools

would not be built in Texas. As a result, Prairie View expanded its courses in classical and scientific studies in 1901.

After graduating, all three Madisons gave back to their community by becoming teachers. Ruth became a home economics teacher and later ascended to the dean of women at St. Phillips College in San Antonio. Laura became a grade school teacher, and John Chester became a teacher and a principal.

Courtesy: St. Philip's Junior College

Charlie, the oldest, ended up moving north, fearing for his life. Oral history tells us that he was the maverick of the family[271]. John Chester, the next (sixth) *griot,* added his older brother's story to the Madison family's history. One evening, when Charlie was leaving his job at the stockyard, he and a group of friends and coworkers were confronted by a group of white men who accused Charlie of stealing a horse. A fight broke out, and one of Charlie's accusers was killed. No one knew who was responsible for the man's death, but afraid for their lives, Charlie and his friends fled town.

Charlie sought refuge at a friend's house in the city of Denison, about 200 miles north of Cedar Creek. He hid for several weeks, eventually changing his name to John Miller, and secured work constructing the railroad.

For months, Martha and Mack endured harassment from white residents of Cedar Creek, who wanted to know where their son was. Things eventually quieted, and the family was finally left alone. Charlie, now

---

[271] Bettye Kearse, The Other Madisons, March 24, 2020

known as John, continued to keep in touch with his family, but to protect both himself and his family, he never traveled back home.

***

John Chester was Bettye's grandfather. Mack chose the baby of the family to be the next *griot* because he had deep love for the family's history and a flair for storytelling. Affectionately referred to as "Gramps" by his grandchildren, he would wait at the door of the Elgin public library so he could be there when it opened. The library allowed the town's Black citizens access only once a month, so Gramps spent the entire day reading and researching information on the slave trade, West Africa, and any available information that existed regarding U.S. slavery.

John Chester gathered additional research to help fill in the blanks of his family's history:

"These stories are important , and they're the reason that we are who we are… they still influence who we are, what's important to us, what kind of values we have," stressed John Chester.

John Chester told stories with his signature flair. His vibrant voice filled the room, telling the stories in foreign accents, like a thick drawl, and with lively gestures. Gramps had an uncanny ability to bring the family's ancestors back to life:

Giles was out chopping wood and heard this loud noise behind him. He turned around and saw a huge bore (sic) coming down the hill, charging at him. Giles jumped behind a tree next to the chopping block and came out with an axe. The next thing the family knew, they were having a great barbecue.

As a child, John Chester had dreams of becoming a doctor. His father offered him money for tuition to encourage him, but John Chester refused. Mack had been free for just a small portion of his life and had worked hard for those savings. Instead, Gramps made the decision to work while attending school, not realizing the work he was able to secure wouldn't be enough to enable him to graduate in four years. But he persevered, and after twenty years, John Chester earned a bachelor's degree in agriculture. He never went to medical school, becoming a teacher instead.

After just two years, John was chosen to become the principal of the Booker T. Washington School in Elgin. This was the only school for Black children in the surrounding area, exacerbated by a shortage of Black teachers to instruct all twelve grades.

During his first year as principal, a beautiful, young woman named Ruby Massey became a teacher at the school. The two started to court and eventually became engaged. Tragically, just a few months after their engagement, Ruby died after her appendix ruptured. At her funeral, one of Ruby's sisters, Birdie Jo, tried to console a distraught John Chester. The two had never met until that day. Birdie Jo was also a teacher, albeit in another town. After the funeral, the two would meet and reminisce about Ruby. John struggled for months over Ruby's death, and Birdie Jo would provide an ear and shoulder for support. Several months later, John and Ruby realized they had two things in common: a love for Ruby, and a love for teaching. A year after Ruby's funeral, John Chester and Birdie Jo were married. They would both teach at Booker T. Washington School. Birdie Jo was serious; John Chester was more fun-loving. They had three children: Ruby, John Jr., and Mack. Birdie Jo was called "Grandmuddy" by Bettye and her brother Biff.

The family lived in the Black part of Elgin in a two-bedroom, five room, white-frame house with a front porch. The house was situated on a dirt road, separated from its similar-looking neighboring homes by small patches of grass. The Madison's plot was small, but the twenty-foot backyard held a dozen chickens and three huge hogs. Gardening tools rested against the back of the home. The railroad track for the Missouri-Kansas-Texas Railway ran just beyond their back fence.

The three children named the train "Katy" and would watch her pass by every day. The ground rumble under their feet let them know the train was approaching. Items on the walls of the house vibrated as the powerful train passed by. The massive steam engine and its railroad cars created strong breezes, blowing the pungent, sharp smell of the farm animals, slop, and dust into their house.

John used the trains as an educational opportunity for his children. He would teach them colors by having them point them out when freight cars passed by. When they were older, they learned the alphabet, in part by identifying letters on the cars. Finally, they learned to read using the words that graced the sides of the cars. Their father would describe the various landscapes the trains traveled through and told his children that someday, they would travel and see some of those same sights.

The siblings loved to imagine the destinations of the passengers on the train. They wondered what the white men and women were talking about, dressed in colorful outfits, and enjoying their food in the dining cars. Their love for trains came from their father. John Chester fell in love with them as a child—imagining where they were headed allowed him to use his imagination and wonder what the rest of the world was like.

Ruby, the shyest of the three children, noticed no Black men were working as train engineers or caboose men—those positions were all held by white men. The men who pumped the handcars up and down the tracks were Mexican. Texas not only segregated Blacks but also Mexicans. In fact, today, the state laws have come to be known as "Juan Crow,"[272] patterned after Jim Crow laws except that they discriminated against Mexican Americans.

***

In 1923, the Madisons walked to the train station to board a train to visit relatives in El Paso. Grandmuddy wore a brown cotton dress; Ruby wore a dark blue dress with white plastic buttons down the front, and the two boys wore brown wool jackets and knickers[273].

---

[272] The term "Juan Crow" was created by journalist Robert Lovato who used the term in an article he wrote for Nation Magazine in 2008. Since then, the phrase has been used in university academics and reporting.
[273] "Knickers", also known as Knickerbockers are full or baggy trousers gathered at the knee or just below the knee. They were usually fastened with either a button or buckle.

The car they were riding in was directly behind the engine. It was crowded, but the young children looked through the windows to see the less-crowded car behind them for white travelers. The Black passengers always wore dark-colored clothes so that the soot coming in from the engine wouldn't be as noticeable. John Chester's children once asked why the Black car was the dirtiest car on the train, and the white cars were always clean and never crammed with people. "Racism" was his one-word answer. He would then go on to explain that experiencing racism was as much a part of them as their name.

I'm glad we colored people have to fight it," he told them. ... Racism made the Black community stronger because it had to be cohesive to fight against it... Racists are scared, and racism is just another challenge, and challenges make us strong... Racism is a feeble leftover of slavery.

The children also noticed that the train's porters and waiters were Black. They watched in delight as the Black waiters gracefully served passengers and wondered at the strength of the porters assisting passengers with their luggage. When the kids asked their father why there were no Black train engineers or caboose men, he told them, "Jim Crow[274]---Ol' Jim- makes the rules.

Later that night, the siblings wanted to see more and quietly walked through their car to take a peek through the door of a stateroom that happened to be open. They saw a little white boy eating vanilla ice cream from a crystal bowl. The little boy noticed the siblings, stuck his fingers into the ice cream and licked his fingers one by one, taunting them. Once he was done, he stuck his tongue out.

The porter saw what had transpired and shooed the Madison children away. Mack stuck his tongue out at the little boy. Ruby cried, not understanding why the porter was reprimanding them instead of the white boy. Their father later explained the porter was doing what he had to do to keep his job: "Railroad work is hard, but it pays well ...and a colored man is much safer on a train than in any southern town, where Ole' Jim runs the show."

John Chester knew his young children were not old enough yet to fully understand the ugliness and the hate that went along with the Jim Crow laws.

***

Years later, John Chester explained the deadly consequences of the Jim Crow laws once his children were in their teens. He told them a Black porter could only briefly glance at a white woman while serving her on a train. However, once he was no longer on that train, he would most certainly be killed if his glance lingered. Ruby was terrified at the thought. When she was older, she understood what her father meant.

One hazy summer day, an adult Ruby was riding in an automobile with the windows down. The hot Texas air blew against her face as she looked across a cotton field. Something caught her eye. Her stomach dropped, and her heart lurched into her throat. A Black man was hanging from a tree at the edge of that field. She remembered what her father told her. Had he looked at a white woman too long?

---

[274] Jim Crow Laws were state and local laws enforcing racial segregation in the Southern United States.

The man's head fell at an abnormal angle away from the hangman's noose. Right then, Ruby knew that when she was older, she would get away from the "Ole South"[275] and move north to get away from the hate.

***

John Chester loved to learn about the world. For thirty years, he subscribed to *National Geographic*, savoring and saving every issue. The knowledge he gleaned from those magazines helped him as a teacher by enabling him to expand his lessons to include geography and culture.

The older students in John Chester's class also learned the entire business cycle of farming: planting, harvesting, selling, and accounting. Bettye always said her grandfather was a scholar who dressed like a farmer. Knowing the power of books and the knowledge they contained, he gave his students access to his large library of books and magazines. He also made his farm tools available to students if they needed them.

Gramps and his family, circa 1935

Gramps passed along his philosophy that if you wanted something, you had to work for it. You controlled your destiny through hard work. When the Madison children wanted money, they worked in the fields and picked cotton. Their father would go along with them and work as well. He encouraged his children and grandchildren to embrace their inner strength and use it to overcome challenges—just like Mandy had done all those years ago.

As *a griot*, John Chester made sure Mandy, Coreen, Jim, and all their loved ones who had been enslaved would never be forgotten. While he was proud to be descended from a president, he was prouder of how his father, grandfather, and other ancestors had overcome enslavement:

Without Madison, we would not have our name. Without Mandy, we would not have our strength.

Gramps added two words to the credo—the same credo the family uses today:

You come from African slaves and a president.

---

[275] "Ole South" is a term used by Black men and women who grew up during Jim Crowe or had relatives were descendants. The saying refers to the hate of the whites who wanted to keep Blacks on unequal footing.

Chapter Three
Always remember--you're a Madison. You come from African slaves and a president.

When John Chester was the *griot*, there was no box to keep the family documents secure and safe, but there was a family Bible that held them. He cherished the book, made of aging black leather, with a cracked and worn binding.

When he accepted a position as principal of a school in Navasota, Texas, John and his family moved. During the process of packing, he wrapped the family's precious Bible in newspaper and secured it with string. He placed the wrapped package on a bookcase that was to be moved to his new home. When the bookcase arrived, the Bible was missing. John assumed the movers thought it was trash and discarded it. He never forgave himself. He purchased a new Bible and set out to locate all the documents that had been stored in the book. Ruby helped her father and began gathering and storing those precious documents and photos in a cardboard box. When he passed away, the box was half full.

***

Ruby was chosen by her father to take over as *griotte* because she was the one most interested in the family's history. In an effort to find the historical documents that had been lost, she scoured libraries and read through miles of microfiche. After five years of researching, Ruby was able to find old letters, photographs, and many of the lost documents. They are now stored in a box to keep them safe.

Ruby was "daddy's girl," and the two were very close. She knew she did not have her father's gift of storytelling, but she was a savvy presenter. As was the case with each *griot* or *griotte* before her, Ruby wanted to add her own mark when telling the family's history.

In the 1980s, Ruby created a slide presentation that she shared with family and friends, as well as genealogical organizations in Texas, Virginia, California, Massachusetts, and New York. Madison family members lived in all these states, so it was important for these state organizations to have the materials.

Ruby attended Prairie View College and majored in home economics, just like her namesake. She vowed she would never work in someone else's kitchen or clean someone else's house. She wanted to be her own woman and have a career like her Aunts Laura and Ruth, both of whom were teachers. Ruby also longed to live in a city where she could wear fashionable clothes and travel on trains, like the ones that passed her house when she was growing up.

When Ruby graduated from college, her father gave her Aunt Ruby's engagement ring, telling her, "Here is something I want you to have." Ruby never felt more special or connected to the woman she had been named after.

Achieving one of her goals, Ruby got her second teaching position when she secured a teaching assignment outside of Texas as a nutritionist and home economics teacher in Arkansas. Her career eventually took her to Kansas City, Missouri. When she was twenty-four, Ruby visited her brother John, a trained physician at Homer G. Phillips Hospital in St. Louis. One of her aunts, Estelle Massey, was the head of the nursing department.

Ruby walked into an elevator where Dr. Clay Morgan Wilson, III, was waiting to go to the obstetrics floor. He was immediately smitten. On the ride up, he memorized her outfit out of the corner of his eye and then asked the nurses if anyone knew her. He later found out she was Dr. Madison's sister and Estelle Massey's niece. After a three-month courtship, the two wed on a blazingly hot August day. Ruby wore a pale blue suit, and Clay wore his wool Army uniform. Joining the armed services in the medical corps was the equivalent of a medical residency. He would have been drafted as a private if he had not enlisted voluntarily. Shortly after their wedding, the couple left for Fort Huachuca, Arizona, the army base for Black soldiers. Bettye was born in Arizona, but once her father left to serve as a lieutenant in the medical corps in the Philippines, Ruby took her daughter to Pasadena to visit Clay's mother and sister. It was there Ruby fell in love with California.

Almost immediately, Ruby noticed there were no filthy public toilets or corroded drinking fountains with signs designating them "COLORED," as had been the case in Texas. Schools were integrated in Oakland. No one living in the city picked cotton. Oakland was the opposite of the "Ole South" Ruby had experienced growing up. She now understood why her husband loved Oakland and why his family still resided there.

Ruby sensed the friendships Oakland residents had with each other. The city reminded her of the tight-knit Black community in Elgin where she grew up—neighbors looked after each other, and community organizations helped parents teach their children values and moral behavior. Resources and support were pooled together to help everyone.

But living in California did not insulate Ruby and Clay's children from racism. Both Bettye and her younger brother Biff experienced racial slurs and epithets directed at them. The Black adults told them to ignore the insults—those words only reflected that person's ignorance.

When young people were unjustly arrested, they were bailed out by funds collected by the Black churches in the community. When grocery stores refused to hire Black students for summer jobs, owners of Black-owned shops created positions for Black students, including Bettye. During her senior year of high school, she saw an ad for a summer job as a clerk. After contacting the company, an interview was scheduled. The night before her interview, Bettye ironed her dress and polished her saddle shoes, wanting to look her best.

But when she arrived at the interview the next day, the white man conducting the interview looked her up and down and, through puffs of cheap cigar smoke, told her, "I'm not about to have no colored gal working in my store."[276]

---

[276] Bettye Kearse, The Other Madisons, March 24, 2020

Bettye felt her cheeks get hot. Then, she heard Gramps's voice: "Racism is just another challenge, and challenges make us strong." She looked the man in the eye and, full of confidence, responded, "Your loss." She turned around and walked out the door, proud of herself for taking a stand.

These kinds of moments reminded Ruby and her family that the plague of racism still existed and would continue to infect the minds of some. The brazen racism, sanctioned vigilante murders, and humiliation of segregation as a child and young adult in Texas still haunted Ruby.

Even so, Ruby, Bettye, and the rest of the family would not allow those memories to control them. Just like her ancestors, Ruby and her family created amazing lives and gave back to the community. They were all grateful for their freedom and, most of all, the love of family. There was light in the darkness, and as *griotte*, it was her responsibility to continue and tell that story.

***

Ruby Laura Madison Wilson and Bettye, circa 1948

When Bettye was five, she accompanied her mother on a trip back to Texas. As was the case with her mother, the train ride became Bettye's most vivid memory of her childhood. It also showed her how little things had changed in the "Ole South."

The pair traveled from Berkeley, California, to Navasota, Texas. At the station in Berkeley, Bettye smiled at the Black porters. She can still picture their smart uniforms adorned with gold braid. Each porter wore a

96

dark blue cap emblazoned on the front with *SPR* (Southern Pacific Railroad). Bettye liked how they all wore their hats a little differently to make themselves look unique.

Her father had a special appreciation for Black railroad workers and provided them free medical care. He worked as a chef and dishwasher on the trains during summer breaks from college. The porters respected his kindness. When Bettye and her mother arrived at the train station, the porters knew who they were, and as a result, they received special treatment. Their bags were picked up first and escorted to the train.

Unlike all those years ago when Ruby had to wear a dark colored dress because Blacks were forced to sit behind the engine, Ruby wore the latest fashion. An elegant hat rested on her perfectly styled hair, and she sported a smart sage-green suit, with pin-straight stocking seams running down the back of her legs. Shiny high-heeled black pumps and soft black gloves completed her outfit. Bettye always got bored and impatient waiting for her mother to make sure her stockings were perfect, but when she was finally ready, Bettye always smiled at how beautiful her mother looked.

One of the porters flashed a smile at Bettye and pulled her up in his arms. Her pigtails bounced in the air as he swung her up over the steps to the train's landing. Her feet landed softly, and she giggled at the porter. He bowed to her as if she was royalty. Bettye felt like a princess. Ruby smiled, wishing she could freeze that moment in time. Bettye was young and innocent. She didn't notice that other passengers were watching them, even though her mother was fully aware. Black passengers laughed in delight over the fuss being made over Bettye. But several white passengers scowled at the porter's gesture, their lips curled up in a contortion of hate.

Railroad cars in California were not segregated. Since they were on a journey that would take days, they stayed in a Pullman car. The railcar's hallway was long, and there were windows on one side, doors on the other. Bettye's mother opened the door to their compartment. The interior was gray, and the air smelled of wheel grease and recently cleaned carpeting. They had their own stainless-steel water fountain. Bettye stood on her toes to reach it. She saw a tall Black man in the hallway wearing a starched white jacket and matching white shirt with a high tight collar and a bow tie. His dark blue pants had perfectly ironed creases. Bettye was just learning how to read at the time and asked her mother what the words were on his cap. "Pullman Porter," she responded.

"You can call me Harold," the porter said, smiling slightly. He handed Bettye a glass of apple juice from a silver tray. Ruby was thankful her young daughter could experience something as a child she never could.

The rocking of the train was soothing to Bettye, and the sounds of the iron wheels traveling over the rails lulled her to sleep. She dreamed of her family in Texas and the adventure that awaited.

The next morning, the porter knocked on the door, announcing breakfast was going to be served. When Bettye opened the door, she saw a little white girl hugging a doll with blue eyes and Shirley Temple curls.

The doll was a twin of the girl. The girl's mother looked at Bettye and smiled. Ruby motioned to both mother and daughter to come into their compartment. Behind the women, Harold watched.

It turned out that Susan and her daughter, Mary, were also traveling to Texas. Over the next two days, the mothers played canasta in the club car. The girls shared crayons and drew pictures. Mary and Bettye giggled as they ate their roast beef and turkey sandwiches together. They did not eat in the dining car because Ruby deemed it "outrageously expensive." But what was more outrageous to Ruby was that once the train entered the South, Black diners who were once free to move around and eat wherever they wanted in that train car were now forced to sit behind a curtain. Bettye thought it would be fun eating behind a makeshift curtain—she did not understand why her mother was so angry.

During one dinner, Ruby surprised Bettye when she ordered fried chicken from the dining car, and then invited Susan and Mary to their compartment to dine with them. The waiter came balancing a large silver tray on one shoulder. On that tray, silver domes and glasses sparkled. When he lifted the domes, young Mary squealed with delight when she saw little paper ruffles decorating the chicken legs like anklets. Bettye smiled at the site. Ruby had already told her about the fancy decorated chicken legs.

When the train arrived in Texas the next day, the joy of the previous evening quickly soured. Bettye wanted to play with Mary but was no longer allowed to—she didn't understand. In California, white and Black children played together. At the next stop, Bettye pressed her face against the window to see the passengers coming on the train and noticed Mary and her mother on the platform. Mary was holding her pink plastic doll case. Bettye could see she was scanning the window, and their gazes were locked. A broad smile appeared on Mary's face. Bettye smiled. The two little girls waved with tears in their eyes. The children tried to wave goodbye, but their moms stopped their innocent children from waving. When Ruby moved away from the window, she saw her mother's cheeks were wet. Harold walked into the open cabin and knelt down to hug Bettye.

Looking back, Bettye said this was her introduction to "Ole Jim." When Bettye became the *griotte*, she added this story from 1948 so future generations would be aware of the racial adversity they encountered.

When Bettye arrived at her grandparent's house, her grandfather delighted her with stories. Gramps told his children and grandchildren America may have been founded by Madison and the other "founding fathers," but it never would have become what is without the tens of millions of slaves like Mandy.

Ruby taught Bettye and Biff to not only recite her Grandfather's words but to know the meaning behind them:

Our white ancestors laid the foundations for this country, but our dark-skinned ancestors built it. They worked the fields, nursed babies, preached sermons, and fought in wars. They played music, owned businesses, cured sickness, and worked on railroads. They taught their children everything important about life in this world. They taught their children about God.

Many of the family history conversations Ruby had with her daughter took place around Ruby's sewing machine. Bettye was a fidgety child and did not like to wait while her mother sewed. For Ruby, telling these stories was not only about teaching her child about their past; it was about the message of love for family.

While each *griot* or *griotte* told the story a little differently, the facts were the same. In the miles of fabric Ruby stitched on her machine, she also stitched together a family's brilliant tapestry. It was woven together with love, loss, pain, strength, suffering, and perseverance. Humor as well.

One of those stories was Bettye's favorite, and Ruby loved Bettye's reaction when she told it to her. Ruby's eyes were full of joy as she remembered that day in her childhood when her humorless mother was the butt of her father's wit:

One day, when I was nine or ten, Mother sent Mack and John to Daddy's library to get some liquid ink eraser. The boys returned empty-handed. Twitching and stomping, they were trying so hard not to laugh. I thought they were going to explode. Somehow, they managed to pass on Daddy's message: He told them, to ask their mother why she was so greedy. Mother looked perplexed. Mack and John explained, 'Look at us!!! You already have two inky racers!'

They fell out on the parlor floor, rolling, giggling, clapping hands, slapping knees, clutching their bellies. Meanwhile, Daddy and I were hiding in the library, trying to muffle our lighter. Our cheeks were bursting, and tears rolled down our faces. When I peeked into the parlor, I saw Mother. She was livid. She had not gotten the ink eraser, and worse, far worse, the decorum of her home had been undermined yet again.

Bettye loved how clever her grandfather was and appreciated his skill playing with words. His humor outshined her grandmother's rigid rules.

***

One of the gifts each *griot* or *griotte* possessed in the Madison family was the innate ability to know when a family member was mature enough to hear—and understand—the stories of Mandy and Coreen.

When Bettye was eleven, she asked her mother what Coreen's father's name was. Ruby, hunched over her sewing machine, never looked up. Instead, as she focused on the needle going up and down through the fabric, she spoke these words: "He was James Madison Sr. His son, the one who became president, was James Madison Jr." Ruby asked how Mandy and the president's father met each other.

Ruby told Bettye Madison Sr. was Mandy's master. He was called "Massa" because he owned the Black people who worked for him—they were his property. She explained to Bettye that Mandy was his slave and had to follow his every order, take care of his every need, and fulfill his every desire: "Whenever he felt like it, Massa could walk into any cabin where slaves lived and visit whichever woman he wanted."

"Visit?" Bettye asked.

"Yes. Massa went from cabin to cabin. That's the way it was back then."

"Like when gentlemen visited before you met Daddy?" Bettye asked.

"What I'm talking about is very different."

"What's different?" Bettye did not understand. "What happened to Mandy? What happened to her?!"

"Mandy attracted her master's attention because she could pick cotton fast." The sewing machine continued to constantly hum as she spoke.

"Did Mandy get a reward for being a good worker?"

"No. Massa punished her."

"Why?"

For the first time, her mother's eyes left the sewing machine. Her normally bright brown eyes now looked sad. She stopped sewing, and there was an uneasy silence in the room.

"She was his slave."

"How did he punish her?" Eleven-year-old Bettye couldn't understand why someone would be punished if they were doing a good job.

There was a pause. Ruby looked away, her eyes eventually drifting back to her sewing.

"I'll tell you later. Not now. You're too young."

"I'm almost twelve!"

"I know," Ruby stopped sewing again. "When I was your age, I was curious, just like you."

When Ruby was Bettye's age, her father would change the subject every time she brought up the topic.

Bettye finally learned the complete story when she was waiting to get fitted for her senior prom gown, one that had belonged to her mother. Now that she was almost eighteen, Ruby knew her daughter was ready for the truth. She told Bettye the entire story while she made alterations to the dress.

When Ruby spoke about Mandy becoming pregnant, her voice fell flat—she never once looked up from her machine.

***

Growing up watching her mother as *griotte*, Bettye was aware of the responsibilities that went with being the family's historian. Her mother and grandfather each contributed different talents to the role, expanding the research and ways of presenting that information. Each generation provided a wealth of stories of strength, inspiration, and pride. These were pillars of their family's foundation. The fundamental building block of the Madison legacy was knowing your self-worth. Only you owned you. Your strengths, dreams, and self-worth started and ended with you.

Bettye and Biff were always encouraged to do their best. They were never told they couldn't achieve whatever it was they were aspiring to. Bettye was never told she couldn't do something because of her gender. For the Madison descendants, there were no roadblocks they couldn't overcome. The only roadblocks preventing someone from achieving their dreams were of their own making.

Bettye followed in her father's footsteps and became a doctor. She was a pediatrician and had a successful practice. Ruby would proudly tell people her daughter was a "double doctor." After graduating from the University of California in Berkeley, Bettye earned her PhD in biology from New York University, where she also met her husband, Lee. After a couple of years working in a lab, and as a young mother of a toddler, she decided to join Lee, who was in medical school at Case Western Reserve University and became a doctor specializing in pediatrics.

Bettye was the second Madison descendant in her line to become a doctor and have her own pediatrics practice. Her Uncle John, her mother's older brother, was the first. Her brother Biff, a dentist, also had his own practice.

Bettye, Lee, and their daughter Nicole built their life in Boston, where the Madison credo and family stories filled their home. When Bettye was forty-seven, her mother called, informing her that she would be bringing over "the box."

The box.

Bettye could not believe what she was hearing. Ruby never told her she would be the next *griotte*. The enormity of the responsibility hit her hard. Each generation elevated the stories of their family's history through their talents for preservation, research, and storytelling. What would Bettye contribute?

When her mother arrived with the box of treasures, in her classic direct style, she simply said to her first born, "I want to give you plenty of time to write the book." Bettye knew this was going to be her *griotte* legacy: To find even more information on Mandy and Coreen and record the family's complete history.

It was important for Bettye to document how remarkable her enslaved ancestors were. Their belief in themselves enabled them to survive as property, often treated worse than the farm animals they were forced to care for. She wanted to convey how their abilities enabled them and succeeding generations to overcome slavery, Reconstruction, Jim Crow, and racism.

Once, when Bettye was pulling out of the hospital she worked at in Boston, the blinkers of her BMW stopped working, so she used hand signals. A car pulled up alongside her, and the driver shouted, "Get your fucking Black hand back in your fucking car!" and sped off. It happened so fast Bettye could not see the driver's face. At that moment, she wondered what kind of hate she would encounter once she ventured to the South to learn more about Mandy and Coreen. She would soon find out.

***

On her trip to Virginia to learn more about her family, Bettye encountered a white, middle-aged woman at the front desk of the Virginia State University library. The woman ignored her, continuing to focus on filing index cards in a metal box. After a few minutes, Bettye finally said, "Excuse me. I'm looking for any documents and books you might have on Montpelier, President Madison's former…"

But before she could finish, the woman interrupted her: "I know what Montpelier is."

"I came down from Boston to do some research on the plantation," Bettye continued. At that point, the librarian sat up straight and rudely responded, "Really? Well, you'll have to come back some other time."

"*This is the South,*" Bettye reminded herself. It was thirty years since the civil rights movement, yet for some attitudes persisted as if the movement never happened.

Thankfully, Bettye heard a voice from behind a stack of books. "Hello. I'm Alice. I have a minute or two to help you if you'd like."

Alice was also a librarian and also white. To her, Bettye was someone in need of research help—she could care less if Bettye was Black or white.

"My ancestors were slaves at Montpelier," Bettye said to Alice.

"Figured as much," the first librarian mumbled, but loudly enough for others to hear.

Ignoring the comment, Alice gestured Bettye to a table and chair near her desk. "Have a seat, please."

Alice disappeared, returning with a cart full of books and binders.

"This should get you started," Alice said.[277]

Bettye poured over documents that shed light on pre-Civil War Virginia. She found photos of mansions and slave shacks, letters, slave bills of sale, even "free papers" some Blacks carried. There was so much it was overwhelming.

Those documents confirmed what her mother and grandfather had told her. Enslavers viewed the family's enslaved ancestors as property. A value was placed on each enslaved person based on their ability to make their white enslavers wealthy through their work in the fields. Women were assessed based on age and childbearing years, as well as their ability to cook, clean, and take care of their enslaver's children. Document after document shed more light on what Mandy, Coreen, Jim, Emanuel (and his family) endured.

---

[277] Bettye Kearse, The Other Madisons, March 24, 2020

After her day at the library, Bettye drove to the inn where she had reserved a room. Based on how she was treated by the first librarian, Bettye was apprehensive about how she would be received. As an adult, Bettye Kearse, MD faced two different types of reactions: pleasant and warm over the phone, surprise and aloofness in person.

Bettye called the inn to let her hosts know she would be arriving shortly. She decided it was a good time to "warn" them she was Black and explained the purpose of her visit.

"How exciting!" the innkeeper replied. Bettye was relieved.

When she arrived, her hostess, Pat, came bounding down the walkway to meet Bettye. Her smile put Bettye's mind at ease.

On the last day of her trip, Bettye was having breakfast at the inn when she was approached by a couple who asked to join her. The husband and wife both appeared to be in her thirties and smiled—Bettye invited them to sit down. The typical pleasantries were exchanged, and the husband told her he was a dentist in Baltimore. Bettye told him she was a pediatrician from Boston. His face lit up when he explained he had lived in a town near Boston.

The conversation waned a little, and while Bettye was pouring maple syrup over her waffle, the dentist cleared his throat and said, "I have to change the subject to something sticky. Black people and white people can't seem to get along," he said looking at her face for a reaction.

"Really?" Bettye said. She looked over at his wife, who was focused on the butter melting on her waffle.

"In Baltimore, a large part of the inner city is Black. The mayor is a Black man. People like and respect him. So why doesn't he just tell everyone they should put racism behind them and work together."

"It's complicated," Bettye responded, trying not to come across as preachy or argumentative. "Racism is systemic. This country wouldn't look the same without it."

"Oh, come on," the dentist pushed back. He moved closer to Bettye. "Blacks have it made. Kurt Schmoke graduated from Harvard Law School. Now, he's mayor of Baltimore. It's a southern town, you know. I voted for him." The dentist grinned. "And…. Look at you. You're a doctor."

Bettye calmly placed down her fork.

"Blacks can do anything and be anything they want," he continued, oblivious to Bettye's non-verbal language. "Discrimination is a thing of the past," the dentist said while tapping the table. "When something doesn't go their way, Blacks blame race."

Bettye clenched her jaw.

"Take that incident with those Black Secret Service men in that Denny's restaurant in D.C.," he continued. "They claimed they weren't being served because they were Black. I've eaten in Denny's myself; the service is bad. That's all."

"Other customers who came in after them were served first," Bettye responded.

"You're wrong. A group of white Secret Service men came in at about the same time and happened to be served before the Black guys."

"That's not what the newspapers reported," Bettye said. "Denny's ended up losing a class-action lawsuit. The courts fined the company and required it to give sensitivity training to every employee."

The dentist shook his head, "See, this is the problem. This is what I'm saying."

Bettye leaned in, "Regardless of what did or did not happen at Denny's, discrimination is not a thing of the past. In that same city, the capital, no less, and in many others, Black professional men and women wearing business suits and carrying briefcases complain that taxis will pass them by to pick up white passengers a few yards up the street. Blacks throughout the country experience this kind of treatment every day in restaurants, shops, hotels, at work, on the street, everywhere."

"Calm down. No need to overreact," the dentist replied.

"This is a bed and breakfast. I paid my money and, like you, I'm a guest here. I am not going to be a sounding board on which you can try out your ignorant, arrogant ideas about race relations, and I will certainly not validate your notion that racism is only in my head."

With her heart pounding in her ears, Bettye pushed her chair away from the table, stood up, and left the room.

She returned to Boston. The conversation with the dentist echoed in her mind. Even though California did not have segregation, racism did exist, and that conversation brought up some ugly memories from her childhood. Bettye relived the times in elementary school where she was called "Brownie." Even in her well-regarded and racially diverse school, she was called "Brownie." In Junior High, her nickname was "Fuzzy." When she was in high school, Bettye was popular and had good grades. She knew racism would limit her future unless she outperformed her fellow white students academically. Her inspiration? Mandy, Coreen, and Elizabeth Madison. They were her spiritual guides and source for strength and grace.

After years of research, Bettye traveled to Virginia to learn more about—and visit—Montpelier. Being at Montpelier was a defining moment for Bettye. She was standing on the same ground her ancestors had stood on. This motivated her to become the *griotte* she wanted to be—to add more to the stories of Mandy and Coreen by being at the very place they had worked in bondage. Bettye walked the grounds and learned more about her ancestors from Lynne Lewis, the head archeologist at Montpelier at that time.

Bettye was able to see the excavation of the outdoor kitchen the archeological team had uncovered. The foundation was visible, as well as parts of the hearth. The rocks of the hearth were caved in, but Bettye could envision Coreen tending to that sweltering fire so many years ago.

Lynn showed Bettye a path that had been worn into the ground by the footsteps of the enslaved cooks as they made their way from the kitchen to the mansion, serving thousands of meals to the Madisons and their guests. The path was a physical reminder of their labors.

Bettye stepped onto the path Coreen once walked countless times a day for years. As she walked, her eyes teared up. The significance of the moment hit her: she was the first free Madison to walk on that path, the same path her great-great-great-great-grandmother walked on each day more than 240 years ago.

Bettye's experiences and the knowledge she attained on that visit would help strengthen her ability to provide more detail when discussing Mandy and Coreen's lives.

***

Two years after her first trip to Montpelier, Bettye traveled to Elmina, Ghana. Her goal was to trace Mandy's journey from Africa to America.

In Elmina castle, a former 15th-century slave-holding fortress, Bettye joined a group of tourists from distant parts of the world. The tour guide led the group through a system of hot, humid, dark tunnels and dungeons carved out below a former Catholic church. Thousands of Black women and children were beaten, shackled, and starved here before being loaded onto slave ships as human cargo.

Towards the end of their tour, the docent led the group to the "room of deep sorrow." The dark room had two tunnel entrances. This was where men and women said goodbye to each other—and their homeland.

The docent explained that after their goodbyes were said, the men and women were led to separate storerooms. One was for men, the other for women. Each windowless space held between 150 and 300 people. He explained that the kidnapped men and women were held anywhere from days to weeks with little food or water. Bettye felt her chest tighten as she envisioned what Mandy went through. Those who survived were moved to a final room with some daylight filtering in. They were then steered to a narrow exit with a heavy iron gate that led out to the beach and the waiting slave ship. This doorway is known as "The Gate of No Return."

Bettye knew this emotionally painful journey would help fill in the blanks of Mandy's story. She wanted to learn more about the "Middle Passage" journey that took her great-great-great-great,-great-grandmother to America.

Bettye's friends knew about her ongoing research. One day, she received a call from her friend Bonnie, who told Bettye she needed to visit Baltimore because a replica of a slave ship was part of an exhibit at the National Great Blacks in Wax Museum.

Bonnie drove Bettye to the Museum. Once inside, they saw the imposing replica. Bettye's heart was racing. They crossed over a plank, just as the kidnapped men and women would have done, and descended the stairs to the areas below deck. She saw wax figures of little boys chained together in one area, the women in another, and the men in a third, more distant part of the ship's hull. Bettye did not realize she was shaking. Bonnie gently wrapped her arms around her. The longtime friends then continued on the slave journey and reviewed exhibits on the slave auctions. After two sobering hours, the pair left.

Bettye had heard these stories growing up, but to be able to physically experience the space and imagine the journey was invaluable. Anne L. Miller, a research scientist and historian for the Virginia Transportation Research Council, told Bettye the stench of the slave ships approaching the harbor was so strong it could be smelled miles away.

This trip and her subsequent research helped Bettye understand more intimately the meaning of this part of her family's credo: "You come from African slaves."

"It's our duty as family storytellers to make sure the complete story gets passed down to future generations," Bettye said. "Every family should have someone responsible for keeping family history. You can also ask relatives if they have artifacts, any information you can think of to add to that history. Just keep searching for old letters and pictures. Family pictures are especially important. Now, you can also record stories. There's nothing like hearing a loved one's voice. I wish I had recorded Gramps, just to hear his voice. Have your loved ones tell you stories about themselves and those that came before them."

Bettye's daughter Nicole will be the next *griotte* when Bettye is ready. Nicole has two children whom she will have to choose between to assume that responsibility.

"It's been very important to have one person in each generation of my family to take on this role. The *griotte* or *griot* is the keeper of *our* story. The keeper of *our* history."

PART THREE

The Quander Family- "One of America's oldest and consistently documented Black families."

Judge Rohulamin Quander was interviewed for this story. Judge Quander is the family historian and founder of the Quander Historical Educational Society.

"Perseverance will be king!"- James W. Quander

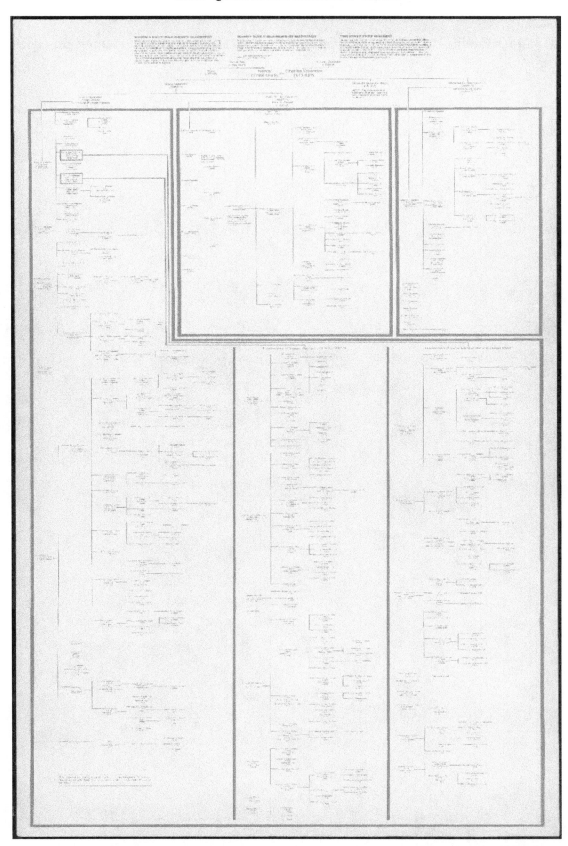

Chapter One
One Family, Three Family Trees

The journey of the Quanders starts with the evolution of their last name.

The Quander family can trace back their lineage to the Fanti tribe in Ghana. Oral history and confirming research say a man by the name of Egya Amkwandoh , or his two sons were kidnapped in the late 17th century and brought to America on a slave ship. Many of the current generation of Quanders believe that when slave owners asked Egya or his son for his name, he answered "Amkwandoh," which was misheard as "I am Quando.' The next several generations of Quanders went by the name Quando. There were other variations after that, such as Quandoe, Quandoo, and Kwando. During the 19th century, the last name changed to the present-day spelling, "Quander."[278]

Once the brothers arrived in Maryland, they were apparently separated and sold to different enslavers. During the sale of the African men and women, the enslavers changed the African names of the men, women, and children to give them European given names.[279]

One son was sold to a Maryland British tobacco planter, county legislature, justice, and sheriff named Henry Adams. Henry renamed the young man to Henry Quando after his first name. Henry's brother, thought to be re-named "Benjamin," was sold to an enslaver in Virginia. The two brothers never saw each other again.

The Maryland and Virginia Quanders found each other in the early to mid-1800s when there was word of a family who had a similar story of brothers separated.

What linked them once they discovered each other was the story of the brother's kidnapping and separation. The stories told by the different branches of Quanders were nearly identical throughout history.

Another part of the Quander family tree is indirectly traced to Mount Vernon, where Nancy Carter, a freed enslaved worker for President George Washington, met Charles Quander, a free Black man who the family believes was a descendant of Henry Quando in Maryland.

The biggest difference between the Maryland and Virginia Quanders was freedom.

While initially based in Maryland (17th Century), the Quanders soon expanded into Virginia (18th Century), and eventually, their presence was noted in Pennsylvania, New Jersey, New York, and other places in the United States.

---

[278] Rohulamin Quander, "The Quanders", January 11, 2021
[279] Paulette Brown-Hinds, "Salve Names in the Americas", October 12, 2010 https://blackvoicenews.com/2010/10/14/slave-names-in-the-americas/

Maryland Quander Tree

On October 12, 1684, Henry Adams, the enslaver of Henry Quando, had a will written where he stated that, after he died, Henry, along with Margaret Pugg, (who became his future wife), would receive manumission.[280] Henry Adams passed away, and on Thursday, July 4, 1686, Adams' will was filed for probate. It was in this document that the name "Quando" was entered into the public record.

This document is the reason why the Quanders are one of the oldest and largest Black American families recorded in the United States. At the time of manumission, Henry was around 9 years old, and Margaret Pugg was around 16. The two worked as indentured servants in farming.

In addition to their freedom, Henry Adams bequeathed Henry Quando one flock bed[281] and a small chest with a Dutch lock. Margrett Pugg was given one cow or calf.

1684 Last Will and Testament of Henry Adams

Source: "The Quanders", Rohulamin Quander

The young Quander and Pugg became part of the small population of free Blacks in Maryland.

---

[280] Manumission means to be legally released from slavery. Manumission is different than emancipation. Manumission is the legal release of certain enslaved people whereas emancipation is the abolishing of slavery and freedom for all enslaved through government action.

[281] A flock bed was a mattress filled with woolen or cotton refuse. Flock was used for stuffing furniture and mattresses

As a freeman, Henry capitalized on his skills in farming and learned as much as he could despite being illiterate. In 1691, he displayed his business acumen when he registered his cattle mark so his property, along with any future property he would amass, could be identified in the event it was stolen.

Henry Quando's cattle mark was described in Charles County registration records as a "swallow fork on both ears and underkeeled on the right ear."[282] Henry was around 16 or 17 at the time. Henry dreamed of prosperity, and he, along with Margrett Pugg, saved enough money from their eight years of indentured servitude to lease land. On February 4, 1695, at the age of 20, Henry signed a 99-year freehold lease for 116 acres of land from Ignatius Wheeler, a large plantation owner in Port Tobacco, Charles County.[283] Henry signed the document with an "X."

In the 18th century, Black women, regardless of their status as free or enslaved, had their men pay taxes on them. On June 13, 1702, Henry made history as the first Black man to petition a high court.[284] Henry filed an appeal in the High Court of Chancery, arguing that he should not have to pay taxes on Margrett, for she was free and his wife. He did not own her, and, therefore, should not have to pay taxes for her. The court ruled the tax was universally applied to all Black females. It did not matter if they were enslaved or free. Henry paid the tax, but that did not stop him from challenging the tax in succeeding years.[285]

Henry, Margrett, their son Henry II, and their three daughters, Victoria, Mary, and Elizabeth faced unfavorable legal action throughout the entirety of their lives.

In 1705, a grand jury indicted Victoria Quando for having a child out of wedlock. In the Court and Land Records of Charles County, the name of the father is never mentioned once. It was ruled Victoria's fault for having a baby out of marriage, not the father's. She appeared in court on January 8, 1706 and pleaded guilty. The fine was ten lashes at the whipping post. However, Henry stepped in her place. The baby's racial classification in reports was mulatto, making the father's child White.

Henry died between 1714 and 1718, leaving Margrett and her children to continue his work on the land on which they lived. Like their parents, oral history says the children could not read.

In 1718, Ignatius Wheeler's brother, Thomas, tried to take advantage of Henry's passing by tricking the two daughters into indentured servitude. The scam started after a grand jury began proceedings against a White indentured servant named Anne Rannes for having a child out of wedlock.[286] Rannes asked Thomas Wheeler, a planter and bondsman, to help her escape the humiliation by leaving the state. She promised him two indentured servants in return for his help.

---

282 Rohulamin Quander, "The Quanders"
283 Rohulamin Quander, "The Quanders"
284 Rohulamin Quander, "The Quanders"
285 Rohulamin Quander, "The Quanders"
286 Rohulamin Quander, "The Quanders"

Thomas and Rannes created a plan where Mary and Elizabeth would co-sign Rannes' bond as a high-risk defendant. If Rannes did not appear in court, the two teens would fulfill the remaining time on Rannes' indentured contract. The length of servitude was seven years.

Wheeler helped Rannes leave Maryland to live in Virginia. When Rannes failed to make her court appearance, Thomas told the court he was wronged by Rannes and the Quando sisters, who had co-signed the bond that labeled her as a flight risk pledged in the legal document, which stated that they would complete the remaining seven years of Rannes' indentured contract.

Margrett appeared before the court, contesting the agreement. For years, Wheeler tried to delay proceedings. Almost four years later, on June 6, 1722, the court ruled in Quando v. Wheeler in favor of Margrett. She was awarded 2,148 pounds of tobacco as punitive damages and costs. The value of tobacco at that time was 1.15 pence per pound.[287] The total value of that tobacco is 2,470.20 pence. Today, that would be the equivalent of $27.49.

Margrett's fight for civil action did not stop with her litigation against Wheeler. As a "free 'negro' woman,"[288] she petitioned the court in 1723, asking for tax levy relief, citing the lack of monetary funds.[289] Unfortunately, her petition was denied. In 1724, she tried again, pleading for relief of the annual 616 pounds of tobacco levy, detailing her and her daughter's hardship, and the courts ruled in her favor. Future tax relief petitions, however, showed Margrett was unable to sway the courts. It was ruled her "poor circumstances" were found unproven.[290]

During this time, Margrett's other daughter, Mary, went before the court three times for having children out of wedlock. The corporal punishment for her offense was, "15 lashes on her bare body well laid on so that blood appears"[291]. George Hardy, identified as a bondsman, agreed to pay the fine on behalf of Mary, and the case was closed.[292] No father was identified.

In 1724, Mary went before the court for a second time and faced lashings on her back as punishment, but this time, the court identified the father, Thomas Edelene. He had to pay the county for the fees of the crime. Thomas Edelene paid three pounds in currency and pledged his property until the debt was paid.

In Mary's third court case, a jury found her guilty of having another child out of wedlock. She put herself at the mercy of the court, admitting her guilt. The judge gave her a lecture on personal responsibility and chastity, demanding her to divulge the name of the father, which she refused to do. The court gave her the maximum corporal punishment in a way to coerce a name: "39 lashes well laid on so that blood appears,"

---

[287] Antebellum Plantations in Prince George's County, Maryland, Table One Commodities Price Index for Tobacco, Wheat, and Corn,1710-1730
https://www.mncppcapps.org/planning/publications/pdfs/206/6%20Agriculture%20and%20Slavery%2009.pdf
[288] Rohulamin Quander, "The Quanders"
[289] Rohulamin Quander, "The Quanders"
[290] Rohulamin Quander, "The Quanders"
[291] Rohulamin Quander, "The Quanders"
[292] Rohulamin Quander, "The Quanders"

along with unrecorded fees to the present case and the two cases before. Mary still refused. A White planter[293] named John Winn paid the debts.

Henry II, Margrett and Henry's son, was a businessman and entrepreneur. Just like his parents and siblings, he was involved in various litigations fighting for his legal rights. Henry II would win the litigations; however, the payments he was meant to receive never happened. He would take the offenders back to court, and the courts would rule in his favor. The White plaintiffs, though found guilty, refused to pay what was due to Henry II.

One case involved a commercial sale of linen, ladies' shoes, tobacco, silk handkerchiefs, stockings, and shipping and packing. The all-White jury handed a judgment in Henry's favor. Unfortunately, it was never paid. Henry died in debt in 1742. The value of his estate inventory was a mare, colt, broad axes, carpentry tools, two rugs, clothing, and smaller items, and was worth 11.6 pounds. That was less than the 50 pounds in sterling that he owed. His only son, Adam Henry Quando, was the recipient of Henry II's estate.

No matter what the results were in court, the stories of Henry and Margrett's fight for justice influenced future Quander generations to never be afraid to speak up and defend themselves. The first chapter of the free Quanders showed the dark reality of free Blacks in Colonial America. Freedom was given to them, but freedom did not mean equality. While the first Quander family might not have had monetary success, oral history said they were rich in love, faith in themselves, and their family. During this time period, the Quando name became very sparse in written records but did not quite disappear, as there was one probate case in July 1776, just about the time of the Declaration of Independence, for Margaret Quando Godfrey, recently deceased.

Mount Vernon Quander Family Tree

The Quander family tree expanded to Mount Vernon with the marriage of Nancy Carter and a free Black man named Charles Quander, whose ancestral line is believed to have come from Maryland.

Oral history says Nancy was a spinner and worked behind the slave quarters at Mount Vernon. Nancy was the daughter of Sukey Bay. Sukey, Nancy, and her sister, Rose, were enslaved to President George Washington. Sukey worked in the fields on River Farm, which George Washington owned. Her father was an enslaved man with the last name of Carter. He lived at the plantation of Washington's closest neighbor, Abednego Adams.[294]

Historical records show George Washington demanded high productivity from his enslaved workers.[295] According to Mount Vernon documents; Sukey's work expanded beyond River Farm. George Washington noted in his diary entry on June 24, 1788, that she was working at the Mansion House. Washington was

---

[293] Planter: is a manager or owner of a plantation.
[294] Jessie MacLeod, Mount Vernon, "Washington's Slave List," 1799, n7 Founders Online, National Archives. (Original source: The Papers of George Washington)
[295] Jessie MacLeod, "Field Labor", Digital Encyclopedia of George Washington, https://www.mountvernon.org/george-washington/slavery/field-labor/

cultivating a new plot of land near the Mansion House and was moving enslaved people around from other farms to work on the land.[296]

In Washington's 1799 list, Nancy was recorded with other enslaved people working in the fields of River Farm. At that time, there were 317 enslaved men, women, and children at Mount Vernon's five farms. They made up more than 90 percent of the estate's population. The entire Mount Vernon plantation had 8,000 acres of land overall.[297]

A scale overlay of Washington's 1793 survey of Mount Vernon on modern aerial imagery shows the five farms shaded in blue with plantation roads marked in red.

Source: Mount Vernon Ladies' Association

In Washington's last will and testament, William Lee, George Washington's personal attendant, was freed immediately after Washington's death. The other 122 enslaved men, women, and children he owned, however, would not be released until Martha died. Afraid for her own life, and a slave uprising, Martha released Washington's enslaved on January 1, 1801. This was just over one year after his death on December 14, 1799.

Nancy Carter was between 12 and 13 years old when she was freed. Little is known about Nancy after she was freed as a child. What is known about her is that Nancy met Charles Quander. and between 1802 and 1810, they were married. Nancy was between 14-22 years old. Together, the couple had at least three children: Gracy (1811), Elizabeth (1815), and Osmond (1825). Charles is most likely a direct descendant of Henry Quando; however, documents linking the two men have yet to be found.

---

[296] Author Email correspondence with Jessie MacLeod, associate curator, George Washington's Mount Vernon April 11, 2022
[297] "Growth of Mount Vernon", Digital Encyclopedia of George Washington,
https://www.mountvernon.org/library/digitalhistory/digital-encyclopedia/article/growth-of-mount-vernon/

Nancy's mother, Sukey, was documented to be in the care of the Washington estate in the early 1830s because she was blind and in need of nursing care.[298]

In 1835, Nancy, along with others formerly enslaved at Mount Vernon, and their children, including her nephew, George Lear (her sister Rose's son), and her son-in-law, William Hayes, returned to Mount Vernon to help with the landscaping for the new tomb of Washington. Nancy was the only woman. She cooked meals for the men who were working on the landscape. The men who were formerly enslaved under Washington, including: Sambo Anderson and Dick Jasper, William Anderson, Berkley Clark, Morris Jasper, William Moss, Joe Richardson, Levi Richardson, Joseph Smith, her son-in-law William Hayes, who was also a former Washington enslaved, along with her nephew, George Lear (her sister Rose's son and a descendant of Tobias Lear, George Washington's personal secretary), came with her to help. Their work on the tomb was written in *The Alexandria Gazette*. Five of the 12 people were children of formerly enslaved workers of George Washington.[299]

The children of Nancy and Charles were the first born free under the Nancy Carter line.

Since the Quanders were free before Emancipation, they were required to register with the Free-Negro Registers. This record was created after the Virginia General Assembly passed legislation on December 10, 1793. All free 'negroes' and 'mulattoes' had to register their name, age, color, and physical stature where they resided. They also had to cite if they were born free or emancipated.

Hundreds of years later, Judge Quander would use this database to find his loved ones. The physical descriptions were priceless. For example, Nancy Quander's daughter, Elizabeth Quander Hayes, was documented at four feet five and a half inches, around 21 years old, and she had a dark complexion, and her right cheek had a smallpox scar. [300] This was priceless information for the Quanders to discover when they wanted to learn more about their ancestors.

Virginia Family Tree

Virginia descendant, West Ford, who was emancipated by the last Will and Testament of Hannah Bushrod Washington, was the grandfather or great-grandfather of several Quanders. Hannah Washington was married to George Washington's brother, John Augustine Washington. Ford's mother was named Venus, and the father was unknown.[301] According to research by Mount Vernon Research Historian, Mary V. Thompson, West Ford was born between March 3, 1783, and June 22, 1784, at Bushfield Plantation in Westmoreland County, Virginia, 95 miles from Mount Vernon.[302]

---

[298] Rohulamin Quander, "The Quanders"
[299] Jessie MacLeod, "Nancy Carter Quander", Digital Encyclopedia of George Washington, https://www.mountvernon.org/library/digitalhistory/digital-encyclopedia/article/nancy-carter-quander/
[300] Rohulamin Quander, "The Quanders"
[301] Rohulamin Quander, "The Quanders"
[302] Mary Thompson, "West Ford", Digital Encyclopedia of George Washington, https://www.mountvernon.org/library/digitalhistory/digital-encyclopedia/article/west-ford/

Although some members of West Ford's family oral history believe that George Washington was his father, but Mount Vernon says there are no records which indicate that George Washington visited his brother's plantation from his time in Mount Vernon on December 24, 1783, to the end of the Revolution, until his brother's death in early January of 1787.[303]

The only trip, according to Mount Vernon records, where Venus accompanied Hannah to Mount Vernon, was in October of 1785.[304] Venus' visit was after Ford's birth.

Mount Vernon records also show George Washington was not in Virginia between November 1781, because he was in Yorktown. He returned to Mount Vernon on Christmas Eve of 1783 at the end of the Revolutionary War.[305]

Historians suspect Ford's father may be George Washington's brother, John Augustine, or one of his sons because of West's favorable treatment.[306] The Washington family provided special opportunities for him, such as reading and writing, and he was also inoculated for smallpox once he was set free at age 21. Ford was the only enslaved person freed by Hannah.

Hannah also asked for Ford to be trained in a skill, so he could support himself once he was free.[307] Ford was taken to Mount Vernon when Hannah's son, Bushrod Washington, became the owner. He worked for the Washington's at Mount Vernon even after he was freed in 1805.[308] He took care of George Washington's manumitted valet, the now elderly William Lee, as well as supervised the enslaved workers, and helped with the Washington family business.

---

[303] "Mt. Vernon Responds to the Ford Family", Frontline, PBS
https://www.pbs.org/wgbh/pages/frontline/shows/jefferson/video/tofords.html
[304] "Mt. Vernon Responds to the Ford Family", Frontline, PBS
[305] Mary Thompson, "West Ford"
[306] Mary Thompson, "West Ford"
[307] Mary Thompson, "West Ford"
[308] Mary Thompson, "West Ford"

Source: Mount Vernon Ladies' Association

Ford was given over 100 acres of land in Fairfax County, Virginia, by Bushrod Washington when he died in 1829. He later used the profits from the sale of that property to purchase a larger section of land, which later became the center of Gum Springs, a free black community. Ford would later become the second wealthiest black man in Fairfax County, Virginia.[309]

Knowing Your Worth

The exact location of Charles Henry Quander's birth is not 100 percent certain. Still, it is believed he was born in Maryland and sold to a Virginia Lawyer, Dennis Johnston, who was Fairfax magistrate and sheriff for Fairfax County. Still, Charles Henry Quander allegedly referred he was born in VA. He learned to read and write from Union Soldiers during the Civil War.[310] The gift of education was an arrangement between the young Quander and the soldiers as payment for his offerings of food.

[309] Mary Thompson, "West Ford"
[310] "Tancil, Gladys Quander", Historical Interpreter, Encyclopedia.com https://www.encyclopedia.com/education/news-wires-white-papers-and-books/tancil-gladys-quander and Whitney Redding, "Neighbors", Washington Post, Feb. 28, 1991

Charles Henry Quander
Source: "The Quanders",
Rohulamin Quander

He was the property of Dennis Johnston and worked on the grounds of the Johnston's plantations in Fairfax County, VA.[311] [312] According to oral history, no one told Charles Henry about the Emancipation Proclamation and how it was in effect on January 1, 1863. Therefore, Charles Henry continued to be enslaved. Eventually, he found out, and in 1867, he went to the Johnstons and told them he was aware slavery was over and that he was leaving. The Johnstons did not want to lose the strong twenty-something-year-old Charles Henry and agreed to pay him. Knowing his worth, he pressed for back pay for his work during 1863-1867. They agreed, and once he was given his lump sum back pay, he quit working for the family and purchased two acres of land from his former enslaver.[313]

Between the late 1870s through the early 1880s, Charles Henry expanded his land through additional purchases. He eventually amassed 88 acres. Charles Henry had a successful dairy business. He died in 1919, leaving several adult children as his heirs. The muddy path that stretched along Charles Henry's property eventually expanded into a well-traveled road as the population grew. When Fairfax County officials approached Charles Henry's family in about 1926 about what they should formally name the road, James Henry Quander, one of Charles' sons, said, "Just call it Quander Road."[314]

Charles Henry sold his dairy products to the local community and Mount Vernon. After his death, eventually, some of the land was distributed to his heirs, and other portions were broken off and sold. The land where Charles Henry's farm was located is now the location of Quander Road School and West Potomac High School, where the middle building of the three building campus is name Quander.

---

[311] Rohulamin Quander, "The Quanders"
[312] Rohulamin Quander, "The Quanders"
[313] Whitney Redding, "Neighbors", Washington Post, Feb. 28, 1991
[314] Rohulamin Quander, "The Quanders"

A Voice for the Voiceless

Gladys Quander Tancil, the granddaughter of Charles Henry, was passionate in her fight to tell the lives of the enslaved people from Mount Vernon. She grew up on the family's dairy farm. Learning about the lives of her ancestors, and telling their stories was a passion for Gladys.

A civil rights leader in her community, Gladys was a staunch advocate for Black women. She was a member of the National Advancement Association of Colored People (NAACP), and a founding member of the Alexandria Society for the Preservation of Black Heritage and the Black Women United of Fairfax County.[315]

Her parents, James Henry Quander, and Alice Cordelia Smith, worked and lived on the land of her grandfather, Charles Henry. Gladys' father sold produce grown and products made on their farm to Mount Vernon.

Growing up in a time where Jim Crow laws dictated the lives of black men, women, and children, Gladys attended segregated public schools. Around 1939/40, Gladys attended Miner Teacher's College. She was the first free Quander in her immediate family line to attend college.

Gladys would work in the U.S. government for 33 years, and, during this time, she would take off from work for up to two weeks in the Fall for the Mount Vernon Ladies' Association Council meeting. She served as the Ladies' maid. This role was personal to Gladys, for her mom was the ladies' maid from 1930-1962.[316]

Gladys Quander Tancil and other fellow museum
attendants modeling their official uniforms, 1975

Source: Mount Vernon Ladies' Association

---

[315] Trevor Vann George Mason University "Gladys Quander Tancil" Digital Encyclopedia of George Washington
https://www.mountvernon.org/library/digitalhistory/digital-encyclopedia/article/gladys-quander-tancil-1921-2002/
[316] Trevor Vann George Mason University "Gladys Quander Tancil"

Her aunt, Cordelia Randle/Randal, was recognized by the Mount Vernon Ladies Association in 1951 for her 40 years of work in various roles as a "maid" or "extra servant" during several council sessions.[317] Cordelia was presented with $50 as a gift upon her retirement.

When Gladys retired from the government, she received a call from her friend, Christine Meadows, who was a curator at Mount Vernon and had questions about Washington dinner menus. [318]

Gladys's knowledge was immense, and Christine suggested Gladys should apply for a job as an interpretive guide at Mount Vernon. In 1975, Gladys was hired and became the first African American woman guide. Gladys became a champion for the enslaved workers of Mount Vernon.

Through the decades, Gladys was on hand for the evolving telling of history at Mount Vernon. Embracing the dark history of slavery, and telling the story of bondage, and forced labor was not acknowledged properly even after the Civil Rights movement. It took years of constructive discussions with the Mount Vernon Ladies' Association (MVLA), which owned the estate, to incorporate a more balanced telling of American history. The MVLA was made up of rich, high-society, white women. The word "enslaved" at the beginning of these tours, in which the MVLA approved the language, was never said.[319]

Gladys was selected to conduct the first guided tour focused on the lives of the enslaved in 1995. Her first "Slave Life Tour" was in April of that year.[320]

The MVLA crafted the terms and language of that tour with staff directed to adhere to the text they were given and to present to visitors.[321]

For example, the hundreds of men, women, and children who worked in the fields from sunup to sundown, made the food, tended to the needs of the family and hundreds of guests that visited each year, as well as raised the livestock, made materials, like forged ironworks and clothing, were called, "servants".[322] It took decades for Mount Vernon, like other historic sites, to expand the scope of colonial life to add more African American history to its tours and educational programs.[323] Gladys was a big part in making sure the inclusion of African Americans' participation at Mount Vernon was added accurately.

The focus of her tours was to talk about her ancestors and other enslaved men and women who built Mount Vernon and labored on the land. She would emphasize they were the unsung heroes of American History. It was their hard labor that supported George Washington. Quander family historians have emphasized this message. Judge Rohulamin Quander, who is the family historian today, emphasized, "It's

---

[317] "Minutes of the Council of the Mount Vernon Ladies' Association of the Union (Mount Vernon, Virginia) 21, 1951.
[318] Rohulamin Quander email correspondence with author
[319] Rohulamin Quander, "The Quanders"
[320] Trevor Vann, "Gladys Quander Tancil"
[321] Rohulamin Quander, email correspondence on May 31, 2023
[322] "Plantation Structure" Digital Encyclopedia of George Washington Digital Encyclopedia of George Washington
[323] Trevor Vann, "Gladys Quander Tancil"

not Negro History. It is *American* history. This history has a proper place, and that proper place is everywhere."

Source: Mount Vernon Ladies' Association

Gladys would recall specifics of the Mount Vernon enslaved life, from countless stories told to her by her elders. She wanted to make sure the stories she told, or the physical examples of how the enslaved lived that were portrayed, were authentic. When a supervising historian was putting together a reproduction of a meal for an enslaved family, Gladys pointed out the chicken was too plump. Her daughter, Gloria, recalled in a newspaper article on her mother, that "Things were not so good for the slaves, she knew." [324]

Gladys took her endless knowledge of enslaved life and personalized the tours with enriched detail. When she led the tour to the spinning room, Gladys called it her ancestral home, saying, "Two centuries ago, (my) relative Nancy Quander spent her days spinning yarn for the Father of Our Country."[325]

Her two children never got tired of hearing the family stories. In their mind, their loved ones came to life. Their voices, physical statures, and personalities were described in vivid detail, creating indelible pictures in their minds and hearts. They could picture the dancing flames of Charles Henry's lantern, which lit his way in the country darkness on Quander Road. Her children knew they were rich in family. Gladys was considered the family historian, and she would share her stories at family reunions so that relatives who lived in Pennsylvania and New Jersey could learn more.

---

[324] "Slaves' Descendant Told Their Stories at Mount Vernon" The Washington Post, December 1, 2002
[325] Trevor Vann "Gladys Quander Tancil"

121

Connecting with Her Roots

A total of five farms made up Mount Vernon, and Gladys loved walking the grounds and visiting the burial grounds. It was part of her reconnecting with her deceased family members.

There were several locations at Mount Vernon where enslaved men, women, and children were buried. The primary cemetery was located down the hill from George and Martha Washington's tomb, in a peaceful wooded hillside above the Potomac River. Most of the enslaved people buried there were assigned to Mansion House Farm.

This land, where some of her loved ones were laid to rest, had no markers to indicate where up to 155 graves of enslaved persons were buried. The Mount Vernon Ladies' Association erected a modest memorial, identifying the enslaved burial ground in 1929, but Gladys, and other descendants who had loved ones buried on the land, wanted something more.

Giving a voice to the voiceless, Gladys and the other men and women lobbied the Mount Vernon Ladies' Association to erect a proper memorial.[326] In 1983, a formal, and more significant memorial, was dedicated. The granite structure, designed by architecture students from Howard University, featured the words, "Love, Hope, and Faith. " Each actionable word was featured in biblical scriptures that the enslaved men and women would hear when they gathered on Sundays to celebrate their faith.

In 2014, the Mount Vernon Ladies' Association commissioned a project using ground-penetrating technology called LIDAR to survey the cemeteries[327]. LIDAR is an acronym *for Light Detection and Ranging.* It uses a high-density laser that is so strong it can penetrate through the tree canopy and scan and map the Earth's surface.

This laser technology peels away the layers of years and helps identify old roads, graves, boundaries, as well as old farming fields that are obscured to the naked eye. The archeological team had a Lidar device mounted on a single-engine Cessna, which flew at a low altitude across the 8,000 acres of Washington's land.[328] To date, 85 burials have been identified in the slave cemetery.[329]

It was discovered the graves were positioned on an east-west axis. This burial placement was according to local African American tradition, so the bodies, which were buried in simple wood coffins, would face Africa.[330] This symbolized the enslaved desire to go home.

---

[326] Rohulamin Quander, "The Quanders"

[327] Joe Downer RPA Archaeological Field Research Manager, George Washington's Mount Vernon email correspondence with author.

[328] Joe Downer RPA Archaeological Field Research Manager, George Washington's Mount Vernon email correspondence with author

[329] Joe Downer RPA Archaeological Field Research Manager, George Washington's Mount Vernon email correspondence with author

[330] "Slave Memorial", Digital Encyclopedia of George Washington
https://www.mountvernon.org/the-estate-gardens/location/slave-memorial

Source: Mount Vernon Ladies' Association

Source: Mount Vernon Ladies' Association

In 1997, Gladys, along with Rohulamin Quander, a descendant of Henry Quando, and founder of the Quander Historical and Educational Society, Inc., a contingent of the membership of Black Women United for Action, were invited to the White House to meet President Bill Clinton and Vice President Gore. The meeting was initially set at the memorial but was moved to the White House due to inclement weather.

123

President William J. Clinton, with a group, including
Gladys Quander Tancil and Rohulamin Quander in
the White House Oval Office, September 1997

Source: "The Quanders", Rohulamin Quander

Gladys was a fixture at Mount Vernon until she was diagnosed with cancer. She passed on November 5, 2002.

Gladys was not the only Quander who worked at Mount Vernon.

Tom Quander was an employee at Mount Vernon from 1893 to 1936[331]. He started working at Mount Vernon as a day laborer. Tom also worked as a Coachman. Tom was later promoted to a gardener in the propagating house, where he worked in the position until he was no longer able to physically handle hard labor. Not ready to retire, he briefly served as a guard.

---

[331] Photograph, Tom Quander, July 1932, Fred W. Smith National Library for the Study of George Washington digital collections, http://catalog.mountvernon.org/digital/collection/p16829coll31/id/344/rec/29

Thomas Edison plants an elm tree in the edge of the woods near the tomb during his visit to Mount Vernon on September 19, 1916. Assisting Edison are Tom Quander (foreground) and an unidentified male.

Source: Mount Vernon Ladies' Association

Other Quanders worked temporarily or seasonally: Norman Quander, a day laborer in the 1890s; James Quander, a day laborer from the 1890s-1900; Elwood Quander, a day laborer in 1900; Jackson Quander, a day laborer in 1905; Robert Quander, house employee during the 1950s, Lucy Quander, laundress in 1902, and Essie Quander, from 1938-1939.[332]

First Quander Reunion

The idea for the first Quander reunion was in 1925 after the deaths of James A. and Alcinda Lear Quander. James A. was the great-grandson of Nancy Carter and Charles Quander, and Alcinda was the great-granddaughter of Tobias Lear, George Washington's personal secretary. Descendants from the Mount Vernon family line lived in and out of state (in Pennsylvania), and family members thought coming together after these passings would provide a fruitful opportunity for Quanders to learn more about their history.[333]

The reunion took place on a steamy summer day on August 15, 1926, on the Woodlawn Virginia farm of Emma Harris, the oldest child of James and Alcinda, and her husband Thomas Harris, another mulatto descendant of Tobias Lear.[334] The motto of the reunion from that day and for future VA reunions was "Stick Together."[335] Children ran and played on the 25-acre property, and the women worked in the kitchen preparing the feast. The men were outside, some drinking Tom Harris' corn whiskey he made for the event.

---

[332] Rebecca Baird, Archivist, The Fred W. Smith National Library for the Study of George Washington, email correspondence with author, October 12, 2022
[333] Rohulamin Quander, "The Quanders"
[334] Rohulamin Quander, "The Quanders"
[335] Rohulamin Quander, "The Quanders"

Because it was Prohibition, the whiskey was hidden in a tub on ice by the woodshed behind the house.[336] Fried chicken, succotash, mashed potatoes with gravy, and homemade ice cream were on the menu.[337]

The next three Quander Family Reunions only included the Pennsylvania and Virginia Quanders. According to oral history, the Mount Vernon Quanders did not want to include other Quanders who were not directly connected to Mount Vernon. They wanted to keep their unique bond and circle tight.[338] The Maryland and Virginia Quanders did not understand this exclusion. In 1930, at the fifth reunion, the "other" Virginia Quanders were invited for dessert. It was not until the 43rd reunion in 1968, that some family members of the Maryland Quander Family tree, James W., his wife Joherra, and son Rohulamin, were formally invited. There are some family conversations about a few Maryland Quanders visiting their Virginia cousins in the 1930's and 1940's, but they were not considered invited guests or attendees of a planned reunion.

---

[336] Rohulamin Quander, "The Quanders"
[337] Rohulamin Quander, "The Quanders"
[338] Rohulamin Quander, "The Quanders"

Chapter Two
Fighters for Freedom

The Quander and extended Quander family members have a long history of serving in the country. The earliest documented Quander to serve was John Pierson Quander, who fought in the Civil War.

John Pierson was born July 7, 1845, to Lewis Quander, a free Black man and grandson of Nancy Carter Quander and Charles Quander, and his wife Susannah Russell Pierson Quander, enslaved to Levi Burke[339].

Even though Lewis was born free, he knew Susannah. Both were from the Mount Vernon area. Levi Burk agreed to the marriage, and the couple was married in the home of her enslaver by Episcopal minister Rev. Johnson on June 11, 1842.[340]

Lewis and Susannah lived together, and in the early days of their marriage, Susannah continued her enslaved work, and Lewis was a farmhand saving his money to buy land for himself. They welcomed James A. (1843), John Pierson (1845), Charles Hillman (1847), Thomas H. (1861) and Susana (1863). Virginia's enslavement law was based on what was called, *partus sequitur ventrem,* meaning a child born to an enslaved mother inherited her enslaved status.

Lewis saved the money he earned as a farm hand to buy land. In 1853, Quander purchased 28 acres from Charles Gillingham for $560. He was a Quaker, and Quakers were known to engage in land sales with free Blacks. In 1855, he next purchased 163 acres from Chalkley Gillingham for $4,227.71. Three years later, he purchased an adjoining tract of land from Gillingham for $75. The total value of that land in today's dollars is $178,402.16.

Lewis Quander was a successful farmer and reported owning a wide variety of farm animals and growing vegetables in 1860. Listed in the paperwork, eighteen hogs, four milk cows, six horses, three heads of cattle, oats, potatoes, hay, wheat corn, and other produce. The farm was also producing 300 pounds of butter.[341]

According to the 1860 Census, Lewis Quander was listed as a farmer who owned land. His wife and three children born during the time the Census was taken were not listed as a part of his household because they were considered the property of Levi Burk.

On January 1, 1863, President Abraham Lincoln issued the Emancipation Proclamation, which declared all enslaved people were free in states that were "in rebellion against the United States." But the reality of the proclamation relied on enforcement. This meant freedom could only be upheld in areas where the Union Army controlled. The area of Virginia, where the enslaver of Susannah and her children lived, was within

---

[339] Colston v. Quander, 1 Va. Dec. 283 (1877) https://cite.case.law/va-dec/1/283/
[340] Colston v. Quander, 1 Va. Dec. 283 (1877) https://cite.case.law/va-dec/1/283/
[341] Curtis L. Vaughn, A Dissertation Submitted to the Graduate Faculty of George Mason University, "Freedom is not enough: African Americans in Antebellum Fairfax County" Freedom Is Not Enough: African Americans in Antebellum Fairfax County (gmu.edu)

the jurisdiction of the Union Army.[342] Susannah was still enslaved until April 7, 1864, when the "Alexandria Constitution" was adopted, which abolished and prohibited slavery in the state of Virginia forever.

In May 1863, the U.S. Government established the Bureau of Colored Troops to manage the growing numbers of black soldiers in the Civil War.[343] These Black regiments were called U.S. Colored Troops or USCT.

The USCT was led by white officers. As the war continued, more African Americans enlisted in the Union Army. One of those soldiers was John Pierson Quander.

It is unknown where John Pierson lived during this time or if his enslaver gave him permission, but on John Pierson's 18th birthday in July of 1863, he enlisted with the Union Army and was part of the 1st US Colored Infantry.

John Pierson Quander, Sr. (1845-1925)
Posing in Civil War Uniform
Grand Army of the Republic reunion
1915, Washington, D.C.

Source: "The Quanders", Rohulamin Quander

He was a Private in the 1st Regiment of the United States Colored Heavy Artillery Infantry Company G.[344] This regiment was comprised of both the Virginia and North Carolina forces.

The 1st Regiment fought in five battles south of the James River and against Petersburg and Richmond, VA.[345] Some of their heroic operations included the Battle of the Crater[346], the Battle of Chaffin's Farm in

---

[342] Colston v. Quander, 1 Va. Dec. 283 (1877) Nov. 1877 · Special Court of Appeals of Virginia 1 Va. Dec. 283
https://cite.case.law/va-dec/1/283/

[343] War Department issued General Order No. 143 on May 22, 1863 which created the Bureau of Colored Troops.

[344] National Park Service. File Number: M589 ROLL 70, Index to Compiled Service Records of Volunteer Union Soldiers Who Served With U.S. Colored Troops.

[345] National Park Service, 1st Regiment, U.S. Colored Infantry Service The Civil War

[346] U.S. Army: A History of African American Regiments in the U.S. Army

the Richmond-Petersburg Campaign, Fort Fisher in North Carolina, and the fall of Wilmington, Delaware.[347] John was an aide-de-camp[348] in the Union Army and carried the Union flag into battle.

Approximately 10 percent of the Union Army by the end of the Civil War were Black men.[349] At the end of the war, the 1st Regiment lost a total of 185 men to either disease or mortal wounds.[350] John Pierson rose to the rank of Corporal in 1864. President Lincoln credited the Black soldiers for helping turn the tide of the war.[351]

After the war, John Pierson returned and married Hannah Bruce Ford, the granddaughter of West Ford. Hannah's father, William Washington Ford, was a gardener at Mount Vernon.[352] In the 1870 census, John Pierson was listed as a farmhand, and Hannah was a homemaker. Both were able to read and write but had no formal education.

Together they had eight children. Born in Mount Vernon were Lewis M., who died at the age of two from inflammatory rheumatism[353] (1870), Henrietta "Hettie" (1872), Maggie Baker (1874), John Pierson, Jr. (1875), and Howard Milton (1877). Later, Nellie May (1880), Susie Russell (1882), Henry Harry (1885), and Charles Calvin (1886) were all born in Washington, DC.

The family moved to Washington, D.C, so all of their children could attend high school. There were no high schools for Black students in the Mount Vernon area where they lived.[354] [355] Only one room schoolhouses where elementary education was taught were available. The first high school for Black students in Fairfax County was not established until 1938.

---

[347] National Park Service, 1st Regiment , U.S. Colored Infantry Service, The Civil War, Duty at Norfolk, Portsmouth and Yorktown, Va., till April, 1864. Expedition from Norfolk to South Mills, Camden Court House, etc., N. C., December 5-24, 1863. Butler's operations south of James River and against Petersburg and Richmond, Va., May 4-June 15. Action at Wilson's Wharf May 24. Assaults on Petersburg June 15-18. Siege of Petersburg and Richmond June 16 to December 7, 1864. Explosion of Mine, Petersburg, July 30. Demonstration on north side of the James River September 28-30. Battle of Chaffin's Farm, New Market Heights, September 28-30. Fort Harrison September 29. Battle of Fair Oaks October 27-28. Expedition to Fort Fisher, N. C., December 7-27. 2nd Expedition to Fort Fisher, N. C., January 7-15, 1865. Assault on and capture of Fort Fisher January 15. Sugar Loaf Hill January 19. Sugar Loaf Battery February 11. Fort Anderson February 18-20. Capture of Wilmington February 22. Northeast Ferry February 22. Campaign of the Carolinas March 1-April 26. Advance on Goldsboro March 6-21. Occupation of Goldsboro March 21. Cox's Bridge March 23-24. Advance on Raleigh April 9-13. Occupation of Raleigh April 13. Bennett's House April 26. Surrender of Johnston and his army. Duty in the Dept. of North Carolina till September. Mustered out September 29, 1865.
[348] aide-de-camp, (French: "camp assistant"), is an officer on the personal staff of a general, admiral, or other high-ranking commander who acts as his confidential secretary in routine matters.
[349] National Archives, "Black Soldiers in the U.S. Military During the Civil War". Roughly 179,000 black men served as soldiers in the U.S. Army and another 19,000 served in the Navy.
[350] National Park Service, 1st Regiment, U.S. Colored Infantry Service The Civil War
[351] American Battlefield Trust, The U.S. Colored Troops
[352] U.S. Census, 1870, Virginia, Fairfax, Township: S O & A R Road, Sheet 30, Family 227
[353] Fairfax County Register of Deaths within Fairfax County, Lee Township, year ending December 31, 1872
[354] History of U.S. 1: Early Schools along Route One, Part 3, http://scottsurovell.blogspot.com/2013/03/history-of-us-1-early-schools-along_31.html
[355] "The story behind Fairfax County's first public high school for Black students" https://www.wusa9.com/article/news/local/virginia/the-story-behind-fairfax-countys-first-public-high-school-for-black-students/65-e191b928-ee36-4997-b4e0-a05eb21b0653

When the family relocated to Washington, DC. John Pierson worked as a waiter.[356] Their children would become the first generation from their family lines to receive a formal education and graduate from college.

These lessons in leadership from John Pierson's military service inspired their children. Nellie was an active participant in the women's right's movement. Their son Charles Calvin served in a Black Militia after the WWII for three years in Washington DC, and when he moved to New York, he served in the New York 15th Regiment militia, retiring with the rank of Captain in 1950.[357] These militia were volunteers. The NY Regiment was a part of the New York State Guard. John Pierson Quander, Sr. was buried at Arlington National Cemetery with full Military honors on May 25, 1925.

Lewis Lear Quander

Lewis was a Quander born in Pittsburgh, Pennsylvania. He was great-nephew of John Pierson as well as the great-grandson of Nancy Carter Quander, Tobias Lear, and West Ford. This lineage of Quander, Lear, and Ford came from Lewis' father, Frank Quander.

Frank's mother, Alcinda Quander, was from the Lear family. Frank's father was James Quander, John Pierson's brother who had family ties to Nancy Quander. Lewis Lear's mother, Lillian Martin Quander, was white. Interracial marriages at that time were not widely accepted.

Even though Pennsylvania did not outlaw interracial marriages, that did not mean society embraced these unions. Even in 1919, when Lewis Lear was born, the bigotry against interracial unions was strong. So much so, that it strained the marriage, and Frank Quander eventually walked out. Lillian, a homemaker, was unable to support the family, so her children were sent to different family members to be raised.

Lewis lived with family friends throughout the years and eventually moved to Virginia to live with his aunt Emma Quander Harris as a young teen. But at age 15, Lewis did now want to live under the stern rules of his aunt and uncle's home and left for a life of riding the rails and performing in a washboard and jug band in New York at the age of 15.

In 1941, Lewis enlisted in the U.S. Army and was a combat engineer for the 91st Engineers, which was a segregated unit. On his WWII enlistment card, it said he had three years of high school education, and his civil occupation at the time was semi-skilled mechanics and repairmen for motor vehicles.

When family members asked Lewis about his time in the war, he would say he "specialized in building air strips and bridges and blowing things up." Lewis reenlisted in 1947 with the U.S. Air Force, which was founded that same year. He was assigned to Special Services. In this role, he coordinated entertainment programs for the airmen. Lewis also studied voice, and as he honed his craft, he entertained the troops as a traveling singer. He also won the Air Force signing championship in 1953. He retired as a staff sergeant in

---

[356] U.S. Census, June 14, 1880, Washington District of Columbia
[357] U.S. Military Service Cards, 1816-1979

1956 and used his voice in a different capacity. As president of the Norwalk Connecticut NAACP. Lewis was a champion for Black home ownership and fought against segregation in the community.

Tuskegee Airmen

America's military was segregated, and many Black Americas were subjected to the Jim Crow Laws[358]. In World War I, Black men who asked to serve as aerial observers were rejected. The National Association for the Advancement of Colored People (NAACP) advocated for twenty years for Black Americans to be given the opportunity to be trained as aviators.

In March of 1942, young Black men volunteered to become part of the country's first Black military airmen. These men, if they passed mental and physical qualifications, were accepted for aviation cadet training. The men were trained to be either pilots, navigators, or bombardiers.[359]

In World War II, 355 Black men served as miliary fighter pilots, forming the 332nd Fighter Group and the 477th Bombardment group of the U.S. Army Air Forces. These men were called the Tuskegee Airmen after the location of where they trained--Tuskegee, Alabama.

The group was active between 1941-1946. A total of 992 Black pilots[360] graduated from the program. 355 of those graduates actively served in WWII as fighter pilots. Two members of the first all-Black military group were Quanders.

Charles J. Quander was a twin engine flight officer[361] and graduated from pilot training on August 4, 1944.[362] He was one of 348 graduates that year.[363] Charles was a descendant of the Maryland side of the family tree. His father, Charles J. Quander, Sr., distinguished himself as the principal of the National Training School for Boys, located in Washington, D.C.

Charles J. Quander,Jr. far right with fellow Tuskegee Airmen
Source: "The Quanders", Rohnlamin Quander

---

[358] Jim Crow Laws were laws created and adopted in the South beginning in the early 19th century. Segregation in public accommodations and voting were enforced. Jim Crow laws were enforced until 1965
[359] Tuskegee Airmen Legacy
[360] Tuskegee Airmen Legacy
[361] Tuskegee Airmen Pilot Roster, CAF Rise Above
[362] Tuskegee Airmen: The African-American Military Pilots of WW II
[363] Tuskegee Airmen Legacy Airmen Statistics

His Virginia family tree cousin, Donald Victor Quander, was a mechanic for the Tuskegee Airmen. As a child, Donald loved airplanes and read manuals. This knowledge enabled him to become an airplane mechanic. Donald also taught both engine and radio mechanics to students who wanted to learn how to fly. He joined the U.S. Army Air Corps in 1941. He was assigned to aircraft maintenance as a mechanic and an electronics instrumentation specialist for the Tuskegee Airmen. He served with the 332nd Fighter Group and the 99th Pursuit Fighter Squadron in Tuskegee, Alabama.

Despite his service to his country while in Alabama, Donald experienced racial hatred and violence. In the streets of Montgomery, military police pointed their guns at the Black troops.[364] As a proud member of Prince Hall Masons[365], America's oldest civil rights organization, Donald was outspoken on civil liberties. His refusal to move to the back of the bus in Montgomery led to a severe beating.[366]

He re-enlisted with the Air Force during World War II and worked on planes for Black pilots. Eventually, the need for Black mechanics to work on planes for white pilots was needed. Donald was reassigned to the mostly white pilot group, the 79th Fighter Group, and was stationed in Europe. This group of pilots took part in Allied operations that defeated the Axis forces in North Africa, conquered Sicily, and captured Pantelleria.[367] The Group received Distinguished Unit Citations for their campaigns in North Africa, Sicily, and Italy.

Donald was a composite character in the movie *Red Tails*, which was about the Tuskegee Airmen. After the war, he was assigned to the staff that maintained Air Force One and other U.S. Presidential aircraft. After a thirty-year military career, Donald V. Quander retired as a Chief Master Sergeant for the U.S. Air Force.

James Simmons, Jr., a Maryland Quander, was Private First Class for the U.S. Army, serving in the 320th Anti-Aircraft Artillery Battalion. James was the only Quander to have died during service. He was killed in action during the Allied invasion of Normandy on D-Day, June 6, 1944.

---

[364] Rohulamin Quander, "The Quanders"
[365] Donald V. Quander was a member of the Euclid Lodge No. 70 in New York CIty
[366] Rohulamin Quander, "The Quanders"
[367] 79th Fighter Group, Army Air Corps Library and Museum

James Simmons, Jr.
Source: Simmons Family Archives

In an interview with 400 Years of African American History Commission's special 400 HOUR program: "African American Fallen Heroes," Charlotte Chase, sister of James S. Simmons, said she remembers the day her mom received word he died in battle.

"I remember when the soldiers arrived at my house, and I heard my mother scream," said Charlotte Chase, sister of James S. Simmons. "I remember running into the living room to see what was going on, and I saw her crying, and crying, and crying, and I turned and left the room. I am very proud of my brother. He gave his life for his country."

Simmons was a part of the 320th Barrage Balloon Battalion, which was an all-Black American Army unit that saw combat during World War II in Europe. It was also the first Black unit in the segregated Army to go ashore on D-Day. This barrage balloon battalion was considered VLA (Very Low Altitude). Their first assignment was on D-Day in both Utah and Omaha.

The balloons were 35 feet in length and were used to protect soldiers on the ground from air attacks. They were flown at varying altitudes and intervals, forcing aircraft to shoot from higher altitudes. It was a passive form of defense, but it made it harder for the enemy aircraft to hit a target.

Barrage Balloons protected dozens of
ships off the beaches of Normandy as
soldiers, material, and munitions needed
to expand the beachhead were unloaded.
NARA 342-FH-3A17185-71287AC
Source: Air and Space Musesum
Smithsonian

The men of this unit realized they needed to create a smaller balloon so it could be easily moved from a landing craft. A standard balloon crew weighed half a ton because of the winch the balloon was tethered to. Normally, five men operated the balloon, but because of the weight, the 320th feared it would sink in the water. The 320th retrofitted a lighter 35-pound cable winch to control the balloons. The crews were also reduced to three and four men.

There were a total of 621 soldiers in this group. Their mission was to raise hydrogen-filled barrage balloons to protect the US infantry and armor from being shelled by enemy aircraft.

Supreme Allied Commander Gen. Dwight D. Eisenhower said the men flew at an altitude of around 200 feet. General Eisenhower commended the unit for conducting "its mission with courage and determination and proved an important element of the air defense team."

Four Generals

Through the decades, some of the Quanders have continued the legacy of their forefathers in serving their country. According to U.S. Army officials, the extended Quander Family is the only Black American family to have four Generals in the U.S. Military.

Three of these officers are from the same immediate family. They are Brigadier General Leo Austin Brooks, Sr., Brigadier General Leo Austin Brooks, Jr., and General Vincent Keith Brooks. They retired from the military in 1984, 2006, and 2019, respectively. According to Army officials, the Brooks family is the only Black American family to have three generals in two generations.

The Quander connection is through marriage. Leo A. Brooks, Sr., married Naomi (Nee Lewis) Brooks. Naomi was a descendant of Mount Vernon enslaved person Nancy Carter. BG Brooks, Sr., and Naomi's two sons, Leo, Jr., and Vincent, and their daughter Marquita are direct Quander descendants. The complete Brooks story is told in the following section.

The fourth General in the Quander family tree is Brigadier General Mark Christopher Quander. General Quander has served as the 79th Commandant of Cadets of the United States Military Academy since May 2021. This position was also held by Leo A. Brooks, Jr. from 2002 to 2004 when he was the 69th Commandant of Cadets. Brooks Jr. was the second African American commandant in West Point History. General Mark C. Quander, along with Leo A. Brooks and Vincent K. Brooks, are all West Point Graduates.

BG Mark Quander is the second of three sons of Lt. Col. Francis Augustine Quander, Jr., a Washington native, and Gail Quander. BG Quander's grandfather, Francis Augustine Quander, Sr., was born in Maryland and was a clerk for the Internal Revenue Service.[368] Francis Sr. served in the European Theater of Operations during World War II. After his service, Francis went to college using his GI Bill. His grandmother, Bethel, was born in Virginia and, according to the 1950 U.S. Census, was a money counter for the U.S. Treasury.[369] Bethel also worked for the IRS. Before moving to Washington, DC, she was an English teacher in Lynchburg, VA. Francis and Bethel valued education and worked multiple jobs so they could afford to enroll BG Quander's father, Francis, Jr., in Catholic School in DC.

BG Quander was born at the old Walter Reed Hospital in 1974. His father, Lt. Col. Quander, had his first assignment in the 3rd Infantry Regiment, the "Old Guard," at Fort McNair in Washington, D.C. They lived in Grant Hall, which is known in history books as the location where the Lincoln co-conspirators were hung at the top of Grant Hall. Like all military families, the Quanders moved around the globe.

Lt. Col. Quander graduated from Norwich University, Northfield, Vermont, in 1971 and joined the Amy the following year. Later in his career, he served in one of the airborne assault divisions[370]. His service took him to Hindenburg, Germany, Fort Bragg, North Carolina, and the Pentagon. As a youth, Mark played soccer when his family was stationed in West Germany.

The family moved to Fayetteville, North Carolina, in the summer of 1985 and lived at Fort Bragg. Then twelve-year-old BG Quander asked his parents if his bedroom could be painted "Carolina Blue". [371] He fell in love with the North Carolina Tar Heels and the legendary coach Dean Smith. From seventh to tenth grade, he would watch the classic Duke vs. Carolina basketball games. He loved the competition between the two teams.

BG Quander had his heart set on becoming a civil engineer, and his mother would describe him in interviews as a "book nerd"[372] and the least likely of her sons to follow in his father's military footsteps. In 1988, his father was deployed for Operation Golden Pheasant[373] in Honduras. BG Quander went to high school as if it were any other day.

[368] 1950 U.S. Census
[369] 1950 U.S. Census
[370] Arlington Cemetery.net Francis A. Quander Jr., BURIED AT: SECTION 11 SITE 246 LH
[371] BG Quander conversation with authors, February 7, 2023
[372] "Myron B. Pitts: Former 71st student makes military history with rise to general" The Fayetteville Observer, April 4, 2020
[373] Operation Golden Pheasant was an emergency deployment of U.S. troops to Honduras. The deployment was in response to Nicaraguan attacks on Contra logistics in Honduras. 82d Airborne Division Brigade task force of two battalions conducted a

That night, the family knew something was going on when Francis did not return home from work. On the evening news, they saw that his unit was a part of the deployment of intermixed troops heading to Honduras. The different units were a part of what was being called rigorous "training exercises" at the border of Honduras and Nicaragua to deter the Sandinista troops, who were invading the Honduras border.[374]

The training exercises accomplished what the US military set out to do: have the Sandinista troops withdraw. The Sandinista government and the Contra leaders negotiated a truce, and by the end of March, the 27th Infantry had returned to Fort Ord, California, and the paratroopers of the 504th had returned to Fort Bragg.

The next family move would be a pivotal point for BG Quander. The family headed north to Washington D.C., where Lt. Col. Quander was working at the Pentagon. BG Quander was in eleventh grade when the Gulf War broke out. This was a turning point for the teenager. Operation Desert Storm was under way. The video of those men and women overseas, coupled with living in the Capital region, the heart of democracy, made a powerful impression on him. He believed the U.S. service members' work was laudable and admirable. It was then he decided he would follow in his father's footsteps.[375]

When he told his father, the response he received was not expected. His father wanted to make sure he was joining the military for the right reasons and told BG Quander not to go into the military just because he was in it. He wanted to make sure BG Quander wasn't doing it for him and that he was doing it for himself. There were multiple conversations on the subject. His father encouraged him to apply to universities to become a civil engineer.

But BG Quander was adamant about attending a military school. His dad took him to West Point where he could see what life was like at a military academy. It was at West Point where he fell in love with the mission of the academy. He was hooked.

BG Quander was accepted to West Point, where he received his Bachelor of Science in Civil Engineering. During his time at West Point, two professors had a significant impact on his academic and military life.

The first was Fred Black. He was instrumental in helping cadets like BG Quander transition to the Military Academy and grow and develop. Black would take time out of his day to chat with Quander to let him know he was there to help develop him.

---

parachute insertion and airland operation- Globalsecurity.org https://www.globalsecurity.org/military/ops/golden_pheasant.htm
[374] Operation Golden Pheasant (1988) Hillsborough County Veterans Memorial Park, Historical Marker Data Base. https://www.hmdb.org/m.asp?m=194762
[375] BG Quander conversation with authors. February 7, 2023

The teachings and leadership of Fred Meyer, a Civil Engineer professor, strengthened and supported BG Quander to becoming an engineering officer. BG Quander credits both men for making him the successful student he was and the soldier he has become.

BG Quander says it takes a village to nurture cadets. He always knew if he was having a bad day, he had Black to speak with, as well as his classmates. He credited his company mates as being "absolutely instrumental" in his development at West Point.

After he graduated, he was commissioned as an engineer officer in 1995. He attended the Engineer Officer Basic Course at Fort Leonard Wood, Missouri, and then completed Ranger School enroute to his first assignment, the 82nd Airborne Division at Fort Bragg, North Carolina. His career in the military took him overseas to the Republic of Korea, the Middle East, and Central Asia. He had several command and staff positions in the United States.[376]

Operation Blind Date

During his mid-tour leave from South Korea, BG Quander flew back to visit his parents in North Carolina, where his dad was working as a Junior ROTC Instructor. It was a two week leave. His dad told him he wanted him to accompany him to his boss' headquarters. BG Quander went along to spend some time with his father.

While at his boss's headquarters, BG Quander walked into a building with his father, who had to go upstairs to his office. In the lobby was Captain Melonie Ingram. She was a stunning, friendly, outgoing woman. They had nice conversation, and he made sure he was very formal, very stoic, and very respectful since she was of higher military rank. He was a first lieutenant at the time.

The two talked for about 45 minutes when his father came down. BG Quander gave a cordial goodbye to Captain Ingram, and they left in his father's car. His dad asked what BG Quander thought of Captain Ingram. BG Quander said that she was nice and pleasant. His dad was a bit more direct and asked BG Quander if he asked Captain Ingram out on a date. BG Quander said no because it would have been too forward, and she was a Captain, and he was a First Lieutenant. His dad then asked if he would like to go out with her. BG Quander said yes but did not know how to go about it after just an initial conversation.

When the two arrived at the Quander house, BG Quander's father called Captain Ingram.

"Captain Ingram, I've got a personal question to ask you," said his father. "How would you like to go out with my son?"

BG Quander could not hear what was being said on the landline phone.

Captain Ingram told his father she would like to go out with BG Quander.

---

[376] United States Military Academy, West Point, 79th Commandant, U.S. Corps of Cadets, Biography

Once she said yes, he put her on speaker phone, turned to BG Quander, and said loudly, "Hey, Mark, she said yes." BG Quander turned beat red. They agreed to a first date, which would happen a few days later. One week later, he flew back to South Korea.

In 1999, BG Quander was back in the United States. It was a whirlwind romance for Captain Ingram and BG Quander. The blind date that sparked their relationship would be the last and most personal operation for BG Quander's father. He passed away in March of 1999.

BG Quander proposed to Captain Ingram in July and then married short time after. The two spent the first three years of their marriage apart. BG Quander served in the 101st Airborne Division at Fort Campbell, Kentucky, while his wife, Melonie, attended graduate school in Philadelphia. Soon after BG Quander assumed company command, the twin towers were hit in New York. It would be an early test of their relationship and BG Quander's leadership. BG Quander would deploy to Afghanistan as part of Task Force Rakkasan in support of Operation Enduring Freedom. As a Company Commander, he would take part in one of the first operations where U.S. Soldiers were called to strike back at the Taliban and Al Qaeda forces.[377] BG Quander served again in Afghanistan, supporting Operation Enduring Freedom in 2002.

BG Quander's military career took him to Afghanistan and several tours in Iraq, where he saw the devastation and casualties of war. When reflecting on his numerous deployments, BG Quander said the mission to Haiti was the most impactful because of the devastation.[378]

The earthquake in 2010 left an indelible impression on BG Quander. He said the loss of life was on a magnitude he had not seen before.[379] The subsequent devastation in Turkey and Syria after a magnitude 7.8 earthquake in 2023, followed by the crackdown on developers[380] in Turkey, reminds him of that mission to Haiti.

His brigade spent a lot of time clearing and opening roads and doing surveys. They also had a dive detachment working to get the Port-au-Prince open, because most of the commerce in Haiti arrives through the port, not the airfield.

---

[377] Operation Anaconda SGM Patrick R. McGuire OEF, Operation Anaconda, Afghanistan, Unclassified. 03/07/2002-08/22/2002
[378] BG Quander phone conversation with author, February 7, 2023
[379] BG Quander phone conversation with author, February 7, 2023
[380] Natasha Turak, "Turkey's devastating earthquake comes at a critical time for the country's future", CNBC   https://www.cnbc.com/2023/02/09/turkey-earthquake-comes-at-a-critical-time-for-the-countrys-future.html

It's not what you think, it's how you think

BG Quander's love for learning made him the perfect candidate for advancement. The military always encouraged military personnel to pursue education and professional certifications to develop their skills.

Through the years, BG Quander earned his Masters in engineering management from Missouri University of Science and Technology to sharpen his technical skills and thinking.

When he was part of the Joint Chiefs of Staff Internship program, he attended Georgetown for one year, where he earned his Masters in policy management. The engagement of currently serving practitioners in their field, and their adjunct professors there at night, helped sharpen his thinking. They were taught it's not *what* you think; it's *how* you think, and how you address something.[381] These teachings were not new to BG Quander, whose grandparents stressed to him the value of education and critical thinking.

Prior to attending Georgetown, BG Quander approached his thinking from a tactical perspective. His godfather used to tell him when you go from Captain to Major, it's like you're a horse racing with its blinders on. But then, when the horse is done with the race, the blinders are taken off, and the horse realizes there's so much more around it. BG Quander says this analogy described what he experienced when he learned how to change his way of thinking at Georgetown.

BG Quander was taught it wasn't about his company, platoon, brigade, or operation. It was about the nation, and it was about the Treasury Department and the State Department and other departments in the United States government he had never even heard of before. This whole world approach to solving complex problems became a part of his critical thinking. The military was just a small piece of it. They were at Georgetown to sharpen their thinking, which would enable them to sharpen their opinions.

This education was reinforced by the experiences he had while working at the Joint Chiefs Staff, or the Secretary of Defense Staff. During that time, he was working on policy issues for the Iraq division of the Joint Staff. He would visit various departments like the State Department and, Treasury Department, and other federal agencies weekly. These experiences helped him see the big picture in the breakdown and allotment of the federal budget.

His educational journey and accomplishments led him to become commandant of the U.S. Army Engineer School at Fort Leonard Wood, Missouri, in July 2019.

---

[381] BG Quander conversation with authors, February 7, 2023

Quander Connection

It would be during one of his deployments that BG Quander would make the connection of just how vast the Quander family was. When he would go to the Quander family reunions as a child he did not understand the size and scope of how large his family was. Serving in the 307th Engineer Battalion, which supported the *504th Infantry Brigade*, he met Leo A. Brooks, Jr., who was one of the battalion commanders. The two men chatted and Brooks, Jr. casually mentioned he was related to the Quanders. Then it clicked. BG Quander remembered when he was deployed to Korea, he was to support a battalion that was previously led by BG Vincent K. Brooks, the younger brother of Leo A. Brooks, Jr. He had crossed paths with cousins and didn't even realize it.

BG Mark Quander and BG Vincent Brooks in Al Faw Palace in Baghdad on August 13, 2007.

The connection grew stronger when BG Quander was on the Joint Chiefs of Staff. Vincent was leaving the Joint Chiefs when BG Quander came on. The cousins have built a relationship today where their families were represented in BG Quander's Brigadier General promotion ceremony.

Before his confirmation, BG Vincent Brooks mailed a package to BG Quander. Inside the package was a warm note and several items, including a pair of Brigadier General epaulets, 1 subdued one-star rank, and 1 silver one-star rank. In the note, BG Brooks explained the insignia of an Army Brigadier General were all family heirlooms – having been worn before in their family. The subdued insignia was on Vince's uniform in Qatar and Iraq. The epaulets were also Vincent's. The silver 1 star was first worn by his father, Leo A. Brooks, Sr., during his promotion on 1 July 1978. BG Brooks explained he proudly donned it upon his frocking on 6 October 2002.

BG Mark C. Quander Promotion Ceremony February 14, 2020.
(From Left to Right) BG Vincent R. Brooks, BG Mark C. Quander, Major General Linda A. Singh, BG Errick Services
Source: Lynda Yezzi

BG Quander wore the epaulets on his white shirt and placed the silver 1 star on his beret during his promotion ceremony on 14 February 2020.

His wife Melonie and mom placed BG Vincent Brooks' epaulets on his Army Service Uniform.

Melonie Quander (wife) and Gail Quander (mother) placing the epaulets on BG Mark Quander's Army Service Uniform. Daughter Grace looking on. February 14, 2020
Source: Lynda Yezzi

In his promotion speech, BG Quander acknowledged those who came before him, and his loved ones who were a part of his journey.

"(I am) a product of my many influences — mostly my faith, my family, and my friends, with the latter two really only being differentiated by relation," Quander said. "My faith, which is strong and important for me, has given me strength and perseverance to endure the tough times, but also grounded in the good ones. My family — both immediate and extended — have allowed me to serve my country in ways that have made this possible."[382]

A year later, on May 24, 2021, another Brooks/Quander connection was made when BG Quander assumed duties as the 79th Commandant of Cadets at West Point. Cousin Leo A. Brooks, Jr. was West Point's 68th Commandant.

It was a warm welcome home for BG Quander, who was thrilled at the opportunity to give back to the institution that helped shape him. BG Quander hoped he could nurture and support the cadets just as Fred Black, did for him. One of the cadets he was in charge of was his niece on his wife's side. She graduated West Point in 2022.

BG Quander hopes his daughter, who wants to be a computer software engineer, and the cadets he is responsible for, learn that the greatest lesson in life is simple.

"Do what you're passionate about, and if you find out what you're passionate about and you follow your passion, you'll never work a day in your life. Also, take advantage of the opportunities you may have that others may not have."

---

[382] "Making history: Quander pins on brigadier general, his family's fourth general officer". February 20, 2020, U.S. Army Fort Leonard Wood Press Center https://ftleonardwoodpresscenter.com/making-history-quander-pins-on-brigadier-general-his-familys-fourth-general-officer/

Chapter Three
Defender of Civil Rights and Liberties

Nellie May Quander was one of the leading Black voices in the women's suffrage movement and education. Her drive and determination were fueled by the lessons she learned from her parents, Civil War veteran John Pierson Quander, a direct descendant of Nancy and Charles Quander, and Hannah Bruce Ford Quander, a direct descendant of West Ford.

Nellie was described as an eager student graduating with honors from Miner Normal School in 1901. The educational institution was created to train young Black American women to become teachers. That year, in September, she taught first and second grade at Garrison Elementary school. Nellie continued to work as a teacher when she enrolled and attended Howard University in 1910. She majored in history, economics, and political science. When Quander attended college, only a third of one percent of Black Americans and five percent of White Americans attended college.[383]

During her time at Howard, she became a member of the Alpha Kappa Alpha (AKA) in 1910. AKA was the nation's first Black sorority and was founded at Howard University on January 15, 1908. The sorority was rushing[384] for members for their second pledge class. Nellie signed up and was initiated 4 to 6 weeks later. Nellie liked the group of women because they represented her beliefs in helping the community and women's rights. Their symbol, the three-leafed ivy plant represented what they stood for: strength, endurance, and vitality.[385] These three qualities would be seen throughout Nellie's life. She became chapter president in 1911 and graduated magna cum laude in June of 1912 with a BA in history, economics, and political science at age 32.

Alpha Kappa Alpha's future became uncertain when there was a vote to change the name of the sorority as well as the symbols and standards. The disagreement led to some women withdrawing from the sorority. Those women who left formed the Delta Sigma Theta Sorority.

Not to be deterred, Nellie reached out to alumni members of the sorority who graduated to support her in her pursuit to incorporate the sorority. According to AKA history, Nellie researched the structure of Greek organizations and came up with the conclusion that Alpha Kappa Alpha must become incorporated as a non-profit to guarantee its future. Incorporating AKA, it gave the sorority the ability to create additional chapters around the country and the world. This would help the sorority expand on its mandate for community service support for Black Americans. Quander, along with six other women, incorporated Alpha Kappa Alpha on January 29, 1913.

---

[383] African American Registry, Nellie Quander
[384] Rushing is a term used by both sororities and fraternities to advertise their group in hopes of attracting possible members.
[385] Erica Williams, "To (Not) Be on One Acord: The Ivy Leaf Footwear and Mobility Alpha Kappa Alpha" endnotes, May 11, 2020 https://humanities.wustl.edu/news/not-be-one-accord-ivy-leaf-footwear-and-mobility-alpha-kappa-alpha-sorority-incorporated#:~:text=This%20is%20the%20official%20symbol,their%20entrance%20into%20the%20organization.

Alpha Kappa Alpha photo, 1913
Nellie Quander, fourth from left bottom row
Source: Howard University

Nellie was elected as the sorority's first national president in 1913 at the first Boulé[386] at Howard University. For the next six years, she appointed members to help implement the sorority's national expansion plan; she created and wrote the sorority constitution's preamble.

Fighting to Be Included

Nellie may have been petite in size (5/1' 100 pounds)[387] , but that did not mean she was a push over. If Nellie believed in something, she would go all in. When it came to a women's right to vote, Nellie believed it would benefit communities of color, because Black women would vote for candidates who they believed would help their communities through legislation and representation. Nellie believed women's electoral equality included Black women regardless of Jim Crow Laws.

In 1912, the National American Woman Suffrage Association (NAWSA) appointed woman suffragist Alice Paul to organize a suffrage parade.[388] Alice, along with Lucy Barns, were the chairs of NAWSA's Congressional Committee, which planned the parade.

---

[386] Boulé means Greek Council meeting
[387] Clare M. Sheridan, "Biographical Sketch of Nellie M. Quander"
https://search.alexanderstreet.com/view/work/bibliographic_entity%7Cbibliographic_details%7C4078813/biographical-sketch-nellie-m-quander
[388] National Park Service, "Alice Paul"

The date of the event would be March 3, 1913, the day before President Woodrow Wilson's inauguration. The plan was to have thousands of female suffragists march down Pennsylvania Avenue. The procession of participants was laid out to show the accomplishments of women worldwide. Delegates marched representing their states, organizations, professions, and universities. But Black women were not initially invited due to White female suffragists from the South objecting to their inclusion. They threatened not to participate.[389]

Alice Paul wrote about her concerns about having Black women participate in the parade to Alice Stone Blackwell, recording secretary of the NAWSA and chief editor of the *Woman's Journal*, America's leading women's rights newspaper.

In a letter dated January 15, 1913, Alice explained her concerns were not based on race, for she was raised a Quaker and supported Black men and women's rights. But she was afraid, given the location of the March in the South, the racial discrimination against Black women might spark unneeded controversy.

"...I hope that I am viewing this present question with an unbiased mind. It seems to me that it would be unfortunate if we have any large number of negroes in our Suffrage Procession. The prejudice against them is so strong in this section of the country that I believe a large part, if not a majority, of our white marchers will refuse to participate if negroes in any number formed a part of the parade.

"However, the participation of negroes would have a most disastrous effect, as far as our cause is concerned, upon the host of spectators gathered here at the time of the Inauguration, and there the Southern element in the crowds at Washington will be unusually large would make it particularly difficult for us to have any considerable number of negroes in our procession. The feeling against them here is so bitter that as far as I can see, we must have a white process, or a negro procession, or no procession at all. I can see no way in which we can affect a compromise on the subject.

"It is extremely sad, it seems to be, that our women are so prejudiced. We cannot, however, ignore the fact that such prejudice exists and that it makes it impossible for a procession of both white and colored people marching together to take place. I think this suffrage proclamation will help the suffrage cause, and therefore I wish to see it go through..."[390]

During this time, in her role as president of Alpha Kappa Alpha, Nellie Quander wrote to Alice Paul to let her know she had women interested in participating and requested a place in the procession. That letter was dated February 15, 1913.

"...there were a number of college women of Howard University who would like to participate in the women suffrage procession," but *"do not wish to enter if we must meet with discrimination on account of race affiliation."[391]*

---

[389] National Park Service, "Places of Alice Paul"
[390] Library of Congress
[391] Library of Congress

Nellie did not receive an answer from Alice Paul.

Two days later, Nellie followed up with a second letter demanding the participation of the 18 women. She requested the group of women to be included in a "desirable place in the college women's section."

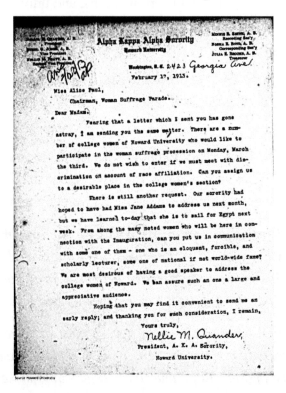

Nellie's unanswered requests from Paul were just one example of what the NAACP's newspaper wrote about:

"The women's suffrage party had a hard time settling the status of Negroes in the Washington parade. At first, Negro callers were received coolly at headquarters. Then, they were told to register but found that the registry clerks were usually out. Finally, an order went out to segregate them in the parade, but telegrams and protests poured in, and eventually, the colored women marched according to their State and occupation without let or hindrance."- The Crisis, *vol 5, no. 6, April 1913, page 267.*[392]

The news of this discrimination reached the national office. Anna Howard Shaw, the president of NAWSA, sent a telegram on February 28th to Alice Paul, ordering her to stop discouraging black participation.[393]

---

[392] "The Easter Crisis" April 1913 The Crisis, Vol. 5, No. 6 (April, 1913) (brown.edu)
[393] Library of Congress

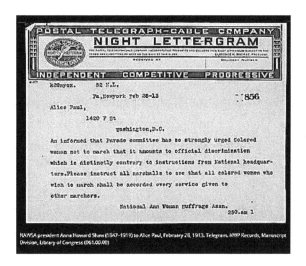

NAWSA president Anna Howard Shaw (1847-1919) to Alice Paul, February 28, 1913. Telegram. NWP Records, Manuscript Division, Library of Congress (061.00.00)

To appease both the Black American and the Southern White suffragists, Paul segregated the parade.[394] She asked African Americans to march at the back and strategically positioned white men between white and Black women.

It is unclear if Alice replied to Nellie personally, but on March 3, 1913, Nellie and her 18 fellow suffragists marched that day. According to the NAACP newspaper, *The Crisis,* twenty-five students from Howard University who were members of the Delta Sigma Theta sorority also participated and marched in their cap and gown with the university women, and six graduates of universities, including Mary Church Terrell[395].

There is mixed reporting on all Black American women marched in the back of the procession. Stories of Black women like journalist, civil rights advocate, and feminist, Ida B. Wells were not welcomed by their state to march (in her case, Illinois). But once the procession started and the group marched by her, Ida joined that group and marched with two white women who supported her fight for their common cause.

Expanding Alpha Kappa Alpha

Nellie Quander's mission to grow her sorority and its influence and charity around the nation continued as she went to Howard part-time and worked at Garrison Elementary as a teacher. She served as the sorority's Supreme Basileus,[396] where she worked with Founder Beulah Burke in the founding and organization of the Beta, Gamma, and Delta Chapters. On November 25, 1916, she personally established the sixth chapter of the sorority, the Zeta Chapter, at Wilberforce University. The dream of her beloved sorority expanding to further its support of Black American women at colleges and in communities was

---

[394] National Park Service, "Places of Alice Paul"

[395] Mary Church Terrell was one of the nation's leading Black American suffragists. She was the first Black American woman to graduate with a Bachelor's degree, rather than a 2-year ladies' degree. Mary was the first African-American woman in the United States to be appointed to the school board of a major city, serving in the District of Columbia until 1906. Terrell was a charter member of the National Association for the Advancement of Colored People (1909) and the Colored Women's League of Washington (1892). She helped found the National Association of Colored Women (1896) and served as its first national president, and she was a founding member of the National Association of College Women (1923).

[396] Supreme Basileus is the highest office in the sorority.

quickly becoming a reality. Incentivizing education, in 1913, Quander established at Howard University the first Alpha Kappa Alpha scholarship for a senior graduating from the liberal arts school who had the highest-grade point average.

Nellie relinquished the office of Supreme Basileus and was elected the first Eastern Region organizer in 1919. After graduation, Ms. Quander advised her Alpha chapter long before the graduate advisor role was established and was a member of the Xi Omega chapter in Washington, D.C.

Mississippi Health Project

Some of the Xi Omega sisters joined other members of AKA to help set up mobile clinics to inoculate Black children and adults against diphtheria and smallpox, as well as provide supplies, treatment, and health education in the 1930s. The program they created and sponsored was called the Mississippi Health Project.[397] The Health Project emphasized access to basic healthcare, and benefitted both social and economic planning for the country. Thomas Parran, U.S. Surgeon General (April 6, 1936-April 6, 1948), recognized the Mississippi Delta Health Project as the first volunteer health project in the rural South, calling it, "one of the greatest efforts of volunteer public health."[398]

The program ran for six years up until the start of World War II. Because of Jim Crow Laws, Black women were not allowed to stay in hotels in the South. A network of black homeowners welcomed the women into their homes so they could help their community.

The sorority's health committee created a series of reports on the health and education of rural Black Americans.[399] This project was so successful, that, in October 2021, AKA revisited resurrecting the program and, along with partners Delta Health Center, Walgreens, and Mallory Community Health Center, established Mississippi Health Project II, where they created clinics that provided COVID-19 testing, COVID vaccines, flu vaccines, HIV testing, vital signs screening and breast examinations to community residents in rural Mississippi.[400]

---

[397] The Alpha Kappa Alpha Sorority Health Project. Alpha Kappa Alpha Sorority, Incorporated. 1938.
[398] National Institute for Health, NIH Record, Volume LVIII, No. 6, March 24, 2006
[399] The Alpha Kappa Alpha Sorority Health Project. Alpha Kappa Alpha Sorority, Incorporated. 1938.
[400] "AKA revisits its Model for Community Health Care", National Museum of African American History & Culture, https://www.searchablemuseum.com/the-mississippi-health-project-ii-aka-revisits-its-model-for-community-health-care

Love of Teaching

Nellie continued to teach at Garrison Elementary for 20 years between 1901 and 1921 before becoming a teacher at Robert Gould Shaw[401] Junior High School in Washington, D.C. where in 1921 she was assigned to help create the junior high school level in the D.C. public Schools, Colored Division. After the creation of the junior high, Nellie was reassigned to Shaw Junior High School. It was there that she organized the city's first School Safety Patrol Unit (crossing guards) in the mid-1920s. She continued to sponsor the activity for 25 years. Her creation and support for the crossing guard unit garnered an award from the American Automobile Association. During her years of teaching, Nellie was granted time off to enhance her education and perform economic research.

Nellie took a one-year leave of absence in the 1914-15 school year to study at Columbia University's Washington, DC, extension campus. Her thesis title was: *A Study of Insurance Among Negroes in the State of Virginia.*[402]

She was granted a second leave of absence in the 1916-17 school year to serve as a special field agent for the Children's Bureau of the Department of Labor.

During this time, Nellie spearheaded a study requested by the Women's Clubs of New Castle County, Delaware, which was looking to create an institution that would serve the disabled. The study would be used in the preparation of that institution. Nellie studied the social and economic conditions among mentally disabled persons in the county for them.

While teaching summer school, Nellie earned a certificate in social work from New York University. To expand her knowledge in economics so she could advocate and be a stronger voice for the Black community, Nellie studied economics at the University of Washington State for two summers. All of this education helped her in her community affairs roles, and in finding solutions to help.

In 1936, Nellie's educational path took her overseas, where she graduated with a certificate in economics from Uppsala University in Sweden.[403] While in Europe, she attended the International Conference on Social Work held in London. These experiences and lessons helped her in her fight for racial and economic equality and opportunity when she came back home.

Community Champion

Never marrying or having children of her own, Nellie dedicated her life to helping strengthen communities of color. She was active in the Readers Research Club, which promoted women's intellectual

---

[401] Robert Gould Shaw served as colonel of the 54 Massachusetts, one of the first Black regiments to fight in the Civil War. National Park Service. He believed the 54th Regiment could prove itself in battle and refused to have his men used for manual labor or raiding. https://www.nps.gov/people/robert-g-shaw.htm
[402] Columbia University
[403] Biography of Nellie M. Quander, 1880-1961, Biographical database of Black Women Suffragists
https://search.alexanderstreet.com/view/work/bibliographic_entity%7Cbibliographic_details%7C4078813/biographical-sketch-nellie-m-quander

growth.[404] In making sure Black History was told and supported, she was a founding member of the Afro-American History Story Telling Association. Her life's work advocating for educational and social equality could be seen through her participation and membership in the NAACP, the National Association of Colored Women, and the Republican Party.

One of the organizations she worked with was the Young Women's Christian Association (YWCA). This non-profit was one of the oldest and largest multicultural organizations that dedicated its efforts to bettering the lives of women, girls, and families.[405] Nellie was a board member and chairman of the Young Women's Department of the YWCA; she was also a member of the board of directors of the Phillis Wheatley YWCA, which operates an independent living facility for low-income, formerly homeless women. She was also chairman of the Business Professional and Industrial Committee of the Phillis Wheatley YWCA.

Nellie served as a special industrial field secretary of the National YWCA to shed light and push for reform of improving the working conditions of women. As a member of the Women's War Work Council for the national YWCA, she helped support military troops with sites for rest and recreation. In the summer of 1918, The Women's War Work Council assigned her to conduct a survey of the social and economic conditions affecting Negro women in Detroit.[406]

During her time at YWCA, the organization encouraged its members to speak out against lynching and mob violence, as well as push for interracial cooperation and to protect Black people's basic civil rights.[407] The YWCA pledged it would work for the integration and full participation of minority groups in every phase of life in the United States.[408] Nellie served for more than 50 years with the YMCA until her passing in 1961.

In the 1940's women represented 6 percent of all boards.[409] Nellie was the first woman trustee and secretary of the Board of Trustees of Lincoln Temple Memorial Church (Congregational).[410] She was also the director of the Miner Community Center, which served women and children.

An active supporter of unions, Nellie was a delegate from the teacher's union to the Women's Trade Union League and was president of the teacher union's Center for Racial Justice. In the 1930s, Black teachers were paid roughly half of what white teachers were paid in the District of Columbia and the

---

[404] Clare M. Sheridan, "Biographical Sketch of Nellie M. Quander"
https://search.alexanderstreet.com/view/work/bibliographic_entity%7Cbibliographic_details%7C4078813/biographical-sketch-nellie-m-quander
[405] YWCA, About YWCA
[406] Biographical Sketch of Nellie Quander, Clare M. Sheridan. Fl. 2021
[407] YWCA, About YWCA USA History
[408] YWCA, About YWCA USA History
[409] OECD, "What big data can tell us about women on boards" https://www.oecd.org/gender/data/what-big-data-can-tell-us-about-women-on-boards.htm
[410] Clare M. Sheridan, "Biographical Sketch of Nellie M. Quander"
https://search.alexanderstreet.com/view/work/bibliographic_entity%7Cbibliographic_details%7C4078813/biographical-sketch-nellie-m-quander

seventeen states that mandated segregated public schools.[411] By the end of World War II, the average pay of Black teachers rose to 56% of what white teachers were paid. 85% of Black teachers were paid the same amount by 1950.[412]

Her AKA sisters always sought her advice. In the 1961 issue of the official magazine of AKA, *Ivy Leaf*, Nellie Quander offered her sorority sisters a passage from the great national Latin epic poem "Aeneid"[413] on blazing a trail and making your own destiny, something Nellie strove to do in all areas of her life.

When I'm asked to give AKA a message for the future, I think of Virgil's advice to Aeneas, 'Only go on, and where the way leads, direct thy path.'

---

[411] Cambridge University Press, "Do We Have Any Men to Follow in Her Footsteps?" February 14, 2018
[412] Cambridge University Press, "Do We Have Any Men to Follow in Her Footsteps?" February 14, 2018
[413] Virgil, "Aeneid" is an epic poem which tells the story of the Trojan prince Aeneas who fled after the destruction of Troy to go to the Italian shores to create a new city (called Alba Longa).

James W. Quander a fighter for social equity, was no stranger to adversity. When he was about to turn six, his parents, John Edward and Maude Pearson Quander, were told their young son would not live past his tenth birthday because he was diagnosed with juvenile diabetes.

The parents hoped insulin, which was discovered in 1921 and manufactured on a mass scale by Eli Lilly in October 1923,[414] would help extend their son's life. James. W. was offered insulin in 1925 and was one of the earliest users. James W. said throughout his life, "Diabetes is not a death sentence, but rather a challenge to live."[415]

James W. grew up in Washington, D.C., which had Jim Crow laws mandating segregation in public schools, recreation facilities, and churches. These laws would fuel James W. to voice his demands for change as a child through his adulthood.

In 1913, Blacks and European Americans immediately fought back against President Wilson's institution of re-segregation in all federal government agencies. Five years later, on April 19, 1918, James W. was born into the revived system of rigid racial segregation and a new era most identified as "The New Negro," describing the Black men and women who resisted the Jim Crow Laws in the 1920s and 1930s.[416]

This term started when the Negro soldiers were returning home after fighting in World War I; they were hailed as heroes and liberators for democracy. When they returned from battle, these men were not welcomed with equality. Instead, they were faced with rigid racism, and they were determined to resist the impact of President Wilson's policies with a new and more forceful attitude. These men were called, "The New Negro," a term which would define the movement for Black equality. Later in life, James W. would also be considered a "New Negro."

James W. had no hesitation in voicing his opposition to segregation. One day, when he was around 11 or 12, James W. walked into St. Paul's Catholic Church to pray a novena.[417] He walked into the church and dipped his right pointer finger and middle finger in the cool holy water held in the holy water font located on the right side of the door frame. He solemnly placed his two wet fingertips and blessed himself with the sign of the cross, by quickly taping his forehead, the center of the chest, the left side of the chest, and the

---

[414] Diabetes UK, "100 Years of Insulin"
https://www.diabetes.org.uk/research/research-impact/insulin#:~:text=15%20October%201923%20%E2%80%93%20insulin%20produced%20on%20a%20mass%20scale&text=Eli%20Lilly%20become%20the%20first,first%20commercial%20supply%20of%20insulin

[415] Author correspondence with Rohulamin Quander, January 4, 2023

[416] Marya Annette McQuirter, PhD. "A Brief History of African Americans in Washington, DC", Cultural Tourism DC
https://www.culturaltourismdc.org/portal/a-brief-history-of-african-americans-in-washington-dc

[417] A novena is a prayer that is made up of nine days of prayer usually to ask God for special prayer requests or petitions. It's a practice that goes back to the times of Apostles. "How to pray a Novena- Novena Prayers & Catholic Devotion."
https://www.praymorenovenas.com/how-to-pray-a-novena

right side of this chest. The hostilities of the outside world would melt away for the young religious man when he entered God's house.

Somberly, he walked down the center aisle towards the front of the church, where he chose a pew. It was then that an usher stopped James W. to move to the back of the Church. James W. refused.

The priest who was going to lead the prayer also walked up to James W. and told him, "To go to his own church".[418] The young Quander responded with conviction, "I *am* in my own church. This is a Catholic church, and I am a Catholic, and I am making this novena… I'm not going anywhere."[419]

James W. was encouraged at a young age by his family to stand up for himself and be the best he could be in every facet of his life. This included his faith and education. His parents and grandparents stressed to him that education was one way he could enhance his life. Neither one of his parents went to college. They wanted him and all his siblings to have that educational opportunity.

James W. graduated from Paul Laurence Dunbar High School, the first all-academic high school for Blacks in the United States, which was based in D.C. The high school was founded in 1870 and originally called the Preparatory High School for Colored Youth after the Black community requested the all-white school board to create a high school opportunity for Black students.[420] This high school curriculum required four years of Math, Science, History, English, and Latin. This was unusual for Black higher education. High Schools for Black students varied anywhere from 1-3 years. In North Carolina, for example, most high schools were limited to one or two years.[421]

Unlike some high schools for Black students, which taught trades, Dunbar was about providing a classics-based education.[422] The four-year curriculum was highly successful, and the proof was in the graduating classes. Around 90% of those students who graduated from Dunbar attended college.[423]

The school's performance was one of the reasons why some Black families moved to Washington, D.C., so their children could attend it. Those who attended Dunbar High School were a select group of children whose parents saw the value of formal education.[424]

[418] "One Blessing Upon Another for Trailblazing Couple Who were Among First Students to Integrate Sacred Heart School in 1950." Catholic Standard, July 2, 2022

[419] "One Blessing Upon Another for Trailblazing Couple Who were Among First Students to Integrate Sacred Heart School in 1950." Catholic Standard, July 2, 2022

[420] "Dunbar History", P.L. Dunbar Bar Middle School for Innovation https://www.lcsedu.net/schools/dms/about/dunbar-history

[421] Flora Hatley Wadelington, "Segregation in the 1920's "Assigned Places" https://www.ncpedia.org/history/20th-Century/segregation-1920s

[422] "Dunbar, H.S. (Washington, D.C.)", African American Registry (AAREG), Dunbar H.S., (Washington D.C.) Opens - African American Registry (aaregistry.org)

[423] "Dunbar, H.S. (Washington, D.C.)", African American Registry (AAREG), Dunbar H.S., (Washington D.C.) Opens - African American Registry (aaregistry.org)

[424] "Dunbar History", P.L. Dunbar Bar Middle School for Innovation

New Negro"

James W. graduated from Miner Teachers College in 1940 and was handpicked to be groomed for a professional position within the FBI. This was part of "the New Negro Movement." School administrators helped him craft his resume and prepared him for an expected "hostile" interview.[425] James W. knew there would be little chance of getting a job at the FBI, but he had to try. His interview would make the point that a Black man was just as qualified as a White man to do the job.

James W., wearing his best suit, walked in for his interview. At the end of the conversation, the White interviewer said, "We do not hire Negroes for these (FBI) positions. We will refer your application to the U.S. Post Office."[426]

Not surprised by the statement, James W. replied, "If I had wanted to work for the Post Office, I would have applied there."[427] The interviewer, a woman, stood up and, facing James W. said, "Young man, you're too uppity and apparently don't know your place. Good day!" James W. did get hired by the U.S. Post Office and worked in several other federal governmental agencies during his 33-year federal service career.

James W.'s fights against discriminatory hiring practices and racial segregation took him to the picket line. He participated in a peaceful campaign led by the New Negro Alliance (NNA)[428], against Sanitary Grocery, a white-owned business where Black customers were allowed to shop but were not employed. The protest was part of the Alliance's "Don't Buy Where You Can't Work."[429]

The Sanitary Grocery protest was a key peaceful picket in civil rights history. The company took the NNA to court and won an injunction to stop the protests. The NNA would not back down, and the court battle went all the way to the Supreme Court. *New Negro Alliance v. Sanitary Grocery Store* became a key court case in Black Americans' fight against discriminatory practices.

Sanitary Grocery's argument was the NNA had no legal right because the picketers did not work there. In 1938 the court, citing the First Amendment to the U.S. Constitution, i.e., freedom of speech, declared the NNA had the legal right regardless of the protestor's employment status at the grocer.[430] James W. also participated in smaller pickets against District Grocery Stores (DGS) and Piggly Wiggly for their hiring practices.[431]

---

[425] Rohulamin Quander, "The Quanders"
[426] Rohulamin Quander, "The Quanders"
[427] Rohulamin Quander, "The Quanders"
[428] The New Negro Alliance was formed in 1933 after John Aubrey Davis, boycotted the Hamburger Grill, a white-owned business which fired its three Black employees and replaced them with white workers. The protest was successful and within two days the establishment rehired those workers
[429] "New Negro Opinion Newspaper", Anacostia Community Museum, Smithsonian, https://anacostia.si.edu/collection/archives/sova-acma-10-012-3
[430] New Negro Alliance v. Sanitary Grocery Co., 303 U.S. 552 (1938) Justia US Supreme Court https://supreme.justia.com/cases/federal/us/303/552/
[431] Rohulamin Quander email correspondence with Author, January 8, 2023 and January 27, 2023

Joherra

James W. was working at the Post Office when a friend of his, introduced him to a woman named Joherra. It would be a meeting that would change his course in life.

Joherra Theresa Amin migrated to the United States from Barbados, British West Indies, on December 4, 1934, the first-born child of Oquindo O'Bryan and Mohammed Abdul Rohualamin. Oquindo's parents were Frederick Orlando O'Bryan and Florence Craigwell O'Bryan. Both parents were of mixed racial background, primarily Irish and Scottish, with an Afro-Caribbean mixture.

When Oquindo was 16, she was married in an arranged union to 32-year-old Mohammed Rohualamin Amin, an immigrant from Calcutta, India. Mohammed, along with his nine-year-old son, Elias, immigrated to Barbados when Mohammed was in his early 30's. Mohammed was a cloth merchant.

There was no Mosque in Barbados during that time, so Oquindo traveled to a friend's home, where an Imam[432] performed the ceremony. She wore a simple light white dress her sister-in-law Florence made. Mohammed wore his best traditional Muslim clothing. After the ceremony, the Indian neighborhood erupted in cheer. Men ahead of the carriage shouted happily, tossing candies to those watching.

The couple welcomed Joherra in 1920. She was the first of seven children born to the couple. Although Mohammed was a practicing Muslim, Oquindo's strong will determined that her children should all be raised as Catholics. He was always unhappy about her decision in that regard, and regularly introduced his children to Islam as they grew up.

Oquindo was not familiar with or raised in a home that practiced Indian culture or made Indian cuisine, so she cooked non-Indian food. Their servants and her husband would cook traditional meals. The warm, spicy aroma of the cooked goat or lamb would perfume the tropical breeze. Mohammed would cook it over a low fire in the front yard. The Indian community where they lived was small, and everyone knew each other. In 1929, Oquindo threw Mohammed out of their home for having a relationship with another woman. She would not stand for his disrespect. Having no money of her own, no job, and lacking the means to support her seven children, all under the age of 10 years, she yearned to go to America and find some type of job, so that she could provide her family a better life.

The family migrated to the United States over time. Oquindo immigrated in 1929, and the last of the seven children arrived in the United States in 1952/53.

Joherra lived in Manhattan and graduated from Julia Richmond high school in 1940. She was hired for a clerical position at the Urban League, but Joherra wanted more. Her goal was to work in the federal government. There would be more opportunities for her to grow.

---

[432] Imam is the title for a Muslim religious leader or chief

Under the Federal Fair Employment Law for African Americans[433], there was a push by the federal government to hire Black workers because economic studies showed the country's economy would be stronger as a direct result of Black Americans shifting from low-paying agricultural jobs to more skilled and better-paying jobs.[434] During World War II, Black Americans were hired in the defense industry.[435]

U.S. Census categories during that time did not include "Afro-Caribbean," which was Joherra's ethnicity, so she selected the "other" category as her race and ethnicity. As a result, Joherra was put in the "Black" category.

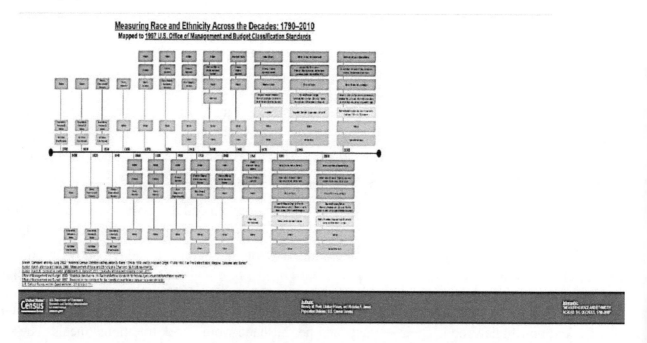

To this day, "Afro-Caribbean" is not included in the U.S. Census. In the 2020 Census, almost 50 million, or more than 1 in 7 people living in the U.S., filed in the "Other" category.[436]

Joherra filed her paperwork and was placed on a waiting list, but the wait was not long. A week after the bombing of Pearl Harbor, and the U.S. declared war, she received a telegram to report to her new job in Washington, DC, at the War Department (now the Department of Defense). Joherra would become one of

[433] "Employment for African Americans in the 1940s and 1950s: Hartford's G. Fox Department Store:, Document One "Federal Fair Employment Law for African Americans in the 1940's and 1950's. CT.gov Connecticut's Official State Website, https://portal.ct.gov/SDE/Publications/Labor/Employment-for-African-Americans-in-the-1940s-and-1950s-Hartfords-G-Fox-Department-Store/Documents
[434] Mary S. Bedell, "Employment and Income of Negro Workers- 1940-52" Bureau of Labor and Statistics https://www.bls.gov/opub/mlr/1953/article/pdf/employment-and-income-of-negro-workers-1940-52.pdf
[435] "Employment for African Americans in the 1940s and 1950s: Hartford's G. Fox Department Store:, Document One "Federal Fair Employment Law for African Americans in the 1940's and 1950's. CT.gov Connecticut's Official State Website, https://portal.ct.gov/SDE/Publications/Labor/Employment-for-African-Americans-in-the-1940s-and-1950s-Hartfords-G-Fox-Department-Store/Documents
[436] Hansi Lo Wang, "1 in 7 People are 'some Other Race' on the U.S. Census. That's a Big Data Problem", NPR, WAMU 88.5 American University Radio https://www.npr.org/2021/09/30/1037352177/2020-census-results-by-race-some-other-latino-ethnicity-hispanic

the many incoming civilians employed by the federal government. Between 1940-1945, the number of federal employees almost quadrupled.[437]

Not knowing a soul in Washington, D.C., Joherra looked to apply for housing through the Government Girl Housing Project. The location she hoped to live in was Arlington Farms, which had ten dormitories on the 108-acre site on the historic 1,100-acre grounds of the Custis-Lee family estate. But because of the color of her skin, she would not be allowed to apply there. All Black women, regardless of African heritage, were directed to apply at the Negro Girl register. The office was in the Northeast section of Washington, DC, where many Black families lived.

Joherra settled in nicely in the neighborhood and met a gentleman named Saxton Howard. He was her neighbor and was fond of her. Already engaged, he had a friend in mind for her to meet. It was his colleague in the Government Printing Office. James W.

On a chilly January 1942 day, James W. met Joherra. He was coming off a recent romantic breakup, and she was looking forward to meeting new people. There was no pressure on either one to make a love connection.

Little did they know after several Sunday visits, which included mass, their relationship would blossom. On Valentine's Day, 1942, Joherra asked him to be her guest at the Phyllis Wheatley YWCA (colored) dance. The night was full of laughter. It was that night she told her friends there, "I think that I have met my future husband."[438] The two were engaged several months later, in June. James W. popped the question while the two were walking past Gallaudet College in Washington, DC. They were married in December 1942 at St. Augustine Catholic Church by Father Hamilton.

James W. was told because he was a diabetic, fathering a child would be difficult, if not impossible.[439] But on December 4, 1943, Rohulamin was born in the segregated Black section of Garfield hospital.

Considered a little miracle, Rohulamin was his grandfather, John Edward Quander's little sidekick. John Edward adored Rohulamin, taking him everywhere and showing him off to all of his neighbors and friends. When Joherra went back to work after maternity leave, John Edward and Maude, his wife, cared for baby Rohulamin.

Between 1943-1954, James W. and Joherra welcomed three additional miracles, Joherra Quander Harris, (June 26, 1948); John Edward Quander, III, (February 13, 1951), and Ricardo Vincent Quander (December 26, 1954). The young Quander family during the early to mid-fifties would be witnesses and participants in history.

---

[437] Claudia Swain, "Standing Room Only: DC's WWII Housing Crunch" https://boundarystones.weta.org/2014/04/08/standing-room-only-dcs-wwii-housing-crunch
[438] Rohulamin Quander, email correspondence with author, January 24, 2022
[439] Rohulamin Quander, email correspondence with author, January 24, 2022

But, being a young father did not slow down James W. and his passion for voicing his support of equal rights. Because James W. had a young family, he was determined to fight for equality so his children and grandchildren would not have to grow up in a segregated world. One of those protests was the famous demonstration at the opening of the play, "Joan of Lorraine."

James W. joined protestors in front of George Washington University's Lisner Auditorium on October 29, 1946. "Joan of Lorraine" was a play from New York that was traveling to other theatres.

When lead actress Ingrid Bergman found out about the theater's segregation policies, she told reporters at a press event the day before the play's opening, "I will not come back here again until black people, just like white people, can come to the theater. We play for everybody. Everybody!"[440]

Bergman and her cast members joined forces and organized boycotts and protests with the Dramatists Guild and the Actors Equity Association. A letter in protest was signed by 22 of the cast members, including Bergman.[441]

Performers in the first production at the Lisner Auditorium, "Joan of Lorraine" signed a petition protesting the theater's segregation.
Courtesy: GWU Archives

The show did go on, but protests continued against the theater's racial segregation policies. The public pressure was effective, and in 1947, the University Board of Trustees announced the University would no longer racially bar Blacks from attending.

---

[440] "The Desegregation of George Washington University and the District of Columbia in Transition, 1946-1954 https://diversity.smhs.gwu.edu/sites/g/files/zaskib891/files/2021-11/Desegregation%20GWU%281%29.pdf
[441] "The Desegregation of George Washington University and the District of Columbia in Transition, 1946-1954 https://diversity.smhs.gwu.edu/sites/g/files/zaskib891/files/2021-11/Desegregation%20GWU%281%29.pdf

Changing Times but Challenges Remain

Demonstrations against racial segregation in DC proved to be effective in the early fifties for the Black community. James W. would read about protests organized by civil rights advocate, 88-year-old Mary Church Terrell, chairman of the Anti-Discrimination Committee coordinating committee. In 1952, Terrell led rallies where over 1,000 supporters would join her in her pursuit of ending segregation, targeting establishments that would refuse to serve Blacks.[442] A nine-month boycott and six-month picket line protest that year at Hecht's department store, whose basement lunch counter refused to serve Black customers, was successful. The store was desegregated. Terrell then set her sights on Thompson's cafeteria, which denied her service for the color of her skin.

Terrell's fight took her to the courts. The District of Columbia represented Terrell, and the company's lawyers fought the cases up to the Supreme Court. In 1953, *District of Columbia v. John R. Thompson Co., Inc.*, jurisdiction was only the District of Columbia, which meant it did not interfere with the Brown versus the Board of Education case they were currently hearing. In a unanimous 8-0 decision in 1953, the Supreme Court ruled to end segregation in all Washington, D.C., establishments that served the public.[443]

While segregation was no more and Blacks were legally granted equal admission, that did not mean the transition was easy. James W. would call the reluctance of some white establishments in opening their doors, the "unwelcome mat."[444]

Attitudes of some white proprietors did not change. The Quanders were selective in visiting new venues. They would eat at the Blue Mirror restaurant and enjoy movies at the downtown movie theaters. But Joherra and James W. were very protective of their young children, trying to shield them from racial hatred.

They frequented Highland Beach, a previous all-Black recreation site in Anne Arundel County, Maryland, that was founded in 1893 by Charles Douglass, a son of Frederick Douglass, Longview Beach in St. Mary's County, Maryland, where they owned a beach lot. The intentionally limited circle surrounding their children extended beyond their social circles. The parents would associate with families, and their children were highly educated. Most of those families had education tied to Dunbar High School, Howard University, or Miner Teacher's College background.

James W. and Joherra also made sure the children's friendship circle was representative of their Catholic faith. Both believed the combination of a solid faith in God and a good education were pillars of a solid foundation in life. They were active in church and community-sponsored events. James W. was determined his Black family would participate in the integrated festivities.[445] Joherra supported her

---

[442] Jackie Mansky, "How One Woman Helped End Lunch Counter Segregation in the Nation's Capital" June, 8, 2016, Smithsonian Magazine https://www.smithsonianmag.com/history/how-one-woman-helped-end-lunch-counter-segregation-nations-capital-180959345/
[443] Jackie Mansky, "How One Woman Helped End Lunch Counter Segregation in the Nation's Capital" June, 8, 2016, Smitsonian Magazine
[444] Rohulamin Quander email correspondence with author, January 8, 2023
[445] Rohulamin Quander email correspondence with author, January 4, 2023

husband, and they were determined to make a statement by using the facilities that were finally available for them.[446]

The family would pile into the station wagon and visit Joherra family in Brooklyn or Long Island. Joherra's family was fun-loving and very close. James W. enjoyed this connection because his own family was much more reserved.[447] The families would come together for holidays, Caribbean and West Indian celebrations, and summer vacations, renting a home in Atlantic City, New Jersey. The Quander family only vacationed in the South once because the environment was still very hostile towards Blacks.[448]

Dinners in the Quander home reflected the Caribbean, and Southern union of James and Joherra. Sunday dinners made by Joherra would vary. Southern fried chicken served with homemade hot rolls, pigeon peas, and rice mixed with meat gravy could also be served, or roast beef with gravy would fill the family table. The children's favorite, Joherra's yellow cake with chocolate icing, would always bring smiles.[449] Not a fork would be picked up until grace was said.

Joherra embraced American cooking and took a baking class to learn pastry making and cookie decorating. She would make a large variety of cookies for her children, family, and friends. The crowning baking jewel on Christmas would be the traditional Caribbean Rum cake, West Indian black cake. James W and Joherra made the cake together, which was a nod to her Barbados English heritage. The cake was filled with a variety of ground fruits and a good dose of rum.[450]

"Be the Best"

The Quander children were taught by their parents to "Be the Best," but the philosophy behind that family mantra was different because of their upbringing: James W. was raised under racial segregation, and Joherra, who was raised in Barbados, did not face the harsh segregation.

Joherra encouraged their children with more mystical encouragement based on her Caribbean roots, "The cosmos and your personal karma will direct where you go in life and what you will achieve. So, always focus on the good and look for the good in others as well. Where possible, avoid conflict."[451]

James W. would often inspire his children with the words of encouragement he heard from his father, John Edward.

"Never give up, for God has blessed you in so many ways. So, always remember that to whom much is given, the Bible likewise says, much is required."[452]

---

[446] Rohulamin Quander email correspondence with author, January 4, 2023
[447] Rohulamin Quander email correspondence with author, January 4, 2023
[448] Rohulamin Quander email correspondence with author, January 8, 2023
[449] Rohulamin Quander email correspondence with author, January 8, 2023
[450] Rohulamin Quander email correspondence with author, January 8, 2023
[451] Rohulamin Quander email correspondence with author, January 4, 2023
[452] Rohulamin Quander email correspondence with author, January 4, 2023

In addition to the words of falling back on one's faith for encouragement, there were talks and advice on the stark reality of growing up in a xenophobic world.

"As a Black man/woman, don't ever lose sight of the many challenges that are imposed upon you to just keep your head above water and survive. This is a racist place and a racist time in this place, and if you lose sight of that fact, you may well be an unwitting party to your demise or destruction."[453]

Fortifying the family mantra included the continual and conscious effort to surround their children with like-minded families in striving for higher education and faith. This was how James W. was raised, and both James W. and Joherra hoped their friendship circles would support their children.

They also hoped these circles would cushion them from discrimination by both Whites who were racists and any potential Black backlash. Some Blacks who wanted to excel in school and society were called "Uncle Tom" by Black people who did not support this ideology. These Blacks would accuse those Blacks who were striving for more to be looking to win approval in white society.

---

[453] Rohulamin Quander email correspondence with author, January 4, 2023

Breaking Educational Barriers

In 1947, the Archdiocese of Baltimore was divided into Washington, D.C., and Baltimore. Archbishop Patrick O'Boyle became the first Archbishop for the newly created Washington, D.C. Archdiocese. One of his main objectives was to end desegregation within his diocese, including the Catholic private school system. In a thoughtful, deliberate process, O'Boyle was successful in having the parochial schools in his Diocese have varying degrees of integration. This was four years (1950) before the Supreme Court's landmark Brown v. Board of Education ruling, which struck down segregation in all schools.[454]

James W. and Joherra wanted their oldest child, six-year-old Rohulamin, to be a part of this moment of educational inclusion. In September 1950, Rohulamin, along with three other students, including his future wife Carmen, who was in kindergarten, bounded up the steps of Sacred Heart Elementary School.

The innocent children were excited for their first day of school. They did not understand the significance of their admission. For them, it was about learning and meeting new friends. The children played on the playground together. The young children were color blind. The color of Rohulamin's skin didn't matter to his fellow young students. Unfortunately, the bubble James W. and Joherra tried to place around young Rohulamin to lessen the blows of racism would quickly implode. The White parents of these children still harbored racist feelings and attitudes.

One day after school, Rohulamin walked with one of his fellow second graders to go to their house to play. But when they arrived, the boy's grandfather stopped Rohulamin from entering, saying, "You can't come in here." The friend was upset, and Rohulamin's heart broke.

The next day at school, his friend explained, "My grandfather said he didn't want any colored people in his house unless they worked there." The apology could not repair Rohulamin's devastated feelings. He would talk to his father, who would encourage him to press on despite the racial hate.

The following year, racial animosity would be directed at Rohulamin's parents when they attended the Catholic school's annual card party to raise funds for the school's Parent Teacher Student Association. James W. had guests from work who were White. He, along with Joherra, and his work colleagues, was looking forward to a night of playing card games, taking a chance at winning the 50/50, and having a good time. When the organizers saw the mixed-race group come in, they put them behind a column away from public view.

---

[454] "History- Brown v. Board of Education Re-enactment, Plessy Decision", United States Courts
https://www.uscourts.gov/educational-resources/educational-activities/history-brown-v-board-education-re-enactment

Integrated but Not Equal

Rohulamin learned at a tender age that while the school he attended or the church he went to on Sundays may be integrated, that did not mean Blacks were equal. He would find out about birthday parties that happened over the weekend at his White friend's house that he was not invited to because of the color of his skin. The kid's parents would not allow it.

Saturday matinees were out of the question because those times, films were only available to White customers. Even walking home with friends became an issue. In fourth grade, he was walking home with a little girl who lived near his home. One day, she told him she was not allowed to walk with him anymore because he was Black. The little girl's mom objected to it. No law would be able to change the minds or hearts of some people.

But what hurt Rohulamin the most was his denial of becoming an altar server. Rohulamin, along with several other White boys, attended the first class on how to become an altar boy. There was no mention during that day of a follow-up class. Rohulamin quickly realized several weeks later that there were meetings, he was just never invited to them.

Sitting at Mass one Sunday, he saw some of those White boys he was in the introductory altar server class, wearing the altar server robe and loose white linen vestment, helping the priest at mass. His heart fell to his stomach in a complex bundle of anger and sadness. No matter how hard James W. and Joherra tried to shield their children from the hurtfulness of segregation, they could not. This infuriated James W. because he could identify with his son's disappointment after his segregation problems with the Church he faced as a young man.

Rohulamin remembered the story of his father telling the story of being asked to leave the church by a priest, and he refused. Like his father, Rohulamin wanted to rise above racism. Being denied did not shake his faith. It made him stronger. Seeking new opportunities, Rohulamin wanted to participate in the school's 1956 Christmas Nativity and tried out. He was chosen to be Balthasar (one of the Three Wisemen).

Power of the Written Word

Growing up, the Quander children would see their father writing. James W. was a prolific letter writer to the newspapers. In his writings, he would voice his dissent against the injustices that were a result of segregation. In one Letter to the Editor, he wrote about the injustice he witnessed against four young Black boys at the hands of a White and non-White police officer.

Monday, Sept. 25, 1967 THE WASHINGTON POST

Poor Judgment

On Sept. 1, I witnessed a most disturbing and potentially dangerous happening.

Four young delivery boys between the ages of 9 and 11 were throwing a miniature rubber football to each other in front of the Safeway store located in the 3500 block of 14th Street nw. Their play was interrupted by the appearance of two uniformed policemen, one white, the other non-white.

The Negro cop took the football from the boys and began to chastise them for breaking the law. When one of the youngsters stated that they did not know that they were breaking the law, the Negro policeman told him to shut up before he mopped the street up with him.

This man showed poor judgment in his choice of words, as well as lack of wisdom in dealing with youth still in the formative years of proper attitude development towards law enforcement personnel. Such thoughtless behavior on the part of a mature adult certainly does not now aid or contribute towards future accomplishment of needed good police-community relationship based on mutual respect.

JAMES W. QUANDER,
Adult Moderator, Los Jeunes Hommes (French community service club).
Washington.

Source: Quander Family

This left a great impression on Rohulamin. The lessons he learned: the power of words and how never to give up. Growing up seeing his father in action and using his intellect to dispute the racial disparity gave Rohulamin confidence to rise above his injustices at school.

Make Your Opportunity

James W. and Joherra did not let bigotry or segregation stop them from offering their children the same experiences as their White friends. They would find them the opportunity to participate. When young Rohulamin wanted to join the Cub Scouts, James W. enrolled him in Cub Pack 559, which was associated with the all-Black church, Mt. Airy Baptist Church. When Sacred Heart School did eventually integrate its Cub and Boy Scout Troop, they initially participated in a lot of events in Maryland where segregation was still in practice, which meant Rohulamin would be excluded. James W. also had White fathers as friends in that troop. Rohulamin and his White friends at school did not understand at that time why they were not in the same Cub Scout troop but that, instead, he belonged to another troop that was located at a Baptist church. The innocence of youth did not connect the dots of racial division in a group whose "Do Your Best" oath was a contradiction to segregation and bigotry:

On my honor, I will do my best to do my duty to God and my country and to obey the Scout Law; to help other people at all times; to keep myself physically strong, mentally awake, and morally straight[455].

---

[455] Cub Scout Motto, "Do Your Best"

164

As Rohulamin got older, he eventually learned and appreciated the reason behind his parent's enrollment in Cub Pack 559.

When he became a Boy Scout, James W., and Joherra enrolled him in Boy Scout Troop 544, which was associated with the All-Black Peoples Congregational Church. They wanted Rohulamin to have a full experience in scouting. Rohulamin attended all Black summer camps run by the Boy Scouts and other organizations. Eventually, in about 1955/6, Rohulamin enrolled in the then recently integrated Sacred Heart 301 Boy Scouts around seventh, and eighth grade.

In June of 1957, Rohulamin was graduating from the eighth grade. The scars of segregation were still deep and far from healing just four years after the local District of Columbia courts struck down segregation in Washington, DC, in 1953.

Sacred Heart always had a traditional post-mass graduation breakfast at the Ugly Duckling Restaurant. Unbeknownst to the graduates and their families, after the 1957 post-graduation breakfast, the owner of the restaurant told the school never to come back there for their celebratory breakfast. Their Black students were not welcomed in his restaurant.[456] When James learned about this, he was mad but knew there was nothing the school could do about it. A year later, 1958, Sacred Heart found a new restaurant owner who did not hold such racial prejudice.

Don't Just Survive, Thrive

James W. and Joherra always impressed upon their children, not to just survive when faced with adversity but to thrive.

Rohulamin was in Archbishop Carroll High School in 1959 when he attended his father's fraternity, Omega Psi Phi's Grand Conclave in New York City. He left that event invigorated and wanted to create a youth group that would internalize the community service values of the fraternity and give back to their community. Studying French at the time, Rohulamin came up with the name "Les Jeunnes Hommes," which means "The Young Men." The idea of belonging to a group that would have a profound impact on their community was important to both Rohulamin and his friends who were from the neighborhood and his boy scout troop.

James W.'s advice to Rohulamin helped guide him and fuel his passion for rising above adversity during his formative high school years.

"As a Black man, don't ever lose sight of the many challenges that are imposed upon you just to keep your head above water and survive. This is a racist place and a racist time in this place, and if you lose sight of that fact, you may well be an unwitting party to your own demise or destruction."[457]

These would be words Rohulamin, and his younger brothers would internalize for the rest of their lives.

---

[456] Rohulamin Quander email correspondence with author, January 13, 2023
[457] Rohulamin Quander email correspondence to author, January 4, 2023

In the early sixties, racial tensions in DC and around the nation were high. Rohulamin and his close friends called themselves, "the Soul Brothers." This group of friends was both Black and White. One day, a Carroll student called Rohulamin a "Black monkey" and told him to, "go back to Africa!" He turned around and could not believe what he heard. The student was not born in America; rather, he immigrated from another country. Rohulamin's family had been living in the U.S. since the 1600s. Rohulamin heard his father's words and mother's encouragement in his mind, but that did not make the racial epithet hurt any less.

Unlike Rohulamin, who went to Catholic School, his siblings were educated in a mixture of Catholic Schools and DC public schools. They, like their older brother, embraced their family's mantra of "Be the Best" in the paths of life they chose.

Rohulamin earned his B.A. and his J.D. at Howard University. He was inducted into his father's and uncle's fraternity, Omega Psi Phi, in 1964. Rohulamin attained promotions through the years, and he retired as a Senior Administrative Law Judge for the District of Columbia.

Joherra Quander Harris graduated from Hampton University, Hampton, Virginia, and went on to the University of District of Columbia, where she received her Masters and served many years giving back to her community as a social worker for the DC government.

John Edward Quander, III, graduated from Tuskegee University and went on to achieve his Master's in Environmental Science from George Washington University, Wash., DC. He worked for the Environmental Protection Agency (EPA), where he researched and wrote reports on hazardous waste site remediation, the proper removal of refuse[458] , and soil vapor remediation, and soil vapor extraction.[459]

Their youngest child, Ricardo Vincent Quander, who had a love of research and animals, graduated from Georgetown University in Washington, D.C., and earned his Doctor of Veterinary Medicine at Tuskegee University. Dr. Quander focused on animal medical research, animal diseases, and vaccines designed to prevent, control, or reduce illness.

---

[458] John E. Quander, Michael Forlini, Physical/chemical treatment technology resource guide and physical/chemical treatment technology resource matrix." Record Display for the EPA National Library Catalog, Record Number 494 of 760 https://cfpub.epa.gov/ols/catalog/advanced_brief_record.cfm?&FIELD1=SUBJECT&INPUT1=Soil%20pollution&TYPE1=EXACT&LOGIC1=AND&COLL=&SORT_TYPE=MTIC&item_count=494&item_accn=207632

[459] John E. Quander, Michael Forlini, "Soil vapor extraction treatment technology resource guide and soil vapor extraction treatment technology resource matrix " Record Display for the EPA National Library Catalog, Record Number 128 of 155 https://cfpub.epa.gov/ols/catalog/advanced_brief_record.cfm?&FIELD1=SUBJECT&INPUT1=CERCLA&TYPE1=EXACT&LOGIC1=AND&COLL=&SORT_TYPE=MTIC&item_count=128&item_accn=276797

Quanders and the March on Washington

The Quander children often heard their father saying, "Perseverance will be king!" This attitude was the thread woven through the family's tapestry of life. So, when the March on Washington for Jobs and Freedom was convened on August 28, 1963, the entire Quander family participated.

James W. coordinated with his Cub Scout and Boy Scout troops as well as with his fraternity brothers. Both Joherra and James W. helped in the coordination of food for marchers because there were no local restaurants close to the National Mall.

The group congregated at the predetermined meeting site, and James W. gave small American flags and handed them to the children to wave as they marched. The Quander family, along with 300-plus people, left together and marched down 13th St. NW to Constitution Avenue. There, they were joined with the thousands of other marchers on Constitution Avenue.

The hot sun beat down on the shoulders of the marchers and bystanders, but that did not diminish their energy. Flags waved, people cheered, and the Quanders knew they were participants in a turning point in history. The energy of that day was indescribable.

The Lincoln Memorial grew larger and larger as they walked. The white bystanders were peaceful, and never once did any of the Quanders feel danger despite comments alluding to threats of violence.[460] Instead, you heard the singing of 'Glory, Glory Hallelujah' by the marchers.[461]

The parade route for the Quander family was around four miles. They arrived at the Lincoln Memorial grounds, found a place to sit on the hot grass, and had a picnic as they listened to the innovation of now Cardinal Patrick O'Boyle, the speech of John Lewis, the fiery songs by Queen of Gospel, Mahalia Jackson, and of course Reverend Doctor Martin Luther King.

It was Mahalia Jackson, whose impromptu comment, "Tell them about the dream, Martin",[462] emboldened Dr. King to improvise his comments and go off script. Five years later, at King's funeral, she sang "Take My Hand, Precious Lord."[463] In the Black community the song is generally known as *Precious Lord, Take My Hand,* giving deference to God first and man second.[464] It would be a day the Quander children would pass down to their children and grandchildren, telling them of the day when the message of hope, pride, and love helped unify and empower the Black community in their fight for equal rights.

---

[460] Rohulamin Quander email correspondence with Author, January 4, 2023
[461] "An Oral History of the March on Washington", Smithsonian Magazine, July 2013
https://www.smithsonianmag.com/history/oral-history-march-washington-180953863/
[462] "An Oral History of the March on Washington", Smithsonian Magazine, July 2013
https://www.smithsonianmag.com/history/oral-history-march-washington-180953863/
[463] "Dream Songs: The Music of the March on Washington", August 28, 2013, The New Yorker
https://www.newyorker.com/culture/culture-desk/dream-songs-the-music-of-the-march-on-washington
[464] Commentary from Rohulamin Quander, May 31, 2023

Fortified with Faith

Faith was a big part of the Maryland Quander family tree.[465] James W.'s faith in God and his desire to give back to the Black community were influenced by the actions of several descendants. His grandfather, Gabriel Quander, was a delegate for the first Colored Catholic Congress (now the National Black Catholic Congress), which took place on January 1-4, 1889, at St. Augustine Church in Washington, DC. 200 delegates met for four days and called for equality in all parts of society, including education, the workplace, and the church.[466]

"Colored Catholics Meet- A notable Convention Begun- Cardinal Gibbons Present
New York Times, January 2, 1889   (public domain)

Their message was the Black community should not be considered as a category in society. Around 100 delegates met with President Grover Cleveland at the White House.[467] The highlight of the first meeting was a cablegram from Pope Leo XIII's secretary of state, Cardinal Rampolia, who said the Pope had sent them his apostolic blessing.

---

[465] Rohulamin Quander, "The Quanders"
[466] "Black History Month", The Catholic University of America, Cultural engagement
https://cultural.catholic.edu/resources/bchm.html
[467] "Black History Month", The Catholic University of America, Cultural engagement
https://cultural.catholic.edu/resources/bchm.html

John Henry Quander (1830-1896) who was enslaved to Mordecai Plummer of Prince George's County[468], once freed, was one of the founders of the St. Mary's Beneficial Society Colored which offered assistance for Black parishioners in 1880.

C1875-constructed home of John H. Quander and Henrietta Tilghman Quander, and c1880s site where St. Mary's Beneficial Society Colored, the Knights of St. John Commandery #74, and the Ladies Auxiliary #21 were each founded and held their earliest meetings
Source: "The Quanders", Rohulamin Quander

The church-related association helped parishioners with their needs in food assistance as well as education. In May of 1889, the Knights of St. John was created by Gabriel Quander, which also served the needs of the poor Black community.[469]

Charles Johnson Quander, his wife Alyce; John Edward Quander and his wife, Helen Orena Stuart Quander; and their daughter, Evelyn Quander Rattley, band together to create their church for the Black community. Tired of sitting in the back of the local Catholic churches, denied communion until all of the whites had received, and likewise not having full access to the respective churches' facilities, they and others of their group, worked with the Josephites[470], an interracial and intercultural, religious community of Catholic Priests and Brothers. Committed to serving the Black American community and the advancement of the church teachings within the Black Community[471], they presented their proposal to the Archdiocese of Washington's Archbishop Curley, who agreed. The Quanders would be founders of St. Benedict the Moor.[472] On April 17, 1946, the first mass was celebrated with James W., his wife, Joherra,

[468] Rohulamin Quander, "The Quanders"
[469] Rohulamin Quander, "The Quanders"
[470] "About", Saint Benedict the Moor Catholic Church, https://sbmdc.org/about-us
[471] "The Josephite Mission Statement", The Josephites, https://www.josephites.org/mission-statement/
[472] Rohulamin Quander, "The Quanders"

and young son Rohulamin in attendance.[473] The Quanders were also involved in the construction of other Churches.[474]

This family history fueled James W.'s desire to do more for the Black Catholic Community. He was given that opportunity when the Second Vatican Council (1962-1965) announced it would re-establish the diaconate as a permanent rank of the hierarchy of the Church.[475] In the United States, Bishops would receive approval to restore the diaconate in 1968. James W. was thrilled. He would study to receive his sacrament of Holy Orders. He studied while working full-time. On September 11, 1971, James W. was in the first group of permanent Catholic Deacons who were ordained in the United States.

James W. Quander, front row, far right. Permanent Deacons are posing with Patrick Cardinal O'Boyle, then the archbishop of Washington, DC. September 11, 1971
Source: "The Quanders", Rohulamin Quander

As Deacon, James W.'s door was always open for those who needed an ear to listen or a voice of comfort. He helped senior citizens as well as celebrated love in marriages he performed and consoled those with his words at the funerals he presided over.

He once told a reporter, "Being a Christian and particularly a Catholic is more than going to mass on Sunday because I've seen too many people that run to mass every Sunday and are hellraisers during the week. It goes far deeper than that. It's human behavior and interrelationships. ... Every person has to seek. We have different paths to glory. Some are very difficult, but I think that if you seek, you will find. But a

---

[473] Rohulamin Quander, "The Quanders"
[474] Rohulamin Quander, "The Quanders"
[475] Immaculate Conception Seminary School of Theology, Seton Hall University, "Celebrating 50 Years of the Permanent Diaconate", https://www.shu.edu/diaconal-formation/celebrating-50-years-of-the-permanent-diaconate.cfm

lot of temptations are thrown in your way, and people who will try to deter you from doing, knowing what your mission happens to be. But at this stage in life, I am going to stick to my guns, stick to them." [476]

In addition to serving his church and community, James W. was asked to assist in two papal Masses. The first mass was in Rome in 1975 for Pope Paul VI and again in 1979 for Pope John Paul II at the Mass on the National Mall in Washington. It was the first time any sitting Pope visited the nation's capital. This Mass completed the Pope's "seven visits'' tour of the U.S. Amongst the 175,000 spectators on the National Mall that day was James W.'s family. The words the Pope spoke that day would forever be engrained in their hearts and minds.

"All human beings ought to value every person for his or her uniqueness as a creature of God, called to be a brother or sister of Christ by reason of the Incarnation and the universal Redemption. For us, the sacredness of human life is based on these premises. And it is on these same premises that there is based our celebration of life-all human life. This explains our efforts to defend human life against every influence or action that threatens or weakens it, as well as our endeavors to make every life more human in all its aspects. And so, we will stand up every time that human life is threatened." -Mass on the National Mall[477]

[476] Rohulamin Quander in email exchange with Author, January 4, 2023, extracted from a March 26, 1984, interview by Cecil Bushell, on behalf of the Abby Aldridge Rockefeller Museum, Williamsburg, Virginia.
[477] Catholic News Agency Staff, "Recalling St. John Paul II's Seven Visits to the United States"
https://www.catholicnewsagency.com/news/44069/recalling-st-john-paul-iis-seven-visits-to-the-united-states

Throughout James W.'s work as a deacon, he always tried to inspire and support. He loved the many hats he wore in life, and finally, at the age of 73, after 20 years of active diaconate service on record and the sustained and debilitating challenges of his diabetic condition, he decided to retire. In his retirement homily, he told the congregation of the Shrine of the Sacred Heart, that he tried to live a life exemplifying the Beatitudes for Friends of the Aged[478]:

Blessed are they who understand
my faltering steps and shaking hands.

Blessed are they who know that my ears today
must strain to catch the words they say.

Blessed are they who seem to know
that my eyes are dim and my reactions slow.

Blessed are they who look away
when my coffee gets spilled during the day.

Blessed are they with a cheery smile
who stop to chat with me for a while.

Blessed are they who never say
"You've told that story twice today."

Blessed are they who know the ways
to bring back lovely yesterdays.

Blessed are they who make it known
that I am loved, respected, and not alone.

Blessed are they who know the loss
of strength I need to bear the cross.

Blessed are they who ease the days
of my journey home in loving ways.

In his last homily on October 6, 1991, Deacon James W. offered these words of encouragement:

"One basic fact I pray, I never forget is that I, as an individual I am not independent of others, and I am not an island unto myself, but I too belong to the mainland of humanity, needing the love and concern

478 Rev. James W. Quander, "Diaconate Retirement Homily", Shrine of the Sacred Heart, Washington, D.C. October 6, 1991

of others. Also, let me not forget that along with you, I, too, am a partner of the "eternal triangle" consisting of God, you, my fellow men, and myself. May I also, along with you, always realize that this "Christian triangle" is fixed, and despite efforts to the contrary, is unchangeable."

Reunions for All Quanders and the Creation of Quanders United

James W. heard about the stories of the Virginia family unions from his father, and after being invited to the 43rd reunion in 1968, he yearned to coordinate a large reunion with both the Maryland and Virginia family trees.

Rohulamin, who was in favor of the idea, asked his father why the Maryland Quanders did not have reunions like their Virginia and Pennsylvania cousins. He explained the families got together around church-related events, not a designated reunion date.[479]

In 1974, after he retired from the federal government, he reached out to some Maryland and D.C. relatives to see if there was interest in having an intergenerational Quander reunion of their own. They said yes.

This was a passion project for James W. because his father, John Edward Quander, became an orphan at a young age, and he and his siblings were split up and divided among relatives. In October of that same year, James W. mailed a letter to the Quanders he knew about the reunion and asked for information on the family's history. This would be the first-ever reunion by this side of the family tree that was a church event. On December 28, 1974, approximately 150 family members got together. The menu was a nod to their Maryland and Virginia ancestors, "with plenty of fried chicken and everything that goes with it."[480] Through the years, Rohulamin compiled a detailed family history. By the third Maryland-DC reunion, he presented the family with his first detailed family history. The response was positive.

James W. wanted everyone to unite at a reunion so everyone could get to know each other. The younger members of the Quanders did not know the extent of the history and contributions their family had made in history. James would happily tell everyone in their family, that this was an event of celebration and paying homage to what it means "To Be a Quander!"[481]

The first reunion of all the Quander family trees was held on December 28, 1974, in the parish center of Sacred Heart Catholic Church, Washington, DC. The reunion was with Maryland and DC Quanders. This event would later be called, The Quanders United, Inc.

---

[479] Rohulamin Quander, "The Quanders"
[480] Rohulamin Quander, "The Quanders"
[481] Rohulamin Quander, "The Quanders"

Carrying the Family Torch

After his first reunion, Rohulamin was driven to learn more about his family. In his spare time, he would research his family history. In 1978, the family was notified by historians from Charles County, Maryland, that their family was one of the oldest consistently documented African American Families in the United States.[482]

For the family's Tricentennial Celebration (1684-1984), held at Howard University, Washington, DC, in June 1984, James W. wanted all the Quanders from the different family lines to come and celebrate together. Rohulamin, who had been researching the family history, wanted to present the Maryland, Virginia, Washington, D.C., and Pennsylvania relatives with a souvenir journal filled with history and photos of their family. Instead of being embraced by this, there were members of the Virginia and Pennsylvania clans who wanted nothing to do with it. Each side claimed they were the original Quanders.[483]

Despite their original demurrer, Rohulamin, along with his Virginia cousin Gladys Quander, presented information on how her grandfather Charles Henry Quander (the mid-1840s – 1919), who was born a slave, apparently in Maryland, was sold to a Virginia enslaver as a child. Charles married Amanda Rebecca Bell, and together, they, and their several children, developed and maintained an 88-acre dairy farm in Alexandria, Virginia. Slowly, a few of the Virginia Quanders signed up to celebrate.

Maryland, and Washington, D.C. Quanders were in favor of Rohulamin compiling their family history, but the older Pennsylvania and Virginia Quanders were still reluctant and not in favor.[484] Some of the Pennsylvania and Virginia Quanders wanted proof they were distantly related. Despite significant and growing evidence to the contrary, some of the Virginia and Pennsylvania Quanders still claimed they were the "original" Quanders. [485]

Both the Pennsylvania and Mount Vernon Quanders had the same initial connection. One example of that connection was Lewis Lear Quander. Lewis was born in Pittsburgh, Pennsylvania on February 9, 1919. He was the son of Frank and Lillian Quander. Frank's ancestors were enslaved at Mount Vernon Plantation.[486] Lewis was one of the original 42 Quander family members who attended the first Quander Family Reunion in 1926.

Although some of the Pennsylvania Quanders initially wanted to boycott the event, as the date for the 300-year celebration drew closer, a handful of Pennsylvania Quanders were open to the idea and registered for the reunion.[487] As a result, the Tricentennial Celebration had all the branches of the Quanders participate. Veteran Lewis Lear Quander wrote a Poem, "To Be a Quander," for the celebration.

---

[482] Rohulamin Quander, "The Quanders"
[483] Rohulamin Quander, "The Quanders"
[484] Rohulamin Quander, "The Quanders"
[485] Rohulamin Quander, "The Quanders"
[486] Lewis Lear Quander, "To Be A Quander" https://static.wamu.org/d/links/11038.pdf
[487] Rohulamin Quander, "The Quanders"

Each Quander Clan had its own motto. Rohulamin and a group of Maryland-based relatives were tasked with creating a coat of arms that they hoped would unite the different branches of Quanders. They needed to create a motto to symbolize the coming together of the families and selected: "We are Many, but We are One." The Virginia-Pennsylvania components of the family rejected the effort and results, creating their own coat of arms for the first time, and added to the design, "Blessed Be the Ties that Bind," which has been their motto since the first Quander Family Reunion which they held in Woodlawn, Virginia on August 15, 1926.

The responsibility of keeping Quanders United strong now rests in the hands of James W.'s son, Rohulamin. Devoted and passionate about his family's history, Rohulamin has taken a cue from his father and has taken to the written word to immortalize the history of his family.

He has written and published several books on his family and founded the Quander Historical and Educational Society, Inc., in 1985. The purpose of the non-profit foundation is to document, educate, preserve, and share the history of the Quander Family.

In a nod to his mother's heritage, Rohulamin works to address the civil and human rights inequities among the Dalit (the Untouchable) population of India, of which he and his mother Joherra are quite possibly descendants. In 2014, during a joint meeting held in the U.S. Capitol that addressed the limitation of human rights in India, The Quanders, along with descendants of Booker T. Washington, Thomas Jefferson Frederick Douglass, and Benjamin Banneker signed the "Declaration of Empathy," which addressed modern-day oppression and enslavement of the Dalit in India.

Coordinating the yearly Quander United reunion is as personal for Rohulamin as it was for his father. Just like he experienced all those years ago, Rohulamin wants his relatives to feel the same joy and awe he had when he met members of his family and learned their history. It was at his first family reunion held in 1968 on Quander Road, Alexandria, Virginia, Fairfax County, that he learned there was a street named after his family and a school. That surge in pride never left him and motivated him to learn more about his lineage. Today that joy has expanded enormously, as there are three other streets named Quander. The original Quander Street was created in about 1890 in Washington, DC. Subsequently, there is a Quander Lane in Bowie, Maryland, Prince George's County, and Quander Court, located in Dale City, Prince William County, Virginia.

Rohulamin wants the younger generations of Quanders to know that while yes, their last name has historical significance and there are buildings and roads named after them, they need to know *who* they are and *where* they came from. The Quander family is about the *people*. Specifically, their loved ones who came before them and whose sacrifices, love, and determination helped pave the way for them to achieve their goals and dreams today.

This is something that he, along with his childhood sweetheart Carmen, who is an accomplished artist, impressed upon their children. Your actions and the words you speak reflect where you came from.

In 2025, the Quanders will have their 100th family reunion. The Centennial Jubilee is historic on many levels for Rohulamin. It not only marks the number of years his family has come together, but it is a time for the Quanders, both young and old, to embrace their past and honor their descendants by the choices they make and contributions in life. Rohulamin said, "You are tomorrow. I am the bridge from the past, and I'm not planning to go away permanently any time soon, but it's not my call. I give you a legacy of love, respect, and focus, and for you to be enthused. I charter you and challenge you to be all you can be, whether it be in formal education, technology, or a manual career. But be the very best of whatever you can be and, on the way, and during that time, remember to take somebody along with you, because if you can help someone, then your living would not have been in vain."[488]

---

[488] League of Descendants of the Enslaved at Mount Vernon Oral History Project, Interview with Judge Rohulamin Quander, Interview conducted by Dr. Julie Sumner, Abby Wallace, Joe Gatlin, and Lori Ann LaRocco, Interview recorded via Streamyard on April 18, 20

PART FOUR

The Brooks Family: The only Black Family in U.S. History to have three Generals (father and two sons) in their immediate family

Major General Leo A. Brooks, Sr., Brigadier General Leo A. Brooks, Jr. and General Vincent K. Brooks were interviewed for this story. All are now retired from the U.S. Army.

"You must be twice as good at whatever you do to get a fair chance." - Henry Curtis Brooks

BROOKS FAMILY TREE

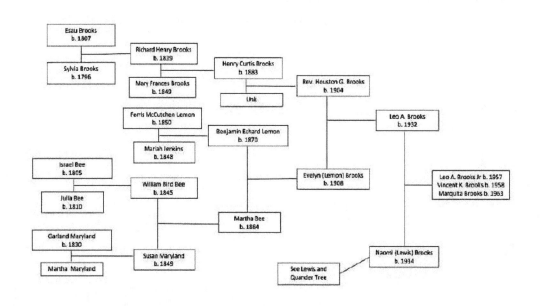

Chapter One
Love of Family and Country

The military accolades and public service, of Major General Leo A. Brooks, and his sons Brigadier General Leo A. Brooks Jr. and General Vincent K. Brooks, all now retired from the United States Army, is long and distinguished but there is more to this family than just military might. Their contributions to education and civil rights have also been extensive.

The foundation of the Brooks family's determination, love of family, and faith was built by Richard Henry Brooks. Richard Henry was born in 1839 and was enslaved to James Dishman.

After Dishman died, Dishman's brother placed Richard Henry in jail to make sure his investment was safe. Richard Henry was considered 'valuable property' because of his age and strength and was placed in jail until he could be sold. Richard Henry was in jail for a couple of weeks until Dr. William Cochran purchased him for the then high price of $1,000 (approximately $38,206.67 today) to be a farm hand. Dr. Cochran's farm was near Middleburg, Virginia.

In March of 1862, Dr. Cochran sent Richard Henry to work for his son-in-law, Thomas Underwood Dudley Jr[489], who was a Confederate Army officer. Richard Henry was a "body servant" [490][491] for the officer.

Richard Henry served as a body servant for approximately 7 weeks near Orange Court House in Orange, Virginia, but did not like the Confederate Army. Richard Henry left Dudley and returned home to Dr. Cochran in Middleburg, VA.

Around a month or two later, Richard Henry heard of reports that the "Rebel Army" was coming to Middleburg, which had been in Union lines. Richard Henry, along with three other enslaved men, escaped the plantation that night enroute to Alexandria, Virginia, 40 miles from Middleburg, VA. They then continued on to Leesburg, VA which was 18 miles away. The three men traveled at night to avoid being captured.

Richard Henry continued on an additional 28 miles by foot until he reached the Union lines at Falls Church. There, he met Freeman McGilvery, captain of the 6th Battery, Maine Light Artillery. Captain McGilvery was looking for a "body servant." Richard Henry told Captain McGilvery of his experience in

---

[489] Thomas Underwood Dudley Jr. served as a Confederate Officer spending most of the Civil War in Richmond in the Quartermaster Department. He and his wife had four children. His wife Fanny Berkeley Cochran Dudley Woodward passed during the childbirth of their fourth child. Dudley Jr. entered the Episcopal priesthood after his wife' death and studied at the Virginia Theological Seminary in Alexandria, Virginia. He advanced within the church to become the second Episcopal Bishop of the State of Kentucky. Dudley became a champion for Black advancement, uplift, and rights. Source: Bishop T. U. Dudley Dies Suddenly in this City: came from Kentucky to attend funeral of his mother-in-law, Mrs. Aldrich"

[490] "Vermonters Fight to Save Battlefields" by Marialisa Calta, Special to the New York Times, January 29, 1989

[491] A body servant is a personal aide and horse handler

the role and Richard Henry was enrolled into the Union Army as his body servant. This relationship would forever change Richard Henry's life and the course of his descendants' lives.

Richard Henry joined the ranks of Black men who were paid to perform labor for the Union. They received $10 a month in pay, which was $3 less than White Union soldiers.[492]

McGilvery was nicknamed "The Captain" because he was a sea captain along with his brother before the Civil War. While on a voyage to Rio de Janeiro, he heard about the Battle at Fort Sumter, and he sailed home to Maine where he raised the "Sixth Battery of Mounted Artillery, Maine Volunteers."

Captain McGilvery and his unit, including Richard Henry, moved up to Harper's Ferry from Washington DC in June of 1862 under the orders of General Banks. They stayed there until August to reinforce and solidify the Union defenses before preparing for an advance on Richmond.

Richard Henry Brooks (circa: 1880-1890)
Source: Brooks Family

Freeman McGilvery

After the unit left Harper's Ferry to go back to Washington DC, McGilvery and Brooks found a pony belonging to the Confederates. It was a good horse, and Captain McGilvery trusted Richard Henry to take the horse back to Harpers Ferry, which was around 50 miles away, and he would join McGilvery's wife, Hannah, who was temporarily staying there, and accompany her back to Maine.

Richard Henry went back to Harpers Ferry as planned, with the pony. But, when he arrived, Colonel Dixon Miles, the Union commander at Harpers Ferry, had imposed a rule restricting the movement of blacks

---

[492] "Black Troops in Union Blue" Constitutional Rights Foundation

beyond the Harpers Ferry military garrison area as they would be considered "contraband." Hannah proceeded home to Maine by train, and Richard Henry would depart Harpers Ferry and head back to Washington to find Captain McGilvery.

This would not be an easy journey, as Richard Henry had to move through numerous pickets[493] that served as outposts for the protected defenses of Washington. In order to gain clearance, you had to produce a pass. And to further complicate matters, Richard Henry's pass was expired. It was issued by Captain McGilvery to move from the front lines back to Harpers Ferry with the pony. Richard Henry took a risk based on the belief that the soldiers he would encounter were illiterate like himself, and unable to determine that the pass was an expired one and they would allow him to proceed.[494]

Following on the Maryland side of the Potomac and using the tow path on the Chesapeake and Ohio (C&O) Canal, Richard Henry successfully passed the first two pickets using the pass. Richard Henry concluded that he was right about their illiteracy. A few miles later, Brooks encountered a group of Union Soldiers bathing in the canal. They yelled at him to stop, but he did not comply with their commands. There were between 8 to 12 of them and fighting them would be problematic. Richard Henry was also concerned someone in the group would likely be literate and would discover the expired pass.

Richard Henry decided his best chances were to run. The Soldiers followed in pursuit. One of the Soldiers hit Richard Henry in the head with a stone. It cut him, infuriating Richard Henry. He stopped, turned around, and began running towards them. This surprised the Soldiers, and they retreated to reorganize.

With the Soldiers retreating, Richard Henry hurried away, trying to increase the distance between himself and the soldiers. Richard completed the 68-mile journey to Washington, DC the next afternoon. It was there he found the Provost Marshal[495] office and an officer who knew of Captain McGilvery and his unit's whereabouts. They were near Warrenton, Virginia. 47 miles back to the west.

Richard Henry was provided with wagon transportation by that Provost Marshal from Washington to Warrenton where he found McGilvery in time for the battle of Cedar Mountain (August 9, 1862). Richard Henry remained with McGilvery, who was promoted to Major after his successive battles of the 2nd Bull Run August 28–30, 1862, and the Battle of Antietam (September 17, 1862), which remains the bloodiest day in American history, with a total of 22,717 dead, wounded, or missing. In November of 1862, McGilvery received furlough to return to Maine. Both McGilvery and Richard Henry started for Maine.

---

[493] A picket is a solider who is stationed near the enemy lines. They are the eyes and ears of the Army where they would alert their fellow soldiers of any enemy movement. They also would prevent desertion.

[494] Provost Marshal was the Union Army officer charged with maintaining order among both soldiers and civilians. They were the Union's military police: Tennessee Secretary of State Library and Archives, Research and Collections, "Union Provost Marshal"

But Richard Henry traveled alone after Major McGilvery changed his mind in Baltimore and returned to Washington in December. Richard Henry separated from McGilvery that month and traveled with McGilvery's brother, William McGilvery – also a sea captain, to Maine.

On Richard Henry's first morning in Maine, William McGilvery's wife, Harriet Hichborn McGilvery, handed him a spelling book and asked him if he could read and write. When he told her he could not, as it was against the law in the South to teach slaves how to read, she said she and her children would teach him how to read and write. This was when literacy and education began for the Brooks family.

Richard Henry was 25 years old at that time and went on to live and work for the McGilvery's for two years. He wrote a handwritten journal on his life during the Civil War. This journal is still in the Brooks family's possession and is treasured by the literate generations who have descended from him.

During the two years Richard Henry was in Maine, he worked in the house, on the farm, and in the shipyard. Freeman McGilvery continued to lead on the battlefield and earned two more promotions and eventually took his furlough and returned home to Maine.

While at home, Colonel McGilvery purchased a horse that was not trained to carry a rider or wear a saddle, and he asked Richard Henry to train the animal. Richard Henry was continuing his horse training when now Colonel McGilvery returned to his place of duty for battle. Colonel McGilvery told Richard Henry to send him word once the horse was trained for saddle riding. The Colonel would then send Richard Henry instructions on where to send the horse. Unfortunately, that horse would never reach Colonel McGilvery.

While awaiting Colonel McGilvery's instructions, the family and Richard Henry received word that "The Captain" died on August 14, 1864, because of a finger wound received at the Battle of Deep Bottom (July 27 - 29, 1864). Sanitation was not the best out in the battlefield, and the injured finger became infected. The doctors had decided to amputate the finger. Colonel McGilvery died during the surgery from excessive chloroform used as anesthesia in September of 1864. Richard Henry wrote about the sad news in his journal.

"(McGilvery) came home and bought a horse which was not broke to the saddle, I trained him until he became a splendid saddle horse and was to take him out to the Capt (sic); but before he wrote his Brother word whare (sic) to send the horse he got wounded and the Doctors started to operate and killed him, he was brought home and buryed (sic) and the Government lost a good Man . . ."

- Journal of Richard Henry Brooks

News from Home

A few months after the burial of "The Captain" in his home village cemetery in Searsport, Maine, Richard Henry received a letter from his mother, Sylvia Brooks, who was in Washington. Sylvia, a free woman of color who was manumitted[496] by her owner, Samuel Dishman, upon his death in 1848, had lived free for 16 years at that point. Her husband, Esau Brooks, as well as her children, had remained enslaved-including Richard Henry.

Sylvia owned land and a house in Middleburg, Virginia. In her letter to Richard Henry, who was now listed as an escaped slave, she wrote that she had been pushed from her property by Confederate guerrillas and took refuge in Washington, which was under the control of the Union Army. While the Emancipation Proclamation declared all slaves in Virginia to be free in 1863, the Proclamation could only be enforced in areas controlled by the Union Army. [497]

Despite the risk of being captured and punished for being a runaway slave, Richard Henry immediately left Maine, and headed to Washington to find his mother. The Civil War was still going on, and escaped slaves, if found, could be sent back to their enslaver, where they could face severe punishment such as amputation or branding.

Once in Washington, Richard Henry found out his mother was living with his brother, John, in Virginia. John was enslaved in the deep South, but was freed when Union forces took control of the area he was enslaved in. Making sure his mother would be ok, Richard Henry purchased a shanty in Alexandria, Virginia and moved in with his mother until the end of December 1864.

During this time, Richard Henry also found the woman he had been engaged to before leaving Middleburg in 1862. Her name was Louisa Bailey, and she, like many blacks in the Middleburg area, sought refuge within the Union-controlled cities of Alexandria and Washington so that she could live free.

It was a reunion she had dreamed of. During the War, Louisa heard news that Richard Henry died, but she did not give up on her faith that her beloved would come home. Richard Henry remained in Alexandria with his loved ones until he left to return to Maine on April 5, 1865. This was just four days before Confederate General Robert E. Lee surrendered to Union General Ulysses S. Grant at Appomattox, putting an end to the Civil War, as well as the institution of slavery. He remained in Maine for six months, spending his time working for the McGilvery's, saving the money he earned from doing so.

In October 1865, as a free man, Richard Henry returned to Alexandria, and then, a few months later, he at last married his 20-year-old bride, Louisa Bailey, on December 29, 1865. In the early spring, Richard Henry set out to find his father, Esau Brooks, who was suspected to still be in Middleburg, Virginia, where he had remained enslaved throughout the war. Richard Henry was successful in finding his father, and

---

[496] Manumitted means released from slavery.
[497] The Abolition of Slavery in Virginia, the encyclopedia of Virginia

brought him back to Alexandria, where he was reunited with Sylvia. The two lived together as husband and wife until his death on May 27, 1867, at the age of 60.

Back to Maine

Once his parents were reunited, newlyweds Richard Henry and Louisa moved back to Maine, where he was an employee of William McGilvery, working again on the farm, in the house, and in the shipyard. Richard Henry and Louisa lived in McGilvery's farmhouse. Unfortunately, since childhood, Louisa was in poor health, and the winters were too harsh. Louisa needed continuous medical attention as a result of the debilitating sicknesses she would suffer from as a result of the sub-zero temperatures. Her doctor suggested the couple move to the warmer weather of the southern Atlantic coast, or the Gulf coast.

The couple first relocated to Alexandria, Virginia, living with Sylvia from April 1868 to February 1873. However, the winters were still too cold for Louisa, so they decided to move to Pensacola, Florida. The couple lived in Warrington, in Escambia County. Richard Henry worked as a shipyard laborer, and Louisa worked as a nurse. However, after only 18 months in Florida, Louisa contracted Yellow Fever, and died at the age of 29 in August 1874. They had no children.

Even though the Civil War was over, Richard never lost the fight to find his family members who were torn away in the slave trade. After the Civil War, former enslaved people posted ads in newspapers or sent postcards to the Freedmen's Bureau in an effort to help find loved ones who were separated during enslavement.

Richard Henry was one of the many who sent postcards. This extra copy was in the Brooks family's possession. In the postcard, Richard Henry was looking for one of his sisters.

WARRINGTON, FLA.

Any person furnishing me with the following information, I had a Sister who was sold, from the Town of Middleburg Loudon Co. Virginia, to a man that followed the slave trade, he took her South for sale, whether he sold her or not and where, I have never known, her name was Mrs. Ann Elizabeth Washington, her husband who was sold sometime before her was William Washington. Our Mother and Father names was Silvay and Esaw Brooks.

There was nine children of us, six boys and three girls, boys William, Stephen, Charles, John, Hiram, and Richard. girls were Mary-Ann, Ann-Elizabeth and Fanny.   Any person giving me the desired information, I will give the sum of ($10) Ten dollars.

R. H. BROOKS

Source: Brooks Family

What was $10 in 1873 is approximately about $247.33 today.

After Louisa's passing, Richard Henry stayed in Warrington, near Pensacola. In the spring of 1875, he traveled to Alexandria, Virginia, to see his family. During his one-month visit, Richard Henry met, and later married, Mary Frances Smith. She was ten years his junior and also had Florida ties with her own property in Pensacola.

Richard Henry and Mary had a total of six children in Warrington County, Florida (the first two children died as infants). Their children were the first Brooks generation to be born free.

In 1884, Richard Henry, Mary, and their four surviving children, Nellie F. (Feb. 4, 1879), William F. (October 8, 1881), Richard Henry Jr., (Feb. 28, 1882), and Henry Curtis (Jun. 27, 1883), moved back to Alexandria, Virginia. The couple welcomed three more children in Alexandria, Mary L. (June 2, 1885) and Whitfield (October 3, 1889). The third Brooks child died in infancy. This would also be the first Brooks generation to receive a formal education. Richard Henry Brooks told his children, "You must be twice as good at whatever you do to get a fair chance." This became a family mantra, which has been passed on to each generation and is embraced to this day.

Henry Curtis Brooks was a gifted musician and loved to play the trombone. On December 24, 1904, his only son, Houston George Brooks, was born. In his twenties, Henry Curtis played the trombone in a vaudeville[498] band, but the wage was not enough to support his infant son and himself, so he moved on to other pursuits.

Knowing how important education was, Henry Curtis enrolled Houston in the first public school for Black boys, the Snowden School for Boys in Alexandria, Virginia. This educational institution was funded by the Freedman's Bureau[499] in 1867. Houston later attended the all-Black Hampton Institute, which was known to educate well known leaders and educators like Booker T. Washington.[500]

Henry Curtis knew the job opportunities for a Black man were constrained. The Jim Crow laws restricted not only the social liberties of Black women, men, and children, it also limited careers where Black men and women could have advancement.

In addition to teaching positions in all-Black schools, one of the major sources of Black employment during this time was the federal government in Washington, DC.[501] This was part of the government's efforts in offering higher paying non-agricultural jobs. While Black workers had a better opportunity within the federal government to advance their careers, wages were still a little less than half [502] of their white counterparts.

---

[498] A Vaudevillian performed in multiple funny, light-hearted skits

[499] Law creating Freedman's Bureau: The Freedman's Bureau was usually referred to as The Bureau of Refugees, Freedmen, and Abandoned Lands. It was established on March 3, 1865 and operated as a U.S. government agency after the Civil War to help direct "provisions, clothing, and fuel...for the immediate and temporary shelter and supply of destitute and suffering refugees and freedmen (formerly enslaved men) and their wives and children". http://www.freedmen.umd.edu/fbact.htm

[500] Library of Virginia, "Students at Hampton Institute, Photograph 1907" https://edu.lva.virginia.gov/dbva/items/show/84#:~:text=The%20primary%20goal%20of%20Hampton,the%20admission%20of%20Indigenous%20students.

[501] National Bureau of Economic Research, "The Competitive Dynamics of Racial Exclusion: Employment Segregation in the South, 1900 to 1950" https://www.nber.org/system/files/chapters/c8796/c8796.pdf

[502] Mary S. Bendell*, "Employment and Income of Negro Workers 1940-52", page 600 https://www.bls.gov/opub/mlr/1953/article/pdf/employment-and-income-of-negro-workers-1940-52.pdf

Henry Curtis Brooks
Source: Brooks Family

Henry Curtis, along with two Black entrepreneurs, saw this push for federal Black employment as an opportunity for a small business. They wanted to create a bus service for Black workers where there were no seat restrictions. The Jim Crow laws forced Black bus passengers to sit in the back of the bus or give up their seats if a White passenger needed a seat.

Henry and his partners believed Black federal workers would be interested in taking bus transportation that would not abide by Jim Crow laws. Their bus line ran from Alexandria to Washington. It was a success, but, unfortunately, the small business was unable to compete with the much larger AB&W (Alexandria, Barcroft, and Washington Rapid Transit Company) Bus Company, which had more buses and additional schedules. Eventually, Brooks and his partners were pushed out of business. The AB&W Bus Company was later acquired and became a part of the WMATA (Washington Metropolitan Area Transit Authority) Metrobus system.

Not one to be discouraged, Henry Curtis and his now young adult son, Houston, relocated to Perth Amboy, NJ, where they would work in the ship building industry.[503] The two hoped this move would provide an employment opportunity, for this coastal area of New Jersey was a key point of transportation and logistics in both the first and second Industrial Revolutions. The waterways in this area moved commodities like coal, as well as raw materials such as bricks, clay, terra cotta, and sand.

One evening after work, Houston went to a dance. There, he met a woman with the warmest smile he ever saw. Her name was Evelyn Lemon. Born in Falling Spring, Virginia (June 14, 1908), Evelyn had a mixed ancestry of African American, and Irish or Scottish heritage. Her paternal grandfather, Ferris

---

[503] Middlesex County, "Maritime History"
https://www.middlesexcountynj.gov/government/departments/department-of-economic-development/arts-institute-of-middlesex-county/division-of-history-and-historic-preservation/maritime-history

McCutchen Lemon, was an Irish or Scottish doctor who had a common law marriage to Mariah Jenkins, a free woman of color mixed African American and Caucasian. Evelyn's parents were Benjamin Echard Lemon of Falling Spring, Virginia, and Martha Anne Bee of Warm Springs, Virginia. Evelyn had nine siblings, and they were the second generation of their family to be born free. Houston and Evelyn fell in love, and got married on April 18, 1927, in Washington, DC, and moved to Chester, PA. A year later, they welcomed Houston George Brooks, Jr. in Pennsylvania, where they resided. The joys of newlywed life quickly came to a halt after the nation entered the Great Depression, the worst economic downturn in industrialized world history, with the stock market crash of October 29, 1929. Their second son, Henry Curtis Brooks, named for his grandfather, was also born that year. The slowdown in consumer spending after the stock market crash led to a pullback in manufacturing, which curtailed manufacturing orders, and impacted the maritime transportation industry. The ripple effects of this downturn would impact millions. Henry Curtis and Houston were among the many Americans who lost their jobs during the Great Depression.

Great Depression

Black Americans, who were considered to be "the last hired, first fired,"[504] experienced the highest rate of unemployment during the 1930's, and had a harder time in making ends meet because their salaries before the Great Depression were lower, and, as a result, they had less of a financial cushion to fall back on. The average U.S. hourly starting wage for unskilled white labor was 45 cents an hour. For Blacks, it was 35 cents.[505]

In pursuit of a job, both Henry Curtis the elder and son Houston Sr. moved back to Virginia. To financially support their family, they started to pick up driftwood from the Potomac River along George Washington Parkway in hopes of selling it. They sawed the pieces of wood into fireplace lengths and sold them. To their surprise, there was great demand for the wood.

Their business grew after a person they knew gave them a used floor sander. Henry and Houston repaired it and started offering floor sanding services. The business then expanded into painting and paperhanging. They were a small business success. Henry Curtis and Houston Sr. called their interior decorating and painting business *H. C. Brooks & Son.*

Black Education Advocacy

The growing population of Black families moving to the DC-area for higher education in the late 1920s to early thirties created a need for additional schools for Black students. The Parker-Gray School, which opened in 1920, was crowded, and there was a need for an additional school in Alexandria for the expanding student body.[506] An existing building would make more sense than building a structure because that would

---

[504] History.com "Last Hired, First Fired: How the Great Depression Affected African Americans"
[505] Wages by race, 1930-1939, Library guides.missouri.edu
[506] Alexandria Times, " Lyles-Crouch school during segregation" September 2, 2010
https://alextimes.com/2010/09/lyles-crouch-school-during-segregation/

take time, and there needed to be an immediate solution. So, the question was, *where was there an existing building that could accommodate this immediate need?*

An abandoned silk factory in Old Town Alexandria was promising.[507] Henry Curtis, who at the time was a leader in the Alexandria NAACP and the "Alexandria Citizens' Association (colored)." wrote a letter that triggered the conversion of the local factory into Lyles-Crouch Elementary School. When the school, which was named after two local free-Black educators, Rozier D. Lyles, and Jane A. Solomon Crouch, opened in 1934, it had 10 classrooms, and could hold 300 students.[508]

The families of Lyles-Crouch students supported their school by organizing benefits to supplement the school's library fund. They were also active in wartime fundraising, supported the Red Cross, and purchased war bonds.[509] The school's Parent Teacher Association, (PTA), also created programs during Negro History Week, which was the precursor of Black History Month.

This was an exciting time for the Brooks family. Henry helped in finding a new school for black students, the family business was growing, and the Brooks family was expanding. In Washington DC, Houston Brooks Sr. and Evelyn added to their family and welcomed Nellie Victoria Brooks (later Quander) (1931), Leo Austin Brooks (1932), and Francis Kenneth Brooks (1943). Henry Curtis would visit the family, and the sons all worked with H.C. Brooks and Son; later, the name changed to Brooks and Sons.

---

[507] "History of Lyles – Crouch Traditional Academy https://lcta.acps.k12.va.us/about-achs/history-of-lyles-crouch
[508] Alexandria Times, " Lyles-Crouch school during segregation" September 2, 2010
https://alextimes.com/2010/09/lyles-crouch-school-during-segregation/
[509] Alexandria Times, " Lyles-Crouch school during segregation" September 2, 2010
https://alextimes.com/2010/09/lyles-crouch-school-during-segregation/

The Brooks family lived in a Black neighborhood called Sunnyside. The community was created on land owned by Black junk dealer and real estate owner, Charles A. Watson. When Watson passed away, his wife, Laura, and his three children inherited the land and established one of the first African American neighborhoods in Alexandria. The community was dedicated in 1905, and the land was subdivided to offer Black families the opportunity to buy a home. The Brooks family was one of the earliest homeowners. There were nine boys and three girls who lived in the neighborhood.[510]

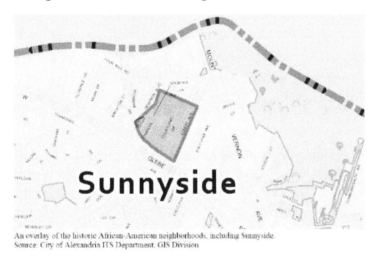

An overlay of the historic African-American neighborhoods, including Sunnyside.
Source: City of Alexandria ITS Department, GIS Division

Unlike their white neighbors who surrounded Sunnyside and had indoor plumbing, residents like the Brooks family did not. They used an outhouse, and once a week, the waste was collected.

"You can only imagine the smell in the neighborhood those days," chuckled Brooks, Sr.

---

[510] Phone conversation with MG Leo Brooks, Sr. with authors on May 16, 2023

Water would also have to be drawn by a hand pump. The children would take turns washing the dishes in the dishpan each week. The Brooks did not have indoor plumbing until Leo Brooks, Sr. was a freshman in High School in 1946.

Their home was on Elbert Avenue, which was considered to be in the center of the neighborhood. All of the streets were named after Watson family members who had died. Some of the professions held by the head of the sixteen households varied from two ministers, a building custodian for the National Press Building in DC, a railroad fireman, a parcel postal delivery man, a barber, and two truck drivers. The women were homemakers and never left the home.

"I cannot remember ever having a key to my house until I was a junior or senior in high school," said Leo Brooks, Sr. "The three girls who included my sister in the neighborhood were all around the same age. The boys were spread out over a 10-to-12-year span," reminisced Brooks, Sr.

Life in Sunnyside was filled with playing softball and touch football in the two vacant lots in the neighborhood, catching lightning bugs and putting them in jars, card games, shooting marbles, and tossing horseshoes until the kids could no longer see the stake.

"When we were around 10 or 11, we would also go to the creek (Four Mile Run[511])with our BB guns and shoot mice and rats. Arlington, at that time, was expanding, and the city was dumping the trash in Four Mile Run. There were always mice and rats around. We would also play soldier."

Four Mile Run would also be the place where MG Brooks, Sr. would learn how to swim. At that time, Brooks, Sr. described the "creek" as narrow and that it had little pools where he could swim. But his parents did not want their children playing in that water.

"My mother and father would warn us and say, 'stay out of that water, someone's going to drown'," said Brooks, Sr. "Well, that's like telling a boy 'don't breathe.' If we would go down to the creek to swim, we would have to skinny dip and put our clothes back on without getting sand in our underwear. Well, when my mother caught us, she would show our father, and he would raise the roof, if you know what I mean."

The Brooks brothers, along with their male adolescent neighbors, were members of the first and only Black Boy Scout Troop in Alexandria; Troop 575. They attended summer camp twice at Camp Benjamin Banneker[512] in Gaithersburg, Maryland.

Summers would include visits to Grandfather Henry Curtis' cottage located in the Patuxent River community of Eagle Harbor. For three weeks in August, the Brooks brothers would feast on their catch of

---

[511] "Four Mile Run" is approximately 20 square mile long stream that lows through Fairfax and Arlington counties and the cities of Falls Church and Alexandria. Belle Haven, Dogue Creek and Four Mile Run Watershed Management Plan DRAFT June 2020

[512] Benjamin Banneker is considered the first Black man of science. He was born in the eighteenth century as a free- Black American in Baltimore county Maryland. This father was a formerly enslaved man and the daughter of a mixed-race couple. He learned how to read and write from his grandmother who was an Irish-born former indentured servant.

the day and crabs caught on the boat. They would also bring their mutt, "Parpoo," who used to love running around on the land. Unfortunately, on one trip, the dog was run over by a car. They never had another dog.

All of the Brooks children would attend Lyles-Crouch Elementary School, the school that their grandfather advocated for. The message they would hear repeatedly from their grandfather and parents would be to do their best in school. It was stressed to them that education was essential in opening doors of opportunity. Throughout their childhood and young adulthood, the Brooks children heard from their great grandmother, Mary Frances Brooks, and grandfather, Henry Curtis, that education could be used as a way out of repression.

When they did not perform up to their parent's educational standards, there were consequences. MG Brooks, Sr. never forgot the stern lecture he received from his father, who was disappointed in his grades in the eighth grade. "They needed to be higher."[513] All the Brooks children took their parents and grandparent's advice on education to heart and excelled in school and in life.

Houston George, Jr. and Henry Curtis (the younger) earned their PhD's in chemistry and psychology, respectively. Nellie was a deputy assistant superintendent of the Fairfax County Public Schools system. Francis K. Brooks served twenty-six years in the Vermont State House and four years in the State Senate. Senator Brooks also taught high school physics and science and was the head of the Science and Technology department. Leo A. Brooks went to college and rose through the ranks of the U.S. Army through education and military service to become a Major General.

"It was always planted in our minds- you are responsible not only for yourself but for the rest of your family," explained MG Brooks, Sr. "All of us Brookses ran into that constantly in school. As a Brooks, you were always under the gun to perform. That message was always there, reminding me. It was the underlying spirit we operated under. Your behaviors affect everyone in the family. If it's good, that's wonderful. If it's bad, Lord Bless us."[514]

While reflecting on his childhood, Leo Brooks found that it was the simple moments that still bring a smile to his face.

"When I was a kid, he (my dad) would take the whole group of us, the boys particularly, we would go to downtown Washington to Hanover Shoe Store, and everybody would get a new pair of shoes before school started. He would sit down and supervise everyone. After I retired, and I came back to the area in Alexandria, he needed a pair of shoes because the ones he wore didn't fit well. So, I took my dad to go get a pair of shoes, and I sat there and thought about the days when I was a child, and I reached over and hugged him. He may not have understood why, but I was just so proud that now here I am sitting, and I'm buying *my* daddy a pair of shoes. It was a very touching moment I have never forgotten."

---

[513] Phone interview with authors, December 29, 2022
[514] Phone interview with authors, December 29, 2022

Family Foundation Based on Faith

The lessons learned by the Brooks children expanded outside of the schoolroom. Before any food was eaten at the family table, prayers were said. To this day, Brooks, Sr. does not touch anything on his plate until he has asked God's blessing.

Houston Sr.'s devotion to God inspired him to become a minister. With the help of Evelyn, Houston balanced religious study, work, and family, and was ordained in 1941 by the Northern Virginia Baptist Association. Since the salary of a pastor was not enough to support a family, Houston continued to work with his father at H.C. Brooks & Son. The hours Reverend Houston Brooks worked were long.

Reverend Houston was on the road a lot- traveling over two and a half hours to serve as a minister successively in the three different Baptist churches in the area in the towns of Gunston, Remington, and Leesburg. During those times, a Black man driving around after dark in the countryside was frowned upon in society, thus making it considerably dangerous.

Evelyn supported her husband's ministerial work and full-time job by staying home to make sure all of the business at home, her children's schoolwork, and extra-curricular activities would all run smoothly. Reverend Houston was on the road a lot.

Later, from 1963 to 1986, when Reverend Houston was the pastor of Mount Calvary Baptist Church in Rockville, Maryland, Evelyn was more active in the church, because the children were all adults now. Black Baptist traditions call on the wife of a church's minister to be the "first lady of the church." Among other roles was her supervision of the cleaning and starching of the communion cloths for Sunday worship services. The first lady of the church was not paid for her service. The congregations beloved Evelyn, and her grace and devotion were praised and appreciated by members of the congregations.

Reverend Houston G. Brooks

Reverend Houston Brooks was the head of the Northern Virginia Baptist Association Youth Program. His influence and passion inspired some 40 young men to become ministers.[515] His son, Henry C. Brooks, would follow in his father's footsteps, and also became a minister.

As a child, Leo A. Brooks would attend the Baptist Church, where his father was minister until he was twelve. He then began attending Alfred Street Baptist Church because it offered more youth-oriented activities. He would sing in the children's choir with Ralph and Richard Wair, twins with whom he grew up in Sunnyside. As a teen, he directed the junior choir and sang in the adult choir.

To Reverend Houston Brooks, the message of faith supporting a person's fortitude and strength was important.

"I want to be able, as the days go by, always to look myself straight in the eye. I don't want to stay under the setting sun and hate myself... If you're a friend of a man, encourage him, tell him! You can make it if you try. I used to love hearing my grandmother say son trust in the Lord. You can do all things! Paul said all things are possible through Him!"- Reverend Houston G. Brooks, sermon on May 1, 1977

When the Brooks sons all reached the age of 12, they would join the family business during the summers. When Henry Curtis retired, Reverend Houston Brooks renamed the firm, H.G. Brooks & Sons. He continued the business until about 1965.

Aside from playing soldier with his brothers and friends, growing up, the young Leo A. Brooks did not have the immediate yearning to join the military. While he was very proud of his great-grandfather Richard Henry, he initially had an interest in something else. Music. Having a grandfather who was a former musical entertainer and a great uncle who was the music director at Alfred Street Baptist Church, their home was constantly filled with music, spiritual and classical.

"There is nothing like a home filled with music," Leo Brooks Sr. said wistfully with a smile in his voice.

As a youth in the fifth or sixth grade, Leo would watch his grandfather, Henry Curtis, give music lessons to his two older brothers, Houston Jr. and Henry, on the trombone and baritone. Young Leo Brooks would sit and listen to every point his grandfather made in those lessons, from how to make a correct embouchure to proper fingering techniques. He was enthralled. After everyone would leave the room, young Leo Brooks would pick up the horn and try to do the same thing. He learned to play the instruments by himself. This natural talent led him to musical pursuits, which provided him several opportunities.

Brooks made the Parker-Gray high school band without ever having had a formal lesson. The band was small and consisted of 25 kids. This was not the only band he played in. Brooks, still a teen, was a member

---

[515] Washington Post Obituaries, October 24, 1987 https://www.washingtonpost.com/archive/local/1987/10/24/mideast-expert-ex-professor-harry-n-howard-dies-at-85/d4aabdd8-085c-467c-b56d-d4b8a5480763/

of two different Elks Lodge bands, one in Washington, and one in Alexandria. It was these experiences in the Elks bands that gave him the inspiration to major in music in college.

Originally, MG Brooks wanted to become a lawyer, but he knew he could not afford to go to college without some sort of scholarship, particularly with three older siblings in college or graduate school at the same time. So, he looked at other fields that he would be happy in. It did not take long to think about music. If he majored in music, there was a $300 teacher's scholarship he could apply for at Virginia State College. If he received the scholarship, it would lower the yearly tuition to $590 (approximately $7,389.35 in today's value). Leo Brooks received the scholarship and majored in music, his solo instrument being the trombone.

In college, Brooks received his first lesson on the trombone from one of his professors, Dr. F. Nathaniel Gatlin. It was there that he excelled on trombone.

As a student, Leo Brooks was active on campus. He was president of the Student Government Association, president of his fraternity Alpha Phi Alpha, as well as other organizations, such as Reserve Officers Training Corps (ROTC), where he received a reserve commission. He was offered a regular Army commission, which he turned down. He wanted to be a music teacher. The pay for teachers at that time in Alexandria was $3,600, which was considered a good wage. When the professor of military science found out young Brooks turned down the Regular Army offer, he was furious.

On the first day of college his sophomore year, Brooks was helping students unload their cars when he saw a familiar face amongst the incoming freshman being dropped off. The stunning 5'11" student's name was Naomi Lewis.

Naomi Lewis

Naomi's statuesque height came from her Virginia Quander heritage. All Virginia Quanders were tall. Her mother, Eunice Naomi, was a Quander who was the granddaughter of Charles Henry Quander. Charles Henry was the former enslaved person who successfully received back pay for his work from 1863-1867 from his enslaver and with those monies, established a successful dairy operation.

As a child, Eunice attended Woodlawn school, which was built on land that was originally part of George Washington's Dogue Run Farm.[516] Quander cousin descendants; Sukey Bay and Nancy Carter Quander, worked that land when they were enslaved by George Washington before they were freed in accordance with his will.

Eunice was a devout Baptist, and attended Alfred Street Baptist Church, the very church Nancy Carter was a member of, as well as dozens of other Quander family members. She attended that church until the

---

[516] Woodlawn Plantation and Pope-Leighey House Historic Overlay District
https://www.fairfaxcounty.gov/planning-development/historic-overlay-districts/woodlawn-pope-leighey#:~:text=Woodlawn%20was%20built%20between%201800,because%20of%20the%20tremendous%20view.

day she died. Her husband, James Lewis, Jr. would attend his own family church, Oakland Baptist Church, where he was Chairman of the Board of Deacons for 37 years. His father held the role before him.

Naomi's father, James Lewis Jr., hailed from "Seminary" a Black community on the edge of Alexandria near the Virginia Theological Seminary, and his Christian upbringing had a huge impact on Naomi's faith and attitude towards life. Naomi also hailed from Seminary. Naomi was active in her father's church: Oakland Baptist Church and also her mother's church: Alfred Street Baptist Church.

James Lewis Jr. was born in 1910 on the grounds of the Virginia Theological Seminary[517][518] James Jr. was the first-born child of James Lewis Sr. and Minnie Roy Lewis. As a young adult, he worked at the Seminary as a janitor or custodian, along with his father, James Lewis Sr.[519] His paternal grandfather, Mack Lewis (b. 1843), was literate, and owned a farm in Gainesville, Prince William County, Virginia. James Lewis, Sr. (b. 1886), along with his siblings, were born and raised on the farm.

James Sr. started to work as a sexton handling horses and maintaining the buildings[520] at the Virginia Theological Seminary (VTS) sometime before 1909; when he married Alexandria native, Minnie Roy. The Seminary was a large employer for Black Americans as laborers. In September 2019 the VTS announced the formation of a designated $1.7 million as *reparations* endowment fund to pay descendants of the enslaved people who worked there as well as descendants of loved ones who were under-compensated laborers as a result of the Jim Crow Laws.[521]

Early in their marriage, James Jr. and Eunice lived in a home provided by the seminary in an area called Donaldson Corner, then owned by James Sr., but eventually moved into homes nearby along Quaker Lane in Alexandria County, (now Alexandria City).

---

[517] Virginia Marriages, 1785-1940

[518] US Census 1910

[519] US Census, 1930

[520] "A conversation with Coach Jimmy Lewis, a Basketball Trailblazer." Julian Brown interview, February 22, 2021

[521] "Reparations" Virginia Theological Seminary Reparations | Virginia Theological Seminary (vts.edu). The initial payments are up to $2,100 cash and given to the descendants, whom the VTS refer to as "shareholders". Along with the money, shareholders are offered access to the on-campus amenities such their loved ones were once prohibited such as borrowing library books and attending programs. They can also eat for free at their dining facilities. The Lewis family is among the families approved by the Seminary to receive reparations.

Mack Lewis (birth est. Sept. 1843)

Source: Brooks Family

Mack Lewis (1843), and Mariah (or, sometimes listed as "Maria" in documents) Foley (1854), were both enslaved and of mixed race. Records show Mack was enslaved in Prince William County, and Mariah's father was her enslaver. Her father was Richard Foley (1830) who married Lucinda Foley (b:1834). Richard's great-grandfather, William Foley (b: 1760- July 23, 1783) served as a Private of the 18th of the Virginia Militia from 1812-1815.[522] A search of Lucinda's family records only began with her marriage license to Richard. Virginia marriage records show Richard and Lucinda married twenty years after Mariah's birth on September 1874[523], and 9 years after the end of the Civil War.

Mack raised Naomi's grandfather James Lewis Sr to have a strong work ethic and be honorable, while also remaining humble. These attributes also carried into the generation of Naomi's father, James Jr. and succeeding generations.

James Lewis, Jr. took pride in his work, and he was known for his trustworthiness and moral character. When he was not working, he enjoyed dressing with a little more flair. For example, seven days a week you could find James Jr. wearing a necktie. He loved to dress well, and always looked impeccable in his chauffer attire. Contrastingly, he also rode a motorcycle as a young man (either Harley Davidson or Indian). He had some physical limitations (abdominal hernias and significantly fallen arches) which prevented him from serving in World War II, but the trusses he wore to support his herniated area and custom designed shoes he had to wear did not slow him down. He refused to let these physical challenges define him. His family, faith, and work did.

---

[522] United States War of 1812 Index to Service Records, 1812-1815, database with images, FamilySearch (https://familysearch.org/ark:/61903/1:1:Q29K-QHVG : 8 March 2021), William foley, 1812-1815; citing NARA microfilm publican M602 (Washington, D.C.: National Archives and Records Administration, n.d); roll 73; FHL microfilm 882,591
[523] "Virginia, Bureau of Vital Statistics, County Marriage Registers, 1853-1935," database, FamilySearch (https://www.familysearch.org/ark:/61903/1:1:DW26-L3PZ : 1 July 2022), Raglis Foley in entry for Richd Foley, Sep 1874; citing Marriage Registration, Prince William, Virginia, United States, Virginia State Library and Archives, Richmond.

When he met the elegant 5'10 Eunice Quander, sparks flew. She was the first May Queen of Parker-Gray High School.[524] James Lewis Jr would ride up on his motorcycle to pick up Eunice at her father, Joseph A. Quander's house, in the Spring Bank area of Fairfax County on Quander Road near Alexandria. They tied the knot on May 7, 1933.[525] Naomi was the first born to the couple on April 14, 1934, while they still lived adjacent to the grounds of the Virginia Theological Seminary. The Black American neighborhood was called by Whites the derogatory term "Mudtown."[526] [527]

James Lewis Jr. riding one of his
motorcycles. circa 1930's

Source: Brooks Family

James Lewis Jr., like his father and several siblings performed labor on the grounds of the Virginia Theological Seminary. In the late 1930's, James Jr., now a married father with a growing family became the driver for the Headmaster of the Episcopal Seminary School. Around 1941, on a tip from one of his brothers who labored at the Seminary, James Jr. applied for the job as driver for the powerful United Mine Workers leader, John L. Lewis.[528] Quickly earning John L. Lewis' trust, James Lewis Jr. became both driver and house manager, as well as trusted confidante, unofficial chaplain, and periodic bodyguard. As the two Lewis men, not related, one White and one Black, traveled to the places where mining was being performed manually in America, including the segregated areas of the South, John L. Lewis always insisted on equal food and accommodations for James Jr. to the chagrin of the segregationists in the areas surrounding them.

---

[524] "A Conversation with Coach Jimmy Lewis, a Basketball Trailblazer."

[525] Virginia, Marriages, 1785-1940

[526] "A Conversation with Coach Jimmy Lewis, a Basketball Trailblazer." YouTube interview Julian Brown -- NOVA and Virginia Legends Podcast, February 22, 2001

[527] Mark Eaton, "Coffee with Krystyn Moon: Exploring Alexandria's real estate history", October 20, 2022 Coffee With Krystyn Moon - by Mark Eaton - About Alexandria (substack.com)

[528] The union leader broke with the American Federation of Labor and set up its own federation. Under Lewis' leadership, the UMW grew to 800,000 members and joined, the CIO (Congress of Industrial Organizations). The UMV was involved in a series of major strikes during World War II as well as threatened walkouts. After WWII, the [528] UMW focused on increasing both medical services, wages, and retirement benefits. The United Mine Workers later joined the combined AFL-CIO in the 50s.

James Lewis Jr. would take care of the residence (Lee-Fendall House in Alexandria, Virginia) as well as the financials, keeping the ledger balanced. The long relationship enabled James Jr. to support his wife and five children and ensure all of them received a solid education well beyond that which he had been afforded. Naomi's father worked for the Union for more than six decades and drove every one of the labor union presidents until he died at the age of 92 in 2003. He was well-known and well-remembered at the Headquarters.[529]

Education was a paramount for the Lewis children. Naomi's early education included the Seminary School for Colored Children, and Lyles-Crouch Elementary School. She then attended the segregated all-Black Parker-Gray High School (PGHS), where she graduated as Salutatorian in 1951. Naomi also excelled in sports, a talent she would pass on to her three children. As the starting forward on the girls' basketball team, Naomi smashed school records, earning and holding records until the school's closing in 1963. The records: the most points scored in a season and scoring the most points in a single game. Even though Naomi and young Leo Brooks were in the same high school geometry class, they were dating other people, so they were only friends.

Naomi was the first in her family to go to college. When her father drove her to Virginia State College, Leo Brooks, now a sophomore, walked over to the car to help her unload her bags. When Naomi's dad was about to leave, Leo Brooks leaned into the car, put his right hand on Mr. Lewis' left shoulder and told him, "I'll take good care of her sir." Naomi's father responded, "I bet you will." and drove away.

During that semester, Leo Brooks was dating another student. On a train ride back home to Alexandria for Christmas break, Naomi Lewis and Leo Brooks sat together and were chatting. She asked him, "I've got a couple of parties I have been invited to. Would you want to go?" Leo Brooks said yes and chose his destiny.

When Brooks arrived back at college in January, he broke up with his girlfriend, and Naomi and Leo started to date. They were college sweethearts. Leo Brooks went on to complete his education and graduated with a Bachelor of Science Degree in Instrumental Music Education in 1954, and he was commissioned as a Second Lieutenant in the U.S. Army and was also a Distinguished Graduate from ROTC. Naomi pinned on his gold bars for Second Lieutenant. She repeated this through seven more promotions in military rank.

[529] Adam Bernstein, "Mine Workers Driver James Lewis Jr. dies", March 3, 2003
https://www.washingtonpost.com/archive/local/2003/03/03/mine-workers-driver-james-lewis-jr-dies/7830ee6d-132c-4cb2-a447-975290a1922f/

Naomi Lewis pins Leo A. Brooks, Sr. 2nd Lieutenant Bars, 1954

Source: Brooks Family

As Second Lieutenant, Brooks reported to Captain James G. Monteith, who counseled the young officer in a way that no one ever else had. He would offer advice like, "Son, what activities do you enjoy? What sports do you play?" then Lieutenant Brooks told him softball and basketball. Captain Monteith told him, "that was fine," but he would need to go buy a tennis racket, bowling glove, and golf clubs, because that's where Army officers make fellowship.

Lieutenant Leo Brooks took his advice and paid $35 for a full set of used golf clubs. Other advice he found extremely useful was how to prepare himself to stay in the Army. He was told there were programs he could enroll in which would help him develop his knowledge and skills, and there was a strong reading program filled with great books. Lieutenant Brooks took Captain Monteith's advice and enrolled into the program and read 10 professional military books in less than six months, while working a ten-hour day.

He received a certificate and other acknowledgements from that program. Major General Brooks says to this day that Captain Monteith's kindness and advice were critical to his development in the Army.

In 1955, Naomi Lewis received her bachelor's degree in education, and the college sweethearts were married on December 24, 1955. Naomi Brooks started teaching at Charles Houston Elementary School in Alexandria.

Her teaching in Alexandria did not last long. Six months after their wedding, the newlyweds were off to Alaska, not yet a State, for MG Brooks' first overseas assignment in the Army's 23rd Infantry Regiment. During their time there, the Brooks welcomed two sons: Leo Jr. and Vincent. The couple thrived in all aspects of Army life despite the distance from their families in Alexandria and the remoteness of the assignment.

As Lieutenant Brooks excelled in his assignments Naomi embraced her role in getting involved in the community and as a mother to two young boys. Naomi was involved in Officers' Wives Club events, sang in the chapel choir as well as taught General Education Development (GED) courses for soldiers at the

Army Education Center. Naomi had a call to action phrase which embraced her Christian upbringing as well as her natural optimism, "Bloom where ye are planted, and God will transplant you to greater things." Naomi was called "the glue" of the family because, no matter how many times MG Brooks Sr.'s military assignments took them to a brand-new place they'd all have to adjust to, she made sure that the family's home life was safe, secure, and full of love. The Brooks family moved a total of 28 times, and MG Brooks left to serve two tours in Vietnam while the family did not move.

The moves did not deter Naomi in her professional and personal pursuits. She continued to teach in the local elementary schools, and also expanded her education, taking courses at Morgan State University, and finishing her Masters in Elementary Education at Virginia State University (VSU). While at VSU, Naomi was a member of Kappa Delta Pi, the Professional Education Sorority, and the International Reading Association. She was also active in Greek Sorority life as a soror of Alpha Kappa Alpha (AKA). Naomi also volunteered for numerous community organizations.

Naomi saw it as her life's mission to serve her children, support her husband, and society, making sure all the lives she touched were filled with comfort, love, compassion, and understanding. Making a difference in each city they lived in was her reward.

She was honored the year before she died, in 2019, when she was awarded the Virginia Theological Seminary Dean's Cross. The award recognizes leaders who live by their baptismal promise to "strive for justice and peace among all people and respect the dignity of every human being." Former First Lady, Barbara Bush, and former US Secretary of State, Madeline Albright, were previous recipients.

Her educational career, which spanned 25 years, was honored posthumously on July 1, 2021, when the Matthew Maury Elementary School in Alexandria was renamed to the Naomi L. Brooks Elementary School.

Continuing Education Created a Foundation of Confidence and Leadership

The next stop for the young family was Central State College in Ohio, where then-Captain Leo Brooks was an instructor teaching military science to ROTC cadets. Brooks Sr. said it was probably one of the two most rewarding jobs in his military service. Naomi also worked at the college teaching remedial reading in the English Department, and Captain Brooks became a student himself and acquired 41 hours of undergraduate Business Administration courses to qualify for graduate school in business administration.

In 1963, the family of four moved back to Arlington, VA, a key year for the Civil Rights Movement. It was a year filled with hopeful messages like the March on Washington[530], and the travesties of violence

---

[530] "March on Washington" History. Officially called the March on Washington for Jobs and Freedom. 250,000 people gathered at the Lincoln Memorial on August 28, 1963. More than 3,000 members of the press covered the event.

like the bombing of the 16th Baptist Street Church[531] where four young girls, Addie Mae Collins (age 14), Denise McNair (age 11), Carole Robertson (age 14) and Cynthia Wesley (age 14) were killed.

Naomi was pregnant with their third child during this move and they were happy to be surrounded by family again. After two months into settling into their neighborhood of Arlington, Virginia and their rented home, Captain Brooks received orders to go to Vietnam. During that time, President John F. Kennedy was assassinated.

In this deployment, MG Brooks, then a captain, was an advisor to a Vietnamese depot commander. In his spare time, on weekends, he would go to a local leprosarium and visit the lepers who lived there. He would also repair items. He and two of his fellow advisors overhauled the French electric generator that lit the compound.

"I had several narrow escapes in my life of trouble and danger," said MG Brooks, Sr. "I give it to faith that I got back."

One of those times was when he was stationed in Qui Nhon, Vietnam, as an advisor. The Chaplain set up a religious retreat in the isolated, rural town of Ban Me Thuot. He was looking forward to going.

They boarded a small plane called an "Otter" and traveled. In the early evening, another plane was supposed to pick them up at an airstrip. The plane never showed up. It was nearly dark. They were in the middle of nowhere, not a soul around. Captain Brooks had no weapons on him. They were stranded.

At dusk the pair heard a hum in the background. A small plane was approaching. It landed and dropped its tailgate. The pilot came out to help get them in. To his surprise, it was a college classmate, and they went on to Ban Me Thuot.

"Later that night I apologized to God I didn't show patience and faith," he said.

In the darkness of war, there was light of joy.

On Father's Day, 1963, Captain Brooks was in Saigon. Normally this would be an easy trip, but the winds were so strong at Qui Nhon, that the pilots couldn't land the plane. So, the plane landed in Da Nang which was another 100 miles away. Captain Brooks was able to make a telephone connection with Naomi to see how she and the boys were, when he found out his daughter Marquita had been born. Being in close proximity to family was a source of help for Naomi, who was busy juggling the boys' activities and a new baby.

When Brooks arrived back home, the family moved several more times, arriving in Baltimore, where for two years, he was chief of the US Army Intelligence Material Support Office. During this time, Brooks

---

[531] Civil Rights Teaching, "Key Events in 1963". Less than three weeks after the March on Washington for Jobs and Freedom, a dynamite bomb planted by Klansmen explodes inside 16th Street Baptist Church on September 1, 1963. https://www.civilrightsteaching.org/1963#freedom

received a promotion to the next higher rank of Major and was a student yet again. He obtained his Master at George Washington University, taking nine hours of courses a semester while working full time.

"The kids were young, so I would go to school at night," explained MG Brooks, Sr. "I would come home 9:30-10 pm, go to bed, wake up at 3 am and study until 7 am until I had to go to work. On weekends and holidays, I would go to the library and study."

This discipline is something his sons still respect and remember to this day.

Then, in July of 1966, the family was packing again for a move, and, this time, they were headed for Kansas. Major Brooks was selected to attend the Command General Staff College in residence. Naomi dove right in, serving the community as a Cub Scout den mother. She had a handful of boys in her pack, including her two sons, and the group would do all kinds of projects in the family's basement.

Around 1966, while still a student at the Command General Staff College in Kansas, then Major Brooks was ordered to a job in the Pentagon where he would be a congressional affairs budget liaison officer in the Office of the Deputy Chief of Staff. The position would start in the Summer after he successfully graduated from Staff College. In April, the Army set up a day where all the real estate agents would come from Washington and meet with Army officers who were relocating there.

The room had tables where they would talk to the mid-career officers. Major Brooks met with one agent who told him about homes he could possibly purchase. Brooks would travel to DC in the Spring around Easter to see those properties and excited for the journey.

The homes he was shown that Saturday were not in Arlington like he had hoped they would be. This suburb was near the Pentagon. All the homes he toured were rundown homes in Alexandria. Brooks was aware White officers relocating were being shown much nicer homes.

Eventually, the realtor showed him a home that was for sale by a homeowner in Bren Mar Park in Fairfax County, Virginia. The drive to the office would be just 15 minutes. The owner of the home was an Army Judge Advocate General Corps (military lawyer) officer who was moving. Major Brooks met with that JAG officer that Sunday and made a deal directly with the seller. In June, when the Brooks family moved in, they were among the first to break the color barrier in this area.[532]

As a Congressional Affairs Officer for Logistics Budget in the Pentagon for the Army Major Leo Brooks would go back and forth to Capitol Hill and meet with Congressional staff members. He would explain to them the Army budget, going line by line to help the staffers understand. These staffers would then prepare their respective members for the hearings.

Brooks would carry a large briefcase, which contained dozens of folders that held numerous fact sheets on separate line items so he would be prepared for any questions.

---

[532] Phone conversation with authors, December 29, 2022

"This was a very stressful experience," said MG Brooks, Sr. "but the communication skills I used during this time, I learned from education. The greatest thing you get out of education is how to deal with people. You learn the technical skills, but it takes time for you to develop as a person to deal with all types of personalities."[533]

MG Brooks, Sr. remembered sometimes, the people he met with were easy to deal with, and at other times, they were not.

"There were some people in our country at that time who did not think a Black person had the skills to excel in finance or technical matters. So, you had to be confident. You needed to be twice as good to do your job. But gradually we've progressively grown to where the Army has gotten past that."[534]

Their neighbors were great, and they had friends throughout the neighborhood. Schools were integrated, but primarily white. The boys attended Bren Mar Elementary School, and little sister Marquita attended a private day school in Alexandria. Their parents emphasized education as the way to open doors for opportunity. Both Naomi and Leo were happy with this move, for this location was pivotal for their children, who were entering their formative years in education.

Each morning, MG Brooks, Sr. would walk by the bedroom his sons shared, and flipped on the switch to their stereo. Music played loudly, following a scurry of activity with the boys getting dressed for school and straightening up their beds and room before heading to the kitchen for breakfast. The children learned at a very young age they had a responsibility to their parents to become self-sufficient.

In June of 1970, MG Leo Brooks, Sr. was told he was going back to Vietnam for a second time, again for a one-year unaccompanied tour. While there, he would be the commander of a battalion. Having been promoted to Lieutenant Colonel with Naomi at his side, he was supposed command the 277th Supply and Service Battalion, but, after five months on the higher headquarters staff, the Army redirected him to the 266th Supply and Service Battalion.[535] Lieutenant Colonel Brooks was able to connect well with the people on the ground because he spoke some Vietnamese.

During that year when Brooks, Sr. was the commander of that battalion, the Army was drawing down the number of soldiers in surrounding battalions, leaving small units of about 50 people to support their area. Major General Walter Woolwine, the senior logistician in Vietnam would tell the staff during this drawdown period, "Give that LSA (Logistics Support Activity)[536] to Leo."[537] This happened several times which greatly expanded the numbers of troops in his battalion, the complexity and the challenges.

---

[533] Phone conversation with authors, December 29, 2022
[534] Phone conversation with authors, December 29, 2022
[535] BG Leo A. Brooks & the 761st Tank Battalion, The Army Historical Foundation
[536] Logistics Support Area (LSA) is a military term which refers to military facilities which act as depot, barracks, and transportation hubs, providing supplies and personnel to facilities closer to or within arenas of armed conflict.
[537] BG Leo A. Brooks & the 761st Tank Battalion, The Army Historical Foundation

As the battalion commander, Lieutenant Colonel Brooks would be responsible to commit the unit to its missions and oversee them as they supplied food, clothing, general supplies, fuel, vehicles and such services as laundry and graves registration to the units in the surrounding area. By the end of his tour of duty the battalion had grown from approximately 800 people to 2,600 people.

There was an additional enemy Lieutenant Colonel Brooks was fighting in Vietnam – heroin. Veterans were recorded saying they used the drug as a way to manage their fear and tensions of war.[538] The drug was popular amongst U.S. soldiers in the early 1970s. Lieutenant Colonel Leo Brooks was awarded the Legion of Merit and a Bronze Star for his service in Vietnam.

Home Life

Outside of his military deployments, MG Brooks, Sr. would still pick up his trombone and play his favorite hymns. His two sons also learned to play, with help from their father. Leo Jr learned trumpet and Vincent trombone. The three of them on one occasion played as a group outside of the house. In the early 1970's, they played at the Quander family reunion. "The Brooks Band" brass trio played two hymns: "Rise Up O Men of God", and "My Faith Looks Up to Thee." Father Leo Brooks, Sr. played trombone, and the younger Brooks brothers played their respective instruments. Leo Brooks, Jr. was 13 years old and Vincent Brooks was 12.

Just like the Brooks home where Leo Sr was raised, music was ever present in the home of Leo and Naomi Brooks. Naomi had a natural talent for playing piano without ever being formally taught. She could play piano by ear. She loved asking a family member to name a song and she would play it. Marquita played the piano and guitar. A nod in keeping the tradition of the Brooks family learning how to use their hands, all three children learned the art of woodworking and other crafts, such as painting and auto mechanics working in do-it-yourself craft shops with their Dad.

Family life was important to both Naomi and Leo Brooks, balancing work and family life, cheering at most of their children's football and basketball games as well as track meets, and tennis matches. Their daughter, Marquita, became the Virginia quarter mile 440-mile champion and played basketball and tennis. Leo Jr. exceled in football and track, and Vincent outclassed his competitors in basketball.

Sundays were reserved for worship and time with family. Naomi loved to sing in church choirs wherever they were stationed. The one closest to her heart was "Guide Me, O Thou Great Jehovah."

Guide Me, O Thou Great Jehovah

Guide me, O thou great Jehovah, pilgrim through this barren land.

I am weak, but thou art might; hold me with thy pow'rful hand.

---

[538] J Mintz, C P O'Brien, B Pomerantz- Am J Drug , The impact of Vietnam service on heroin- addicted veterans, Alcohol Abuse, 1979, National Library of Medicine

Bread of heaven, bread of heaven, feed me till I want no more,

feed me till I want no more.

Open now the crystal fountain whence the healing stream doth flow;

Let the fiery, cloudy pillar lead me all my journey through.

Strong deliv'rer, strong deliv'rer, be thou still my strength and shield,

be thou still my strength and shield.

When I tread the verge of Jordan, bid my anxious fears subside;

death of death and hell's destruction, land me safe on Canaan's side.

Songs of praises, songs of praises I will ever give to thee,

I will ever give to thee.

Connecting with each other around the table, eating their afternoon dinner was important. Opinions were shared on varied topics and each learned to hold his or her own in debate. This day was a reset, and a reaffirmation of the family credo: faith in God and family was the secret ingredient to keeping a family together and strong.

Leo and Naomi believed when their boys were teenagers, that the best way to stay connected with them was through supporting them in their sports and other school activities. Leo Sr. would work his demanding schedule so that he could leave the office at 3 to go see his kids play their sport games and encouraged their participation. He would use those events to keep open communications with his kids when they were going through teenage life when they tried to break away. Naomi and Leo Sr. would always discuss the games with their player children when it was over. Once the game and conversation were over, Brooks, then a Colonel; would often return to his military office, where he would finish his work for the day and arrive home around 10 pm.

During those high school years, Colonel Brooks, Sr. managed to attend all but one of Vincent's basketball games, and he never missed one of Leo Jr.'s football games or any of Marquita's tennis matches.

MG Brooks, Sr. said, "Being a father is tougher than being a soldier because it takes time, patience, love and understanding to be a good father. You need to be there for your children. This is why you see less successful fathers compared to successful career men. It was *my* responsibility to make sure I balanced everything in my life. It was done by using moderation. It was my responsibility as a father to make my family the priority. Was playing golf with friends or staying at work over seeing my children's games more important? I found a way to make the time. Every parent really has this responsibility. Children learn more by what you do than by what you say."[539]

When Brooks, Sr. was on assignment, Naomi ran the house. During the second Vietnam tour the kids were 12, 11, and 6.

"She held their (the kid's feet) feet to the fire when it came to school." At the time she was teaching fifth grade students in a different public school system.

The second trip to Vietnam was much more impactful for the family at home. Memories still linger with the children, now mature adults. The family sent Dad to war at Dulles Airport and negative thoughts remain when the jet-setting children of Leo and Naomi Brooks travel through there. Vincent cried for weeks when his father deployed to Vietnam for the second time. Unlike today, deployed soldiers in the 1970's had few opportunities to have a phone call with family. Handwritten letters from home or from Vietnam, reel to reel tapes that would be weeks old, and one phone call at Christmas time were the methods used by the Brooks family to keep in touch.

While he was in Vietnam, the family car became unreliable, and Naomi needed to buy a new vehicle. Leo Sr. read in one of her letters that she wanted to buy a Volkswagen camper, the preference of the three children.

"I wrote her back and said, 'Don't you dare buy that camper,'" chuckled Brooks. Sr. "I can just see my son's picking up someone's daughter to go to the prom in a camper! So Naomi got a VW Super Beetle which we kept for years and all of the kids got their licenses driving that car."

When their kids were 12 and 13, Brooks, Sr. told them, and continued to tell them, they would not be allowed to drive until they could pay for the car insurance. Brooks, Sr. wanted to make sure their kids developed responsibility as he did as a youth working in his grandfather and father's businesses and in other money-making jobs.

While the sons started mowing lawns for pay around age 11 and 12 and had household chores for a small allowance, MG Brooks believed getting a paid job would further instill their sense of responsibility.

Leo A. Brooks, Jr went to work after school at the home-improvement store The Hechinger Company.

"At first they did not want to hire him," Brooks, Sr. said. "I went down and raised a little bit of hell and they hired him because they had hired a couple of his schoolmates. When he got his paycheck, he would turn it over to me until it reached $300." Unbeknownst to Brooks, Jr. when he gave his father his money, the money was put into savings bonds in his name.

---

[539] Phone interview with authors, December 29, 2022

After returning home from Vietnam in 1971, Leo Brooks Sr. became the deputy secretary of the general staff of the U.S. Army Materiel Command in Washington, D.C. Brooks worked in that role for one year before being selected to attend the National War College in Washington, D.C.

Watching their parents better their careers through education was a common sight for the children of Leo and Naomi Brooks. While faith was the foundation of their spiritual fortitude, education, they saw firsthand, helped open doors for opportunity.

MG Brooks explained, each level of schooling would add to his toolbox of leadership.

"As a second lieutenant, you go to school for about 14 weeks. As a captain, you go to school for six months, then as a major you go and attend school for a year. If you're lucky enough, which not many people are, you get to go to war college, and that's another year. The psychology you learned during this time helped me as a leader and managing people. My father was a master of evaluating people. I wanted to be like him. I became pretty good at measuring individuals (and) their worth."[540]

This knowledge helped MG Brooks both in his military operations and government work.

Rising Above Racial Hate

While the Brooks family had many positive experiences of educational integration and community acceptance, as a Black family in the late sixties and early seventies the Brooks, like many other Black Americans were subjected to racist taunts and threats. One morning, when the boys who were in the later years of elementary school, opened the door to go walk to school, they saw in their front yard a large cross had burned in their yard.

The cross was hard to miss. Gasoline, which was poured and lit charred the ground in the shape of a cross, which was around six feet long, and around three to four feet wide.[541]

"Leo and Vincent showed it to me first," said Leo Brooks, Sr. "I then dug out the spots where the cross was. I said nothing. My daughter never even knew about it. I cut the grass down real low, so nobody knew. I could have made a big federal case out of it but the reason I said nothing is I learned from my parents if you stopped to throw stones at a barking dog, you'd losing time on your journey. So, I knew the best way to handle it that whoever did it would not get the public reaction they were looking for."

We presumed some high school kids were behind the act.

The family pushed forward, and both the boys excelled in sports and in academics. Leo Brooks, Sr., and Naomi raised their children to look at the whole person, not their color. *Be* you, and don't set artificial limits on what *you* can do or what *you* can be.

---

[540] Phone conversation with authors December 29, 2022
[541] Conversation with BG Leo A. Brooks, Jr. December 29, 2022

The Brooks brothers and their sister were college preparatory curriculum students and star athletes like their mom. But while their academic success was celebrated at home, some of the Black students who attended school with them would make fun of Leo Jr. and Vincent using the racial epithet, "Uncle Tom"[542] used among African Americans.

Leo Sr. and Naomi encouraged their children not to listen to the social pressure and taught them that excelling in school was **not** about denying their Black culture or identifying as Black and wanting to be "White". Doing well in school would enable them to achieve their dreams. Their children took this to heart and continued to persevere and excel.

Defining Moment

In the late 1970's, MG Brooks, Sr. was selected for a promotion to colonel and was assigned to the Office of the Joint Chiefs of Staff as the Cambodian desk logistics officer. He was supposed to work in this position for three years, but after 13 months, he received new orders to move to Lexington, Kentucky.

"Vincent was excited because it was a big basketball center" said MG Brooks, Sr. "Then three weeks later I got a second set of orders directing me to Sacramento, California instead."

Colonel Brooks would become the Commander of the Sacramento Army Depot, where he would oversee an electronics rebuild plant and a storage and distribution center operated by 700 government civilians. At first, Leo, Jr. was not happy, for he was going into his senior year in high school, had been elected captain of the varsity football team, and had just attended Boys State as an emerging leader in the Commonwealth of Virginia. He wanted to graduate with his friends.

"I found out the public schools (in Sacramento) at that time were not very strong academically, and I told the boys I was going to put them in the Jesuit High School," said MG Brooks, Sr. "The boys said that was fine because at Jesuit, they love football, basketball, and academics. But when I told them there were no girls in the school, they said to me, 'Why are you going to punish us?'"

Girls attended two nearby Catholic high schools. Marquita attended a Catholic diocesan elementary school (St. Philomene) associated with one of the two high schools.

Once in California, Naomi and Leo, Sr. discussed Vincent and his desire to learn how to drive. Leo, Sr. sat Vincent down, and told him the same story he told his older brother; that he needed to get a job to pay for his insurance. Vincent, grudgingly, got a job at a nearby McDonald's, and Leo Brooks, Sr. put Vincent's money into savings bonds under his name, as well.

When Vincent was finished with his job, Brooks, Sr. sat him down and said, "Son, what have you learned from all of this? He looked at me and said, 'never to eat again at McDonald's.'"

---

[542] A Black person who is overeager to win the approval of whites (as by obsequious behavior or uncritical acceptance of white values and goals)- Merriam Webster

Years later, when MG Brooks, Sr. visited both Leo, Jr. and Vincent, who were both then cadets at West Point. He was sitting on a bench with them and a few of their friends, and the story of the sons working to pay their car insurance arose.

"One of the friends said, 'Sir, is it true you made your sons earn $300 before they could drive your car?' and I said yes. What that told me was that when I required it, they thought at the time it was cruel. But now they are bragging about it because they realized, at this age, the importance of it."

Unlike the family's prior moves, where they had their own house, the family lived on the military base. It was the first time the children saw their father on the job as the top ranking person in the organization, and the respect the fellow officers and soldiers gave him when they addressed him. They always knew his role in the Army was important, but seeing the veneration in person made a large impression on them.

Second Generation Off to College

In Sacramento, both Leo A. Brooks, Jr and his brother, Vincent Brooks, attended Jesuit High School. Naomi and Leo Brooks, Sr. watched their sons being courted by coaches from around the country to play for their colleges. This included West Point. Brooks, Sr. never pressured his sons to go into the military or to the Military Academy. In fact, Vincent Brooks wanted to become a doctor. He took a volunteer job at the University of California, Davis, in the pathology lab to observe autopsies to supplement his courses in anatomy and physiology in high school.

When the opportunity came for their oldest to choose a college, Leo Brooks, Jr decided to go to West Point. Leaving the family for field exercises and deployments to Vietnam was hard on MG Brooks, Sr. but, it was part of his job. He had never experienced his children leaving *him* before. When it was time for Leo Brooks, Jr. to leave for West Point, the family took him to the airport.

"At first, he hugged his sister goodbye, and I could handle that," remembered MG Brooks, Sr. "Then he hugged his mother goodbye, and then I saw my two grown sons hug goodbye, and I couldn't take it very much more and then he hugged me, and the tears just flowed. I got over it pretty quickly. We put him on the airplane, and then we went to a restaurant to have breakfast. We were at the table, and I got ready to pray and started crying. Then everyone else started to cry. We then got up and didn't eat anything. I dropped some change on the table before the food was served and left. It was just that emotional."

Then Colonel Brooks, Sr.'s heart ached, but he knew his son would be near family and friends. His eldest brother Houston Brooks, Jr lived in nearby New Jersey, and agreed to meet Leo Jr. at the airport and drop him off at West Point. He also had a Fort Leavenworth, Kansas classmate, Colonel Roger Edgington, who was assigned as the Comptroller of West Point. Colonel Brooks, Sr. called and asked him to look after his son.

In December of that year, Leo, Jr. came home wearing his West Point uniform. Seeing his big brother wearing the West Point Grey uniform inspired Vincent Brooks, who had already been accepted into pre-medicine programs at three universities. So much so, the lanky, much taller Brooks tried on his brother's uniform, telling his older brother he wanted to go to West Point now but feared it was too late because it was very late the admissions timeline, which normally begins during junior year in high school. Vincent was halfway through senior year.

Not wanting to let his little brother down, on his return to West Point, Cadet Leo Brooks, Jr spoke with West Point's head basketball coach, Mike "*Coach K*" Krzyzewski, about his brother. Vincent applied and placed in two tracks – a recruited athlete as well as a traditional applicant.

The next year, the Brooks family saw off their two sons on the 7 am plane out of Sacramento to San Francisco and from there across the country to LaGuardia airport.

Leo Sr.'s time in California's capital was not to last long. In 1976, after Vincent joined Leo at West Point, Brooks, with Naomi and daughter Marquita, was assigned to Fort Hood, Texas[543], to command the 13th Corps Support Command. He led the organization of eight specialized battalions and 9,000 troops for maintenance, engineering, and logistic services, as well as inventory management of supplies and equipment maintenance to support the Army's mobile armored Corps.

While at Fort Hood, still a colonel, Brooks, Sr. had thirty company commanders, of which two were female. His most vivid memory was of Captain Donna Lightfoot, who commanded a Truck Company that excelled in every task. He would not tolerate gender discrimination and worked hard to thwart any intolerance amongst the male soldiers. Concurrently, Vincent was part of the first class at West Point to include women.

MG Brooks, Sr.'s military and civilian education made him one of the Army's premier logisticians.[544] In 1978, Brooks became an Army general, promoted to the one-star rank of Brigadier General. Naomi assisted in pinning on his first star. Leo and Vincent would later wear those same stars.

The family's two years in Texas were coming to an end. They were off to Fort Lee, Virginia, where, as Commanding General of the U.S. Army Troop Support Agency, he managed the system of 187 Army commissary stores worldwide. For three years, then BG Brooks, Sr would travel to eight foreign countries. Alaska, Hawaii, and Puerto Rico to visit the Army's grocery stores.

Then, on one summer day in 1981, MG Brooks received a call notifying him he had new orders and had one week to travel to Philadelphia to become Commanding General of the Defense Personnel Support Center and promoted to the two-star rank of Major General. The household property would come later.

In this role; he would be responsible for the procurement, storage, and distribution of all of the food, medicine, medical equipment, medical supplies, clothing, and other textile items for all of the military services and the U.S. Department of Veterans Affairs.

---

[543] Fort Hood, Texas was renamed as Fort Cavazos in 2023.
[544] History Makers Brigadier General Leo Brooks, Sr.

He flew back a week later to move Naomi into their temporary housing on base. At the same time as this move, their youngest child, Marquita, was moving to James Madison University to attend college.

The family gathered for the promotion ceremony, and as had been the case when Leo Sr. began his career twenty-eight years earlier, Naomi was there to pin on the second star of a Major General.

Second star Major General Promotion, July 1, 1982

Source: Brooks Family

While serving as Major General, in Philadelphia, he met W. Wilson Goode, Sr., who had just been elected Mayor of Philadelphia. In December 1983, before the inauguration, Philadelphia's first black mayor, Mayor Goode, Sr., offered him the job of Managing Director for the City of Philadelphia. Leo Sr. accepted his offer.

Since he retired before serving three full years at his military grade of Major General, he was required to retire with a reduction of one rank as a Brigadier General. During his retirement ceremony in February 1984, MG Brooks, Sr. was awarded the Army Distinguished Service Medal and the Defense Superior Service Medal, added to numerous awards he received over his 30-year career.

As Managing Director, MG Brooks, Sr. oversaw the operation of the ten different service departments (police, fire, prisons, licenses and inspections, public property, recreation records, human services, streets, and health) of the city. He also negotiated labor contracts.

MG Brooks, Sr. was brought up to speed on the growing tensions between the Black middle-class neighborhood Osage Block Association and the Black liberation organization, MOVE. The Osage Avenue residents expressed to the city they had had enough of the teeming piles of garbage and human waste on its once clean streets and the booming rat population and dozens of dogs as a result of MOVE.[545] They were also fearful for their lives after some neighbors were assaulted and threatened. The group would also use megaphones mounted on their rowhouse at all times of day and night, filling the air with obscene rants and angry speech.

---

[545] Frank Trippet, "It Looks Just Like a War Zone" Time Magazine originally written May 27, 1985, reprinted June 24, 2001.

The group's goal was to win the freedom for nine of their members, known as the MOVE 9. The group was charged with the murder of Officer James J. Ramp, and for injuring 16 officers during a 1978 standoff. Mayor Goode and Police Commissioner Sambor classified MOVE as a terrorist organization due to its terroristic threats.

In 1985, MG Brooks, Sr. learned his father was diagnosed with prostate cancer. He informed the mayor he was resigning so he could take care of his ailing father. The mayor asked him to remain until Summer. MG Brooks, Sr. agreed to do so.

On the morning of May 13, 1985, police initiated its large operation to serve warrants on four MOVE members. The warrants charged the members with making terrorist threats, parole violations, contempt of court, and the illegal possession of firearms.[546] Hundreds of police officers, along with Police Commissioner Gregore J. Sambor, and Managing Director Brooks, arrived at the row house, which was converted into a fortified compound.[547] Neighborhood residents were evacuated prior to the operation.

The police were unable to remove the MOVE members after a long standoff, where rounds of ammo were exchanged between officers and MOVE members.[548] Even teargas was used. It was finally decided a satchel charge containing plastic explosives was to be dropped from a helicopter onto the fortification on the rooftop of the building. Because the roof of the MOVE rowhouse was covered with tar, a fire quickly spread, destroying nearly an entire block of homes. In the end, five children and six adults were killed.[549]

Mayor Goode took full responsibility for the actions of the police that day. Three years later, MG Brooks, Sr. was cleared of all criminal liability by a Philadelphia grand jury in 1988.[550] According to news reports covering the case, the grand jury said, "neither Mayor Goode nor Leo A. Brooks, the city's managing director at the time, were criminally liable because neither took part in the decision to let the fire burn."[551] Neither were suspects at any time and only provided testimony before the Grand Jury as witnesses.

Ten days after the bombing, General Brooks resigned from his position, citing "familial obligations," and moved back to Virginia to take care of his father.[552] [553] MG Brooks, Sr. took care of his father, Reverend Houston Brooks, patriarch of the Brooks family, until he passed away on October 21, 1987.

After his father passed away, MG Brooks, Sr. briefly worked as an independent consultant.

Reflecting on his life and career, MG Brooks, Sr. said his greatest job in life has been being a father. " I enjoyed being called Leo's dad or Vincent's dad or Marquita's dad."

---

[546] Trippett

[547] Gene Demby, "Trying to Make Sense of The MOVE Bombing", NPR, May 13, 2015

[548] Trippett

[549] History.com On This Day in History, May 13, 1985

[550] William K. Stevens, "Grand Jury Clears Everyone in Fata Philadelphia Siege", New York Times, May 4, 1988

[551] William K. Stevens "Grand Jury Clears Everyone in Fata Philadelphia Siege", New York Times, May 4, 1988

[552] Oral History interview with BG Leo A. Brooks, 12/02/2013, The History Makers

[553] Phone conversation with BG Leo A. Brooks, Sr. December 29, 2022

Looking back, he said the advice he was given as a child by his parents and grandparents and passed on to his own children, has never been more relevant for today's youth.

"My first piece of advice is about choices," said MG Brooks, Sr. "You have the choice of succeeding or failing. And you have the choice of joining activities that distract from your journey. You have the choice of getting involved with people who themselves have problems. And so, you get to decide whether you want to distract yourself at any stage of your life. You decided to take the chance to let that trouble into your life. The second piece of advice has to do with your faith. Faith is a choice even for a young person. Having faith in God and being a participant in a congregation is so important because of the mutual support. The third piece of advice has to do with your friends. Certain people can put pressure on you. Because of that, you need to associate with people who share your thoughts spiritually, psychologically, emotionally, and physically. That's the essence of my advice."

Chapter Three
Brigadier General Leo A. Brooks Jr.

Leo A. Brooks, Jr.

Brigadier General Leo Austin Brooks Jr. was born in Anchorage, Alaska on August 15, 1957. The eldest son of Leo Brooks, Sr. and Naomi once said it was engrained in him at a very young age to never limit himself in terms of what he wanted to become or what his goal was to achieve. This advice empowered the young Brooks to create his own path in life and overcome whatever obstacles that were before him.

The Brooks family lived a life focused on faith, personal excellence and mutual love and support. Mom and Dad were loving yet always encouraged and pushed their children to do their best. Leo Jr. was keenly aware no matter what your age, your actions were a reflection of your family. He saw this in the daily actions of his parents and grandparents. His mom was a great influence on him as a child. The demands of the Army on Leo's dad meant his mother Naomi carried a bigger load than many mothers. She had to balance her roles as a mother, teacher, student (if she was taking additional college courses), as well as fulfilling her duties in extracurricular roles, such as a cub scout leader and choir member. Her ability to gracefully handle the pressures that could break others was a constant example to him of love and strength.

"My parents had such a loving and supportive relationship. Dad adored her and she was always proud to be his wife," said Leo Jr. "My mother always said the Army gets two for the price of one. Once my father became more senior, there were constant expected duties of her as an Army spouse in addition to other things she was doing to support us growing up."

"Academics were very important to my parents," explained Leo Jr. My mother would ensure we got our homework completed and check what we did. When my father got home, he would quiz us on what we learned."

We usually looked forward to reviewing report cards with our father and mother. Leo Sr. would say the same words he was told by his father when there were Bs listed, "That's a pretty good report card son. I'm proud of you. Now what are we going to do about those two Bs?"[554]

Living in civilian communities instead of on the military post for the majority of their experiences enabled the Brooks children to "Bloom where ye are planted," as their mom would tell them. Part of the blooming process was knowing your self-worth and believing in yourself.

"We were raised to not focus on our color, but instead focus on being the best at what we do," said Leo Jr.

The brothers were tight, and they played hard together. Living in the various communities around the country, the young Brooks sons and their little sister Marquita were able to meet kids who were raised in different cultural settings.

When the family moved to Bren Mar Park in Fairfax County, Virginia and their family broke the color barrier in their neighborhood. The Brooks children would play with the neighborhood kids. They also learned valuable lessons from their parents on humility and on appreciating your fellow man, taught to them by working-class parents.

In the Bren Mar Park neighborhood, the Brooks as homeowners paid for trash removal. One day, a worker from another trash company accidentally made an unscheduled trash collection at the Brooks home. The children did not think about the hard labor that went into this job. Leo, Jr., then a fifth-grader said to his father, "Look we are getting two trash cans removals for free!"

His father simply replied, "Son, never take advantage of another man's hard toil and labor." Leo Jr. watched his father walk over to the worker telling him he had the wrong house.

Leo Jr. remembers those words as if they were spoken yesterday.

As with many young children, the Brooks sons and their sister were full of energy and spirit. To give Mother Naomi a break, and to find time to bond more with his sons, Leo Sr., would take one or both sons for a half day at work at the Pentagon on Saturdays. Marquita was then too young. The boys learned then to navigate inside the huge, five-sided, multi-floored, labyrinth of corridors and offices, something that gave them immediate advantages when they were both assigned to the Pentagon as officers themselves.

On one of those Saturday trips, it was pouring rain. They saw a woman's car had a flat tire on the side of the Shirley Highway (now called I-395). Then-Major Brooks Sr. pulled off at the next exit and parked the car off the road where he then climbed up a hill and ran across Interstate 395 to help her change the tire while wearing his Army green uniform.

---

[554] Phone interview with authors, December 29, 2022

"That's the kind of guy he is," said Leo Jr. "He's humble, yet proud. He could be cocky when he needed to be, but in the end, he was always humble, and he showed us that all the time."

Athletically inclined like their mother and father, the Brooks children all participated in team sports and their days were filled with attending sports practice. Leo Jr. chuckled, remembering a time when he was entering sixth grade. He walked into the classroom, and he saw his fifth-grade teacher who would now be his sixth-grade teacher. They both looked at each other and said, "Oh no, not you!"[555] Leo Jr. credits Ms. Adeline Waters with having a lasting impact on young Leo's academic development.

Rising Above Social and Racial Backlash

The parenting of Naomi and Leo Brooks, Sr. created a strong base for their children and helped foster inner confidence.

They always watched their father and mother's actions in response to racism. Their parent's actions offered them not only guidance but reassurance. The strength of their father taking the higher road showed the young pre-teenage boys how to act like responsible men. Racism was an unfortunate, albeit infrequently part of their lives, and they learned how to handle it. But Leo Jr. would face something he never did before junior high school, and that was social backlash about his father serving in the Vietnam War.

When Leo Jr. was in junior high (seventh or eighth grade) at Oliver Wendell Holmes Intermediate School in Fairfax County, his father was serving as battalion commander in Vietnam. The anti-Vietnam War sentiment and public demonstrations around the country did not stop in the streets. Anti-war opinions were also expressed in the schools.

Leo Jr. would face or hear criticisms from classmates regarding the War while he was worrying about his father's safety while fighting in that war for the second time. He was told what his father was doing in Vietnam was "wrong, and evil."[556] Leo Jr. knew they were incorrect, but it didn't minimize the effect of their hurtful words.

When his father came back from his second Vietnam tour, Leo Jr would cherish going into the Pentagon with his father on Saturdays for a half-day of work. The remainder of the day would be dedicated to chores and play. During the week, he appreciated his father intentionally carving out time for him and his sporting events. Leo Jr. was a running back on his high school football team and one of the top competitors in Northern Virginia in the triple jump event in track and field. Sports in the Washington DC metropolitan were intensely followed and that passion for the sport occasionally added to racial tensions as integration in the public school systems was still nascent.

The Brooks family grew up in a transitional time for education in America. In the city of Arlington, Virginia where Leo Jr. attended first grade the city was in its' final steps of educational integration and

---

[555] BG Leo A. Brooks, Jr. conversation with authors, November 20, 2022
[556] BG Leo A. Brooks, Jr. conversation with authors, November 20, 2022

there were riots of protest. Despite all U.S. public schools officially desegregating in 1954[557], and, the following year in 1955, where the Supreme Court ruled school desegregation must take place with "all deliberate speed"[558], schools in Virginia had different levels of desegregation and integration. For almost a decade, a series of lawsuits ensued for Black students to be integrated into white schools.[559] There was still unrest in the public school system when the Brooks family returned to northern Virginia, in Leo Jr's case, from fifth grade to eleventh grade in the most consequential and turbulent period of the 1960's and early 1970's. His mother Naomi, an educator, taught at the same time in the City of Alexandria where racial tensions were the highest in the area.

The 1960's was a time filled with civil unrest and racial riots. The assassination of Reverend Martin Luther King, Jr. on April 4, 1968, led to four days of rioting and protesting with buildings in Washington, DC set ablaze. King's assassination was just four days after the delivery of his "Remaining Awake Through a Great Revolution" sermon at the National Cathedral. For student athletes like Leo, Jr. he experienced the paradoxical racism first-hand.

"On the field, race did not matter," said Leo Brooks, Jr. "You were valued as a teammate and what you could contribute to the team. Off the field, however, race was a part of the social scene."

In the Summer of 1971, the city of Alexandria was integrating all three of its high schools (two all-White and one partially-Black) into one high school for the city. T.C. Williams High School would become the 11th and 12th grade high school for both races. The decision to integrate the two schools and sport programs, like football, led to racial unrest. Leo Jr. was in high school at that time, attending, Thomas Jefferson High School. Worries of race riots happening there were not far from the minds of students and teachers.

One day, at Leo Jr.'s high school, a fight broke out around lunch time between 10-15 Black American students and around same number of white students.[560]

Later that day, Leo Jr.'s head football coach pulled him aside after the fight to ask him at practice if he was involved in the fight. "Did someone call you an Oreo or something?'"[561]

---

[557] Brown vs. The Board of Education of Topeka 347 U.S. 483 (1954) Justia US Supreme Court Brown v. Board of Education of Topeka :: 347 U.S. 483 (1954) :: Justia US Supreme Court Center

[558] Brown v. Board of Education of Topeka, 349 U.S. 294 (1955) Brown v. Board of Education of Topeka :: 349 U.S. 294 (1955) :: Justia US Supreme Court Center

[559] "Desegregation of Virginia Education (DOVE), Old Dominion University https://ww1.odu.edu/library/special-collections/dove/timeline

[560] BG Books Jr. conversation with Authors, November 20, 2022

[561] a Black person who is regarded as having adopted the attitudes, values, and behavior thought to be characteristic of middle-class white society, often at the expense of their own heritage.- Dictionary.com

Leo Jr. told him he was not involved in the fight, and no racial slurs were said to him, but he did witness the fight. Leo Jr. knew his teammates were not against him but the racial charge in the environment was unsettling. The school tried to simmer down tensions by separating the students and held conferences regarding the incident.[562]

Leo Jr. would talk to his parents about the school incident. They would reassure him and support him. Reminding the teen, the only thing he could control was what he did. The family mantra of not focusing on your color; focusing on being the best at what *you* do was embraced even harder.

The young Brooks had the tools to deal with racial prejudice but for the first time in his life he received social push back from an unlikely source- his fellow Black students. This was something he did not understand, and the words cut deep in his heart.

Leo Brooks, Jr. was competitive on the field and in the classroom. He was a college preparatory student, and he was proud of his academic achievements. One day he was chastised by some Black students on his good grades, and they called him an "Uncle Tom"[563].

He was taken aback. Just because he wanted to learn and excel in school did not make him want to be White. This did not sit well with young Leo to have his identity challenged and his pride as a young Black man questioned. He was raised to be proud of being Black, but ever vigilant and aware that he would not always be treated fairly due to the color of his skin, and that education and excellence would open doors for him. Why didn't his friends view education the same way?

How could education make you less Black? He believed he was a part of that culture regardless of his good grades. The only "difference" was his family valued education, pursued careers, and pushed him to excel. So how can that be anti-Black?

Throughout the formative years, the continued counsel from his parents was to take the higher road, be unpretentious, not aggressive, and putting your faith in God. His faith was deep and part of his personal foundation and while it helped him make the right decisions, it did not take the sting away from the hurtful words.

Unwanted Change

The summer before Leo Jr.'s senior year, he received word from his parents that no teenager would want to hear. They were moving. But the relocation was not a state or two away where they could still see family and friends. No, they were moving from the East Coast to the West Coast. They would be living on the Army post in Sacramento, California where their father, now a Colonel, would be Commander of the Sacramento Army Depot.

---

[562] BG Brooks, Jr. phone conversation with authors, November 20, 2022
[563] Uncle Tom is a slur used to disparage a black person who is humiliatingly subservient or deferential to white people.

"I did not want to go," said Leo Jr. "I had several families willing to let me stay with them, but my father would have none of that. He said he had done everything in his power through the years to keep us in one place (while my father went to Vietnam and had several different assignments in the Washington DC metropolitan area, the family stayed in one place for seven consecutive years), but we were together as a family for only so long and I was going to California with everyone else. I begrudgingly went."

The family moved in the Summer of 1974, and Leo Jr.'s fear of making new friends would quickly fade away. His parents enrolled the children in private parochial schools to ensure there was a continued focus on academics for college preparation. Word quickly spread he was an accomplished football player and a track standout. He made fast friends and connected with the players and students. The smaller school was rooted in college preparatory academics and excellent sports and BG Brooks, Jr's fellow athletes also valued education and doing well in school. They saw him for who he was, not the color of his skin. There was only one other Black student enrolled in the school at that time. The Brooks brothers and one freshman increased the population to four in the 1974-1975 academic year. The bonds he formed with some of these students were so strong he is still friends with them today. Leo Jr. excelled at Jesuit High School. He played football as a running back and as an outside linebacker, earning for him the team's "Iron Man Award" was awarded annually to the toughest, hardest hitting defensive player.

Even though the Brooks were no longer in the South, that did not mean the darkness of bigotry wasn't present on the West Coast.

After a track meet in early Spring of 1975, Leo Jr. was on a road trip with his teammates. He drove his Volkswagen Super Beetle car with four white track mates. They pulled into a 7-Eleven to get *Slurpees*. A Sheriff's Deputy from the area walked into the store and confronted Leo Jr. who was standing with his friends at the register.

"Let me see your ID," the Sheriff's Deputy said sternly, with no explanation.

Leo Jr. was confused and asked, "What did I do?"

The Sheriff Deputy ignored the question.

"What did I do?" he asked. His friends flashed passing glances at one another. They too were also puzzled.

The Sheriff's Deputy continued to stare at Leo Jr.

Leo asked again, "What did I do?" .

The Sheriff Deputy shifted his weight on his feet. No answer.

"Tell me what I did?" young Brooks asked for a third time.

The Deputy Sheriff finally spoke, "Shut up. I said, show me your ID."

Leo Jr. pulled out his Jesuit High School ID and driver's license. The officer looked at the card and walked back to his patrol vehicle. At no point did he address or look at the other teens standing there with Leo Jr.

Leo Jr. and his friends looked at each other, not saying a word. Time continued to pass. Eventually, his teammates walked back to his car without any interference.

The Deputy Sheriff walked back into the store and found Leo Brooks Jr. standing by himself.

Returning the ID, the Sheriff's Deputy said, "Here."

Not saying a word, Leo Jr., had the presence of mind to read the deputy's name tag.

The Sheriff Deputy said nothing else, and never told him why he stopped him. He walked out of the convenience store and proceeded on his way.

When Leo Jr. got home, he told his parents what happened. His father was furious. Because of his father's role as Commander of the Army Depot, he was an ex-officio member of the Chamber of Commerce for the State Capital of Sacramento.

Unbeknownst to Leo Jr. at the time, his father went through business channels demanding an answer. A few days passed, and one day Leo Jr., received a phone call from the head of the sheriff's office apologizing for the deputy's actions. The Sheriff explained there was a robbery in the area and the suspect was described as a young Black man. Leo Jr. automatically became a target.

To this day, BG Leo Brooks Jr., thinks about the event -- how the situation unfolded, the singling out because of the color of his skin, and the disrespect he felt. He wonders why the Sheriff's Deputy just didn't ask him, "Hey, where have you guys been? We just had a robbery. I'm just checking IDs." If the Deputy was smart," BG Leo Brooks Jr. said, "he would have checked everyone's ID's."

Making the Grade

Living on the Army post gave the Brooks children the ability to see how people in positions of leadership responded to their father who was, at that time, a Colonel and the most senior officer on the post. This was the first time in many years the Brooks children saw their father at work during a work week where there would be interaction. They were not able to see those relationships when their father worked at the Pentagon. This made an impression on Leo, Jr and Vincent who were now in their Senior and Junior year in High School respectively. Marquita was six years younger and in elementary school. "I was very proud," said Leo Jr. "He was a pillar in the community, not just on the post. I would go into the headquarters with him. You would see his picture on the wall depicting his position in the chain of command up to the President. You would then walk the halls until you got to his giant corner office. My dad was a very humble guy, he never saw himself above others, but he commanded tremendous respect because he was so good with people and knew his business. He was raised by my grandfather who was also humble and yet was held with great respect and was very good with people as the Pastor of a church."

Leo Jr. looked at a variety of colleges in his college search. There was one institution in particular he was curious if he could make the grade- West Point. At this point, he was inspired by his father's path and career and was interested in a career as an Army officer as well. To him, the Academy would be a good litmus test to see how he stacked up overall with other students nationally.

He applied for a ROTC scholarship and wanted to run track and play football at several universities, and he also applied at the United States Miliary Academy. The honors student and his athletic ability attracted the attention of several colleges. During his senior year, a couple of West Point officers visited him. One of them was Major Joe Briggs, an African American recruiting officer from West Point Admissions. He told the young Brooks about the opportunities West Point could offer him.[564] Olympic medalist (1968) and Vietnam Veteran, Army Captain Mel Pender, who would later become Leo's track coach, also came to visit. Recruiters also came from the Air Force Academy and Boise State University. He also received letters of interest from football programs at University of Hawaii, Rice University, and Bowling Green State University.

The acceptance made him proud. It was a result of his hard work and following the advice from his grandparents and parents on seizing the opportunity of education and being the best you can be.

His father told him there was no pressure to take an appointment if he received one from West Point. Leo Jr. took his father's advice to heart, and, when he received that appointment, he almost didn't take it because he was not convinced he wanted that type of commitment (five years on active duty in the Army following graduation).

Bowling Green was the university he was most heavily considering. Some of his teachers at his Jesuit High School actively tried to persuade him not to take the West Point appointment because they feared the military academy would try and change his free spirit.[565] In a high school sports article Leo Jr. was asked what he wanted to be. He said, an Airborne Infantry Officer. Leo Brooks Jr. accepted his appointment from West Point to become a Cadet for the Class of 1979, entering in the summer of 1975.

---

[564] West point center for oral history. A record that speaks for itself: excellence across all pillars of the academy experience Leo Brooks
[565] West point center for oral history. A record that speaks for itself: excellence across all pillars of the academy experience Leo Brooks

R-Day

Leo Jr. hugged his family and said goodbye at the San Francisco Airport and landed at Newark, NJ, where he was picked up by his father's older brother, Dr. Houston G. Brooks, Jr who served two years in the Army in occupation of Germany immediately following World War II.[566] Dr. Brooks, Jr. was an accomplished scientist, and had several patents filed on cell fixation[567], and his work was also published in journals such as The Chemical and Biological Aspects of Pyridoxal Catalysis.[568]

Houston G. Brooks, Jr. PhD.

Uncle Houston would take his nephew to the Academy for "R-Day," or Reception Day, the day the Cadet Candidates report to West Point.

Just like his fellow candidates and their families, they entered West Point through either the Thayer or Stony Lonesome Gates.[569] His uncle was directed to parking around Michie Stadium, or alternatively at Buffalo Soldier Field.

"As we drove to West Point in his car, he told me about his own experiences as a draftee and that I should expect for upper class to mess with me. His parting words were, "don't take any shit from those people....play the game."

With those parting words, the mission in the delivery of his nephew was complete, and his Uncle Houston left.

Leo Jr., and other cadet candidates, piled onto shuttle buses to Eisenhower Hall Theater, where the candidates would report and receive a short briefing to begin their processing for Cadet Basic Training (CBT).[570] After a hectic day of processing, Leo Brooks Jr., and the other new cadets, participated in the Oath Ceremony on the Trophy Point.

---

[566] "Footprints of African Americans In Alexandria" by Andrew Winfree
[567] Patents filed with the US Patent Trademark Office (USPTO):
5597688, 5571726, 5514602, 5422277, https://patents.justia.com/inventor/houston-g-brooks-jr
[568] Houston G. Brooks, "Reactions of Pyridoxal-N-Methochloride with Amino Acids",
Chemical Biological Aspects Pyridoxal Catalysis. January 1, 1963.
[569] West Point Academy R-Day FAQ sheet
[570] West Point Academy R-Day FAQ sheet

Plebe (Freshman) Year

Leo Jr.'s father knew the first year of a cadet would be hard. Now, for the first time, Leo Jr. was learning to balance academics, his sports, and contributing to his assigned cadet company of roughly 120 cadets. He was a "Plebe", *(Freshman), who had the extra challenge of being an active* three season athlete. He decided that first summer to focus on Track. After consultation with the football coach, Leo Jr. would work on building speed and size and join the football team as a sophomore in addition running Track. At West Point, the intercollegiate athletes ate at special training tables and were granted exceptions to train with their team vice participating in intramural sports in their respective assigned companies which was required of all cadets. Cadet Leo Brooks Jr. was assigned to the cross-country team in the fall, even though he was not a long-distance runner so that he would be allowed to have access to these intercollegiate privileges. He also ran indoor and outdoor Track. When he was not in his company delivering mail or participating in all activities, he was lifting weights, building strength, and running Track as part of the Academy's efforts to develop him as an intercollegiate athlete.

The lack of face time with his company created a wrongful negative perception of his contribution in the minds of some of the Cadets in his company. This was hard on Cadet Leo Jr, who, for the first time, had to deal with such a perception. To help center and comfort his mind and soul, he turned to the church, attending weekly Bible Study. Chaplain Richard Camp, the associate pastor of the Corps of Cadets, became his mentor.

Leo Jr. leaned on his faith to help him through tough times. During his first year, the honors student found himself struggling with the advanced mathematics of West Point. West Point education excelled in this area, but Leo Jr., quickly realized the math foundation from his high school years did not prepare him academically for this level of curriculum. Not one to be discouraged, he studied hard, sought additional instruction from his professors, and prevailed in the class. After overcoming his lack of confidence in math, he actually began to enjoy applied mathematics and declared his major concentration in mechanical engineering.

Over Christmas break, the young cadet came home for the first time wearing his grey cadet uniform. Cadet Leo Brooks Jr. had no idea his return would have such a profound impact on his younger brother.

One evening, younger brother Vincent Brooks, now a senior at Jesuit High School, walked into the living room, where Leo Jr. was watching television, wearing his older brother's cadet jacket and hat. The sleeves of his dress grey uniform jacket ended several inches above his wrist. While the jacket fit Leo Jr.'s 6' frame perfectly, Vincent, a basketball star, was 6'4". He told his older brother he wished he had applied to West Point as well, but it was too late to start the process, for it was Christmas of his senior year.

"I told him I didn't think it was too late," BG Leo Brooks Jr. said.

After holiday break, Cadet Brooks returned to West Point, and, one day while at indoor Track practice in the field house, he saw "Coach K," Coach *Krzyzewski, who was the head basketball coach at that time.* (The field house contained both the indoor Track facilities and the varsity basketball practice court.)

He walked up to the Coach and said, "Coach, my brother is 6'4" and can dunk with two hands behind his head. He has a 4.0 grade average, and he wants to go to West Point, but he didn't apply." Coach K said for him (Vincent) to send him a tape of his games. I called home that night."[571]

This video tape submission put Vincent in the process of nomination for recruited athletes. The submission was successful. Vincent would receive his acceptance the following Spring.

Turning Point

After a hard year of battling a negative perception regarding his commitment at West Point among some of his classmates, Cadet Leo Brooks Jr. proved his leadership skills during the summer at the start of his second or sophomore year. Cadets beginning their second year spend the summer in intense, focused Army tactical field training. They are randomly assigned to companies, so they are not with the same group of classmates with whom they spent the first year. This training occurs in a wooded preserve near West Point proper called Camp Buckner.

For this training period, he also had a different officer who evaluated each cadet's performance and leadership. These officers, assigned to each company, are called Tactical Officers. They are responsible for the development and evaluation of each cadet. This Tactical Officer had never seen or worked with any of their cadets previously. At the end of the summer he was evaluated as one of the top cadets of the roughly one thousand cadets in his class.

The reviews he received were glowing, and the rating was high. The elder Brooks brother was beginning to make his mark. His Tactical Officer (TAC)[572], Captain Peter J. Ammon, could not believe the freshman report he read by his predecessor. Captain Ammon told Cadet Leo Jr.; it was like the predecessor was evaluating a different person.

Captain Ammon believed in Cadet Leo Brooks and gave him more leadership opportunities; including being one of only two cadets allowed to go to both Airborne and Ranger School in the same summer training period between his sophomore year and junior years.

Ranger School, especially, is one of the Army's toughest leadership development experiences. When Leo, Jr. was a cadet, only one cadet from each of the thirty-six companies was allowed to attempt this grueling leadership and tactical skills training. The practice of allowing cadets attend Ranger School ended

---

[571] West point center for oral history, A record that speaks for itself: excellence across all pillars of the academy experience Leo Brooks

[572] West Point definition of a TAC: A Tactical Officer (TAC) is the legal Company Commander of a Cadet Company and the primary integrator at the United States Military Academy. They assess the potential and oversee the holistic development of cadets as required by the physical, military, academic, and moral-ethical programs. Tactical Officers coach, teach, and mentor the cadet chain of command by empowering them to take ownership and responsibility for their Cadet Company.

approximately five years after Leo graduated due to the high failure rate of this school which was normally attended by Soldiers with more experience. At 19 years old, he graduated the course as an Army Ranger on 3 August 1977.

While most Soldiers celebrated Ranger graduation with a well-deserved break, Leo, Jr. entered Airborne School on the same day. Three weeks later, a little over a week after his 20th birthday, Leo Austin Brooks, Jr. became the Airborne Ranger that he aspired to become while in High School.

That third summer set the path for Cadet Brooks, Jr.'s junior or "Cow" year. Now more focused, and balanced, he took his experiences and applied them to being the best cadet he could be. He carved his own path, despite whatever challenges came up.

LEO AUGUSTINE BROOKS JR.   G-4
California   Captain

Source: U..S. Military Academy.

During his sophomore year, the star Track and football athlete switched to Rugby. It was on a training run up one of West Point's countless mountains where the team stopped by the Rugby pitch to watch a few minutes of practice. Leo Jr. was attracted to the instant decision-making, non-stop play, aggressive physicality, speed of the sport, and the versatility of the players. Brooks said he saw the similarities between qualities of this sport to the essence of what it was to be a soldier.

"Rugby is just like life," said a reflective BG Leo Brooks, Jr. "It's fast moving, quick thinking, and constantly changing. It's about we. In rugby, we don't care who scores. It's about how can we get the ball and work together to get it across the Try (goal) line. It's a great sport to develop a man or woman."

BG Brooks, Jr. said playing the sport absolutely helped him in his career as an officer in the military. The fast-moving game was constantly transitioning and changing to where the players had to be versatile and nimble to respond.

Coming from a high school where football was king, he was not aware of Rugby's popularity. Leo Jr. loved how both the backs and the forwards on the team had to be able to not only run, but also tackle and pass. He played in the backline at center, wing, and fullback.[573]

Leading by Example

Entering his Cow (Junior) year, Cadet Leo Brooks Jr. now an Airborne Ranger, was further distinguished from among his peers. Out of the nearly thousand cadets in his class, only four had the same accomplishment -- two that entered West Point with the qualification from prior Army service, and two, Leo Jr and the other cadet, that went to both schools prior to their Junior year.

In his Firstie (Senior) year, officials at the Academy selected Brooks to serve as one of four cadet Regimental Commanders. He was issued a cadet officer's saber worn only by seniors. He carried that saber through his one year tenure as Regimental Commander of the 4th Regiment. During graduation week when the sabers are returned as property of West Point for reissue to the rising seniors, Cadet Leo Brooks, Jr. had the saber tagged when he returned it, with the hope that his brother, Cadet Vincent Brooks, would be issued it to carry as a senior also.

Source: .U.S. Military Academy

---

[573] Rugbymag.com, archives: 4 April 2004-1 March 2016 "General Leo Brooks, West Point Commandant

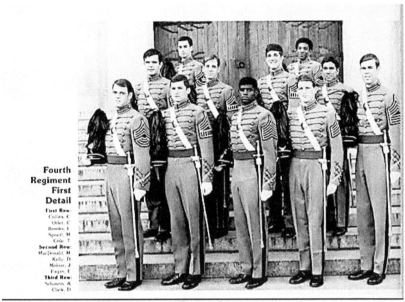

Fourth
Regiment
First
Detail

First Row:
Collins, C
Oslet, C
Brooks, L
Spied, M
Cole, T
Second Row:
MacDonald, M
Kelly, D
Molnar, J
Pagan, F
Third Row:
Schaton, A
Clark, D

Source: West Point Class of 1979 yearbook , U.S. Military Academy

That hope became a reality. Leo Brooks Jr. had attained the highest rank (the six striped rank of cadet captain) held by any Black cadet in the Academy's history. There was only one position higher … the First Captain. In August of 1979, that position had its first Black occupant, Leo Jr's brother Vincent. He was issued the saber Leo Brooks Jr. had tagged before graduating. Vincent carried it throughout his senior year and upon graduation, instead of returning the saber to West Point, Vincent Brooks purchased the saber taking it out of circulation. That saber was used in both brothers' weddings and is an important historical artifact in their family.

Adrenaline Rush

After Leo Jr. graduated from West Point, the first purchase he made was a motorcycle. Owning a motorcycle as a cadet was forbidden by the Academy. So, for Brooks, it was something he wanted to have upon graduating. Like his grandfather James Lewis, Jr., Leo Jr. was proud of his bike. The self-described 'thrill seeker' loved that bike. His parents, however, were not as keen on the acquisition. Within 30 days of owning the motorcycle it was stolen from outside of his apartment. Lieutenant Brooks, Jr. was upset. The bike only had 300 miles on it. When he called home to tell his parents the news, his father responded, "Thank the Lord!"

If it wasn't the motorcycle, it was his skydiving that drove his mom to worry. He logged just short of 200 free fall sport parachute jumps.

Second Lieutenant Leo Brooks, Jr. began his military career in late 1979 when he arrived at Fort Campbell, Kentucky to join the 101st Airborne Division (Air Assault). He was assigned to the 3rd Brigade as a Platoon Leader for an infantry platoon and subsequently an anti-tank platoon. He thrived in these assignments and was recommended to interview as the aide-de-camp to the one-star general serving as the Assistant Division Commander for Operations. Serving as the principal aide to the second in command of the entire Division of fifteen thousand Soldiers was a true honor and gave the young officer tremendous insights into "what right looked like" as a commander. Following this assignment, while still at Ft. Campbell with the 101st Airborne Division (AASLT) he was given command of C Company, 3rd Battalion, 327th Infantry Regiment.

Breaking Barriers

Toward the end of his 18-month Company Command at Fort Campbell, Brooks wanted to apply for assignment with the elite special operations force, the 1st Battalion, 75th Ranger Regiment. He told his current battalion commander who was his immediate supervisor, that he wanted to do this and asked him for a letter of recommendation.

Before writing the letter, his battalion commander had a frank and well-intentioned conversation with the hard-charging Brooks. During that conversation the commander told him how he was about to finish an outstanding tour of command with the 101st so why would he take a chance of going to the Rangers in Savannah, Georgia where he would be the only minority officer in the Regiment of 1,800 men? Additionally, Leo Jr. would be moving there with a white wife and mixed-race daughter. "He foresaw potential problems that I really hadn't viewed as hindrances" said BG Leo Brooks Jr. reflecting back on the experience.

"Why would you want to do that?" questioned the commander. "Because if you go down there and fail, you've derailed yourself on a trajectory that's really, really good."

Now a Captain, Brooks Jr. thoughtfully listened, and then told his commander something that had been his mantra from a young boy . . . strive for excellence.

"Sir, the Rangers are supposed to be the best infantry in the world and I am an infantry officer," said BG Brooks, Jr. "Why wouldn't I want to be in the best infantry unit in the world?"

His commander said, "I can't argue with that, but you're taking a risk."

The letter of recommendation was written by his commander, and Captain Leo Brooks, Jr. was off to the Infantry Officer Advanced Course for six months (in the same class with his brother Vincent), followed by Jumpmaster School before proceeding to his assignment to the 1st Battalion, 75th Ranger Regiment in Savannah, Georgia. For four years, he served in that unit. When he first arrived, he was assigned to a staff position as a logistics and supply officer. His welcome was temperate. Everyone was very professional, very focused but not cordial or welcoming like he had experienced in his previous assignment at Ft. Campbell with the 101st. He quickly realized it wasn't because of the color of his skin. The group was always cool to the new guys. It took Ranger Brooks between six and eight months to prove he could hang with this group of tough guys, and that he added value to the unit's overall mission accomplishment. He served a total of two years on staff and was then given the honor of commanding a Ranger rifle company – Company A, 1st Battalion, 75th Ranger Regiment for almost two years from June 1986 to March 1988. He was the first Black American to command a modern-day Ranger company, within the Joint Special Operations Command.

After four tough years serving with the 75th Ranger Regiment, Brooks was assigned overseas to the Republic of Korea (ROK). His first year was on the 8th Army staff in the Training Division and his subsequent two years were on the Combined and Joint Staff of the ROK-US Combined Command as a Ground Operations Officer. While serving in this joint assignment, he concurrently earned a Masters in Public Administration at night from the University of Oklahoma extension program. He was also promoted to the rank of Major. Brooks tour of duty in Korea was from 1988 through the summer of 1990. His family also expanded.

Major Leo Brooks Jr. with his family of a wife and four daughters headed to Fort Leavenworth, Kansas to attend the Command and General Staff College (CGSC) for a year. Again, he and his brother were in academic programs at the same time which gave them time together and allowed Leo Jr.'s family to recharge after two back-to-back demanding assignments while preparing to go back to a unit with troops . . . which was Brooks' first love as a Soldier.

Upon completion of CGSC the Major Leo Brooks Jr. and family moved to Ft. Bragg, North Carolina for what would be the first of three assignments with the famed 82nd Airborne Division. His first assignment was as the Battalion Executive Officer (second in command of a unit of 600 men) for the 1st Battalion, 504th Parachute Infantry Regiment. He excelled in this position to include a deployment to middle east for duty with the Multi-National Force and Observers Mission positioned between Egypt and Israel. He was subsequently chosen to serve as the Deputy Operations Officer (Deputy G3) of the entire Division. In this role he truly learned how the 82nd Airborne Division worked from top to bottom. At the end of that assignment he was hand-picked by the Chief of Staff of the Army -- the Army's top general – to serve as his Aide de Camp. This was an incredible honor which took Leo Jr. and family to Washington, DC for their first Pentagon assignment.

Major Brooks travelled the world with General Gordon R. Sullivan, Army Chief of Staff. Together they would travel to every spot on the globe where American Soldiers were serving…from war-torn Somalia to genocide ravaged Rwanda. While with General Sullivan, Brooks would meet world political and military leaders. The experience was once in a lifetime. It prepared Brooks for his next assignment back to Ft. Bragg, North Carolina and his second assignment with the 504th Parachute Infantry Regiment in the 82nd Airborne Division where he returned in October 1995. This time the newly promoted Lieutenant Colonel (LTC) was in command of the 1st Battalion of the 504th (PIR).

In addition to the many leadership lessons LTC Leo Brooks Jr. had learned over his 17 years of service, he would remember the words of advice from one of his biggest inspirations – his maternal grandfather,

James Lewis Jr. In an interview, BG Brooks, Jr. said "Lewis' commitment to his family, God, coupled with his hard work, determination, and cheerful disposition, were nothing less than inspiring."[574]

Following two years of successful command which included an emergency deployment to Haiti, as well as Europe, Brooks was assigned as the Chief of Current Operations for the 18th Airborne Corps. In this capacity he coordinated the operations of four Divisions in the Army's rapid deployment Corps. This one-year assignment was a bridge between battalion command and attendance at the prestigious US Army War College. Selection to the War College was an indication that Brooks was destined for positions of greater responsibility. For the fourth time, the Brooks brothers were in the same academic program with brother Vincent attending and Army War College Fellowship at Harvard University, but part of the same War College Class.

In June 1999, Leo Brooks Jr. was promoted to the rank of Colonel in a ceremony at the US Army War College officiated by his father BG (Retired) Leo Brooks. Also promoted to Colonel in that same ceremony was younger brother Vincent. A few weeks later, newly promoted Colonel Leo Brooks, Jr. was headed back for the third time to Fort Bragg, North Carolina and for the third time he was assigned to the 504th Parachute Infantry Regiment and the 1st Brigade of the 82nd Airborne Division, this time as the 31st Colonel Commanding the Regiment since its inception in 1942. Brooks recalls one particular training mission that became an impactful moment in his career and decision making.

The 82nd Airborne Division was participating in the largest airborne assault since Operation Market Garden of World War II. It was called "Operation Purple Dragon," a three-week training exercise where elements of all four Divisions in the 18th Airborne Corps as well as units from the other services conducted forcible entry operations on a grand scale to include large parachute operations.

On the evening of January 29, 1998, approximately 3,000 paratroopers from the 82nd Airborne Division parachuted into Holland and Sicily Drop Zones (DZ) at Fort Bragg. After the paratrooper drop into the Sicily DZ, the heavy equipment drop proceeded where tons of artillery pieces, High Mobility Multipurpose Wheeled Vehicles (HMMWV) and other heavy equipment/vehicles were parachuted from C-130 and C-141 aircraft. In total there were 32 C-130's and 48 C-141 aircraft used.

But this parachute drop almost didn't happen. Colonel Leo Brooks Jr. received notification from the Air Force commander in charge of the aircraft, and Leo's counterpart commander that there was a bomb threat to one of the planes to be used in the parachute operation that evening. As the Parachute Brigade Commander, Brooks also had the role for that mission of Airborne Commander for the operation, meaning it was his overall decision on all things pertaining to the operation. The Air Force asked him what he was going to do. The Air Force leader for the operation gave Brooks and two of his senior leaders an update on the call they had received and said they could call off the drop if that was Colonel Leo Brooks Jr's decision.

---

[574] Rugbymag.com, archives: 4 April 2004-1 March 2016 "General Leo Brooks, West Point Commandant

Brooks reviewed the operation, and went through the process of analyzing the threat probability in his mind:

Have these planes been on the listed green ramp and yellow ramps and secured the whole time? Yes.

Has anybody had access to these planes besides air crew? No.

The next question he would ask himself- *would he tell his troops? No.*

Colonel Brooks chose not to inform the rank and file of his unit in an effort to shield paratroopers from excessive and unnecessary worrying. Jumping out of a plane at 130 miles an hour at 800 feet above the ground in the dark with a thousand of your closest friends was dangerous enough. Only his key staff knew.

With his mental checklist complete, Colonel Leo Brooks Jr. told the Air Force commander they were going through with the operation.

Three hours later, the 1st Brigade Combat Team was rigged up. Paratroopers had their parachutes on and were loading on the planes, including Brooks as the overall commander. Two planes were loading when a military police officer came, driving down the runway in a military police vehicle announcing through their megaphones to get away from the airplanes.

All personnel moved immediately out of the way of the planes. Colonel Brooks, Jr. was in dismay at the unfolding scene. He ran over to the officer and demanded to know what is going on.

The military police officer told him the threat was more specific, and that they wanted to get everyone away from the airplanes. Colonel Brooks, Jr. questioned if the police chain of command made the decision on their own. He took off all his gear and ran to link up with the Air Force counterpart commander.

Colonel Brooks asked if anything changed with regard to the previously reported threat. The Air Force commander said no and recommended they don't go, but, that it was up to Colonel Brooks, Jr. as the Airborne Commander.

He told the Air Force commander they were moving forward.

Colonel Brooks, Jr. called his Commanding General, the Commander of the 82nd Airborne Division for input. Then Major General (later General) Dan K. McNeill responded, "You're the commander on the ground. I'm good with whatever you choose." That answer gave Colonel Brooks, Jr. the confidence he needed to make the final call.

He never considered his decision "cavalier" but a "measured" conclusion based on the review of the process. At this point the paratroopers needed to know what was going on. Their commander, Colonel Leo Brooks, Jr. boarded each plane and explained the situation and gave them encouragement that all was good, it would be fine and to trust him. They knew he would not put them at unnecessary risk. That night Colonel Brooks led his paratroopers on the Airborne operation without incident.

Company Commander of A Company, 1st Battalion of the 75th Ranger Regiment, early Spring 1987, Hunter Army Airfield in Savannah, Georgia.
All the commanders and field grade officers in the Ranger Regiment were there in preparation for a rehearsal of a contingency operation in South America.

Gen. Brooks, Jr. was the first ever and only African American commander in the modern day 75th Ranger Regiment at the time of this photo.

Source: Brooks Family photo

After two years of proudly commanding of the 1st Brigade Combat Team and the 504th Infantry Regiment, Brooks received a surprising call from Washington. He had been selected for Brigadier General and was deploying to Europe as Deputy Commanding General of the 1st Armored Division, U.S. Army Europe and Seventh Army, in Germany in June 2001. This move meant he would be leaving his oldest daughter in the United States as an incoming freshman at the University of North Carolina at Chapel Hill, and uprooting his second daughter, who was entering her senior year of High School. The turmoil his teenage daughter felt, was something he could sympathize with and relate to. Based on his own experience, the family all moved with the exception of eldest daughter Bethany who proceeded to UNC Chapel Hill.

Upon arrival in Germany Brooks was "frocked" to the rank of Brigadier General, which meant he wore the one-star insignia of rank of a BG, but was still a year and 1/2 away from actually getting paid in the grade. This practice requires approval from the Department of Defense and is only done when individuals are serving in critical international or joint positions requiring them to have the rank immediately as part of doing their duties. Brooks helped lead the 1st Armored Division through the attack on 9/11 and securing people and facilities across Europe while simultaneously planning for the invasion of Iraq. Leo Brooks Jr. was the youngest general on his promotion list which made him the youngest general in U.S. Army.

Full Circle

In June 2002, BG Leo Brooks, Jr. received another great honor. He had been selected by the Chief of Staff of the Army, then General Eric K. Shinseki, to serve as the 68th Commandant of Cadets at West Point. He returned to where it all began. The sense of pride of being the Commandant, and the love of soldiering, strongly beat in his heart. He swore in the first class to enter after 9/11. He knew all these young men and women were going to war and he had to ensure they were ready. This was a personal mission for him.

As Commandant, he oversaw the development of the 4,200 member corps of cadets at West Point. He was responsible for developing their moral and ethical training; and making them well rounded Army officers and leaders. This was one of the greatest responsibilities in his career: to prepare, inspire, and support the future leaders of the U.S. Army.

"I would tell any young person coming up always be the best you can be every day," he said. "Some days you don't feel like it, but you work to be the best you can be every day. Don't worry about if you have a failure, you're going to have some. But when you have a failure, sit back, and ask yourself, okay, what can I do next time to improve on what I did? I don't care if it's performance in sports, a test or how you cut the grass and your parents didn't like how you did it. Learn from that experience and be better from it. Make it a lesson."

BG Leo Brooks, Jr. also made sure the perceptions of cadet athletes like he once was, were not diminished and they were fairly evaluated. Brooks stressed success was based on an individual's personal accountability. He would offer encouragement; talking about his time as a young man growing up on military posts back in the 60s and early 70s, that people never treated him as any differently because he was Black. He was, as Martin Luther King stated in his *I Have A Dream* speech, not judged by the color of his skin but rather by the content of his character.

This is what he wanted to impress upon the cadets. He said "The Armed Forces have pushed hard to ensure that all of its service members are viewed that way. We care about what you do and what you say, not about how you look. The Armed Forces pushed for equality among men and women and among all races and have been in the nation's forefront in this regard."[575] During his military service, Leo Jr. was recognized with numerous awards including the Army Distinguished Service Medal for his service during the war on terror from 2004 to 2006 as Vice Director of the Army Staff. [576]

Leading in the Business World

BG Leo A. Brooks Jr. retired from the Army after serving two years as the Vice Director of the Army staff in the Pentagon. He now brought his leadership skills and work ethic to the corporate world and to philanthropic causes. Following the Army, he joined The Boeing Company where he worked for 13 1/2 years. Starting initially as their Vice President responsible for engagement with senior Army leadership, he was quickly identified as a leader who could handle much more. After two years in the Army position, he was chosen to serve as a more Senior Vice President responsible for the engagement, interaction, and counsel to the Chairman and Chief Executive Officer regarding all military departments, the department of Homeland Security, NASA, and the Intelligence Community. For over a decade he served on the board of Boeing.

In public addresses Brooks acknowledges and credits the support and guidance from his family and his faith in God as the foundation for his success and his ability to give back. It is about "we", not "me".

"My grandparents never attended college, but they knew education was the path to opportunity. They inspired and drove my parents and their siblings to never accept average… Work harder than anyone else, with humility…And always thank God for the opportunity to try… I have walked on a path guided by their example of excellence and encouragement.[577] …And to the leaders of tomorrow, recapture those things so hardly fought for in order to give you the opportunity to be free and pursue your dreams."[578]

As for the youth of tomorrow, BG Leo A. Brooks, Jr. offers this advice, which echoes from his parents, grandparents, and great-grandparents:

"Don't limit yourself in terms of what you are or what you think you want to be," urged Leo Brooks, Jr. "Don't focus on what you are going to do next. Focus on being the best at what you are doing now. Then think about what assignment/position/job I'd like to have two moves in the future. What am I doing in my current role that is going to help me prepare ultimately for what I want to do in the future? I think young

---

[575] Rugbymag.com, archives: 4 April 2004-1 March 2016 "General Leo Brooks, West Point Commandant

[576] Other awards include: Other military awards include the Legion of Merit with Two Oak Leaf Clusters representing three times awarded this medal), the Defense Meritorious Service Medal, four awards of the Army, Service Medal, the Army Commendation Medal, and the Army Achievement Medal. He earned the Ranger Tab, Master Parachutist Badge (Distinguished Honor Graduate of Jumpmaster School), the Air Assault Badge (Distinguished Honor Graduate), the Pathfinder Badge, Expert Infantryman's Badge, and Department of the Army Headquarters Staff Badge.

[577] Black Engineer of the Year speech, 2019

[578] African Americans in Time of War Address at Mt. Calvary Baptist Church, February 4, 2017

people today put too much pressure on themselves. They want to be perfect. Yes, you should strive for excellence, but don't beat yourself up if you occasionally fall short . . . learn from it. Do better the next time. Enjoy the journey. Have fun, laugh, enjoy. Don't take life too seriously where you think your life is over if you don't get a certain job or opportunity. Two people can achieve the same thing but take totally different paths in life in order to achieve it, and that's ok."

Chapter Four
Vincent K. Brooks

General Vincent K. Brooks was born in Alaska like his brother, BG Leo Brooks, Jr., on October 24, 1958. At that time, Alaska was not yet a State. Only fourteen months apart, Vincent and Leo were always close. Although Vincent outgrew Leo at an early age, he always looked up to his older brother and tried to maintain pace with him in all activities. They were "thick as thieves" according to Vincent.

No matter how many moves the Brooks family made driven by Leo Sr.'s military career, the one thing Vincent Brooks said you could count on was the family routine. This was the foundation of stability for the young family. The routine never changed.

Sundays were always reserved for family. They always attended church together, and they enjoyed an early afternoon Sunday dinner together. If there were football games on, later in the day, you would find the family hanging out together, watching sports in the family room. The strict routine in life was the law of the land laid out by Naomi and Leo. It was an integral part of Naomi's "bloom where ye are planted" life mandate. Maintaining a schedule to keep a rising military officer, a working mom and her three children in harmony took a lot of planning, and, most of all, patience.

During Brooks, Sr.'s second one-year tour in Vietnam, Naomi was teaching in a different school system than her children. The Brooks brothers were taught in Fairfax County Public Schools based on where they were living, Marquita attended a Day School in Alexandria where she could easily be dropped off and picked up by Naomi who was teaching in the City of Alexandria Public School system. Every day had a cadence to it – wake up, make beds, straighten rooms, personal hygiene, breakfast, and off to school. After school, the boys were expected to go straight home, do homework first, any chores, then relax until Mom and Marquita arrived home from Alexandria.

Vincent said it was his mother's driving strength, love, and determination that kept this family rhythm on track.

"Trying to balance to all that was more like cement, not glue," said General Vincent Brooks about his mother Naomi's impact. "At that age, we were rambunctious. My sister, even though she's five years younger than us, was a Tomboy and always kept up with her brothers. She has that same active and fiery spirit we all had. Ever since she was three, Marquita always called us, 'her boys'. You could always count on her to be with us."

Both parents made sure their sons, who would sometimes play little tricks on Marquita, would take care of their little sister. And they did. The three siblings were latchkey kids, and they were trusted by their parents to complete their daily mission- to be responsible and not create any mischief. The children were expected to get into the home, complete their homework and studies, and then, once they were finished, they would be allowed to go hang out with friends.

During this time, while Leo Sr. was again in Vietnam, the fiery spirit of the boys was leading to squabbles over everything. Testosterone was running high in the adolescent boys, and younger brother Vincent Brooks, wanted to do everything his older brother was allowed to do or experimented with.

"It was second child syndrome to the max," said Vincent Brooks. "I didn't want to be left out. I didn't want to be excluded. I wanted to have the same shot that he's got. But I'm also a year younger and less mature. But I wouldn't want to wait another year until it's my turn. So, I want it now and I did most things with him."

Even with numerous relatives in the area, Naomi rarely called the family for help. But the incessant fighting was adding unwanted stress to an already demanding situation for a working mom trying to do it all. Her husband was overseas fighting in the increasingly unpopular Vietnam War. She turned to her father-in-law Reverend Houston G. Brooks, Sr. for help. He stepped in.

"Our grandfather came over and unemotionally said, 'get in the car boys,'" said Vincent Brooks. "The first thing we did was get in a fight over who was going to sit in the front seat. It just proved the point of why my mom called him. He then said 'Okay, *both* of you sit in the same seatbelt.' So, we are sitting in the same seat, and he tightens the seatbelt so tight we can barely breathe."

The Brooks brothers and grandfather started off on their drive.

"I remember him saying, 'I'm going to tell you the same thing I told your father and his brothers and his sister. I don't care if you get in a fight with somebody else. But if I catch you fighting each other. I'm going to shake the shit out of you.' Now you know if a Baptist preacher says that to his grandkids you know we got the point." It was the first and only time they would hear him use such language.

After that, the boys got along better.

Harnessing the Creative Spirit

The brothers followed the rules most of the time, but General Vincent Brooks chuckled and described his brother and himself, and often their friends and cousins in the area as "explorers by nature".

Their father would try and find ways of harnessing their son's "creative spirit" and he would teach them the value of the trades he learned from his father and grandfather. Brooks, Sr. was a talented carpenter and all-around handyman. He learned and honed his talents while working for his father and grandfather in the family company . Brooks, Sr. would teach the boys how to make wood projects. But, sometimes, the boys would take those tools and use them on their own 'special' projects. They were proud of their accomplishments, but, Naomi, on the occasion, would not be so amused.

The brothers would always find ways to amuse themselves creatively. They came up with a dart game, but they needed darts. They decided to make some.

"We took out our mom's sewing kit and she had a red pin cushion full of pins," said Vincent Brooks. "We wrapped lots of thread around the head of the pin and glued it on. We then cut that thread so it would resemble feathers like you see on blow darts. We would then sit at the top of the stairs and throw them down to the room below to see who could stick the dart into the carpet." On one iteration of the game, Leo Jr. decided to throw a wooden pencil. It stuck in Vincent's arm.

"This is why I say my mom was the cement of the family," chuckled General Vincent Brooks.

In addition to learning woodworking, the Brooks children played sports, especially during high school years. Naomi would spend her afternoons and early evenings driving the children to their various sporting events. Vincent Brooks loved baseball and played in the Little League until one day he was in his grandmother Eunice Naomi Quander Lewis' kitchen and she told him, "you are going to be a basketball player, like your Uncle Jimmy." She was right. Between 8th and 9th grade Vincent began to develop skills. He learned from his uncle, Jim "Jimmy" Lewis, Naomi's brother, who was an All-American basketball player.

Originally, Uncle Jim was a football player, however, he unfortunately suffered a torn ACL during practice. That injury ended his football playing, but he pivoted to another sport he loved- basketball.[579] Uncle Jim was the youngest in the family, and learned from his big sister, Naomi, who broke numerous basketball records in High School.

Uncle Jim broke the color barrier throughout this athletic career. He committed to the University of West Virginia, which at that time never before had a Black player. Jimmy attended the University with his best friend Fritz Williams. Fritz also broke the color line. Jimmy Lewis was also "the first African American basketball player to sign an athletic grant-in-aid".[580] He studied journalism, and then went on to the University of Detroit for his Masters in the subject. He later attended Tennessee State University to obtain a degree in physical education. All of this education and basketball skill were used throughout this career.

"I started playing with Uncle Jim and some of his college and pro-basketball buddies the summer of my freshman year in high school and he accelerated my game," said Vincent Brooks, "When I came back to

---

[579] "A conversation with Coach Jimmy Lewis, a Basketball Trailblazer."
[580] "WVU Recruit", The Morgantown Post (Monday Afternoon edition), March 9, 1964, page 6

school and started playing, one of my friends said to me, 'In your freshman year you weren't worth a damn, but suddenly in your Sophomore year you were on fire!'"

Uncle Jim went on to coach men's and women's basketball several times at the college level, including at Tulane, at Duke University where he was the first Black coach for any sport,[581] and at George Mason University where he founded the Division 1 Women's Basketball program. He also coached women's professional basketball and was the first coach of the Washington Mystics. In addition to college and pro-ball, he was a high school basketball coach, as well as commentator, and was elected to the USA Basketball Executive Committee.

It was this regular level of play with his uncle's friends that General Vincent Brooks credits to him becoming a stellar athlete at Thomas Jefferson High School in Virginia as a sophomore and a standout All-Star at Jesuit High School in California, opening the door for him to be recruited by the famous "Coach K" and make the Varsity team at West Point in his freshman or "Plebe" year. To this day, Vincent is a passionate Duke basketball fan as a result of both his Uncle Jim and Coach K coaching that team in different eras.

A Life Dedicated to Compassion

In addition to sports ability inherited from his mother, General Vincent Brooks also inherited her compassion. Naomi, the eldest, was like a mother to all her siblings, three sisters and one brother while her father was frequently away with the President of the United Mine Workers of America. His Aunt Barbara, who was only 14 months younger than Vincent's mother, battled mental illness her whole life and lived with Vincent's grandparents. The next sister, Janice was very studious and academically talented. She married a young Baptist preacher who had studied under Reverend Houston G. Brooks, Sr., and she went on to attain her doctorate while raising two of Vincent's cousins. The third sister, Ruth, named for her mother's mother, also excelled academically and married a college sweetheart and Army officer.

Vincent was the ring bearer at their wedding and when his officer uncle passed away, Vincent, then a three-star general, presented the folded American flag to his aunt as part of the military honors. Ruth's two sons also served full careers as senior Army officers and Vincent served with both of them.

The mental illness affecting Vincent's Aunt Barbara ran in the Lewis Family. [582] Out of James Lewis, Jr's eleven siblings, two sisters spent most of their adult lives in a State institution. During those times, institutionalization was the common treatment for individuals with mental illness. This was something James Lewis Jr. was sensitive to. He wanted to make sure his daughter, Barbara, would not be institutionalized, and would be cared for.

Barbara lived with James Lewis, Jr. and Eunice, Vincent's grandparents, until she was in her 70's, when it was too much for her parents to handle. Naomi helped her to enter into a long-term care facility. Naomi

---

[581] Alexandria African American Hall of Fame
[582] Phone interview with Authors January 14, 2023

became her care point person, and coordinated all her medical attention with the staff, to make sure no matter what Barbara's financial status was, she received what she needed. After that, when any Lewis family members needed care later in life, or other life preparations like estates that needed to be settled, they came to Naomi. The same family reliance happened on the Brooks side with MG Brooks, Sr.

"My grandfather said to my father, 'take care of your mother and take care of Leola (his first cousin and only living relative)," shared General Vincent Brooks. "My parents fulfilled their promises and set the example for me." Vincent has carried on this tradition of service to the family as he tended to the disposition of his in-laws and his mother Naomi when they passed. "I think my compassion to help comes from having relatives who have mental and emotional issues," he said.

Over Achiever

General Vincent Brooks looked up to his older brother, and always considered him to be a "high performer" which drove him to always raise the bar himself.[583] Yet, he always lived in his high-performing brother's shadow. Known as "Leo's brother" Vincent always strove for excellence and to crave his own notoriety. Academically talented as an "A student" with a perfect attendance record and being a student leader and letter-winning athlete, Vincent was well-prepared for college.

Like his brother had, he successfully applied for admission to several pre-medicine programs and was accepted at University of California – Davis, Creighton University, and Cornell University. Since elementary school, Vincent focused on becoming a doctor, and coupled with Army ROTC and basketball at the collegiate level, he was well on track into his senior year of high school at Jesuit. But all of that changed one December afternoon.

Vincent's brother arrived home after his first semester at West Point for the Christmas holiday break wearing his West Point "dress gray[584]" uniform. His heart fluttered and he was immediately impressed by how West Point had brought out even more excellence in his brother. Vincent Brooks realized then, he wanted to go into the Military Academy and become an Army officer.

During the Christmas break Vincent saw the gray uniform hanging amongst other clothes in his brother's closet. Even on the hanger, the uniform projected an aura. The 6'4", gangly teen, slowly put on the jacket. The lining of the sleeve jacket felt cool on his bare, long arm. He then placed the gray dress cap on his head. The *brass* plate of the *West Point's* coat of arms reflected the light of the afternoon California sun pouring into the room.

Vincent Brooks then walked over to the mirror to see his reflection. His long arms protruded, and it was baggy in the chest given his brother's 6' and stockier built frame. It did not matter that the size did not fit.

---

[583] Gen. Vincent Brooks: Leadership is About People: Leading Authorities, June 11, 2019 speech

[584] The Gray uniform commemorates the victory at Chippewa where a small American Army, led by General Winfield Scott wearing gray, defeated the British in summer of 1814. General Scott was hailed by historians and the military as one of the most accomplished generals in U.S. History. He retired in West Point, NY and when he died on May 29, 1866, he was laid to rest at West Point Cemetery.

For Vincent, looking at his reflection, the image fit perfectly. Then, his heart sank. He knew that the admission process was time consuming and required several tests to gain acceptance. He had taken the physical aptitude test and excelled at it but did not further pursue the application process. High School graduation was six months away. He was sure that he had missed the deadline to apply. Just like he did when he was little, he went to his older brother seeking comfort and advice.

Cadet Leo Brooks Jr. was watching sports on television with the family in the family room, as the Brooks' had always done. He looked up to see Vincent Brooks walk into the room wearing the jacket and hat of a West Point cadet. Their eyes locked. Vincent Brooks told his older brother he wished he applied. But just like his big brother always did, Leo Brooks, Jr. told his little brother he would help him find a way once he returned to the Academy.

Leo Jr. upon returning approached the head basketball coach, Coach Mike Krzyzewski, better known as "Coach K" himself a 1969 graduate of West Point. Coach K had a young team and had only a few graduating seniors whose places needed to be filled. Leo called home first to relay the Coach's response. Vincent sent the video of one of his recent high performing games, and soon thereafter Coach K called the house in Sacramento. Vincent was now on two tracks for admission – the regular application and the recruited athlete application. One failed, and the other succeeded.

In the last few days of Vincent's senior year, he received the first notification that he had not been accepted for admission. Vincent's heart sank. Thankfully, this was not the last word. A few days later Vincent received a second, similar letter. This letter congratulated him on his acceptance for admission in the summer of 1976 with the West Point class of 1980. A month later, the brothers said their goodbyes to their family, and were off to West Point, reunited.

The brothers, along with one of Leo Jr.'s West Point classmates, Essex Fowlks, who also lived in Sacramento and had been a competitor from a different high school before being selected to attend the Military Academy, flew together on the plane bound for LaGuardia Airport, New York. The two older young men were in uniform and faced harassment and heckling from protesters inside the airport as they walked. Vincent, not in uniform, witnessed this and would never forget it.

The three of them then traveled to the Port Authority in New York City and took a bus up to West Point. Leo and Essex knew the way, Vincent was following their lead with a steady stream of unknowns filling his head and making him feel nauseous in the exhaust-fume scented bus.

Upon arriving at West Point, majestic and breath-taking in the summer, the brothers parted ways. Cadets Leo Brooks, Jr. and Essex Fowlks had to report that day for their second-year training camp at a remote area in the mountains surrounding West Point. Vincent was now standing alone on the edge of the parade field near a statue of George Patton. Like all newly arriving students, Vincent Brooks was not allowed in the cadet area of the campus until he had been "received" by West Point. That would happen the next morning. He was picked up by his father's friend, Colonel Roger Edgington who was the Comptroller of the US Military Academy. Colonel Edgington delivered Vincent to Michie Stadium where

1,100 others said goodbye to the families and life as they had known it. Then the well-rehearsed West Point machine took over and Vincent, along with his new classmates from all over the country, and several foreign nations, were molded into the West Point Class of 1980.

Unique to this summer was the addition of 119 women among the young men being converted into cadets. That evening, having been fitted for uniforms, shorn of hair, processed through a flurry of physical and administrative actions, and being taught to follow the beat of the drum while marching, Vincent Brooks wore his own West Point uniform, perfectly tailored to his frame, and marched with his classmates to the awe-inspiring Trophy Point to repeat the oath of office making him a New Cadet. It was a blur for the most part, but punctuated by poignant memories that are indelibly imprinted in Vincent Brooks mind.

Finding Support at West Point from a Historic Role Model

In addition to his brother, Cadet Vincent Brooks was inspired daily by another Black cadet. This cadet attended West Point almost 100 years before him. His name was Henry Ossian Flipper. Brooks admired Flipper's strength, leadership, and resilience.

Henry O. Flipper, Ca. 1877
Credit: National Archives (NAID: 2668824)

Flipper was a former slave, and, in 1877, he became the first Black American to graduate from West Point. His time at West Point was filled with racial discrimination and hostility. The atmosphere at the Academy was charged with prejudice, despite the Academy's efforts to integrate blacks.

Flipper was the fourth Black cadet to enter West Point on July 1, 1873. The first three, unfortunately, did not graduate. Flipper persevered, despite being silenced by many cadets who refused to speak to him. Brooks admired Flipper and his academic accomplishments, graduating 50th in his class of 76 cadets, and being commissioned as the first black officer in the United States Army. He, along with four West Point graduates, were assigned to the 10th Cavalry, where he was stationed at Fort Sill, Indian Territory, (present day Oklahoma), with Company A.

242

In two years, Flipper rose through the ranks to become the commander of Company G at Fort Sill. Because of the number of stagnant ponds on the post, officers were getting sick from malaria.[585] Flipper was assigned duties as the post's engineer and was ordered to survey the area to create and supervise the construction of a drainage system to keep the water moving. The project was successful, and, in 1977, that drainage system was called "Flipper's Ditch", as well as being officially designated a Black Military Heritage site in 1977.

Flipper left Fort Sill with Company A for Fort Davis, Texas, where they secured U.S. citizens along the U.S. and Mexican border which was mostly uncharted. While there Flipper participated in operations in pursuit of Apache leader, Victorio, and his band of warriors who were terrorizing and raiding American and Mexican ranches on both sides of the Rio Grande. Lieutenant Flipper was assigned the additional duties of Acting Assistant Quartermaster and Acting Commissary of Subsistence for Fort Davis.

The young Black soldier's career was promising until the commissary funds he was responsible for became missing. He tried to conceal the loss in order to buy himself time to find the money. He reported to Colonel William R. Shafter, who was known to be a strict disciplinarian.[586] When the concealment of funds became known, he was tried, and court-martialed for embezzlement of commissary funds and for conduct unbecoming an officer. Lieutenant Flipper maintained his innocence.

On June 30, 1882, Lieutenant Flipper was found innocent of embezzlement for which no evidence was discovered, but he was dishonorably discharged from the Army nonetheless with the loss of all benefits on the charge of conduct unbecoming an officer for concealing the loss of funds to his commanding officer. President Chester Arthur upheld the court-martial. Those who had long wanted him purged from the ranks achieved their goal.

Throughout his entire life, Flipper maintained his innocence and continued to make notable achievements. He translated Spanish land documents and surveyed land grants. He became a go-to government witness in court cases for the Court of Private Land Claims. Eventually he served on the staff of a U.S. Senator who became Secretary of the Interior. Flipper joined him in the Department of the Interior as assistant to the Secretary.

In 1976, his case was reviewed by the Army Board for the Correction of Military Records. The board determined it did not have the authority to overturn his court-martial convictions, and concluded the conviction and punishment were "unduly harsh and unjust"[587] and recommended that Lieutenant Flipper's dismissal be commuted to a good conduct discharge.[588] His remains were exhumed and reburied with military honors.

---

[585] "Second Lieutenant Henry Flipper", Fort Davis, National Historic Site Texas, https://www.nps.gov/foda/learn/historyculture/secondlieutenanthenryflipper.htm#:~:text=In%20the%20fall%20of%201881,not%20guilty%20to%20both%20charges.
[586] "Second Lieutenant Henry Flipper", Fort Davis, National Historic Site Texas
[587] "Lieutenant Henry Ossian Flipper", Center of Military History, https://history.army.mil/html/topics/afam/flipper.html
[588] "Lieutenant Henry Ossian Flipper", Center of Military History, https://history.army.mil/html/topics/afam/flipper.html

Identifying with Flipper

A year after Lieutenant Flipper's dishonorable discharge was reversed, a bronze bust of Lieutenant Flipper was placed in West Point's library. Cadet Vincent Brooks, then a Plebe, looked deep into the eyes of the face of Cadet Flipper that day. It was May 3, 1977.

"The first time I saw it, I kind of felt like I was looking at myself," said General Vincent Brooks. "Some of his features are like mine. We both part of our hair on the side and the similar way, although Flipper's hair part was closer to the center. I felt a kinship with him. He also reminded me a lot of my brother Leo."

Vincent Brooks was still learning about Lieutenant Flipper at that time. He would look back as a seasoned officer at this moment in his life and appreciate it more.

Another West Point Cadet and graduate General Vincent Brooks identified with was Charles Young.

"His career also faced gross injustice," said General Vincent Brooks.

Charles Young

BG Charles Young, the third Black American graduate from West Point, graduated from the Academy in 1889.

Portrait of Cadet Charles Young by Pach Brothers, NY
Undated Photo- credit: NAM MSS 03. National Afro-American Museum and Cultural Center, Wilberforce, OH.

BG Young's parents, Gabriel & Arminta Young, were both enslaved. His father who escaped enslavement fought in the Civil War with the 5th Regiment of the U.S. Colored Heavy Artillery.

After the war, BG Young's father urged his son, who graduated from an integrated school with honors and was a teacher, to take the entrance exam to West Point. Young would pass and was accepted to West Point. Like Lieutenant Flipper, BG Young was subjected to the same isolation and racial hostility.[589]

After graduating, he was assigned to the 9th Cavalry as a 2nd Lieutenant, which was stationed at Fort Robinson, Nebraska. The unit was not welcoming, and he was met with that same isolation and hostility he was all too familiar with for the year he was with them.[590] BG Young was then transferred to Fort Duchesne, Utah, where he commanded a unit under the name: the Buffalo Soldiers.[591] He would later become the nation's first Black American National Park Superintendent, and serve in President Theodore Roosevelt's administration in three different diplomatic posts. Vincent Brooks wrote the foreword for the book Black Cadet in a White Bastion: Charles Young at West Point, by author and West Point graduate Brian G. Shellum.[592]

First Captain

Learning the stories of Lieutenant Flipper and BG Young helped Cadet Vincent Brooks develop his own self-confidence and self-worth. He found his place.

In his "Firstie" (Senior) Year, Cadet Vincent Brooks was appointed the highest position a cadet can hold- the First Captain. This was the first time in the 178-year history of the Academy, that the First Captain was a Black cadet.

Initially, Cadet Vincent Brooks had hoped to hold the same position held by his brother Leo the previous year – Cadet Regimental Commander, a position in charge of 1,000 cadets, and subordinate only to the First Captain in seniority. Perhaps being so accustomed to trying to keep up with his brother, Vincent naturally saw that as the goal to achieve. With the appointment to the highest position, Vincent Brooks, for the first time, emerged beyond Leo Jr.'s large shadow into his own light as a history-maker.

As First Captain, Cadet Vincent Brooks would lead the 4,000 Cadet Corps. He was responsible for the leadership of cadets in all four classes of the student body, the overall performance of the cadets, as well as the liaison between the Corps of Cadets and the West Point administration. He was also the first cadet to lead a West Point student body where there were women in all four classes. His historic achievement added to the already historic nature of the West Point Class of 1980. Vincent Brooks knew it was a prestigious position, and that he would be a history maker, but he wanted to make sure his appointment was based on merit, instead of being a political decision.[593]

---

[589] Brigadier General Charles Young, Charles Young Buffalo Soldiers, National Park Service, https://www.nps.gov/chyo/learn/historyculture/charles-young.htm
[590] Brigadier General Charles Young, Charles Young Buffalo Soldiers, National Park Service,
[591] National Park Service: American Plains Indians who fought against the black cavalry troops as "buffalo soldiers" because of their dark, curly hair, which resembled a buffalo's coat and because of their fierce nature of fighting. The nickname soon became synonymous with all African American regiments formed in 1866.
[592] https://www.brianshellum.com/black_cadet_in_a_white_bastion_charles_young_at_west_point_55832.htm
[593] Gen. Vincent Brooks: Leadership is About People: Leading Authorities, June 11, 2019 speech

He asked the Superintendent of the Military Academy at that time, General Andrew Jackson Goodpaster, if he was a "token". General Goodpaster told him no, and emphasized that given West Point's very long history it was not going to take that kind of risk for political purposes.

"You're the First Captain because you should be the First Captain."[594]

When Cadet Vincent Brooks was announced as First Captain, the news media amplified the appointment of the first Black American achieving the distinguished leadership role, the cadet was still faced with racism. He received many letters of support from abroad, and also letters filled with racist epithets from many people, whether they knew him or not. He even received letters from both in and out of the Corps of Cadets "expressing their displeasure" of his appointment.[595] He was surprised, saying as a child growing up in the fifties, sixties, and the civil rights movement, he had an expectation by 1979 all of that was behind the American society.

"I learned then that we cannot let up," General Vincent Brooks, said commandingly. "So, I would go to Henry Flipper and draw inspiration from him. Knowing it would never be too tough for me, because it wasn't for him. And certainly, what I was going through was nothing like what he went through."[596]

Brooks wanted to lead the Cadet Corps, following in the footsteps of Flipper, with his willingness to stand up to pressure, and to demonstrate what he was capable of to anyone who was willing to observe. Like Flipper, he wanted to fight for his good name.[597] Working closely with Army public affairs who managed the numerous interview requests, Cadet Brooks was exposed to and learned of the importance of deliberate, carefully focused communication. Something, later in life, he would use in front of the world as an Army general.[598]

When Vincent Brooks received his diploma on graduation day in 1980, the Class of 1980 applauded. It was reminiscent of Henry Flipper's graduation when he was the only member of his class to receive applause for his accomplishment. Moments later, after all graduates had received their diplomas Vincent Brooks, now a commissioned 2nd Lieutenant, as his father and brother had been, gave the final command to the Class of 1980. He shouted the long-awaited and coveted words, "Graduating Class, Dismissed!!!" as the sky above Michie Stadium, the same Michie Stadium where they had all been received at West Point in the summer of 1976, filled with the white hats of the graduates. The Brooks family was present in great number to witness the event. They all thanked God. Vincent wept in gratitude and at the lifting of a heavy burden.

---

[594] Gen. Vincent Brooks: Leadership is About People: Leading Authorities, June 11, 2019 speech
[595] Gen. Brooks Remarks: Henry O. Flipper Dinner, February 13, 2019
[596] Gen. Brooks Remarks: Henry O. Flipper Dinner, February 13, 2019
[597] Gen. Brooks Remarks: Henry O. Flipper Dinner, February 13, 2019
[598] Gen. Vincent Brooks (RET), Remarks at the 2019 Public Affairs Forum , May 13, 2019

Brigade
Staff

First Row:
K. Gerald
V. Brooks
J. Sisner
Second Row:
K. Wildey
M. Knapp
J. Davis
J. Cox
P. Capstick
S. Snook

Source: U.S. Military Academy

Carol Rene Perry

Six months after graduating from West Point, Lieutenant Vincent Brooks went home to visit his parents and sister for Christmas leave in 1980. Lieutenant Brooks completed the requisite basic courses for an Airborne Infantry officer at Fort Benning[599], Georgia, and after a short break, would report to his first duty assignment as a Parachute Infantry officer in the 82nd Airborne Division at Fort Bragg[600], North Carolina. His family was living in Fort Lee[601], Virginia, where his father was stationed and where they had previously lived as a young family. During his visit, he met college student Carol Rene Perry, eldest of three daughters of his parents' friends, Army Colonel Mervin Eural Perry and Marion Elizabeth Harris Perry.

Carol was an "Army Brat" like Vincent Brooks. She was born in Aschaffenburg, West Germany, in 1960. Carol and her middle sister Robin were home from college visiting her family over the holiday break. Carol and Robin attended the University of Texas, Carol at the Medical Branch in Galveston, where she was studying physical therapy, and Robin at the main campus in Austin. Youngest sister, Susan, was in high school in Petersburg, Virginia, and was a classmate of Vincent's sister, Marquita.

The Perry and Harris family histories, like most African American families, had ties to slavery, and inter-racial conceptions. Carol's family history was also filled with multiple stories of personal courage in the face of racial obstacles and historic achievements, just like the Brooks family.

Carol's father, Mervin Perry, was one of the earliest graduates of Prairie View A&M, long a part of the Perry family educational experience, to achieve the rank of colonel. His twin brother, Ervin S. Perry, PhD, at the age of 28, became the first Black faculty member at any predominantly white university in the former Confederate States at the University of Texas in Austin.[602]

---

[599] Fort Benning, named for a Confederate general, was renamed to Fort Moore in 2023.

[600] Fort Bragg, named for a Confederate general, was renamed to Fort Liberty in 2023.

[601] Fort Lee, named for a Confederate general, was renamed to Fort Gregg-Adams in 2023.

[602] An Accomplished Engineer, Ervin Perry Made History as UT's First Black Faculty Member, The University of Texas at Austin, Cockrell School of Engineering
https://cockrell.utexas.edu/an-accomplished-engineer-ervin-perry-made-history-as-uts-first-black-faculty-member

Carol's mother, Marion, was the daughter of Reverend Odell Greenleaf Harris, a priest of the Protestant Episcopal Church, who led numerous successful efforts to create racial equality in the Episcopal Church in America. Odell used his language and debate skills to write pieces, and publicly supported the right of Blacks to have a voice and equal representation in the Episcopal Church. His battle for equality started in North Carolina with his church, St. Luke's Episcopal Church, built by his grandfather William Paschall Russell and other former slaves, most of whom were relatives. It was one of the first Episcopal churches for Blacks after the Civil War.

From 1943-1947, Harris was the dean of the Colored Convocation in the Diocese of Southern Virginia. In his book, "It Can Be Done," he wrote about his dismay of religious segregation, and how Jim Crow had no place in God's House.[603]

Reverend Harris taught and was a part of pastoral training at Bishop Payne Divinity School, the segregated seminary for producing Black clergy for the Episcopal Church. He was the Warden and Professor of Old Testament and New Testament Greek. Reverend Harris would go on to break color lines in the Episcopal Church, including championing the merger of the Bishop Payne Divinity School with the Virginia Theological Seminary, where Vincent's ancestors in the Lewis family had familial origins. Carol Brooks and her husband Vincent Brooks would donate all her great-grandfather's writings to the school, where they are preciously preserved.[604]

Operation Cupid

General Vincent Brooks characterizes his first meeting with Carol as a "military crossfire." The mothers arranged a college mixer, so that all the kids coming back from college or from their military breaks for the holidays had something to do. The dance mixer was at the Fort Lee officer's club.

"My mother and Carol's mother Marion were having a conversation specifically about their kids," said General Vincent Brooks, "Marion said, 'You know I've got three daughters.' My mother said, 'I have two sons and a daughter. Let's get them together!' "

Unaware of their wives who had been in conversation, then BG Leo Brooks, Sr. and Colonel Mervin Eural Perry were working on their cars in the automobile shop. Both of them work on cars for their daughters.

BG Leo Brooks, Sr. was working on the Volkswagen Beetle his sons once used, and he was giving it to his daughter Marquita. Carol's father was working on a little Chevy hatchback that his daughters were going to use on their drive back down to the University of Texas.

---

[603] Odell Greenleaf Harris, "It Can Be Done: The Autobiography of a Black Priest of the Protestant Episcopal Church who started under the bottom and moved up to the top." Page 33. Edited by Robert W. Prichard (Alexandria: The Protestant Episcopal Theological Seminary in Virginia, 1985
[604] Virginia Theological Seminary, https://library.vts.edu/

"So, the two dads are talking about their kids coming home, and they, too, had an idea to get their sons and daughters together. This is why I call it crossfire because the spouses and husbands were both colluding without a conversation between them!" he laughed.

Lieutenant Vincent Brooks attended that dance, but Carol was busy dancing that night with Frank Underwood, Jr. actor Blair Underwood's brother. The Underwood's father was stationed in Petersburg also, at Virginia State University, as a colonel in charge of ROTC there. Finally, Vincent got his chance and slow danced with Carol. He was smitten. According to Vincent Brooks, she was not as impressed. But she did share her mailing address with Vincent by writing it on a cocktail napkin, an address Vincent, forty-two years later, still remembers.

"That moment is still etched in my mind," said General Vincent Brooks. "203 Morgan Hall, UTMB (University of Texas Medical Branch at Galveston, Texas)."

A few days before Christmas, Leo and Naomi celebrated their 25th Wedding Anniversary with a cocktail party at their on-post residence. Vincent, as the eldest child present, proposed the Anniversary toast in the presence of the attendees, including Colonel Mervin and Mrs. Marion Perry. This toast made an impression on both Colonel Mervin and Mrs. Marion. In fact, Marion decided to double her efforts to match her studious first daughter with the dashing Lieutenant who proposed the toast.

A few days after Christmas, Lieutenant Vincent Brooks was lounging in the family room with his father in front of the TV. They were enjoying the flurry of football bowl games being broadcast on television. The phone rang, and his father picked up the phone. It was Carol's mother. She told him her daughters were still at home, and if one of their sons was still there, perhaps he could come over and "listen to records." BG Leo Brooks, Sr. told her his son would come over . . . then he told Vincent about the call. Vincent protested it was the last few days before he started his assignment. His father encouraged him to, "go on over there and visit."

"If you don't like what you see after about thirty minutes, be a gentleman and excuse yourself, then come home," Vincent recollected.

His father, ever the teaser, added, "But if anything comes out of this, I will never let you forget 'listen to records.'"

When Vincent arrived at the Perry residence about half a mile away from the Brooks home, he was met at the door by Carol's tall Texan father, Colonel Mervin Perry. Marion joined her husband at the door and welcomed Vincent inside.

The evening started slowly, but Carol warmed up to Vincent, and they spent the next few hours listening to records and chatting. Vincent, arriving back at the Brooks home after dark, told his parents he had a good time and "there is something there." His father smiled broadly and laughed. Two days later, Vincent joined the Perry family as they put Carol on the airplane to return to her studies in Galveston. This was a big deal for Vincent to be included in an emotional family moment. Vincent leaned in to kiss Carol goodbye, and to his delight, Carol kissed him back . A week later, when Lieutenant Vincent Brooks returned to join the 82nd Airborne Division as an Airborne Ranger Infantry Officer, still remembering that kiss

About two and a half months passed, and every time the young Lieutenant called home, his parents always asked if he had written to Carol. He would tell them not yet. He did not have a permanent address yet while living with two lieutenants who were his West Point Classmates. He would write when he had a permanent residence. He still had the napkin with Carol's address.

"Son, you've got to follow up with that girl!" his parents would say. The pairs of parents continued to conspire to get the two together. Once Vincent had acquired an apartment, his parents shared his address with Carol's parents.

College student Carol and Lieutenant Vincent both wrote a letter postmarked on the same day. In a few days, they each received their letter and re-established contact. The relationship bloomed from there. On December 27, 1982, two years and two weeks after they were first introduced and six months after Carol's graduation from the University of Texas Medical Branch in Galveston, Texas, as a Physical Therapist, the couple married at Fort Lee on December 27, 1982

By this time, Vincent's parents had been reassigned to Philadelphia. Carol's parents were still in Virginia. The young couple married in the Main Post Chapel, repeating many characteristics of their parents' weddings. While both clergyman grandfathers were present for the wedding, the ceremony was performed by Reverend Henry Curtis Brooks, Vincent's uncle, with elements of the Episcopal tradition and the general Protestant tradition woven into the service.

This was easy work for Henry Curtis Brooks, then a Theologian and Professor at the Andover Newton Theological Seminary. The timing of the wedding during the holiday break enabled families from both sides who were in education and in the military to attend. Big brother Leo, who was married two months earlier, was also in attendance. Vincent, now a First Lieutenant, wore his military dress uniform and had military ushers from his unit. Carol wore the same wedding dress and pearl necklace worn by her mother. The couple cut the cake with the saber both Leo and Vincent carried in their senior year at West Point.

Carol and Lt. Vincent Brooks wedding, December 27, 1982

Marion and (Rank) Mervin Perry's wedding Dec 16 1957

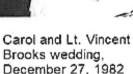

Source: Brooks Family

Carol joined Vincent in Fort Bragg, North Carolina. There, she worked in civilian practice as a physical therapist, and in subsequent assignments, when she was allowed to travel overseas with him, she did. Overseas, Carol worked at military installations, helping patients, including some of her husband's soldiers, recover from injuries.

One of those overseas assignments was their first as a married couple in Germany from 1984-1987. Carol was born in Germany, where her father served two overseas tours of duty; Carol worked at the 5th General Hospital in Bad Canstatt near Stuttgart.

Then Captain Vincent Brooks was in command of 150 soldiers in B Company, 4th Battalion (Mechanized) 16th Infantry, 1st Infantry Division (Forward), and a year later, in a second command of 350 soldiers in Headquarters and Headquarters Company of the same battalion. The 4th Battalion (Mechanized) 16th Infantry, 1st Infantry Division (Forward) was the southern-most combat unit in Germany at the time in Goeppingen, West Germany, during the Cold War.

During these years, Carol treated many of Vincent's soldiers, often before or after some of the long road marches he used to condition the unit, physically. Vincent was always present and led his soldiers on these long road marches.

Education Leading to Opportunity

When looking for the leaders of tomorrow, the U.S. Army takes select individuals who show promise for duties with increasing levels of responsibility and sends them to advanced academic programs before committing them in a subsequent series of assignments to greater and greater roles. Both Brooks brothers, like their father before them, were among this select group.

Just like his parents, General Vincent Brooks furthered his education to expand himself professionally. He and his brother Leo Brooks Jr. would serve together professionally only on two assignments to the Pentagon. Academically, they were together four times.

The brothers overlapped for three years at West Point. Five years later, in 1984, they were stationed together at Fort Benning, Georgia, to attend the Infantry Officer Advanced Course. Leo Jr. stayed an extra year at Fort Campbell to command an infantry company, which took precedence over his academic training. Seven years later, in 1991, they were rejoined at Fort Leavenworth for Staff College. Vincent attended one year before Leo, who spent an extra year in the 1st Ranger Battalion, 75th Infantry. Vincent remained for an extra year at Leavenworth, which overlapped Leo's Staff College year, to attend the prestigious School of Advanced Military Studies (graduates are nicknamed "Jedi Knights"). Vincent earned a master's degree in Military Art and Science.

The brother's fourth time together academically took place at the peak level of their professional military education, Senior Service College. The brothers were in the Class of 1999 at the US Army War College, with Leo in the resident course at Carlisle Barracks, Pennsylvania, and Vincent a War College Fellow at Harvard University John F. Kennedy School of Government in the National Security Fellowship program.

Vincent's journey took him from the School of Advanced Military Studies to key jobs from 1992 to 1998 in combat units in Texas, the Pentagon (where he again served with his brother Leo Jr., who was already there), and in Korea.

Working Together

In addition to education, the Brooks brothers also worked together. They worked in the front office of the Army to aid in the transitions between the outgoing Chief of Staff of the Army and Vice Chief of Staff of the Army to their incoming counterparts. Leo Brooks Jr. was aide de camp to the outgoing Chief of Staff of the Army. Vincent was aide de camp to the incoming Vice Chief of Staff of the Army, General Ronald Houston Griffith. The brothers worked together for about one and a half months.

"Being an aide de camp was a very visible and prestigious position filled with learning experiences at the knee of a serving general," said Vincent Brooks. The positions rarely went to Black officers at the highest levels. The Black officers who held the position prior to Brooks were notable Black military leaders.

One of them was a contemporary of his father, Army Major General Hugh G. Robinson. MG Robinson was a 1954 West Point graduate and had been aide de camp to President Lyndon Johnson from 1965 until the end of Johnson's presidency. He was the first Black officer to hold the position.

Brooks recalls the late 1980s to mid-1990s was a popular time to have Black aides de camp as the military pushed for greater diversity and early identification of diverse talent. One such example is Charles Q. Brown, who, as a Captain and Major, was aide de camp to the Chief of Staff of the Air Force General Ron Fogleman from 1994 to 1996. Today, General Charles Q. Brown is the Chief of Staff of the U.S. Air Force, and the nominee to be the new Chairman of the Joint Chiefs of Staff, which is the country's highest-ranking officer.

"These were door-opening opportunities. Not only for those of us who were trailblazers in holding them, but, more importantly, for many minority officers who held such positions after us. Many proceeded up in rank to become generals and admirals themselves," said General Vincent Brooks.

The development of a military leader is not only education, but the series of deployments that they lead. Each mission builds onto the next one, and the expansion of their skill sets broadens as the knowledge learned in books becomes actionable and used. For General Vincent Brooks, this progression in leadership and military contribution was no different. To give an example of "just one" deployment or mission to define a lesson or his career would be next to impossible. Each mission he participated in, and each leadership role he earned, collectively led him to where he is today.

Korea, Cambridge, Kuwait, and Kosovo

After the Pentagon, then Lieutenant Colonel Vincent Brooks was off to Korea, where he commanded a unit of 800 Americans and South Koreans. This was his first assignment in the country. He was in Korea from 1996 to 1998 as a battalion commander, just south of the Demilitarized Zone (DMZ). Carol went with him but was required to live further away from the DMZ in the capital city of Seoul. They saw each other a few days every two months.

Lieutenant Colonel Brooks learned to read Korean and speak a limited amount (he had also studied Spanish, German, and Arabic prior to Korean). Brooks credited his linguistic abilities to his father, who speaks fluent Vietnamese and Spanish. His brother and sister also speak Spanish.

The Korea assignment was a turning point in Vincent's career. He was forward deployed[605], facing a very real threat from North Korea all day, every day. The soldiers of the unit rotated out of the country each year, making the preservation of readiness and unit cohesion a challenge to be overcome through creative leadership. The unit had soldiers from the United States and from Korea and operated within the combined force of the two countries.

Korea was not at peace, but in a condition of a temporary armistice.[606] Hostilities could have resumed at any time. Lieutenant Colonel Vincent Brooks thrived in this environment, which brought together all he had learned, leading troops in the 82nd Airborne Division ready for worldwide commitment, in the 1st Infantry Division (Forward) in Germany, securing another divided country with an outnumbering enemy force just miles away, and in the 1st Cavalry Division where he learned to maneuver infantry and armored forces supported by artillery and aviation with great effect. All of these were required in the demanding environment of Korea. The unit was the 2nd Battalion (Mechanized), 9th Infantry Regiment, nicknamed

---

[605] "Forward deployed" means a US military base on foreign soil
[606] Armistice is an agreement which serves as a military ceasefire. It is not a peace treaty. On July 27, 1953, a signed armistice agreement between North and South Korea formally ended the war in Korea. It was signed by United States Army Lieutenant General William Harrison Jr. and General Mark W. Clark representing the United Nations Command (UNC), North Korea leader Kim Il Sung and General Nam Il representing the Korean People's Army (KPA), and Peng Dehuai representing the Chinese People's Volunteer Army (PVA)

"Manchus" within the 1st Brigade of 2nd Infantry Division. The Division Commander was then Major General Tommy R. Franks.

Sadly, just over halfway through the two-year assignment, Colonel (Retired) Mervin Perry, Carol's father, died at the age of 62. Vincent was in the field with his soldiers conducting nighttime live fire maneuvers when he was called to the field headquarters to receive the message from Carol. It was also brother Leo's 40th birthday. The date would thereafter have dual meanings.

Before leaving command of the 2nd Manchu Battalion in May of 1998, Vincent received word that he had been selected early for promotion to Colonel. He and Carol were heading to Senior Service College at Harvard. Carol decided to pursue another degree. This was something she had done while Vincent was in Staff College and at SAMS. This time, she would pursue her doctorate in Orthopedic Rehabilitation from a new Doctorate of Science (DSc) program through Rocky Mountain University of Health Professions. Carol stopped clinical practice in Boston to concentrate on her degree.

Two months before the end of the one-year academic fellowship, NATO began combat operations, in Kosovo and Serbia, with ground force deployments to Albania and staged elsewhere in Europe. Naval forces in the Mediterranean Sea and the Aegean Sea were also involved in building a presence and contributing to strikes against targets in Kosovo and Serbia.

Leading NATO operations at that time was the Supreme Allied Commander of NATO, and the Commander of U.S. European Command was General Wesley K. Clark. General Clark nurtured Vincent's early career as a Plans Officer in the Division Headquarters staff of the 1st Cavalry Division and a year later as operations officer of a Mechanized Infantry Battalion. General Clark officiated Vincent Brooks' promotion to Lieutenant Colonel while both served at the Pentagon.

The other leader in the mission, Director of Operations for US Army forces in Europe (USAREUR), was Major General David D. McKiernan, who was, as a lieutenant colonel, Vincent's boss, while both worked for Clark at 1st Cavalry Division.

McKiernan reached out to War College fellow Brooks, two months short of course completion, and asked him to come to the United States Army Europe headquarters right away to assist in some sensitive planning efforts as lead planner. It would be a temporary assignment as Brooks was already on orders to Headquarters, Third Army, to report in late June.

In late April, Brooks passed through the Pentagon on the way, where he was updated by then-Brigadier General George Casey, who was the Deputy Director J-5 for Politico-Military Affairs in Europe. BG Casey was also the Chief of Staff of the 1st Cavalry Division when Major Vincent Brooks was a plans officer for the Division.

Once updated, Lieutenant Colonel Brooks arrived in Germany and reported to Major General McKiernan. It was the fourth job Vincent Brooks had held under McKiernan. The planning efforts were frenetic and bounced between Germany and Brussels, where Vincent was also a special plans officer supporting Clark's NATO Headquarters, which was buzzing with the deployment of forces and the conduct of strike missions in Kosovo and Serbia. Vincent's role was to assist in developing a wider array of options to compel Yugoslav Serbian leader Slobodan Milosevic to cease operations in Kosovo and withdraw his forces. It was the first time for Vincent to operate inside of a high-level command, particularly while conducting combat operations. The experience deepened Vincent's understanding of the military art and brought to life his education at SAMS seven years earlier.

While deployed to Europe, Vincent finished the final course requirements of his one-year academic fellowship. At the end of May 1999, Vincent was back in Cambridge to pack up his home with Carol, and together they headed to Carlisle Barracks, Pennsylvania, for Vincent's promotion ceremony to colonel, a ceremony he would share with his brother also being promoted to colonel.

Vincent's father officiated the ceremony and placed one of his own eagles on the right shoulder of Vincent's tunic. Carol pinned one of her late father's eagle insignia on the left shoulder of Vincent's tunic. The passing of her father made this moment even more poignant.

The two mothers then slipped on a colonel's epaulet on each shoulder of Vincent's shirt. Each epaulet had been placed by them on their husbands when they were promoted to Colonel. Vincent Brooks always wore legacy insignia at each rank until he was promoted to four-star general when he donned his own rank for the first time.

Vincent K. Brooks Colonel Ceremony June 1, 1999
Source: Brooks Family

For eight years, Brooks commanded forces in both Operations Desert Shield and Desert Storm. On September 11, 2001, then, Colonel Vincent Brooks was a Brigade Commander deployed to Kosovo. Colonel Brooks, along with the commanders of a Russian unit under Brooks' supervision and a U.S. unit under Brooks' supervision, were meeting with villagers in a town that had been, historically, mixed with ethnic Serbs who were Christian and ethnic Albanians who were Muslim living in peace. The fire winds of ethno-religious extremism had made the village a battleground.

Initially, the ethnic Albanians were forced out, and the Serbian extremist militias destroyed their homes. After NATO intervened in support of the ethnic Albanians against Serbia, the Kosovar Albanian extremist militias sought revenge and re-entered the village, destroying the homes and displacing the remaining ethnic Serbs.

Under the protection of the US and Russian forces securing the area, many of the villagers felt safe enough to return. They wanted to rebuild the village themselves, along with their neighbors, and some support from KFOR (Kosovo Force[607]), which would provide building materials and security. That village had become the main effort for Colonel Brooks.

Later that afternoon, while in the village, word came to Brooks through satellite telephone that the first plane had hit the World Trade Center in New York. Then, the second. Then, the towers collapsed. The ethno-religious extremism that destroyed that village in Kosovo had just reached the United States homeland.

The world had just changed.

The mission ended for the 1st Brigade, 3rd Infantry Division two days before Thanksgiving in late November. But the war on ethno-religious extremism was a preview of the next twenty years of Brooks' military career. He moved from one senior command to another, most of which were overseas in the Middle East, Central Asia, the broad Indo-Pacific region, and Asia.

These military experiences coupled with the foundational mixture of faith and family, education, and experience, and most of all, excellence.

"I felt like each assignment was a crowning achievement bringing together everything I had learned since my childhood – and then there was another, and another. It was a true blessing to have been able to serve this way and for so long," recalled General Vincent Brooks.

Vincent Brooks was nominated for promotion to Brigadier General in 2002 and was "frocked"[608] in October 2022 since he was in a joint duty assignment for a general. This promotion made him the youngest

---

[607] KFOR is a NATO-led international peacekeeping force in Kosovo.

[608] An officer who is so authorized to wear the insignia of the next higher grade is said to be "frocked" to that grade. Source: 10 USC 777: Wearing of insignia of higher grade before promotion (frocking): authority; restrictions

general in the Army that year (Leo Brooks Jr. was the youngest on the promotion list of the previous year). He was the first member of the West Point Class of 1980 to be selected for promotion to brigadier general and was the only member of his class to be on that promotion list.

The ceremony was officiated by Vincent's new boss, Lieutenant General George Casey Jr., with whom he had served in the 1st Cavalry Division a decade earlier. Vincent Brooks' promotion also made history as it made the Brooks family the first, and only (to this date), Black American family to have three generals within two generations of an immediate family. The promotion occurred shortly after Vincent's arrival in The Joint Staff, the most senior staff in the U.S. Military.

Before Vincent Brooks' promotion to brigadier general, the family shared history with the father and son combinations of Army BG Benjamin O. Davis, Sr. and his son Air Force General Benjamin O. Davis, Jr., and Air Force General Daniel "Chappie" James and his son Air Force Lieutenant General Daniel James Jr.

Once Vincent was promoted to brigadier general, Vincent and Leo Jr. were the second pair of Black American brothers selected to serve as generals or admirals. The first set of brothers was Navy Rear Admiral Lawrence Chambers and Army Lieutenant General Andrew Chambers. After the Brooks brothers, only one other pair has advanced into the flag officer (generals and admirals) ranks, the Gainey brothers – Army Major Generals Sean Gainey and Andrew Gainey, who both remain on active duty.

Raising his Hand

One day at the end of 2002, while walking the corridors of the Pentagon between meetings, the young brigadier general encountered his former commander from Korea and from Atlanta, General Tommy Franks. General Franks was now a four-star general and in command of all military forces in the Middle East and Central Asia, known as U.S. Central Command or CENTCOM.

Franks was already conducting combat operations in Afghanistan. BG Vincent Brooks felt that he was at the "wrong end of the spear" serving in the Pentagon and said to General Franks, "Sir, I feel guilty being here while you are running a war. If I can help in anyway, please 'put me in, Coach.'"

In February 2003, the drum beat of war was increasing in volume. Afghanistan was ongoing, and Iraq was on the horizon. One of his roles in the Joint Staff was the bilateral military policy coordination between the US and Canada through a body called the Military Cooperation Committee. Brooks was the U.S. head of delegation, and he was attending a meeting in Halifax, Nova Scotia.

A snowstorm was raging along the eastern seaboard of the north American land mass. At the end of the first day of the two-day meeting, BG Brooks enjoyed a cold beer with his Canadian counterpart when he received a note from the staff that US Air Force Major General Mike Dunn, acting J5 of the Joint Staff in the Pentagon, needed him to call as soon as possible. MG Dunn told him General Franks wanted him back in DC immediately for new orders.

"It was a story of planes, trains, and automobiles," recalled General Vincent Brooks. "The storm went from Nova Scotia down to New Jersey. I flew as far as possible to Newark, New Jersey. Landing shortly before the airfield was shut down, I moved to a train until being kicked off four stops later for having the wrong ticket. Then, catching the next train, I made it to Washington Union Station, then took the Metro subway to the closest station near the house where Carol and I lived in Virginia." Carol picked him up, and he told her what was unfolding.

Brooks recalled, "I told Carol late on Friday night, called together my staff at the Pentagon on Saturday morning to tell them, and told my parents on Sunday after worshipping with them at church that General Franks called me forward and that I was leaving the next day for an unknown time period."

On Monday, Vincent flew to Tampa to receive updates and introductions to the CENTCOM staff there. Later that week, Carol joined him in Tampa on Friday before he left on Sunday. It was two weeks from the day of notification by Major General Dunn when Brooks left.

Torn

BG Vincent Brooks had mixed emotions heading to the unique assignment. He was an Infantry officer, not a public affairs officer, and didn't want this role to diminish his accomplishments at the tip of the spear since he would likely be viewed in the media as a press secretary. But he knew not to question divine providence, nor hesitate when given a mission, especially when it came from one of his former bosses and mentors. This would mark the third and final time Vincent Brooks worked under General Tommy R. Franks. Brooks had gotten what he asked for.

BG Vincent Brooks told his parents his concerns. His mom told him, "Like I always tell you, don't worry, just pray."[609]

His father's greatest piece of advice, which guided him daily, "Just be yourself. Stay humble. And do your job."[610]

During his time in the Middle East, Naomi would send him email notes of encouragement, and care packages just like she sent him and his brother while at West Point. Naomi's peanut butter blossom cookies with the Hershey kisses on top were popular in the warfighting headquarters.

---

[609] Annie Gowen, "Military Success Runs in Family", The Washington Post, May 25, 2003
https://www.washingtonpost.com/archive/local/2003/05/25/military-success-runs-in-family/7f29c78d-220f-40f1-ba3b-eca567b66ed3/
[610] BG Vincent Brooks conversation with authors, June 20, 2023

From Shock and Awe to Fire and Fury – seventeen years as a general

BG Vincent Brooks arrived in Camp Doha, Qatar, in February 2003, a month before the start of combat operations in Iraq, which would begin with the "The Shock and Awe" precision strike campaign.[611] On February 27, 2003, in CENTCOM headquarters in Qatar, while Vincent was coming up to speed for the imminent start of combat operations, his grandfather, James Lewis Jr., passed away.

"I was thankful that I spent some quality time with him in early January before I was called forward," recalled General Brooks, who noted he was overseas in military service when each of his four grandparents, and his father-in-law, died.

Once combat operations began on March 20, 2003, BG Vincent Brooks moved between the two worlds of operations, as a Deputy Director of Operations (J-3) and the public domain as operations spokesperson. He used his knowledge of operations and converted that knowledge into something that could be shared with a bevy of journalists at the headquarters, and a world seeking information about the operation. He used the communication skills he first developed at West Point when he was First Captain. At this time, he was the youngest general officer in the Army and was not yet being paid a brigadier general's pay.

"The world was hungry for information," said General Vincent Brooks. "We were communicating to media outlets from dozens of countries. The media had their big-name correspondents there with us and embedded with our troops in the line of fire. The pool of journalists was massive. The tension was high."

The media briefings were lively as journalists tried to gather the latest information. Reporters repeatedly asked for General Tommy Franks. They did not want to hear from BG Vincent Brooks. What the reporters didn't know, was Gen. Franks was much more selective about going before the press. In that regard, his approach was not the same as General H. Norman Schwartzkopf, who led the same CENTCOM in combat operations against Iraq in 1991.

Reporters initially asked why BG Vincent Brooks was providing the updates. They wanted Gen. Franks, not him. They would also express their frustration that the information BG Vincent Brooks was authorized to convey at the briefing was disseminated to the press earlier by the Pentagon.[612]

"I did not want to become the story," stressed General Vincent Brooks. "And if my emotions got engaged, I would become the story. And that wasn't fair to the people who were fighting, many of whom I knew personally."

---

[611] Iraq War began on March 19, 2003, when the United States joined forces with the United Kingdom, Australia, and Poland initiated war on Iraq. The coalition vowed to end the dictatorial rule of Saddam Hussein and find and destroy Iraqi weapons of mass destruction (WMD).

[612] In practice, the Pentagon, the White House and the CENTCOM headquarters daily coordinated communications actions to ensure consistency in what was reported. Depending on the time of day when the information emerged, it might be more timely for the Pentagon to release it into the news cycle or it might be part of the CENTCOM update first. Interview with authors.

BG Vincent Brooks explained he took the opposite approach and tried to make sure that his emotions were kept under control.

"That was part of my upbringing, obviously, in my house, at West Point, and in my military career," said General Vincent Brooks, "Keep your emotions under control. No matter how you feel. Do your duty first. And so that's what I was trying to do there."

Then-BG Vincent Brooks always kept his trademark cool demeanor and would deliver the information no matter what journalistic provocation. He would update the world on the big picture: the progress of the war, the context for the reporting coming from the front lines, the methods used in the information domain as well as the physical domain, and refute false information being introduced by Iraq and other governments. He could not give specifics because he could put forces in jeopardy. Reporters did not find satisfaction with that. Naomi and MG Leo Brooks, Sr. would set their alarm at 7 am so they could watch his briefings.

In one of those briefings, they watched him rise above, and not take the bait from a high-profile reporter who questioned the value of the high-level briefings since they were not being briefed by "senior-most officers" and the information they were receiving was "largely information released by the Pentagon…"[613]

Instead, BG Vincent Brooks took the high road as his parents taught him, and, without skipping a beat, told the reporter, "First, I would say it's your choice," he said. "We want to provide information that's truthful from the operational headquarters that is running this war."[614]

Both Naomi and MG Brooks, Sr. were overjoyed at his response, and told a *Washington Post* reporter they raised their children to never apologize.

"The reporter started with the quip, 'no offense,' and growing up as an African American in the 1960's and 70's, anything that started with "no offense" was going to be offensive, so when I heard him start his question with that, I was prepared and on guard," recalled General Vincent Brooks. "You have to learn to regulate the quick retort, and I learned that growing up I usually regretted what I said out of emotion. You need to be thoughtful about what you're saying."

General Vincent Brooks said self-awareness is key to being a leader. While soldiers learn self-awareness in the military, anyone can learn this valuable trait by learning from the hurt that can be caused by "shooting off at the mouth." By learning from the impact your words can have on others, you can help you develop the tools you need to help you learn to hold your tongue and think before you speak. The experience was deeply formative and impacted the approach taken by General Brooks in deliberately joining operations

[613] Annie Gowen, "Military Success Runs in Family", The Washington Post, May 25, 2003
https://www.washingtonpost.com/archive/local/2003/05/25/military-success-runs-in-family/7f29c78d-220f-40f1-ba3b-eca567b66ed3/
[614] Annie Gowen, "Military Success Runs in Family", The Washington Post, May 25, 2003
https://www.washingtonpost.com/archive/local/2003/05/25/military-success-runs-in-family/7f29c78d-220f-40f1-ba3b-eca567b66ed3/

with information for the rest of his career as he became more and more senior with expansive responsibilities over large regions of the world.

When Franks and part of the CENTCOM headquarters moved into Baghdad, occupying the former palaces of the now-destroyed Ba'ath Regime of Saddam Hussein, General Franks released Brooks.

Brooks sought to return to the Pentagon without fanfare. The goal was short-lived. Driven by humility, he carried a sense of embarrassment that he was better known than those who were conducting the fighting at the tip of the spear. This became clear as BG Vincent Brooks boarded a military "rotator" flight, a chartered aircraft that moved military troops and government civilians through several middle east stops and delivered them to the United States on a cycle. Brooks wanted to fly with the troops. Upon boarding, he took his seat in the full aircraft. Being the most senior officer aboard, he sat close to the front next to two other servicemen.

As the door closed, the purser aboard the flight, who had recognized Brooks from his television press conferences, announced through the public address system, "we are honored to have aboard Brigadier General Vincent Brooks." Applause emerged through the aircraft.

A few moments later, the two servicemen in the same row leaned over and said, "Sir, thanks for talking about us. We flew the Air Force F117 stealth fighters that dropped bombs on the first night, including Dora Farms."

The embarrassed general thanked them for what they did in the fight. Their names were unknown to the world. Brooks knew that the debt owed to them would never be repaid.

BG Vincent Brooks resumed his assignment in the Pentagon in May 2003. He would serve in six more positions as a one-star general, including a tour of duty in combat at the tip of the spear in Iraq.

Brooks was waiting to report on a new field assignment in Baghdad when he received a call from mentor George Casey, Jr., now a four-star general and Vice Chief of Staff of the Army, notifying him that his orders had been changed and that he would instead serve as the Chief of Public Affairs for the U.S. Army. Even though he was worried about being type-cast into public communications with this second assignment, Brooks accepted the position and gave it his all. It was imperative he did for the abuses at Abu Ghraib prison in Iraq, as well as the mishandling of the tragic death of Corporal Pat Tillman in Afghanistan, which had just broken into the news. Both had significantly damaged the reputation of the U.S. Army in the public view. It would be BG Vincent Brooks' job to turn that around.

At War and "Spotting Quander"

From May 2006 until 2008, then-BG Vincent Brooks, served as Deputy Commanding General of the Famous 1st Cavalry Division to stabilize Baghdad. This mission is now called, "The Surge" in Operation Iraqi Freedom. But in the darkness of war, there was some light. On several occasions, Brooks served in locations where his cousins were stationed.

In emails to home during the extended time in Baghdad, which grew from a planned 12 months to 17 months, then BG Vincent Brooks would update his family about some positive aspects of his life in the combat zone.

"The scary and, dangerous, and heartbreaking parts were in abundance, but I never shared them with my family since it would multiply their worry," said BG Vincent Brooks. There were family sightings from time to time in Iraq. Three of his relatives were also in Iraq at the same time."

Vincent first connected with Major Lucius Shuler, III, a Lewis and Quander cousin, son of his mother's sister Ruth, in November 2006. They met at a logistics base in central Iraq, where Lucius served as a staff officer.

BG Vincent Brooks and Major Shuler, III
Balad Air Base, Irag
November 2006

Source: Brooks Family

Later, an email home carried the subject line "Spotting Quander."

The email was about the unexpected joy of seeing additional family relatives. BG Vincent Brooks first crossed paths in Iraq with Major Melonie Quander, who was an Army nurse and the wife of Quander cousin, Major Mark Quander, an Army Engineer. These meetings would be a nice surprise for them, especially during the holidays.

"Even a few minutes or less than an hour, if we had contact like that, it was a humanizing moment," reminisced General Vincent Brooks. "It made you feel like you're part of somebody and that you're not going through this hardship alone."

In Taji, which is north of Baghdad, Melonie, a nurse at the field medical unit, and BG Vincent Brooks saw each other on Christmas Eve.

Christmas Eve 2006
Melonie Quander, Army Nurse
Source: Brooks Family photos

Eight months later, BG Vincent Brooks connected with his cousin, and Melonie's husband, Major (later Major General)Mark Quander, in Al Faw Palace in Baghdad, on August 13, 2007.

BG Vincent Brooks (Left) and BG
Mark Quander,
Al Faw Palace, Baghdad, August 13,
2007
Source: Brooks Family photos

Melonie and BG Vincent Brooks overlapped twice in Baghdad. He missed BG Mark Quander by a few days for a second chance meeting. BG Vincent Brooks left Iraq in 2008 to return to the United States for a year. During that time, he briefly commanded the 1st Cavalry Division but left command when a senior Pentagon official held his nomination for promotion to major general.

Brooks left the 1st Cavalry Division and served as the Deputy Commanding General of III Corps and Fort Hood until April 2009, when the promotion hold ended. The Senate proceeded to confirm his promotion. He was promoted that day, with his parents and siblings looking on by video teleconference into the Pentagon. Carol's mother, Marion, and her sisters were present in person for the ceremony. General George Casey, Jr., now Chief of Staff of the Army, ordered Major General Vincent Brooks to move to take command of the 1st Infantry Division "The Big Red One"[615] one week later as the unit was preparing for its second deployment to Iraq.

---

[615] "The Big Red One" is one of the most celebrated units in the Army. The unit gets its name because of its distinctive shoulder patch—a red numeral on an olive-drab shield—

In November 2009, the 1ˢᵗ Infantry Division deployed to Iraq. The division was responsible for securing the country's southern half, which was largely populated by the Shi'ites and adjacent to Saudi Arabia to the southwest, Kuwait to the southeast, and Iran to the east.

Grace of God

General Vincent Brooks said there were many examples where faith mattered, and the grace of God kept him, and most of his soldiers, alive—the holidays provided no respite from danger.

General Vincent Brooks said it didn't dawn on him or Carol until retirement that they never spent a Thanksgiving dinner alone together. They were always with their military family. While there were fewer than a handful of Thanksgiving holidays together with relatives, he served food to his soldiers somewhere around the world almost every other Thanksgiving.

One of those Thanksgivings was in Basra, Iraq, in 2010. He was flying through an area bounded by the Iran, Kuwait, and Saudi Arabia borders throughout the day to serve as many troops as possible at the various bases dining facilities. The Chief of Chaplains for the US Army was visiting Iraq and joined Brooks in the movements. ,. They decided they were not going to eat until every place got served because leaders eat last.

It was a full day, and as they were approaching the final destination, Brooks' headquarters at Basra base, just before dusk, they heard the incoming artillery and missile alarm in the radio background while receiving an update from the operations center. The alarm was the sound of four long horn tones, then the voice alarm "INCOMING, INCOMING, INCOMING" in a continuous and repeating melody of warning. "That alarm normally goes off for a couple of minutes while missiles are in the air and then stops. This alarm kept on signaling," observed General Brooks. Moments later, the airfield controller told the pilots of the UH-60 "Blackhawk" helicopter carrying the Commander of all US Forces in the southern half of Iraq, Major General Vincent Brooks, and the two-star Chief of Chaplains for the entire Army, Major General Doug Carver the base was under attack, and the airfield was closed. The aircraft was low on fuel after the long day of flying.

While in the air and hearing the alarm, Major General Vincent Brooks was thinking of an attack that he experienced in Baghdad in October 2007 during "the surge" in Iraq. Brooks and soldiers were eating dinner in the dining facility, and the same missile alarm going off now was blaring then.

This alarm went off so frequently with attacks on the base during the surge that the soldiers were used to it and were not intimidated by it. But one of the nearby alarms went off longer than normal, signaling that missiles were still in the air, threatening the area where the alarm was sounded. One of those missiles landed right outside the door of the dining facility at night while people were in line to get food. Brooks said, "One missile injured 36 people and killed two. So, I was thinking, here we go again, and on Thanksgiving." Brooks helped to organize the response to the mass casualty event and assisted the medical teams in treating the most grievously injured. The experience was etched in his mind.

After learning not to dwell on negative thoughts in combat, Brooks returned to the present with a strong desire to get on the ground as quickly as feasible to provide leadership.

Once they were allowed to land, they left the helicopters and quickly drove their waiting vehicles straight to the dining facility to serve soldiers there, and to assess what may have been hit in the uncommonly long duration strike.

"It was between 36-38 missiles that impacted us, all launched remotely by Iranian-trained agents with Iranian-provided missiles," said General Vincent Brooks. "All but two of 40 missiles fired; thank God, none caused injuries. They (the Iranian-trained militias) built a shed out of cinder blocks and put these multiple launch missiles into the cinder block shed, covered them, and then, on command, launched them. The missiles were landing all over the base. One landed right in front of the dining facility. People paused (just as had happened in 2007) after it exploded, and then the serving of food resumed. I walked in with the Chief of Chaplains, and we put on our hats and gloves and continued to serve turkey to the troops. Thank God everyone was fine, and after everyone was served, we got to eat. I can count on the Chief of Chaplains being with me to give us a little bit of divine protection."

General Vincent Brooks said one of the things he learned is that "for the families of warriors, who have been to war or had a family member at war, when it's husband or wife, they learn to work through it. When it's the children of that same couple, it's different. It's very different for them and worrisome all the time."

"So, it's harder on parents than it is on warrior and spouse teams who are going through it," said General Vincent Brooks. "My mother told me she wore her knees out with all those years she was praying when I was over in Germany, Kosovo, in the Middle East, throughout the Indo Pacific, and in Korea ."

Vincent Brooks continued to receive promotions and increasing responsibilities as he rose in rank from a two-star Major General in command of over 12,000 troops and their families, to a three-star Lieutenant General in command of over 48,000 troops, and to the top rank that can be held in the U.S. military, the four-star rank of General.

Brooks became the eighth Black American in U.S. Army history to attain the top military rank. His family was present for the ceremony. Carol and Chief of Staff of the Army, General Ray Odierno, under whom Vincent had served three times, including twice in combat, pinned the four-star rank on his tunic. His father and brother unfurled the large red flag with gold trim and four white stars.

"It was a blessing to have many family members there in Hawaii for the ceremony. I had just left command in South Carolina the previous week, and yet they were all present. It was especially poignant that my brother Leo had achieved a 'perfect attendance record' by being present to witness all ten of my promotions over the span of 33 years," General Brooks recalled joyfully.

It was a long way from Richard Henry Brooks serving as a body servant to a Confederate officer and then a Union Officer in 1862.

Not So Fast

After three challenging years, commanding 108,000 Army troops throughout the Indo-Pacific region, General Brooks was preparing to retire in the Spring of 2016. His papers were filed, submitted, and awaiting the approval of the Secretary of Defense. After a larger group meeting, Secretary of Defense Ashton Carter asked Brooks to join him in a side room.

"The Secretary said, 'I heard you intend to retire," recalled BG Brooks on the conversation. "Did the President (Obama) talk to you yet?'".

 Carter told Brooks that he and the President were impressed by Brooks' leadership and wanted Brooks to take command in Korea. Brooks said Carter told him, "But the President wants to talk to you himself."

On March 30, 2016, General Brooks had an office call with President Obama in the Oval Office of the White House. Brooks would take command in Korea three weeks later, returning to a familiar but much more advanced place than the first time serving there in 1996 to 1998. It was an excellent match of the talents and experiences of General Brooks.

On April 30, 2016, General Vincent Brooks was back in Korea as a commander for a second time, this time as the most senior commander in the country leading the United Nations Command, the Republic of Korea and US Combined Forces Command, and U.S. Forces Korea (Army, Air Force, Navy, and Marine Corps). The largest of these three commands was comprised of over 650,000 South Korean and U.S. troops in the Combined Forces Command.

During this time, Brooks served the US President and the South Korean President, two of each, as both democratic nations underwent a political shift during General Brooks' first year in command. On January 20, 2017, U.S. President Barack Obama was replaced by newly inaugurated President Donald J. Trump. Korean President Park, Geun Hye was impeached and removed from office on March 10, 2017, and newly elected President Moon, Jae In, was inaugurated on May 7, 2017. General Brooks was the only foreigner in attendance at the inauguration of the Korean President.

Relations with North Korea, under the leadership of Kim Jong Un, were at the highest level of tension in recent years. The potential for a resumption of warfare in Korea was rising. President Donald Trump described this potential, saying, "North Korea best not make any more threats to the United States. They will be met with fire and fury like the world has never seen."

Affairs with China, Japan, and Russia also were challenging as the countries jockeyed for influence and power in the strategically critical area of northeast Asia. The position required all the skills, innate and learned, that Brooks had available to him. From his linguistic talents (Brooks was well-known in Korea for being able to sing all four verses of the Korean National Anthem ("Aegukga") in the Korean language), to his military diplomacy, strategic planning, warfighting, and communications skills. All were needed to create sufficient pressure to drive North Korea into dialog and negotiations, while not breaking the Korea – U.S. Alliance or the Japan – U.S. Alliance.

By mid-2018, North Korea had shifted to dialogue. Kim Jong Un met with the South Korean President twice, both meetings occurring in the UN Command administered Joint Security Area of Panmunjom under the oversight of General Brooks. North Korea had also engaged in an unprecedented meeting with the US President.

A comprehensive military agreement was signed between North and South Korea, significantly reducing the potential of an incident along the Demilitarized Zone, becoming a spark that reignited direct combat in Korea. It was a 180-degree reversal of the situation facing Brooks upon arrival. It was time to step off the world stage, remove the uniform of the Nation for the last time, and enter retirement with Carol beside him.

"Vince was masterful in crafting and implementing the military dimension of the pressure campaign (against North Korea), and in doing so, he demonstrated extraordinary strategic vision, professional maturity, and judgement," said Chairman of the Joint Chiefs of Staff General Joseph Dunford, US Marine Corps, at the retirement ceremony for General Vincent Brooks in December 2018.

General Vincent Brooks retired from the military on January 1, 2019, but that did not mean he has retired from leading. He now crosses the world, spreading the lessons he learned on leadership in hopes of inspiring others.

Change the World and Influence Others Through Leadership

General Vincent Brooks stresses to this day, leadership needs to change lives, and your actions reflect your honor. His mother's Christian beliefs and way of life shaped him greatly.

"Her message was, 'you always have more to give . . . you need to give of your gifts, give back'," said General Vincent Brooks. "So, from the earliest days, that was part of how we were raised. To recognize our gifts God imbedded in us, and to use them to benefit others."

He saw that from both parents and their siblings and from his grandparents. Their leadership impacted the communities they lived in and brought out the best in others. "*That* is leadership. You do not need to wear a military uniform to be a leader," said General Brooks.

In one of his many speeches, he impressed upon the audience how leadership impacts society because of how the actions of one can inspire many. The outcome of that inspiration is a wave of positive influence. His key message- leadership, if done right, is powerful.

He challenged the audience by asking, "What kind of leader are you? Are you the kind of leader that others want to follow? If not, chances are you're not leading. If no one is following you, you're not leading. So, your example matters a lot." [616]

---

[616] Gen. Vincent Brooks: Leadership Is About People- Leading Authorities Speakers Bureau

"The Long Gray Line"

When it comes to these lessons, General Vincent Brooks often shows the continuity of inspiration by using the phrase, "The Long Gray Line". This saying is used proudly by West Point graduates and others to describe the bond that ties every USMA graduate who has come before, and those who will come after. Brooks described this lineage as a series of handshakes across generations.[617]

In his speeches, he refers to his own experience at West Point and the lineage of handshakes that led him to Lieutenant Flipper.

After a year of hearings that garnered national headlines, he was found guilty in 1881 of staging the attack and was expelled from West Point. Although the verdict was overturned by President Chester A. Arthur in 1882, the son of Abraham Lincoln, Robert T. Lincoln, who was Secretary of the Army at that time, expelled him from the academy based on Whittaker failing an examination in 1880.[619] [620]

He later became a lawyer and also taught at a school. His sons fought in World War I, and his grandson was a Tuskegee Airmen in World War II. On July 25, 1995, President Bill Clinton awarded the posthumous commission to his heirs, saying, "We cannot undo history. But today, finally, we can pay tribute to a great American and acknowledge a great injustice."[621] General Brooks, then a Lieutenant Colonel, was present at the White House ceremony.

Demonstrating The Long Gray Line

In a speech honoring Henry Flipper in 2019, Brooks used "The Long Gray Line" with the life story of General Benjamin O. Davis, Jr., the first Black cadet to attend the academy during the 20th century.

While a cadet, Davis, Jr. faced "the silent treatment" from the Cadet Corps when he attended. He did not have a roommate and ate his meals in silence. Cadet Davis, Jr. was only spoken to if duty required it.

---

[618] "President William J. Clinton's Comments, Honoring LT. Henry O. Flipper, February 19, 1999 https://history.army.mil/html/topics/afam/clinton_flipper.html

[617] Gen. Brooks Remarks: Henry O. Flipper Dinner, February 13, 2019

ITALY-Gen. Benjamin O. Davis pins the Distinguished Flying Cross on his son, Col. Benjamin O. Davis, Jr.
Print received October 17, 1944
Credit: National Archives, (photo no. NAID: 204909500)

Vincent Brooks had a chance to meet and speak with General Davis, Jr. twice. Once was during a dinner where Major Brooks met General Davis and his wife. The second was when they both attended a White House event when President Clinton posthumously commissioned Johnson C. Whittaker as an officer in the US Army.

[619] Johnson C. Whittaker (1858-1931) Black Past
https://www.blackpast.org/african-american-history/whittaker-johnson-c-1858-1931/
[620] John F. Harris "The Late Lieutenant" The Washington Post
https://www.washingtonpost.com/archive/lifestyle/1995/07/25/the-late-lieutenant/e7b7f2ad-31b5-4d40-b316-85df5027e344/
[621] "Remarks at the Posthumous Commissioning Ceremony for Johnson C. Whittaker" The American Presidency Project.
https://www.presidency.ucsb.edu/documents/remarks-the-posthumous-commissioning-ceremony-for-johnson-c-whittaker

During their conversation before the event, they reminisced about their time at West Point. The two men knew each other's accomplishments. It was then that Lieutenant Colonel Vincent Brooks learned how only two handshakes were needed to connect Benjamin O. Davis, Jr., West Point Class of 1936, to Henry O. Flipper, West Point Class of 1877.

General Davis, Jr. wanted to fly after graduation, and he earned his wings in the Army Air Forces, where he became the commander of the 99th Fighter Squadron of the Tuskegee Airmen. Later, he also took command of the 332nd Fighter Group. He became the first Black Brigadier General in the U.S. Air Force. General Davis, Jr.'s inspiration for joining the military was his father. Lieutenant General Davis, Jr. was promoted on the retired roster of the U.S. Air Force to four-star general by President Clinton on December 9, 1998. Davis died three- and one-half years later on the 4th of July, 2002. Vincent's brother, BG Leo Brooks, Jr., then serving as the Commandant of Cadets at West Point, was present at General Benjamin O. Davis Jr.'s military funeral.

Handshake One

General Davis Jr.'s first handshake was with his father, BG Benjamin O. Davis Sr., who was the first Black General in the U.S. Army. As a teen, BG Benjamin O. Davis, Sr. wanted to enter military service. He passed the physical exam, but, because of his age, he was not accepted for an officer's commission. He was later recruited by the African American 8th U.S. Volunteer Infantry and was appointed a lieutenant. Once it disbanded, he lost his status as a lieutenant, and he enlisted as a private in Troop L of the 9th Cavalry Regiment, a regular Army unit based in Nebraska known as the "Buffalo Soldiers"[622]. Davis quickly rose in rank to the top enlisted position in the unit within a short period of time, given his already demonstrated leadership experience.

The Buffalo Soldiers were Black Americans who predominantly served on the western frontier after the Civil War, and they also went on to fight in the Spanish-American War, as well as the Philippine-American War. Buffalo Soldiers also were some of the first care takers of the national parks, and they trained all West Point cadets how to ride horses. His commanding officer was Regular Army First Lieutenant (later Captain) Charles Young.[623]

Handshake Two

Captain Young was the ninth African American to attend the Academy and the third to graduate from West Point with the Class of 1889. He encouraged Sergeant Davis, to expand his education and take the necessary tests to become a regular Army officer. Captain Young tutored Davis Sr on the subjects he would need to know in order to pass the commissioning exam.

---

[622] National Park Service: American Plains Indians who fought against the black cavalry troops as "buffalo soldiers" because of their dark, curly hair, which resembled a buffalo's coat and because of their fierce nature of fighting. The nickname soon became synonymous with all African-American regiments formed in 1866.
[623] "Up From the Ranks", The APPEAL, December 28, 1901, https://www.newspapers.com/article/121354437/ranks/

His instruction helped Davis pass his first test for a commission at Ft. Leavenworth, Kansas, with a score of 91 out of 100 points. Lieutenant Benjamin O. Davis, Sr. was then assigned to the 10th Cavalry Regiment, the second of two all Black cavalry regiments, like the 9th, where he originally served as an enlisted soldier, and served in the Philippines, where he was one of the youngest officers in the Army.

Brooks mentioned in the speech through two handshakes, General Benjamin O. Davis Jr. touched Henry Flipper. Adding Brooks' handshake with Davis, Jr., this extended the "Long Gray Line" to three.

"Stay in the line and make a difference," stressed Brooks in the speech honoring Henry Flipper. "We strengthen each link, each clasp from the previous generations, to the future. We are part of the same line. You are the same as me, and we will always be one…. Your footprints and your walk have an impact that is far broader, far wider, and lasts far longer than you can imagine. Be that person. And if you do that, you will honor Henry Flipper, and you will honor West Point."[624]

Secrets to Being an Effective Leader

In General Vincent Brooks' eyes, a leader has earned subordinates' respect through their listening skills and inspiration. Building a team of people who know and feel like they belong and believe they are a part of something bigger than themselves is an effect leadership has in the eyes of General Vincent Brooks.

During his military career, he saw firsthand the opportunities that could be available in times of uncertainty and challenges. You just need to believe in yourself to try and not be held back by challenges and, thus, avoid any opportunities that could present themselves during the challenge. Taking advantage of education to broaden your skill sets and using those tools to enhance your career is another. Finally, having a strong faith that would support you through good times and challenging times. Collectively, these are pieces of advice that anyone of any age, civilian or military, can learn.

"Make society better," urged General Vincent Brooks. "Don't let anyone take society backward. The way you feel about your friends *that* is the way society as a whole should feel about people. Don't let it go backward. Make it better."

---

[624] "Up From the Ranks", The APPEAL, December 28, 1901, https://www.newspapers.com/article/121354437/ranks/

Afterword

There is so much we can learn from history. The circumstances that shape each individual, and the journey others have taken all serve as a guide that we can learn and grow personally and professionally as we start our own journeys. This book calls out a bold face message – keep the stories of previous generations alive by sharing their stories while building on the stories with your own additions. The honesty in which these stories are told - good, bad, and ugly - is key to the impact your stories will have on future generations.

The stories of these four African American families are truly inspiring. They reflect the worst and the best of American history. It is difficult to imagine the horrific circumstances of the Clotilda while illegally transporting human beings to be sold and traded. America knew better and had laws against the practice, and yet "Polleete," Pollee, and Rose Allen were there and lived to tell the story about the slave ship and their captivity.

Their story did not end with Clotilda being scuttled. Instead, their perseverance and their desire to bring forth a better life for each generation led to accomplishments and achievements that Pollee and Rose could never have imagined for themselves.

The story of Africatown serves as a fantastic example of what it takes to build a community and how that community thrives by creating high standards of excellence, mutual concern for neighbors and their families, and by doubling down on the value of education. Africatown was a model community, and the experience forever shaped the residents and descendants.

Sadly, there is always a darkness that seeks to undo goodness. Racism, practiced and experienced in every generation of America, ultimately undermined the success of Africatown. What remains is the story, so wonderfully told by the descendants of Pollee and Rose and preserved by the authors of this book.

The Madison Family story reminds us that our histories are intertwined. Their journey from the west coast of Africa to the west coast of America is like the history of America itself.

Woven throughout is the story of strong women who never gave up hope for themselves and especially for their children and generations who followed. The role of designated keepers of the family story – the *griots* and *griottes* – keeps the story alive over centuries and vast geographic expanses. It is the stories we are told that inspire us to live up to a level of excellence we might not have otherwise chosen to pursue. Hardships, separations, cruelty, and humiliation intervened with a sad frequency, yet hope, inspiration, identity, expectation, and resilience always overcame.

The Madisons knew who they were, and even when left unacknowledged by the well-to-do family of America's fourth President, they never denied themselves the realization of their impact in building America and seeing the Constitution drafted by their ancestor ultimately fulfilled, despite repeated and concerted efforts to oppose, diminish or not implement. Despite these recurring hindrances, the descendants of the Madison Family strove for excellence and attained greater and greater levels of achievement. And they kept the story of the family intact.

The Quanders story is equally informative and compelling. As one of America's oldest and best-documented African-American families, the Quander journey illustrates the American struggle with slavery and racism. The fracturing of family units, lost contact with branches of the family tree, and the challenges of living in the South as free persons of color well before the Emancipation Proclamation was issued by President Lincoln all presented generational obstacles to be overcome. That is exactly what the Quanders did. They built businesses and purchased larger and larger segments of land, enabling generations to lead their various fields of endeavor. Most importantly, they kept the stories of the family intact and passed from generation to generation. It is amazing that there have been 99 years of Quander family reunions. I wish them success on the 100th in 2024. For such a large family, the number of achievements cannot be quantified to capture the true merits and contributions. Nevertheless, the family continues to highlight several exemplars. The Quander family overcame the obstacles placed before them and have a rightful place in the museums that capture American and African American history.

The Quander and Brooks families overlap. Like the three other families whose stories are told in this book, the Brooks family story also reflects an amazing American journey. I was honored to serve with all three Brooks generals during my career of military service. Our paths moved in parallel and frequently crossed. The family traditions of excellence, faith, and humility are tell-tale characteristics of the Brooks family teachings and expectations. Being the only African American family in American history to have three generals in the same immediate family bears witness to the abilities of each and reflects historical acknowledgements and lessons learned across many generations.

Even though I know the Brooks' personally, I had no idea about the family story. The journey from slavery, to escape to civil war service to trust to literacy and the capturing of the experiences into a journal is a phenomenal record of courage will survive and thrive. Their success as a family not only makes me smile, it makes me proud.

The intervening generations from the mid-19th Century to the 21st Century also had to show determination and grit to overcome the plagues of segregation and racism. Achievements happened in each generation despite systemic efforts to slow down their social advancement. Leading social change, educating others, achieving high academic honors, attaining electoral offices, and leading tens and hundreds of thousands of military people all over the world are among just a few of the generational accomplishments of the Brooks family.

From my own experiences, I know how challenging it can be to strive for excellence when the steady chorus of *"you can't,"* or *"not you,"* or even *"not yet"* can be heard from close associates as well as individuals with opinions who have no knowledge of you.

As an Army child with multiple generations of military service, I knew about the noble calling of wearing the uniform of the Nation. Yet, from the beginning of my own journey to the very end, I had to confront the naysayers and doubters. In my experience, while not without challenges, if you follow the Brooks model of maintaining high standards, delivering exceptional performance, integrity, and top-notch leadership, you can convert the naysayers to believers. You never quit, even when things are unfairly stacked against you. Each hindrance must be confronted by stepping up to the challenge and striving for excellence once undertaken.

When I published <u>A Higher Standard: Leadership Strategies from America's First Female Four-Star General</u> in 2015, I did not realize the degree to which my story would resonate with others – women and men, white and black, military and not military. Certain things seem to transcend the categories superimposed upon us in any era. Family identity – reminders of from whom and from whence you come, family mantras like "Be the best," and "You must be twice as good" are strong multigenerational motivators that propel one generation to strive for and to achieve beyond what was accomplished before them. These timeless and uncategorized realities that are keys to success are captured in <u>Embracing Your Past to Empower Your Future</u>. I am certain that the degree of inspiration and the degree of clarity on what many African American families faced and continue to face will exceed even the highest expectations because of the stories told by these four incredible families. My greatest takeaway from this incredible book is that we must all continue to keep these stories alive and continue to add our stories to enhance the journey.

General Ann Dunwoody is a retired Army four-star general, the first woman in American history to achieve the top military rank.

Acknowledgements

The completion of this book could not have been done without the descendants who spent hours sharing their stories.

Bettye Kearse, your grace, wisdom, and passion for keeping Mandy and Coreen stories alive have inspired us. The love you have for them and for every generation that came after them can be felt in every word you chose to use in telling their story to us.

Vernetta Hansen, thank you for the long talks, sharing your faith, and how the foundation of any successful person starts with family and faith. A smile was left on our faces after our talks. We hope more people will now know more about Pollee and Rose Allen, Africatown, and the Clotilda. Veda, we became fast friends, and I will always cherish our friendship. You are the most caring, supportive daughter I know. Your strength and assistance meant everything to us. You really helped get your family's story to the finish line!

Judge Rohulamin Quander, thank you for your stories, documentation, and passion for encouraging future generations to be the best you can be and contribute to the world. The family members we highlighted, we hope to inspire future generations to see how they can use freedom to make their own opportunities, be fearless, and make this world a better place.

Thank you to the Brooks family. General Leo A. Brooks, Sr., you are a remarkable person. Your stories of your devotion to family and the lessons you learned from your ancestors illustrate how you, your children, and your siblings were able to overcome segregation and Jim Crow laws to be rock stars in society. General Leo A. Brooks Jr., thank you for sharing your stories of perseverance, challenge, and sibling love. General Vincent Brooks, thank you for your historical knowledge of your family, and the wonderful stories you shared about your ancestors and your own remarkable life. It was an honor to collaborate with you all these months!!! I hope the readers are left gobsmacked and inspired by the family story.

Thank you to James Lewis, great-great-grandson of Gumpa (African Peter or Peter Lee); your hospitality was very much appreciated. Your explanation of the property you have kept so beautifully is a wonderful example of what Africatown was built on. Family and sharing.

We would also like to thank Eric Finley, tour director of the Dora Franklin Finley African-American Heritage Trail (DFFAAHT). Thank you for the photos and for sharing your stories of Africatown.

Thank you, Chiquita Howard of Africatown Freedom Tours. We appreciate you taking the time to speak with us and sharing your knowledge of this historic town. May the full story of Africatown be told!

We also appreciate the League of Descendants of the Enslaved at Mount Vernon for accepting our emails on our project, allowing us to present our project to the descendants' group, and for the introduction to Judge Quander. Thank you, Christopher Ullman, for the introduction and for listening to our book idea. We are grateful for your friendship and support.

We would like to thank the historians and archivists of both Montpelier and Mount Vernon for their review of our research and footnoting. Your eye for detail in your review of the information to confirm the accuracy of our book is much appreciated. Our deepest thanks to Hilarie Hicks, Director of Museum Programs at James Madison's Montpelier, Jessie MacLeod, Associate Curator of George Washington's Mount Vernon, Mount Vernon Ladies' Association, Matt Briney, vice president of Media and Communications of Mount Vernon, Allison Wickens, vice president of education of Mount Vernon, Samantha Snyder, research librarian & manager of Library Fellowships, The Fred W. Smith National Library for the Study of George Washington, Mount Vernon Ladies' Association, Dawn Bonner, manager of visual resources George Washington's Mount Vernon, Mount Vernon Ladies' Association, Rebecca Baird archivist at The Fred W. Smith National Library for the Study of George Washington, Mount Vernon Ladies' Association, for going through the extensive archives and answering our long list of questions, and Joe Downer RPA Archaeological Field Research Manager for our questions on LIDAR and the Mount Vernon graveyard archeological site.

Thank you, Llewellyn "Lew" Toulmin, for reviewing our work on the Clotilda and the Pollee Allen family. Your research, knowledge, and assistance helped us augment the lives of the 110 Clotilda survivors. We are appreciative of you taking the time to speak with us.

Thank you so much to our literary agent, Cynthia Zigmund. Your keen editorial eye for detail elevated this project to what it is today. You were our sounding board, our advocate, and our biggest supporter. You are simply the best.

Finally, thank you to Michael Wallace. You are the best father and husband a woman and daughter could ever have. This project has taken years, and you have seen the highs and lows we have been trying to tell these stories. To have had you on this journey means so much. We love you.

About the Authors

Lori Ann LaRocco is an American Journalist who is known for personalized storytelling and her ability to make people feel comfortable and open up. She demonstrates her penchant for tackling complex topics and sensitive material in her articles, columns, and books. LaRocco is also the author of "Trade War Containers Don't Lie: Navigating the Bluster (Marine Money, 2019), "Dynasties of the Sea: The Untold Stories of the Postwar Shipping Pioneers (Marine Money, 2018), "Opportunity Knocking" (Agate Publishing, 2014), "Dynasties of the Sea: The Shipowners and Financiers Who Expanded the Era of Free Trade" (Marine Money, 2012), and "Thriving in the New Economy" (Wiley, 2010). As Senior Editor of Guests and the Global Supply Chain reporter for CNBC, Lori Ann has the ear of some of the world's biggest business minds. She is also a trade columnist for American Shipper.

Abby Wallace is an AP (Advanced Placement) History and English student at West Milford High School in NJ. In addition to co-authoring ***Embracing Your Past to Empower Your Future***, Abby enjoys creating her own stories. When Abby isn't writing, she can often be found reading, drawing, riding horses, performing on stage, playing video games or watching anime. Abby loves to give back to others and enjoys volunteering at Pony Power Therapies, teaching kids and adults alike how to ride horses. She hopes to one day have a therapy barn of her own.

Sylviane A. Diouf, 15n63

T

Tactical Officer (TAC), 224
Tancil, Gladys Quander, 117, 119–124, 174
Tarkar law, 4
Tarkars, 3–4, 6
T.C. Williams High School, 217
Tennessean, Nashville, 13
Tensaw River, 13
Terrell, Church, 147n395, 159
Thomas Jefferson, 7, 16n71, 69, 175, 239
Thomas Jefferson High School, 239
Thompson, Mary V., 115
332nd Fighter Group, 131–132, 270
320th Anti-Aircraft Artillery Battalion, 132
320th Barrage Balloon Battalion, 133
Thurgood Marshall Institute, 42n149
Tillotson College, 88
Timothy Meaher Family Tree, 54n179
Tobacco, Port, 111
Todd, Dolley Payne, 68–72
Trevor Vann, 119–120, 121n325
Trevor Vann George Mason University, 119
Trump, Donald J., 266
Tucker, Pastor Derek, 25
Turner, Aunspaugh "Clara", 30
Turner, Joe, 58
Turner, Lucy, 30, 36
Turner, Ruth, 34
Tuskegee Airmen, 131–132, 268, 270
Tuskegee Airmen Legacy, 131
Twelve Mile Island, 11
266th Supply and Service Battalion, 203
2nd Manchu Battalion, 254

U

Underwood, Frank, Jr., 249
Union Military, 78
United Confederate Veterans, 42
United Daughters of the Confederacy (UDC), 42–43
United States War of 1812, 196n522
Uppsala University, 149
U.S. Army Air Corps, 132
US Army forces in Europe (USAREUR), 254
U.S. Army Troop Support Agency, 210

US Army War College, 230, 252
U.S. Colored Heavy Artillery, 244
U.S Customs, 11
US Patent Trademark Office (USPTO), 222n567

V

Vernon, Mount, 12, 68, 109, 113–116, 124–127, 129, 134, 174, 176n488
Very Low Altitude (VLA), 133
Vickii Howell, 53n175
Virginia Family Tree, 115, 132, 173
The Virginia House-wife, 69
Virginia Marriages, 195n517
Virginia Quanders, 109, 126, 174, 194
Virginia State University (VSU), 102, 200, 249
Virginia Theological Seminary (VTS), 179n489, 195, 197, 200, 248
Vodun, 4

W

Wair, Richard, 193
Walter Reed Hospital, 135
Washington, Booker T., 90–91, 175, 185
Washington, Bushrod, 115–117
Washington, George, 109, 113–116, 124n331, 125, 158, 166, 187, 194, 202
Washington, Hannah, 115
Washington, John Augustine, 115–116
Watson, Reverend, 24
Wesley, Cynthia, 201
Wheeler, Ignatius, 111
Whitney Redding, 117, 118n313
Whittaker, Johnson C., 269
Wicks, Justice, 86
Wiggly, Piggly, 154
Wiley College, 88
William County, 175, 195–196
William Harrison Jr., 253n606
William J. Clinton, 268n618
William K. Stevens, 212
Williams, Fritz, 238
Wilmington Daily Herald, 13
Wilson, Clay Morgan, 95
Wilson, Estelle, 34
Wilson, Ruby, 63
Winfield Scott, 240n584

Womack, Joe, 28, 53, 55, 58n194
Women's War Work Council, 150
Woodlawn Plantation, 194n516
Woodlawn Virginia farm, 125
Woodrow Wilson, 145
Woolwine, Walter, 203
World War I, 27, 33n147, 39–40, 131, 152, 268
World War II, 131–133, 135, 148, 151, 156, 196,
     197n528, 222, 230, 268

Y

Yorba tradition, 15
Young, BG Charles, 244–245
Young, Charles, 244–245, 270
Young Women's Christian Association (YWCA),
     150, 157

Z

Zora Neale Hurston, 9

Printed in the USA
CPSIA information can be obtained
at www.ICGtesting.com
CBHW082018020524
7574CB00005B/16

9 781917 054560